P9-APJ-184

DATE DUE

1 8 NOV 1972

8 DEC 76

DATE DUE

MAY 11 1992	MAR 03 1992
SEP 1 5 1993	JUL 2 6 1993

Demco, Inc. 38-293

Managerial Behavior and Organization Demands: Management As a Linking of Levels of Interaction

Rand McNally Series in the Organization Sciences

Managerial Behavior and Organization Demands:
Management As a Linking of Levels of Interaction

Edited by

Robert T. Golembiewski
University of Georgia

Frank K. Gibson
University of Georgia

Rand McNally & Company   Chicago

Rand McNally Series in the Organization Sciences
Robert T. Golembiewski, Editor

Abrahamson, *The Professional in the Organization*
Cornog, Connelly, Kenney, and Scott, eds.,
EDP Systems in Public Management
Golembiewski, *Organizing Men and Power*
Golembiewski and Gibson, eds., *Managerial Behavior
and Organization Demands*
Press and Arian, eds., *Empathy and Ideology*

Copyright © 1967 by Rand McNally & Company
All rights reserved
Printed in U.S.A. by Rand McNally & Company
Library of Congress Catalog Card Number 67:10338

HD
31
G57
C.2

Preface

This volume attempts to fill what we see as a real need and seeks to fill that need in a relatively novel way. The need is to bring to students and practitioners of administration a representative slice of the several managerially relevant literatures and to do so with a vehicle permitting flexibility of use in executive development programs as well as in regular course work. Our contribution lies not in perceiving this need, for we could hardly have more company. Rather, we stress our dual emphases. The several levels of managerial interaction and the different demands these levels make upon managers breathe a sense of reality into the volume which particularly distinguishes it. After all, life in organizations is in significant senses one of experiencing levels of phenomena, of coping with them, and of tying them together into cooperative effort. Thus any manager, at a minimum, must deal with people and with groups. "Level plus linkage" has received less attention than the "functions" (like accounting) or the "processes" (like leadership) of management, however.

Our hopes may be summarized. We hope to contribute to the dissemination of managerially relevant knowledge, and we also hope to augment the attention given to a significant perspective from which management may be viewed.

Like management, this effort is ineluctably cooperative. Thus we could hardly have given form to the volume had many researchers not labored long and well. Many other workers also contributed. We note particularly the typing and clerical skills of Gloria Hawkins, Renate Black, and Sigrid Sanders.

Robert T. Golembiewski
Frank K. Gibson

Athens, Georgia
June 1, 1967

Contents

Introduction

This volume of readings has a straightforward rationale and an uncomplicated format. The immediate purposes are: to outline this rationale; to sketch and explain the format; and to establish some significant relations between the two.

As for rationale, we live on the knife-edge of an organizational revolution in both business and government. That revolution leaves few untouched, and it leaves almost everyone uncertain of our ability to stay on top of developments. Thus only a few observers see the contemporary burgeoning of organizations as thrusting us into an age of unparalleled good and plenty. The majority has no such benign view. Many see humankind being inexorably dragged toward a thoroughgoing manipulation beyond all experience; still others see society reverting to a kind of modern dark ages of organizations which have grown so bloated that they suffocate in the offal of their own procedures and policies. Both groups of pessimistic observers share a common view of the dilemma of man. The organizational size which was once necessary to achieve more of the good things of life has now reached the point of increasingly small marginal returns. That balance, they judge, will soon reach the point of diminishing returns as innovation and adaptation become increasingly difficult. Indeed, some argue that point already has been reached.[1]

For good or ill, there seems no stopping the organizational world because it is safer to get off. We must ride the tiger of our organization revolution because we rightly fear what it might do to us if we ever tried to get off. Consequently, the managers of our government and business organizations are increasingly hard pressed.

One of the major adaptations to our need to "hold on" to the contemporary developments in organizations is the increasing attention given to managerial training, both in schools and in executive development programs. In this sense, the rationale of this volume is patent. It is a small contribution to increasing our chances that the tiger of the contemporary organizational revolution will not become our master. The format and readings of this volume thus are chosen to transmit information necessary to facilitate managerial training.

We have two basic target audiences. Participants in the typical executive development program constitute one of these target audiences. Editorial selections from the managerially relevant literatures thus were guided by the experience of our considerable involvement

---

[1] Roderick Seidenberg, *Post-Historic Man* (Boston: Beacon Press, 1957).

in a wide variety of such programs for both business and government. The selections of readings also had to suit a target audience composed of students and faculty involved in the wide variety of courses which have a managerial focus and are given in our many schools of public and business administration. Such managerially oriented enrichment is particularly necessary in Public Administration which, for a variety of reasons, has moved but sluggishly toward exploring the relevant literatures.[2] The tragedy is that government administrators have a particularly intense need for such information.

Given this rationale, the basic strategy underlying the format of this volume leans heavily in spirit on the biblical advice given to Moses by Jethro during the great exodus. Relying on antiquity is no sign that we wish to flee to the safety of simpler days. Directly, Jethro's advice to Moses was reasonable under the circumstances. Moreover, almost all contemporary organizations in effect follow Jethro's advice.

What was Jethro's advice? Briefly, the exodus had been going poorly indeed for the Jews, and in large part because Moses had been forced into the role of a Universal Decision Maker. While Moses paused to make decisions both great and small, difficult and simple, the people he was leading out of bondage dawdled along the way. "You are not acting wisely," Jethro was emboldened by events to tell his son-in-law Moses, and Moses listened. The Bible notes that:

> Moses picked out able men from all Israel and put them in charge of the people *as officers over groups of thousands, of hundreds, of fifties, and of tens.* They rendered decisions for the people in all ordinary cases. The more difficult cases they rendered to Moses, but all the lesser cases they settled themselves.

The exodus then went far more quickly, and (we presume) Moses was a less frantic man. But Jethro—wise father-in-law that he was—did not press his luck. His advice having been given and accepted, Jethro "went off to his own country."

We, like Moses, will organize incredible complexity in a simple way. Thus the bulk of this sampling of the vast managerially relevant literatures will be organized around these four themes:

I. Managing by Ones and Twos: Freeing-up Relations Between Individuals

II. Managing by Tens and Twenties: Supervising Immediate Work Units

III. Managing by Hundreds: Middle Management and Departmental Dynamics

---

[2] The point is made, for example, by Bertram M. Gross, *The Managing of Organizations* (New York: The Free Press of Glencoe, 1964), Vol. 1, pp. 226–28.

IV. Managing by Thousands: Developing and Maintaining An Institution

Other guidelines for organizing this volume could have been used, but we do make two major claims for the usefulness of the four themes focusing on different levels of organization and their different demands. Although they are not magical boxes for sorting the total phenomena of management, the emphasis on the four levels of organization does spotlight central tendencies in organizational demands that differ enough that we are ill-advised to neglect them. That is, as we view management, each of the four levels of organization detailed above imposes different demands upon the manager, and the manager must sink or swim in providing appropriate behaviors. These differences in the organizational demands at the several levels are marked enough to appear in public as well as in business organizations. These similar demands at similar levels appear even in organizations doing vastly different work, be it administrative or manufacturing. Hence the title of this volume: *Managerial Behavior and Organization Demands.*

Additionally, although students and practitioners alike recognize that different levels of organization *do* impose different demands on managers, most management texts neglect the point. Thus the focus of texts is likely to be on the major functional areas (such as production, engineering and accounting). Or the focus of texts may be upon general activities performed by all managers (such as leading, planning, and motivating). We will not neglect either such functions or such activities, but we will treat them only as they appear concretely at some specific level of organization. This emphasis upon levels distinguishes this volume from most others. Hence this volume is titled: *Managerial Behavior and Organization Demands.*

The differing demands of different levels of organization may be illustrated simply. For example, one set of organizational demands challenges the supervisor in the face-to-face management of his workunit. Tersely, he manages people and their problems. Quite another set of behaviors must be supplied by the chief executive who, from a distance, attempts to guide an organization in the successful pursuit of its evolving concept of its mission and roles. In a crude but revealing sense, the top-level executive manages an institution and its problems.

Only a few managers can get off cheaply by serving the demands of one level of organization at the expense of others, however. Illustratively, the chief executive usually must be concerned with the face-to-face supervision of his immediate staff as well as with the management of the organization *qua* institution. This, in short, involves him in the management of tens as well as thousands. In addition, every chief executive—like the rest of mankind—can neglect his interpersonal relations only at his own peril. He is perforce involved in managing by ones and twos.

Exaggerations are sudden-death for most arguments, but we need not carefully hedge our statement of the importance of levels in an organization. For much evidence supports the ubiquitous importance of levels in organizations. For example, our organization level may determine what we see, certainly a powerful effect. Sherman approached the point in these terms: "Rarely, if ever," he noted, "is an organizational problem one of 'good guys' vs. 'bad guys.' Rather, it is usually one between or among more or less decent people of different values and different self-interests, who see the problem from different perspectives."[3] And these different perspectives, in large part, have their roots in the particular job and in the particular level of that job in an organization. "Where one stands," Rufus Miles summarized, "depends on where he sits." Or, alternatively, "we see things not as they are, but as we are." As might be expected, then, the impact of where we sit on where we stand often is made starkly plain, as when a person changes jobs or rises in the hierarchy. Sherman tells of the staff man who had a ready explanation for every organizational difference. "If only people would talk to each other," he would lament, "there would be no problem." But the explanation seemed to lose its power when the individual accepted a high-level "line" job. Sherman described the change sharply: "Now he would say that there just wasn't time to talk to all the people who were involved with his operations, and he would bemoan the fact that it was so difficult to imbue the various staff departments with the same sense of urgency and priority that he felt for his operations."[4]

In terms of the mechanics of presentation, each section of this volume in turn will stress two types of materials. First, one or more pieces in each section will outline the kinds of demands typically imposed on managers at some one level of the organization. Second, other pieces in each section will have a multiple focus. They explore specific problems in depth; they trace the interrelations of problem areas; and they particularly highlight the kinds of behaviors and techniques which a manager can use to react successfully to the demands made upon him. Brief editorial comments will help identify the more salient aspects of each piece.

These mechanics of presentation may be illustrated specifically by

---

[3] Harvey Sherman, *It All Depends: A Pragmatic Approach to Organization* (University, Alabama: University of Alabama Press, 1966), p. 62.
[4] *Ibid.*, p. 63.

the three readings that complete this introductory section. In gross terms, this section is a microcosm of what is to follow. Thus one article stresses the general demands that organizations make upon the very substance of men, their personalities. Two other articles—within the area of significance established by the first piece—comprehensively indicate more specific difficulties in organizing. These two articles also sketch the progress that has been made in coming to grips with these demands upon men in ways that permit some degree of conscious control over the conditions of our organizational experiences.

We may usefully provide more specific introductory substance. Professor Ivar Berg's "Do Organizations Change People?" briefly summarizes the relatively firm evidence converging toward the conclusion that an organization tends to shape its members in its own image. Evidence is drawn not only from organizations producing goods or services but from anthropological studies of various levels of social organizations as well. The shaping-to-form involves more than superficial qualities. Berg writes of "personality," that is, of the very essence of what man-in-society is.

Although available evidence is "more suggestive than definitive" to Berg, these findings build toward a conclusion and suggest the enormous stakes for the individual and society implicit in our organizational revolution. Tersely, these stakes are implicit in one massively important datum. Directly, it is the increasingly rare individual who is not somehow affected by gargantuan organizations of business or government or union that can significantly affect his destiny. Organizational design and policy will have increasingly widespread and irrevocable consequences, and the tolerable margin for error will become smaller and smaller as we go further and further down the expressway of our organizational revolution. Do not forget that diminishing tolerable margin for error applies to the ultimate worldly material, man and his psyche.

If organizations do mold their human products, however, we still have the opportunity, within limits, of determining what the shapes of the molds shall be. William Scott and Herbert Kaufman both provide valuable perspective on who and what is involved in attempting to develop safeguards against the ultimate error. Their two contributions have "internal" and "relational" emphases. Thus Scott's "Organization Theory: An Overview and An Appraisal" comprehensively traces the variety of major approaches attempting to make theoretical and practical harmony of the cacophony of phenomena associated with life in organizations. In this sense, Scott's effort has an "internal" bias. He sketches the advantages and disadvantages of three major contending and partially overlapping approaches to the analysis of orga-

6 *Managerial Behavior and Organization Demands*

nizations: the Classical Doctrine; the Neoclassical Theory; and Modern Organization Theory. The latter is distinguished by its comprehensive and integrative features. Thus Modern Organization Theory attempts to develop theoretical relations which permit comprehensive applied use by the integration of these levels of phenomena: the individual; the formal organization; the informal organization; the fusion process of the welding together of role expectations; and the physical setting within which work is performed.

The perfect world of Modern Organization Theory, however, is a composite of a clear concept of what things must be done and of the very uneven advances toward them. Thus Scott conceives dual goals for Modern Organization Theory: the development of sets of "linking processes" integrating the several levels of phenomena listed above and the development of a "general systems theory" to encompass the whole of the linkages of all of the appropriate levels of phenomena. However, actual advances toward such clear goals are conspicuously rare. Scott traces this datum directly to the disinclination of students to give solid attention to the goal of a general systems theory. Scott observes with some feeling: "The irony of it all is that a field dealing with systems has, indeed, little system. Modern organization theory needs a framework, and it needs an integration of issues into a common conception of organization."[5]

Scott protects himself against charges of utopianism by noting that "this is a large order," but the dimensions of the "order" are even broader than he acknowledges. Some of these broader dimensions are dealt with directly by Kaufman in his paper "Organization Theory and Political Theory." Kaufman dwells on the actual "parallels between political theory, probably the oldest of the social sciences, and organization theory, perhaps the newest such discipline," and he finds these parallels "so totally unexpected." Kaufman's original expectations stood in stark opposition to his findings, these expectations emphasizing as they did isolation and discontinuity. As he explained:[6]

> If there is any conscious agreement between the two fields, it is on their separateness from each other: political theorists and organization theorists alike seem to take for granted the impossibility of encompassing within a single theoretical framework propositions about states . . . and propositions about other forms of human association. In the literature of organization theory, one rarely finds references even to contemporary political theorists and almost never to

[5] William G. Scott, "Organization Theory: An Overview and An Appraisal," *Journal of the Academy of Management*, Vol. 4 (April, 1961), p. 24.
[6] Herbert Kaufman, "Organization Theory and Political Theory," *American Political Science Review*, Vol. 58 (March, 1964), p. 5.

those who wrote in the past. By the same token, political theorists rarely seem to find anything relevant to their interests in the work of students of organization.

Kaufman traces a uniform picture of similar problems similarly coped with, and he explains the similarities of both kinds in terms that imply an enormous scope for the problems of organization theory. Kaufman isolates three major parallelisms in organization theory and political theory: accounting for the obedience of man to man; explaining the coordination of human efforts; and reconciling individual needs and collective requirements. He accounts for the similar treatment of these theoretical problems in political theory and in organization theory in terms of three explanatory themes. First, similar treatment of similarly perceived problems could not be avoided because of the broad and overlapping areas covered by political theory and organization theory. "When all is said and done," Kaufman explains, "they both treat of phenomena that encompass vast areas, if not all, of human life."[7]

Second, parallelisms are products of this major datum. Both governments and businesses face similar problems of governance. Policy formation, succession, loyalty and revolution are among the major common components. Institutional differences notwithstanding, these significant common components encourage common approaches in the two areas of study.

Third, Kaufman explains the parallelisms he observed by stressing common normative problems. That is, both political theory and organization theory face common questions. For what purposes should man be organized? What are the acceptable limits on enforcing compliance to some definition of the collective purpose? Since they drew on the common heritage of the western tradition in attempting to cope with such common questions, both political theory and organization theory generated a range of solutions that overlap closely.

We may boldly note one implicit conclusion from these three pieces. The stakes are high in our contemporary organizational revolution, and the game is as narrow as an individual's life history or as broad as man's total political and social existence.

---

[7] *Ibid.*, p. 10.

Do Organizations Change People?[*]

Ivar Berg

In approaching this question of "what people are like" in terms of their compatibility with the large organization, we may first ask whether there is any evidence that the organization changes people, particulary in the direction of making them more pedestrian, less innovative, less willing to take assertive action.

Research on the relationship of organizational experience to individual personality has been more suggestive than definitive. Students generally describe an organization in terms normally used to delineate one or more personality traits, and then they measure the personalities of a sample of the organization's members under the same categories. In the most representative study of this type, two Harvard investigators characterized three organizations as autocratic, democratic, or "transitional" (between autocratic and democratic) according to the way they allocated authority and reached decisions.[1] The investigators then developed scales to measure the democratic-autocratic beliefs as well as personality traits of the organization's members. They found that the personalities and the beliefs varied with the type of organization so that there were authoritarian beliefs held by authoritarian people in the autocratic organization, democratic beliefs and democratic people in the democratic organization, and a mixture of authoritarian and democratic beliefs and people in the transitional organization.

I attempted to repeat and to elaborate upon this Harvard study by studying another autocratic organization in addition to those studied by Levinson and Gilbert and by adding a behavioral dimension to the attitudinal and personality dimensions used in the earlier study.[2] I found, as they had at Harvard, that the personalities of the people fitted in with the character of the organization, and also that behavior was similarly consonant with the organization, the beliefs, and the personalities of the people. In this investigation, personality, belief, and behavior were measured independently.

[*] From a paper prepared by Professor Ivar Berg, Graduate School of Business, Columbia University, for the Arden House conference. Reprinted with permission of author and publisher from Leonard Sayles, editor, *Individualism and Big Business* (New York: McGraw-Hill Book Company, Inc., 1963), pp. 61–65.
[1] D. Gilbert and D. J. Levinson, "Role Performance, Ideology and Personality in Mental Hospital Aides," in M. Greenblat, D. J. Levinson, and R. Williams (eds.), *The Patient and the Mental Hospital,* The Free Press of Glencoe, New York, 1957, pp. 197–208.
[2] Ivar Berg, "Role Personality and Social Structure: The Nurse in the General Hospital," PhD. dissertation, Harvard University, Cambridge, Mass., 1960.

The difficulty with these studies is that they used crude measures of personality and somewhat intuitive judgments (based upon clinical rather than statistical evidence) about the character of the organizations. This type of study seldom tells us whether the organization "stamped" once diverse personalities, after the fashion of a cookie cutter, in order to ensure an identity between people and organization, or whether the organization recruited congruent types.

I examined this possibility by comparing "old" with "new" members of the organization. I found that there was more homogeneity in personality, in behavior, and in attitude in the seasoned group with long service—in the direction of harmony with the environment—than there was in the newer group. This observation, however, does not tell us directly whether the organization had wrought any change in the senior group. It may be that organizational experience had changed the personalities of the long-service employees. Or it may be that the organizational contemporaries of long-service employees, whose personalities, beliefs, and behavior were "different" left the organization long before my study, either because they were intolerant of an environment unsuited to their personalities or because they were selected out by an uncongenial environment. In short, we do not know whether the organization changed, repelled, and/or selected people or, more likely, whether all these processes interacted. Only a future study that would reveal whether congenial employees among the short-service group stay or whether the uncongenial ones change, will enhance our confidence that it is possible to study the impact of organization upon basic personality structure.

This particular investigation is especially relevant in the present context in that one of the personality scales I used in my research aspired to measure a personality trait which should be associated, on theoretical grounds, with autonomous behavior. I tried to measure employees' propensities to accept and act upon their impulses.[3] Thus I asked indirectly whether imaginative, innovating, resourceful people were among those who stay or leave the organization, an organization which was not notably hospitable to nonconforming acts of individual judgment and creativity. The organization was a hospital, and while "creative surgery" and "ground-breaking medicine" were proud boasts, it squelched other innovations with very formidable efficiency. New patterns of diabetic nursing care, for example, were restricted. Ingenious

---

[3] My measure was one developed by Kenneth Kenniston and Arthur Couch of Harvard's psychological clinic. Constructed on the basis of a careful analysis of the mathematical properties of over 100 personality "tests" administered to thousands of people, the two investigators were able to validate their measure in a clinical setting.

systems for simplifying antiquated patient billing procedures met considerable antagonistic pressure, as did other inventive new approaches to old problems.

I found, as I had in examining other personality traits, that there was a close fit between senior members and their organization. Once again the problem of personality change, self-selection, and organizational selection could not be resolved with the data available. The available evidence then does not conclusively support either the "organization man" criticism or the position that organizations have little or no effect on personality.

Other studies are, in their basic design, near carbon copies of the two described, except that some investigators substitute such environments as Indian tribes and universities for more conventional organizations. Results are almost always the same. Thus it was found in a comparative study of Menominee Indians that those who stayed on the reservation, living the traditional tribal life of the Menominee, had personality traits conforming to the social-psychological character of tribal life.[4] Menominee who left the reservation were found characteristically to differ from reservation residents in the direction of non-Menominee town dwellers. Again, however, we are not sure whether the Americanized Menominee had changed *after* his acculturation and assimilation or whether he differed from Menominee who remained on the reservation even *before* leaving the reservation.

Many writings on organization and personality, stemming from earlier studies of national character, reflect more a particular intellectual persuasion than a proved theory. Columbia sociologist Robert Merton, describes, in a speculative though suggestive way, what he terms a "bureaucratic personality" and implicitly assigns great force to prolonged experience in a bureaucratic structure as a stimulant in generating tendencies widely alleged to be associated with bureaucrats—rigidity, compulsive preoccupation with rules, impersonality, and acceptance of hierarchical relationships.[5] While recognizing both the logic and the charm of his analysis, we must nevertheless express reservations about this writer's implicit conclusion that priority goes to the organization as cause and bureaucratic behavior as consequence.

We are not prepared to draw any final conclusion on the basis of the evidence then as to the impact of organization on personality. The personality tests used are not demonstrably valid and the fit usually

[4] Alex Inkeles, "Personality and Social Structure," in Robert K. Merton, R. Brown, and L. Cottrell, *Sociology Today,* Basic Books, Inc., Publishers, New York, 1958.
[5] Robert K. Merton, "Bureaucratic Structure and Personality," in Robert K. Merton et al. (eds.), *Reader in Bureaucracy,* The Free Press of Glencoe, New York, 1957, pp. 361–371.

found to exist between men and organizations may grow out of the test used: other traits, measured by other tests, might be found to be *less* typical of a sample of persons in an organization and less closely correlated with the character of the organization. On this score we might anticipate future studies of the impact of organization on personality by those who operate with a more general conception of personality than the one contemplated by the trait approach and who measure personality from its behavioral manifestations rather than from pencil-and-paper tests.

If we can only anticipate future studies of the impact of the organization, we are fortunate in having at present some data on the impact of personality (as measured by specific behavioral indicators of deeper-lying traits) on performance in organizational positions. Unpublished research by anthropologist Eliot Chapple and his colleagues indicates that personalities are not randomly chosen to fill organizational positions, that the aggregate of interaction patterns in an organization will be affected by the personalities of role incumbents, and that social structure will be massively influenced by the different qualities of role performance within the behavioral repertoire of people located at strategic positions in the work flow of organizations. Since there is a high correlation between role performance and interaction "style," on the one hand, and personality on the other, and since performance patterns affect social structure, it is entirely reasonable to assume that personality has a considerable impact on social structure. These findings are entirely consistent with those reported in a highly imaginative investigation by Hemphill and his colleagues at Teachers College, Columbia University.[6] In this particular research organizational demands were simulated in a weeklong intensive study of the performance and personalities of over 200 school principals.

Prof. Alex Inkeles, in a careful review of studies dealing with the modern equivalent of the old heredity-environment question, writes of personality and social structure that ". . . both social structure and personality must be treated as important independent but interacting variables influencing the flow of the social process."[7]

---

[6] J. K. Hemphill, D. E. Griffiths, and N. Frederiksen, *Administrative Performance and Personality,* Bureau of Publications, Teachers College, Columbia University, New York, 1962.
[7] Inkeles, *op. cit.,* p. 267.

Organization Theory: An Overview and an Appraisal[*]

William G. Scott

Man is intent on drawing himself into a web of collectivized patterns. "Modern man has learned to accommodate himself to a world increasingly organized. The trend toward ever more explicit and consciously drawn relationships is profound and sweeping; it is marked by depth no less than by extension."[1] This comment by Seidenberg nicely summarizes the pervasive influence of organization in many forms of human activity.

Some of the reasons for intense organizational activity are found in the fundamental transitions which revolutionized our society, changing it from a rural culture, to a culture based on technology, industry, and the city. From these changes, a way of life emerged characterized by the *proximity* and *dependency* of people on each other. Proximity and dependency, as conditions of social life, harbor the threats of human conflict, capricious antisocial behavior, instability of human relationships, and uncertainty about the nature of the social structure with its concomitant roles.

Of course, these threats to social integrity are present to some degree in all societies, ranging from the primitive to the modern. But, these threats become dangerous when the harmonious functioning of a society rests on the maintenance of a highly intricate, delicately balanced form of human collaboration. The civilization we have created depends on the preservation of a precarious balance. Hence, disrupting forces impinging on this shaky form of collaboration must be eliminated or minimized.

Traditionally, organization is viewed as a vehicle for accomplishing goals and objectives. While this approach is useful, it tends to obscure the inner workings and internal purposes of organization itself. Another fruitful way of treating organization is as a mechanism having the ultimate purpose of offsetting those forces which undermine human collaboration. In this sense, organization tends to minimize conflict, and to lessen the significance of individual behavior which deviates from values that the organization has established as worthwhile. Further, organization increases stability in human relationships by reducing uncertainty regarding the nature of the system's structure and the human roles which are inherent to it. Corollary to this point,

[*] Reprinted with permission of author and publisher from *Journal of the Academy of Management*, 4 (April, 1961), pp. 7–26.
[1] Roderick Seidenburg, *Post Historic Man* (Boston: Beacon Press, 1951), p. 1.

organization enhances the predictability of human action, because it limits the number of behavioral alternatives available to an individual. As Presthus points out:

> Organization is defined as a system of structural interpersonal relations . . . individuals are differentiated in terms of authority, status, and role with the result that personal interaction is prescribed. . . . Anticipated reactions tend to occur, while ambiguity and spontaneity are decreased.[2]

In addition to all of this, organization has built-in safeguards. Besides prescribing acceptable forms of behavior for those who elect to submit to it, organization is also able to counterbalance the influence of human action which transcends its established patterns.[3]

Few segments of society have engaged in organizing more intensively than business.[4] The reason is clear. Business depends on what organization offers. Business needs a system of relationships among functions; it needs stability, continuity, and predictability in its internal activities and external contacts. Business also appears to need harmonious relationships among the people and processes which make it up. Put another way, a business organization has to be free, relatively, from destructive tendencies which may be caused by divergent interests.

As a foundation for meeting these needs rests administrative science. A major element of this science is organization theory, which provides the grounds for management activities in a number of significant areas of business endeavor. Organization theory, however, is not a homogeneous science based on generally accepted principles. Various theories of organization have been, and are being evolved. For example, something called "modern organization theory" has recently emerged, raising the wrath of some traditionalists, but also capturing the imagination of a rather elite *avant-garde*.

The thesis of this paper is that modern organization theory, when stripped of its irrelevancies, redundancies, and "speech defects," is a

[2] Robert V. Presthus, "Toward a Theory of Organizational Behavior," *Administrative Science Quarterly*, June, 1958, p. 50.
[3] Regulation and predictability of human behavior are matters of degree varying with different organizations on something of a continuum. At one extreme are bureaucratic type organizations with tight bonds of regulation. At the other extreme are voluntary associations, and informal organizations with relatively loose bonds of regulation.
This point has an interesting sidelight. A bureaucracy with tight controls and a high degree of predictability of human action appears to be unable to distinguish between destructive and creative deviations from established values. Thus the only thing which is safeguarded is the *status quo*.
[4] The monolithic institutions of the military and government are other cases of organizational preoccupation.

logical and vital evolution in management thought. In order for this thesis to be supported, the reader must endure a review and appraisal of more traditional forms of organization theory which may seem elementary to him.

In any event, three theories of organization are having considerable influence on management thought and practice. They are arbitrarily labeled in this paper as the classical, the neo-classical, and the modern. Each of these is fairly distinct; but they are not unrelated. Also, these theories are on-going, being actively supported by several schools of management thought.

For lack of a better method of identification, it will be said that the classical doctrine deals almost exclusively with the *anatomy of formal organization*. This doctrine can be traced back to Frederick W. Taylor's interest in functional foremanship and planning staffs. But most students of management thought would agree that in the United States, the first systematic approach to organization, and the first comprehensive attempt to find organizational universals, is dated 1931 when Mooney and Reiley published *Onward Industry*.[5] Subsequently, numerous books, following the classical vein, have appeared. Two of the more recent are Brech's, *Organization*[6] and Allen's, *Management and Organization*.[7]

Classical organization theory is built around four key pillars. They are the division of labor, the scalar and functional processes, structure, and span of control. Given these major elements just about all of classical organization theory can be derived.

(1) *The division of labor* is without doubt the cornerstone among the four elements.[8] From it the other elements flow as corollaries. For example, *scalar* and *functional* growth requires specialization and departmentalization of functions. Organization *structure* is naturally dependent upon the direction which specialization of activities travels in company development. Finally, *span of control* problems result from the number of specialized functions under the jurisdiction of a manager.

(2) *The scalar and functional processes* deal with the vertical and

---

[5] James D. Mooney and Alan C. Reiley, *Onward Industry* (New York: Harper and Brothers, 1931). Later published by James D. Mooney under the title *Principles of Organization*.

[6] E. F. L. Brech, *Organization* (London: Longmans, Green and Company, 1957).

[7] Louis A. Allen, *Management and Organization* (New York: McGraw-Hill Book Company, 1958).

[8] Usually the division of labor is treated under a topical heading of departmentation, see for example: Harold Koontz and Cyril O'Donnell, *Principles of Management* (New York: McGraw-Hill Book Company, 1959), Chapter 7.

horizontal growth of the organization, respectively.[9] The scalar process refers to the growth of the chain of command, the delegation of authority and responsibility, unity of command, and the obligation to report.

The division of the organization into specialized parts and the regrouping of the parts into compatible units are matters pertaining to the functional process. This process focuses on the horizontal evolution of the line and staff in a formal organization.

(3) *Structure* is the logical relationships of functions in an organization, arranged to accomplish the objectives of the company efficiently. Structure implies system and pattern. Classical organization theory usually works with two basic structures, the line and the staff. However, such activities as committee and liaison functions fall quite readily into the purview of structural considerations. Again, structure is the vehicle for introducing logical and consistent relationships among the diverse functions which comprise the organization.[10]

(4) *The span of control* concept relates to the number of subordinates a manager can effectively supervise. Graicunas has been credited with first elaborating the point that there are numerical limitations to the subordinates one man can control.[11] In a recent statement on the subject, Brech points out, "span" refers to ". . . the number of persons, themselves carrying managerial and supervisory responsibilities, for whom the senior manager retains his over-embracing responsibility of direction and planning, co-ordination, motivation, and control."[12] Regardless of interpretation, span of control has significance, in part, for the shape of the organization which evolves through growth. Wide span yields a flat structure; short span results in a tall structure. Further, the span concept directs attention to the complexity of human and functional interrelationships in an organization.

It would not be fair to say that the classical school is unaware of the day-to-day administrative problems of the organization. Paramount among these problems are those stemming from human interactions. But the interplay of individual personality, informal groups, intra-organizational conflict, and the decision-making processes in the formal structure appears largely to be neglected by classical organization theory. Additionally, the classical theory overlooks the contributions of the behavioral sciences by failing to incorporate them in its doctrine

[9] These processes are discussed at length in Ralph Currier Davis, *The Fundamentals of Top Management* (New York: Harper and Brothers, 1951), Chapter 7.

[10] For a discussion of structure see: William H. Newman, *Administrative Action* (Englewood Cliffs: Prentice-Hall, Incorporated, 1951), Chapter 16.

[11] V. A. Graicunas, "Relationships in Organization," *Papers on the Science of Administration* (New York: Columbia University, 1937).

[12] Brech, *op cit.*, p. 78.

in any systematic way. In summary, classical organization theory has relevant insights into the nature of organization, but the value of this theory is limited by its narrow concentration on the formal anatomy of organization.

Neoclassical Theory of Organization

The neoclassical theory of organization embarked on the task of compensating for some of the deficiencies in classical doctrine. The neoclassical school is commonly identified with the human relations movement. Generally, the neoclassical approach takes the postulates of the classical school, regarding the pillars of organization as givens. But these postulates are regarded as modified by people, acting independently or within the context of the informal organization.

One of the main contributions of the neoclassical school is the introduction of behavioral sciences in an integrated fashion into the theory of organization. Through the use of these sciences, the human relationists demonstrate how the pillars of the classical doctrine are affected by the impact of human actions. Further, the neoclassical approach includes a systematic treatment of the informal organization, showing its influence on the formal structure.

Thus, the neoclassical approach to organization theory gives evidence of accepting classical doctrine, but superimposing on it modifications resulting from individual behavior, and the influence of the informal group. The inspiration of the neoclassical school was the Hawthorne studies.[13] Current examples of the neoclassical approach are found in human relations books like Gardner and Moore, *Human Relations in Industry,*[14] and Davis, *Human Relations in Business.*[15] To a more limited extent, work in industrial sociology also reflects a neoclassical point of view.[16]

It would be useful to look briefly at some of the contributions made to organization theory by the neoclassicists. First to be considered are modifications of the pillars of classical doctrine; second is the informal organization.

---

[13] See: F. J. Roethlisberger and William J. Dickson, *Management and the Worker* (Cambridge: Harvard University Press, 1939).

[14] Burleigh B. Gardner and David G. Moore, *Human Relations in Industry* (Homewood: Richard D. Irwin, 1955).

[15] Keith Davis, *Human Relations in Business* (New York: McGraw-Hill Book Company, 1957).

[16] For example see: Delbert C. Miller and William H. Form, *Industrial Sociology* (New York: Harper and Brothers, 1951).

Examples of the Neoclassical Approach to the Pillars of Formal Organization Theory

(1) The *division of labor* has been a long standing subject of comment in the field of human relations. Very early in the history of industrial psychology study was made of industrial fatigue and monotony caused by the specialization of the work.[17] Later, attention shifted to the isolation of the worker, and his feeling of anonymity resulting from insignificant jobs which contributed negligibly to the final product.[18]

Also, specialization influences the work of management. As an organization expands, the need concomitantly arises for managerial motivation and coordination of the activities of others. Both motivation and coordination in turn relate to executive leadership. Thus, in part, stemming from the growth of industrial specialization, the neoclassical school has developed a large body of theory relating to motivation, coordination, and leadership. Much of this theory is derived from the social sciences.

(2) Two aspects of the *scalar and functional* processes which have been treated with some degree of intensity by the neoclassical school are the delegation of authority and responsibility, and gaps in or overlapping of functional jurisdictions. The classical theory assumes something of perfection in the delegation and functionalization processes. The neoclassical school points out that human problems are caused by imperfections in the way these processes are handled.

For example, too much or insufficient delegation may render an executive incapable of action. The failure to delegate authority and responsibility equally may result in frustration for the delegatee. Overlapping of authorities often causes clashes in personality. Gaps in authority cause failures in getting jobs done, with one party blaming the other for shortcomings in performance.[19]

The neoclassical school says that the scalar and functional processes are theoretically valid, but tend to deteriorate in practice. The ways in which they break down are described, and some of the human causes are pointed out. In addition the neoclassicists make recommendations, suggesting various "human tools" which will facilitate the operation of these processes.

[17] See: Hugo Munsterberg, *Psychology and Industrial Efficiency* (Boston: Houghton Mifflin Company, 1913).
[18] Probably the classic work is: Elton Mayo, *The Human Problems of an Industrial Civilization* (Cambridge: Harvard University, 1946, first printed 1933).
[19] For further discussion of the human relations implications of the scalar and functional processes see: Keith Davis, *op. cit.*, pp. 60–66.

(3) *Structure* provides endless avenues of analysis for the neoclassical theory of organization. The theme is that human behavior disrupts the best laid organizational plans, and thwarts the cleanness of the logical relationships founded in the structure. The neoclassical critique of structure centers on frictions which appear internally among people performing different functions.

Line and staff relations is a problem area, much discussed, in this respect. Many companies seem to have difficulty keeping the line and staff working together harmoniously. Both Dalton[20] and Juran[21] have engaged in research to discover the causes of friction, and to suggest remedies.

Of course, line-staff relations represent only one of the many problems of structural frictions described by the neoclassicists. As often as not, the neoclassicists will offer prescriptions for the elimination of conflict in structure. Among the more important harmony-rendering formulae are participation, junior boards, bottom-up management, joint committees, recognition of human dignity, and "better" communication.

(4) An executive's *span of control* is a function of human determinants, and the reduction of span to a precise, universally applicable ratio is silly, according to the neoclassicists. Some of the determinants of span are individual differences in managerial abilities, the type of people and functions supervised, and the extent of communication effectiveness.

Coupled with the span of control question are the human implications of the type of structure which emerges. That is, is a tall structure with a short span or a flat structure with a wide span more conducive to good human relations and high morale? The answer is situational. Short span results in tight supervision; wide span requires a good deal of delegation with looser controls. Because of individual and organizational differences, sometimes one is better than the other. There is a tendency to favor the looser form of government, however, for the reason that tall structures breed autocratic leadership, which is often pointed out as a cause of low morale.[22]

The Neoclassical View of the Informal Organization

Nothing more than the barest mention of the informal organization is given even in the most recent classical treatises on organization

[20] Melville Dalton, "Conflicts between Staff and Line Managerial Officers," *American Sociological Review,* June, 1950, pp. 342–351.
[21] J. M. Juran, "Improving the Relationship between Staff and Line," *Personnel,* May, 1956, pp. 515–524.
[22] Gardner and Moore, *op. cit.,* pp. 237–243.

theory.[23] Systematic discussion of this form of organization has been left to the neoclassicists. The informal organization refers to people in group associations at work, but these associations are not specified in the "blueprint" of the formal organization. The informal organization means natural groupings of people in the work situation.

In a general way, the informal organization appears in response to the social need—the need of people to associate with others. However, for analytical purposes, this explanation is not particularly satisfying. Research has produced the following, more specific determinants underlying the appearance of informal organizations.

(1) The *location* determinant simply states that in order to form into groups of any lasting nature, people have to have frequent face-to-face contact. Thus, the geography of physical location in a plant or office is an important factor in predicting who will be in what group.[24]

(2) *Occupation* is key factor determining the rise and composition of informal groups. There is a tendency for people performing similar jobs to group together.[25]

(3) *Interests* are another determinant for informal group formation. Even though people might be in the same location, performing similar jobs, differences of interest among them explain why several small, instead of one large, informal organizations emerge.

(4) *Special issues* often result in the formation of informal groups, but this determinant is set apart from the three previously mentioned. In this case, people who do not necessarily have similar interests, occupations, or locations may join together for a common cause. Once the issue is resolved, then the tendency is to revert to the more "natural" group forms.[26] Thus, special issues give rise to a rather impermanent informal association; groups based on the other three determinants tend to be more lasting.

When informal organizations come into being they assume certain characteristics. Since understanding these characteristics is important for management practice, they are noted below:

(1) Informal organizations act as agencies of *social control*. They generate a culture based on certain norms of conduct which, in turn, demands conformity from group members. These standards may be at

---

[23] For example: Brech, *op. cit.*, pp. 27–29; and Allen, *op. cit.*, pp. 61–62.

[24] See: Leon Festinger, Stanley Schachter, and Kurt Back, *Social Pressures in Informal Groups* (New York: Harper and Brothers, 1950), pp. 153–163.

[25] For example see: W. Fred Cottrell, *The Railroader* (Palo Alto: The Stanford University Press, 1940), Chapter 3.

[26] Except in cases where the existence of an organization is necessary for the continued maintenance of employee interest. Under these conditions the previously informal association may emerge as a formal group, such as a union.

odds with the values set by the formal organization. So an individual may very well find himself in a situation of conflicting demands.

(2) The form of human interrelationships in the informal organization requires *techniques of analysis* different from those used to plot the relationships of people in a formal organization. The method used for determining the structure of the informal group is called sociometric analysis. Sociometry reveals the complex structure of interpersonal relations which is based on premises fundamentally unlike the logic of the formal organization.

(3) Informal organizations have *status and communication* systems peculiar to themselves, not necessarily derived from the formal systems. For example, the grapevine is the subject of much neoclassical study.

(4) Survival of the informal organization requires stable continuing relationships among the people in them. Thus, it has been observed that the informal organization *resists change.*[27] Considerable attention is given by the neoclassicists to overcoming informal resistance to change.

(5) The last aspect of analysis which appears to be central to the neoclassical view of the informal organization is the study of the *informal leader.* Discussion revolves around who the informal leader is, how he assumes this role, what characteristics are peculiar to him, and how he can help the manager accomplish his objectives in the formal organization.[28]

This brief sketch of some of the major facets of informal organization theory has neglected, so far, one important topic treated by the neoclassical school. It is the way in which the formal and informal organizations interact.

A conventional way of looking at the interaction of the two is the "live and let live" point of view. Management should recognize that the informal organization exists, nothing can destroy it, and so the executive might just as well work with it. Working with the informal organization involves not threatening its existence unnecessarily, listening to opinions expressed for the group by the leader, allowing group participation in decision-making situations, and controlling the grapevine by prompt release of accurate information.[29]

---

[27] Probably the classic study of resistance to change is: Lester Coch and John R. P. French, Jr., "Overcoming Resistance to Change," in Schuyler Dean Hoslett (editor) *Human Factors in Management* (New York: Harper and Brothers, 1951) pp. 242–268.

[28] For example see: Robert Saltonstall, *Human Relations in Administration* (New York: McGraw-Hill Book Company, 1959), pp. 330–331; and Keith Davis, *op. cit.,* pp. 99–101.

[29] For an example of this approach see: John T. Doutt, "Management Must Manage the Informal Group, Too," *Advanced Management,* May, 1959, pp. 26–28.

While this approach is management centered, it is not unreasonable to expect that informal group standards and norms could make themselves felt on formal organizational policy. An honestly conceived effort by managers to establish a working relationship with the informal organization could result in an association where both formal and informal views would be reciprocally modified. The danger which at all costs should be avoided is that "working with the informal organization" does not degenerate into a shallow disguise for human manipulation.

Some neoclassical writing in organization theory, especially that coming from the management-oriented segment of this school, gives the impression that the formal and informal organizations are distinct, and at times, quite irreconcilable factors in a company. The interaction which takes place between the two is something akin to the interaction between the company and a labor union, or a government agency, or another company.

The concept of the social system is another approach to the interactional climate. While this concept can be properly classified as neoclassical, it borders on the modern theories of organization. The phrase "social system" means that an organization is a complex of mutually interdependent, but variable, factors.

These factors include individuals and their attitudes and motives, jobs, the physical work setting, the formal organization, and the informal organizations. These factors, and many others, are woven into an overall pattern of interdependency. From this point of view, the formal and informal organizations lose their distinctiveness, but find real meaning, in terms of human behavior, in the operation of the system as a whole. Thus, the study of organization turns away from descriptions of its component parts, and is refocused on the system of interrelationships among the parts.

One of the major contributions of the Hawthorne studies was the integration of Pareto's idea of the social system into a meaningful method of analysis for the study of behavior in human organizations.[30] This concept is still vitally important. But unfortunately some work in the field of human relations undertaken by the neoclassicists has overlooked, or perhaps discounted, the significance of this consideration.[31]

The fundamental insight regarding the social system, developed and applied to the industrial scene by the Hawthorne researchers, did not

---

[30] See: Roethlisberger and Dickson, *op. cit.*, Chapter 24.

[31] A check of management human relations texts, the organization and human relations chapters of principles of management texts, and texts on conventional organization theory for management courses reveals little or no treatment of the concept of the social system.

find much extension in subsequent work in the neoclassical vein. Indeed, the neoclassical school after the Hawthorne studies generally seemed content to engage in descriptive generalizations, or particularized empirical research studies which did not have much meaning outside their own context.

The neoclassical school of organization theory has been called bankrupt. Criticisms range from, "human relations is a tool for cynical puppeteering of people," to "human relations is nothing more than a trifling body of empirical and descriptive information." There is a good deal of truth in both criticisms, but another appraisal of the neoclassical school of organization theory is offered here. The neoclassical approach has provided valuable contributions to lore of organization. But, like the classical theory, the neoclassical doctrine suffers from incompleteness, a shortsighted perspective, and lack of integration among the many facets of human behavior studied by it. Modern organization theory has made a move to cover the shortcomings of the current body of theoretical knowledge.

Modern Organization Theory

The distinctive qualities of modern organization theory are its conceptual-analytical base, its reliance on empirical research data and, above all, its integrating nature. These qualities are framed in a philosophy which accepts the premise that the only meaningful way to study organization is to study it as a system. As Henderson put it, the study of a system must rely on a method of analysis, ". . . involving the simultaneous variations of mutually dependent variables."[32] Human systems, of course, contain a huge number of dependent variables which defy the most complex simultaneous equations to solve.

Nevertheless, system analysis has its own peculiar point of view which aims to study organization in the way Henderson suggests. It treats organization as a system of mutually dependent variables. As a result, modern organization theory, which accepts system analysis, shifts the conceptual level of organization study above the classical and neoclassical theories. Modern organization theory asks a range of interrelated questions which are not seriously considered by the two other theories.

Key among these questions are: (1) What are the strategic parts of the system? (2) What is the nature of their mutual dependency? (3)

---

[32] Lawrence J. Henderson, *Pareto's General Sociology* (Cambridge: Harvard University Press, 1935), p. 13.

What are the main processes in the system which link the parts together, and facilitate their adjustment to each other? (4) What are the goals sought by systems?[33]

Modern organization theory is in no way a unified body of thought. Each writer and researcher has his special emphasis when he considers the system. Perhaps the most evident unifying thread in the study of systems is the effort to look at the organization in its totality. Representative books in this field are March and Simon, *Organizations*,[34] and Haire's anthology, *Modern Organization Theory*.[35]

Instead of attempting a review of different writers' contributions to modern organization theory, it will be more useful to discuss the various ingredients involved in system analysis. They are the parts, the interactions, the processes, and the goals of systems.

The Parts of the System and Their Interdependency

The first basic part of the system is the *individual*, and the personality structure he brings to the organization. Elementary to an individual's personality are motives and attitudes which condition the range of expectancies he hopes to satisfy by participating in the system.

The second part of the system is the formal arrangement of functions, usually called the *formal organization*. The formal organization is the interrelated pattern of jobs which make up the structure of a system. Certain writers, like Argyris, see a fundamental conflict resulting from the demands made by the system, and the structure of the mature, normal personality. In any event, the individual has expectancies regarding the job he is to perform; and, conversely, the job makes demands on, or has expectancies relating to, the performance of the individual. Considerable attention has been given by writers in modern organization theory to incongruencies resulting from the interaction of organizational and individual demands.[36]

The third part in the organization system is the *informal organization*. Enough has been said already about the nature of this organization. But it must be noted that an interactional pattern exists between

---

[33] There is another question which cannot be treated in the scope of this paper. It asks, what research tools should be used for the study of the system?

[34] James G. March and Herbert A. Simon, *Organizations* (New York: John Wiley and Sons, 1958).

[35] Mason Haire, (editor) *Modern Organization Theory* (New York: John Wiley and Sons, 1959).

[36] See Chris Argyris, *Personality and Organization* (New York: Harper and Brothers, 1957), esp. Chapters 2, 3, 7.

the individual and the informal group. This interactional arrangement can be conveniently discussed as the mutual modification of expectancies. The informal organization has demands which it makes on members in terms of anticipated forms of behavior, and the individual has expectancies of satisfaction he hopes to derive from association with people on the job. Both these sets of expectancies interact, resulting in the individual modifying his behavior to accord with the demands of the group, and the group, perhaps, modifying what it expects from an individual because of the impact of his personality on group norms.[37]

Much of what has been said about the various expectancy systems in an organization can also be treated using status and role concepts. Part of modern organization theory rests on research findings in social-psychology relative to reciprocal patterns of behavior stemming from role demands generated by both the formal and informal organizations, and role perceptions peculiar to the individual. Bakke's *fusion process* is largely concerned with the modification of role expectancies. The fusion process is a force, according to Bakke, which acts to weld divergent elements together for the preservation of organizational integrity.[38]

The fifth part of system analysis is the *physical setting* in which the job is performed. Although this element of the system may be implicit in what has been said already about the formal organization and its functions, it is well to separate it. In the physical surroundings of work, interactions are present in complex man-machine systems. The human "engineer" cannot approach the problems posed by such interrelationships in a purely technical, engineering fashion. As Haire says, these problems lie in the domain of the social theorist.[39] Attention must be centered on responses demanded from a logically ordered production function, often with the view of minimizing the error in the system. From this standpoint, work cannot be effectively organized unless the psychological, social, and physiological characteristics of people participating in the work environment are considered. Machines and processes should be designed to fit certain generally observed psychological and physiological properties of men, rather than hiring men to fit machines.

---

[37] For a larger treatment of this subject see: George C. Homans, *The Human Group* (New York: Harcourt, Brace and Company, 1950), Chapter 5.

[38] E. Wight Bakke, "Concept of the Social Organization," in *Modern Organization Theory,* Mason Haire, (editor) (New York: John Wiley and Sons, 1959) pp. 60–61.

[39] Mason Haire, "Psychology and the Study of Business: Joint Behavioral Sciences," in *Social Science Research on Business: Product and Potential* (New York: Columbia University Press, 1959), pp. 53–59.

In summary, the parts of the system which appear to be of strategic importance are the individual, the formal structure, the informal organization, status and role patterns, and the physical environment of work. Again, these parts are woven into a configuration called the organizational system. The processes which link the parts are taken up next.

The Linking Processes

One can say, with a good deal of glibness, that all the parts mentioned above are interrelated. Although this observation is quite correct, it does not mean too much in terms of system theory unless some attempt is made to analyze the processes by which the interaction is achieved. Role theory is devoted to certain types of interactional processes. In addition, modern organization theorists point to three other linking activities which appear to be universal to human systems of organized behavior. These processes are communication, balance, and decision making.

(1) Communication is mentioned often in neoclassical theory, but the emphasis is on description of forms of communication activity, i.e., formal-informal, vertical-horizontal, line-staff. Communication, as a mechanism which links the segments of the system together, is overlooked by way of much considered analysis.

One aspect of modern organization theory is study of the communication network in the system. Communication is viewed as the method by which action is evoked from the parts of the system. Communication acts not only as stimuli resulting in action, but also as a control and coordination mechanism linking the decision centers in the system into a synchronized pattern. Deutsch points out that organizations are composed of parts which communicate with each other, receive messages from the outside world, and store information. Taken together, these communication functions of the parts comprise a configuration representing the total system.[40] More is to be said about communication later in the discussion of the cybernetic model.

(2) The concept of *balance* as a linking process involves a series of some rather complex ideas. Balance refers to an equilibrating mechanism whereby the various parts of the system are maintained in a harmoniously structured relationship to each other.

---

[40] Karl W. Deutsch "On Communication Models in the Social Sciences," *Public Opinion Quarterly,* 16 (1952), pp. 356–380.

The necessity for the balance concept logically flows from the nature of systems themselves. It is impossible to conceive of an ordered relationship among the parts of a system without also introducing the idea of a stabilizing or an adapting mechanism.

Balance appears in two varieties—quasi-automatic and innovative. Both forms of balance act to insure system integrity in face of changing conditions, either internal or external to the system. The first form of balance, quasi-automatic, refers to what some think are "homeostatic" properties of systems. That is, systems seem to exhibit built-in propensities to maintain steady states.

If human organizations are open, self-maintaining systems, then control and regulatory processes are necessary. The issue hinges on the degree to which stabilizing processes in systems, when adapting to change, are automatic. March and Simon have an interesting answer to this problem, which in part is based on the type of change and the adjustment necessary to adapt to the change. Systems have programs of action which are put into effect when a change is perceived. If the change is relatively minor, and if the change comes within the purview of established programs of action, then it might be fairly confidently predicted that the adaptation made by the system will be quasi-automatic.[41]

The role of innovative, creative balancing efforts now needs to be examined. The need for innovation arises when adaptation to a change is outside the scope of existing programs designed for the purpose of keeping the system in balance. New programs have to be evolved in order for the system to maintain internal harmony.

New programs are created by trial and error search for feasible action alternatives to cope with a given change. But innovation is subject to the limitations and possibilities inherent in the quantity and variety of information present in a system at a particular time. New combinations of alternatives for innovative purposes depend on:

(a) the possible range of output of the system, or the capacity of the system to supply information.

(b) the range of available information in the memory of the system.

(c) the operating rules (program) governing the analysis and flow of information within the system.

(d) the ability of the system to "forget" previously learned solutions to change problems.[42] A system with too good a memory might narrow its behavioral choices to such an extent as to stifle innovation.

---

[41] March and Simon, *op. cit.*, pp. 139–140.
[42] Mervyn L. Cadwallader. "The Cybernetic Analysis of Change in Complex Social Organization," *The American Journal of Sociology*, September, 1959, p. 156.

In simpler language, old learned programs might be used to adapt to change, when newly innovated programs are necessary.[43]

Much of what has been said about communication and balance brings to mind a cybernetic model in which both these processes have vital roles. Cybernetics has to do with feedback and control in all kinds of systems. Its purpose is to maintain system stability in the face of change. Cybernetics cannot be studied without considering communication networks, information flow, and some kind of balancing process aimed at preserving the integrity of the system.

Cybernetics directs attention to key questions regarding the system. These questions are: How are communication centers connected, and how are they maintained? Corollary to this question: what is the structure of the feedback system? Next, what information is stored in the organization, and at what points? And as a corollary: how accessible is this information to decision-making centers? Third, how conscious is the organization of the operation of its own parts? That is, to what extent do the policy centers receive control information with sufficient frequency and relevancy to create a real awareness of the operation of the segments of the system? Finally, what are the learning (innovating) capabilities of the system?[44]

Answers to the questions posed by cybernetics are crucial to understanding both the balancing and communication processes in systems.[45] Although cybernetics has been applied largely to technical-engineering problems of automation, the model of feedback, control, and regulation in all systems has a good deal of generality. Cybernetics is a fruitful area which can be used to synthesize the processes of communication and balance.

(3) A wide spectrum of topics dealing with types of decisions in human systems makes up the core of analysis of another important process in organizations. Decision analysis is one of the major contributions of March and Simon in their book *Organizations.* The two major classes of decisions they discuss are decisions to produce and decisions to participate in the system.[46]

Decisions to produce are largely a result of an interaction between individual attitudes and the demands of organization. Motivation analysis becomes central to studying the nature and results of the inter-

---

[43] It is conceivable for innovative behavior to be programmed into the system.
[44] These are questions adapted from Deutsch, *op. cit.,* pp. 368–370.
[45] Answers to these questions would require a comprehensive volume. One of the best approaches currently available is Stafford Beer, *Cybernetics and Management* (New York: John Wiley and Sons, 1959).
[46] March and Simon, *op. cit.,* Chapters 3 and 4.

action. Individual decisions to participate in the organization reflect on such issues as the relationship between organizational rewards versus the demands made by the organization. Participation decisions also focus attention on the reasons why individuals remain in or leave organizations.

March and Simon treat decisions as internal variables in an organization which depend on jobs, individual expectations and motivations, and organizational structure. Marschak[47] looks on the decision process as an independent variable upon which the survival of the organization is based. In this case, the organization is viewed as having, inherent to its structure, the ability to maximize survival requisites through its established decision processes.

The Goals of Organization

Organization has three goals which may be either intermeshed or independent ends in themselves. They are growth, stability, and interaction. The last goal refers to organizations which exist primarily to provide a medium for association of its members with others. Interestingly enough these goals seem to apply to different forms of organization at varying levels of complexity, ranging from simple clockwork mechanisms to social systems.

These similarities in organizational purposes have been observed by a number of people, and a field of thought and research called general system theory has developed, dedicated to the task of discovering organizational universals. The dream of general system theory is to create a science of organizational universals, or if you will, a universal science using common organizational elements found in all systems as a starting point.

Modern organization theory is on the periphery of general system theory. Both general system theory and modern organization theory study:

(1) the parts (individuals) in aggregates, and the movement of individuals into and out of the system.

(2) the interaction of individuals with the environment found in the system.

(3) the interactions among individuals in the system.

(4) general growth and stability problems of systems.[48]

[47] Jacob Marschak, "Efficient and Viable Organizational Forms" in *Modern Organization Theory,* Mason Haire, editor, (New York: John Wiley and Sons, 1959), pp. 307–320.
[48] Kenneth E. Boulding, "General System Theory—The Skeleton of a Science," *Management Science,* April 1956, pp. 200–202.

Modern organization theory and general system theory are similar in that they look at organization as an integrated whole. They differ, however, in terms of their generality. General system theory is concerned with every level of system, whereas modern organizational theory focuses primarily on human organization.

The question might be asked, what can the science of administration gain by the study of system levels other than human? Before attempting an answer, note should be made of what these other levels are. Boulding presents a convenient method of classification:

(1) The static structure—a level of framework, the anatomy of a system; for example, the structure of the universe.

(2) The simple dynamic system—the level of clockworks, predetermined necessary motions.

(3) The cybernetic system—the level of the thermostat, the system moves to maintain a given equilibrium through a process of self-regulation.

(4) The open system—level of self-maintaining systems, moves toward and includes living organisms.

(5) The genetic-societal system—level of cell society, characterized by a division of labor among cells.

(6) Animal systems—level of mobility, evidence of goal-directed behavior.

(7) Human systems—level of symbol interpretation and idea communication.

(8) Social system—level of human organization.

(9) Transcendental systems—level of ultimates and absolutes which exhibit systematic structure but are unknowable in essence.[49]

This approach to the study of systems by finding universals common at all levels of organization offers intriguing possibilities for administrative organization theory. A good deal of light could be thrown on social systems if structurally analogous elements could be found in the simpler types of systems. For example, cybernetic systems have characteristics which seem to be similar to feedback, regulation, and control phenomena in human organizations. Thus, certain facets of cybernetic models could be generalized to human organization. Considerable danger, however, lies in poorly founded analogies. Superficial similarities between simpler system forms and social systems are apparent everywhere. Instinctually based ant societies, for example, do not yield particularly instructive lessons for understanding rationally conceived human organizations. Thus, care should be taken that analogies used to bridge system levels are not mere devices for literary enrichment.

---

[49] *Ibid.*, pp. 202–205.

For analogies to have usefulness and validity, they must exhibit inherent structural similarities or implicitly identical operational principles.[50]

Modern organization theory leads, as it has been shown, almost inevitably into a discussion of general system theory. A science of organization universals has some strong advocates, particularly among biologists.[51] Organization theorists in administrative science cannot afford to overlook the contributions of general system theory. Indeed, modern organization concepts could offer a great deal to those working with general system theory. But the ideas dealt with in the general theory are exceedingly elusive.

Speaking of the concept of equilibrium as a unifying element in all systems, Easton says, "It (equilibrium) leaves the impression that we have a useful general theory when in fact, lacking measurability, it is a mere pretence for knowledge."[52] The inability to quantify and measure universal organization elements undermines the success of pragmatic tests to which general system theory might be put.

Organization Theory: Quo Vadis?

Most sciences have a vision of the universe to which they are applied, and administrative science is not an exception. This universe is composed of parts. One purpose of science is to synthesize the parts into an organized conception of its field of study. As a science matures, its theorems about the configuration of its universe change. The direction of change in three sciences, physics, economics, and sociology, are noted briefly for comparison with the development of an administrative view of human organization.

The first comprehensive and empirically verifiable outlook of the physical universe was presented by Newton in his *Principia*. Classical physics, founded on Newton's work, constitutes a grand scheme in

---

[50] Seidenberg, *op. cit.*, p. 136. The fruitful use of the type of analogies spoken of by Seidenberg is evident in the application of thermodynamic principles, particularly the entropy concept, to communication theory. See: Claude E. Shannon and Warren Weaver, *The Mathematical Theory of Communication*, (Urbana: The University of Illinois Press, 1949). Further, the existence of a complete analogy between the operational behavior of thermodynamic systems, electrical communication systems, and biological systems has been noted by: Y. S. Touloukian, *The Concept of Entropy in Communication, Living Organisms, and Thermodymamics,* Research Bulletin 130, Purdue Engineering Experiment Station.

[51] For example see: Ludwig von Bertalanffy, *Problem of Life* (London: Watts and Company, 1952).

[52] David Easton, "Limits of the Equilibrium Model in Social Research," in *Profits and Problems of Homeostatic Models in the Behavioral Sciences,* Publication 1, Chicago Behavioral Sciences, 1953, p. 39.

which a wide range of physical phenomena could be organized and predicted. Newtonian physics may rightfully be regarded as "macro" in nature, because its system of organization was concerned largely with gross events of which the movement of celestial bodies, waves, energy forms, and strain are examples. For years classical physics was supreme, being applied continuously to smaller and smaller classes of phenomena in the physical universe. Physicists at one time adopted the view that everything in their realm could be discovered by simply subdividing problems. Physics thus moved into the "micro" order.

But in the nineteenth century a revolution took place motivated largely because events were being noted which could not be explained adequately by the conceptual framework supplied by the classical school. The consequences of this revolution are brilliantly described by Eddington:

> From the point of view of philosophy of science the conception associated with entropy must I think be ranked as the great contribution of the nineteenth century to scientific thought. It marked a reaction from the view that everything to which science need pay attention is discovered by microscopic dissection of objects. It provided an alternative standpoint in which the centre of interest is shifted from the entities reached by the customary analysis (atoms, electric potentials, etc.) to qualities possessed by the system as a whole, which cannot be split up and located—a little bit here, and a little bit there. . . .
> We often think that when we have completed our study of *one* we know all about *two*, because "two" is "one and one." We forget that we have still to make a study of "and." Secondary physics is the study of "and"—that is to say, of organization.[53]

Although modern physics often deals in minute quantities and oscillations, the conception of the physicist is on the "macro" scale. He is concerned with the "and," or the organization of the world in which the events occur. These developments did not invalidate classical physics as to its usefulness for explaining a certain range of phenomena. But classical physics is no longer the undisputed law of the universe. It is a special case.

Early economic theory, and Adam Smith's *Wealth of Nations* comes to mind, examined economic problems in the macro order. The *Wealth of Nations* is mainly concerned with matters of national income and welfare. Later, the economics of the firm, micro-economics, dominated the theoretical scene in this science. And, finally, with Keynes' *The*

[53] Sir Arthur Eddington, *The Nature of the Physical World* (Ann Arbor: The University of Michigan Press, 1958), pp. 103–104.

General Theory of Employment Interest and Money, a systematic approach to the economic universe was re-introduced on the macro level.

The first era of the developing science of sociology was occupied by the great social "system builders." Comte, the so-called father of sociology, had a macro view of society in that his chief works are devoted to social reorganization. Comte was concerned with the interrelationships among social, political, religious, and educational institutions. As sociology progressed, the science of society compressed. Emphasis shifted from the macro approach of the pioneers to detailed, empirical study of small social units. The compression of sociological analysis was accompanied by study of social pathology or disorganization.

In general, physics, economics, and sociology appear to have two things in common. First, they offered a macro point of view as their initial systematic comprehension of their area of study. Second, as the science developed, attention fragmented into analysis of the parts of the organization, rather than attending to the system as a whole. This is the micro phase.

In physics and economics discontent was evidenced by some scientists at the continual atomization of the universe. The reaction to the micro approach was a new theory or theories dealing with the total system, on the macro level again. This third phase of scientific development seems to be more evident in physics and economics than in sociology.

The reason for the "macro-micro-macro" order of scientific progress lies, perhaps, in the hypothesis that usually the things which strike man first are of great magnitude. The scientist attempts to discover order in the vastness. But after macro laws or models of systems are postulated, variations appear which demand analysis, not so much in terms of the entire system, but more in terms of the specific parts which make it up. Then, intense study of microcosm may result in new general laws, replacing the old models of organization. Or, the old and the new models may stand together, each explaining a different class of phenomenon. Or, the old and the new concepts of organization may be welded to produce a single creative synthesis.

Now, what does all this have to do with the problem of organization in administrative science? Organization concepts seem to have gone through the same order of development in this field as in the three just mentioned. It is evident that the classical theory of organization, particularly as in the work of Mooney and Reiley, is concerned with principles common to all organizations. It is a macro-organizational view. The classical approach to organization, however, dealt with the gross anatomical parts and processes of the formal organization. Like classical physics, the classical theory of organization is a special case. Neither are especially well equipped to account for variation from their established framework.

Many variations in the classical administrative model result from human behavior. The only way these variations could be understood was by a microscopic examination of particularized, situational aspects of human behavior. The mission of the neoclassical school thus is "micro-analysis."

It was observed earlier, that somewhere along the line the concept of the social system, which is the key to understanding the Hawthorne studies, faded into the background. Maybe the idea is so obvious that it was lost to the view of researchers and writers in human relations. In any event, the press of research in the micro-cosmic universes of the informal organization, morale and productivity, leadership, participation, and the like forced the notion of the social system into limbo. Now, with the advent of modern organization theory, the social system has been resurrected.

Modern organization theory appears to be concerned with Eddington's "and." This school claims that its operational hypothesis is based on a macro point of view; that is, the study of organization as a whole. This nobility of purpose should not obscure, however, certain difficulties faced by this field as it is presently constituted. Modern organization theory raises two questions which should be explored further. First, would it not be more accurate to speak of modern organization theor*ies*? Second, just how much of modern organization theory is modern?

The first question can be answered with a quick affirmative. Aside from the notion of the system, there are few, if any, other ideas of a unifying nature. Except for several important exceptions,[54] modern organization theorists tend to pursue their pet points of view,[55] suggesting they are part of system theory, but not troubling to show by what mystical means they arrive at this conclusion.

The irony of it all is that a field dealing with systems has, indeed, little system. Modern organization theory needs a framework, and it needs an integration of issues into a common conception of organization. Admittedly, this is a large order. But it is curious not to find serious analytical treatment of subjects like cybernetics or general system theory in Haire's, *Modern Organizational Theory* which claims to be a representative example of work in this field. Beer has ample

---

[54] For example: E. Wight Bakke, *op. cit.*, pp. 18–75.
[55] There is a large selection including decision theory, individual-organization interaction, motivation, vitality, stability, growth, and graph theory, to mention a few.

evidence in his book *Cybernetics and Management* that cybernetics, if imaginatively approached, provides a valuable conceptual base for the study of systems.

The second question suggests an ambiguous answer. Modern organization theory is in part a product of the past; system analysis is not a new idea. Further, modern organization theory relies for supporting data on microcosmic research studies, generally drawn from the journals of the last ten years. The newness of modern organization theory, perhaps, is its effort to synthesize recent research contributions of many fields into a system theory characterized by a reoriented conception of organization.

One might ask, but what is the modern theorist reorienting? A clue is found in the almost snobbish disdain assumed by some authors of the neo-classical human relations school, and particularly, the classical school. Re-evaluation of the classical school of organization is overdue. However, this does not mean that its contributions to organization theory are irrelevant and should be overlooked in the rush to get on the "behavioral science bandwagon."

Haire announces that the papers appearing in *Modern Organization Theory* constitute, "the ragged leading edge of a wave of theoretical development."[56] Ragged, yes; but leading no! The papers appearing in this book do not represent a theoretical breakthrough in the concept of organization. Haire's collection is an interesting potpourri with several contributions of considerable significance. But readers should beware that they will not find vastly new insights into organizational behavior in this book, if they have kept up with the literature of the social sciences, and have dabbled to some extent in the esoteria of biological theories of growth, information theory, and mathematical model building. For those who have not maintained the pace, *Modern Organization Theory* serves the admirable purpose of bringing them up-to-date on a rather diversified number of subjects.

Some work in modern organization theory is pioneering, making its appraisal difficult and future uncertain. While the direction of this endeavor is unclear, one thing is patently true. Human behavior in organizations, and indeed, organization itself, cannot be adequately understood within the ground rules of classical and neo-classical doctrines. Appreciation of human organization requires a *creative* synthesis of massive amounts of empirical data, a high order of deductive reasoning, imaginative research studies, and a taste for individual and social values. Accomplishment of all these objectives, and the inclusion

---

[56] Mason Haire, "General Issues," in Mason Haire (editor), *Modern Organization Theory* (New York: John Wiley and Sons, 1959), p. 2.

of them into a framework of the concept of the system, appears to be the goal of modern organization theory. The vitality of administrative science rests on the advances modern theorists make along this line.

Modern organization theory, 1960 style, is an amorphous aggregation of synthesizers and restaters, with a few extending leadership on the frontier. For the sake of these few, it is well to admonish that pouring old wine into new bottles may make the spirits cloudy. Unfortunately, modern organization theory has almost succeeded in achieving the status of a fad. Popularization and exploitation contributed to the disrepute into which human relations has fallen. It would be a great waste if modern organization theory yields to the same fate, particularly since both modern organization theory and human relations draw from the same promising source of inspiration—system analysis.

Modern organization theory needs tools of analysis and a conceptual framework uniquely its own, but it must also allow for the incorporation of relevant contributions of many fields. It may be that the framework will come from general system theory. New areas of research such as decision theory, information theory, and cybernetics also offer reasonable expectations of analytical and conceptual tools. Modern organization theory represents a frontier of research which has great significance for management. The potential is great, because it offers the opportunity for uniting what is valuable in classical theory with the social and natural sciences into a systematic and integrated conception of human organization.

Organization Theory and Political Theory*

Herbert Kaufman

If two men of similar talents, identical training, shared values, and common interests were to study the same phenomena it would not be at all remarkable if they approached the phenomena in the same way, described them in the same terms, employed the same logic in analyzing them, drew the same conclusions from them, and formulated the same theories about their causes.

If, however, two men of similar talents but of rather divergent training, professing differing objectives, and displaying varied (perhaps even conflicting) concerns were to pursue studies of phenomena each believed to be quite distinct from the other's field of inquiry, it would be most astounding if their findings and inferences should turn out to be closely parallel in many important respects, particularly if there were little evidence of communication between them.

That is why the parallels between political theory, probably the oldest of the social sciences, and organization theory, perhaps the newest such discipline, are so totally unexpected. If there is any conscious agreement between the two fields, it is on their separateness from each other: political theorists and organization theorists alike seem to take for granted the impossibility of encompassing within a single theoretical framework propositions about states—that is, the relation of governments to subjects, and the relations of governments to each other— and propositions about other forms of human association. In the literature on organization theory, one rarely finds references even to contemporary political theorists and almost never to those who wrote in the past. By the same token, political theorists rarely seem to find anything relevant to their interests in the work of students of organization. Measured by the acknowledged exchange of information between the disciplines, the gulf between them is wide and seldom bridged.

Perhaps such a gulf is inescapable. Political theorists draw heavily upon history, philosophy, and personal experience for their ideas and evidence; organization theorists rely heavily upon sociology, social

* A paper delivered at the Annual Meeting of the American Political Science Association, New York City, September, 1963. I should like to acknowledge the patient criticism and instruction given me by my colleague, Professor Roger Masters, who saved me from many errors, misinterpretations, and oversights, and tried vainly to save me from those that remain in the text. Reprinted with permission of author and publisher from *American Political Science Review,* 58 (March, 1964), pp. 5–14.

psychology, economics, and, when possible, on controlled experimentation. Political theorists are frankly normative; organization theorists generally believe their work is value-free. Political theorists deal willingly with the intangible aspects of human associations, for it is difficult to measure the outputs of governments and governmental agencies; organization theorists are more at home with organizations producing tangible products and measuring their performance ultimately in terms of profit. The fields do seem to have quite different traditions, methods, goals, and subject-matters.

But all this merely makes the similarities in the problems they investigate and in their findings more surprising and intriguing.

I

For example, both organization theorists and political theorists encountered the same enigma: In order that the human systems may come into being and continue, men often have to do, at the behest of others, tasks that are unpleasant or even hazardous (such as working on assembly lines or going to war), and must refrain from doing what they would greatly enjoy(such as helping themselves to the property of others or saying whatever they please wherever and whenever the spirit moves them). What accounts for obedience and docility entailing such self-sacrifice, self-restraint, self-denial, without which neither states nor other associations could long survive?

Political philosophers and organziation theorists have offered essentially the same range of explanations: the rationality of men and the conditioning of men's minds.[1]

Because men are rational, they can calculate what they would lose if everyone were to follow his own impulses and preferences without restraint. They can also see that collective action will be taken against individuals who disobey. Out of fear of the consequences, they submit. They can calculate, too, the advantages they may gain from organized life and activity. They can see that the gains usually outweigh the

[1] A third explanation, offered initially by political philosophers of classical antiquity, was that some men are by nature followers and others are by nature rulers. The followers obey because it is their nature to do so, just as leaders command because that is *their* nature. This argument has few defenders among contemporary political theorists, and it is seldom articulated by organization theorists. But one may wonder whether the batteries of personality and aptitude and intelligence tests used for selecting executives do not rest ultimately on the assumption that there are "natural" leaders who should be identified, separated from the "naturally" subservient mass, and elevated to their "natural" managerial roles.

costs. Out of hope for the benefits, then, as well as out of fear, rational men yield to the wills of others.[2]

At the same time, according to many political and organization theorists, men obey because obedience to certain commands from certain sources is a conditioned reflex. Even in infancy, every individual is introduced to the exercise of authority; maturation is in many ways a process of learning when to obey, whom to command, and under what circumstances to do either. That is, from his social environment generally, and also by virtue of the deliberate drill and indoctrination to which he is subject, every man is prepared for his social roles. He comes to yield to others because he learns it is right and proper to do so, and he may even come to cherish his submission. The will to obey is implanted in him; depending on the discipline one draws upon for appropriate language, he is educated, indoctrinated, trained, socialized, acculturated, programmed, or brainwashed.[3]

---

[2] This reasoning underlies most social-contract philosophies of the origins of civil and political society. The emphasis was placed in some cases on escape from the risks and uncertainties of anarchy (as in Hobbes and Locke), in others on ascension to a higher, richer, distinctively human and civilized life (as in Rousseau, whose logic, in turn, parallels that of classical political theory). The hypothesized reasoning in men's decisions to form or join groups in which they must then submit to others is not far removed from the analysis by J. G. March and H. A. Simon, *Organizations* (New York, 1957), of individual calculations regarding "the decision to participate" in organizations (ch. 4). See also Simon's assertion that a distinctive feature of organization theory is its treatment of joining an organization as an "all-or-none choice of participation or non-participation," in *Models of Man* (New York, 1957), p. 74 and chs. 10 and 11.

Organization theorists and most political philosophers exhibit little confidence in fear as a long-range mode of eliciting obedience. But for a few political theorists (Hobbes, for example), and for more than a few rulers and managers, it is the cornerstone of theory and practice.

[3] Many political theorists recognized this. For example, according to H. V. Jaffa ("Aristotle," in L. Strauss and J. Cropsey, eds., *History of Political Philosophy* (Chicago, 1963), p. 75, Aristotle held that "Trained obedience, as distinct from brute direction, is the characteristic of being ruled politically or royally." Hume, says R. S. Hill ("David Hume," *ibid.*, pp. 511–12), considered that "The main support of the rule of the few over the many . . . is the opinion that those in authority have a right to that authority. This opinion is usually the fruit of time and habit. Custom is the great guide of human life; most men never think of inquiring into the reasons for the authority of the form of government to which they have become habituated." Rousseau (see A. Bloom, "Jean-Jacques Rousseau," *ibid.*, pp. 527, 531) believed "the manners of society are of as much or more concern than the institutions of government because manners underlie institutions and give them their force," and he saw an advantage in the ancient city "because it is small enough . . . for citizens to share a common heritage and a common way, because the particular wills can more easily be submerged in custom, and because the statesman can control the entirety." Burke (see F. Canavan, "Edmund Burke," *ibid.*, p. 603) also ascribed obedience to governments and laws to "opinion, habit, and acquired sentiment," and to the fact that "men think

Interestingly enough, political theorists have from the very beginning made more strenuous efforts to incorporate the non-rational (*i.e.*, the conditioned) elements of men's behavior into their hypotheses than have the organization theorists. For men are born into political systems, and the possibilities of withdrawal are much more limited. It is not clear that joining or remaining in a political system is really a matter of rational choice at all, except in isolated instances. Organization theorists, on the other hand, deal more extensively with associations that men presumably choose to enter and may leave at any time. To explain membership and all it entails, students of organization lean toward a rather literal application of social-contract theory and utilitarianism; many eighteenth- and nineteenth-century political philosophers, who employed these concepts as metaphors to aid in understanding the rational component of behavior, would find little in most modern organization theory with which to quarrel. And some organization theorists would doubtless be surprised to discover how many political philosophers in ancient and medieval times were aware there were social norms and group loyalties that a ruler dared not violate without risking extensive disobedience.

At any rate, more or less independently of each other, drawing in different ways on different bodies of experience, political theorists and organization theorists have dealt in very similar fashion with the obedience of man to man.

II

They have also dealt similarly with organizational structures for the achievement of coordination. For purposes of this discussion, coordination means ordering the direction, volume, and timing of flows of activities, goods, and services so that the functioning of one element

---

it right to submit to them," and Bentham (see H. M. Magid, "Jeremy Bentham," *ibid.*, p. 623) explained political society as arising from "the habit of obedience."

These interpretations may be compared with similar formulations by H. A. Simon, D. W. Smithburg, and V. A. Thompson in their *Public Administration* (New York, 1950), at pp. 188–201, attributing obedience in part to the authority of confidence (or expertise), of identification (or group loyalty), and of legitimacy (the feeling that one ought to obey). In like fashion, P. M. Blau and W. R. Scott, *Formal Organizations* (San Francisco: Chandler, 1962), at pp. 27–32, 140–45, stress "culturally defined role expectations" (p. 30) and internalization of social values (p. 144). R. V. Presthus, "Authority in Organizations," in S. Mailick and E. H. Van Ness, eds., *Concepts and Issues in Administrative Behavior* (Englewood Cliffs: Prentice-Hall, 1962), at p. 125, emphasizes socialization, or the acceptance of societal or group norms and values, as a key process producing acceptance of authority.

in a system at least does not prevent or negate or hamper the functioning of other elements, and at best facilitates and assists the functioning
of other elements. Coordination is not always a goal of system designers; the separation of powers, for example, encourages some contradictions and deadlocks in order to protect other values. But it is often
among the principal values, and practically never is a matter of total
indifference. And when political theorists and organization theorists
discuss methods of promoting coordination, they end up in much the
same positions.

Fundamentally, coordination is accomplished by two processes: central direction, which means that the activities of the elements of a
system respond chiefly to cues and signals from some common source,
and reciprocal relations, which means that the elements respond to
cues and signals from each other. Every system employs some blend
of the two processes. Moreover, the systems are not mutually exclusive;
an increase in reliance on one does not necessarily produce a decrease
in the other. On the contrary, effective central direction often permits
a higher degree of reciprocal cueing, as in a well-trained platoon, and
vice versa. Whatever the blend of modes of coordination and whatever
the general level of coordination in any system, these may be explained
in terms of the relative weight assigned to each of the two underlying
processes.

Political theorists who believe men are inclined to take advantage of
one another tend to stress central direction as the best means of coordinating them. Without an overriding central figure, according to
them, any system breaks down in disorder, confusion, and internal
warfare. Hobbes, of course, presented this argument in its purest, most
logical form.[4] On the other side, philosophers who assume the interests
and tendencies of men are harmonious emphasize the possibility and
desirability of coordination through reciprocity, and regard central
direction as an exploitative or disturbing factor in what would otherwise be a highly coordinated system distributing maximum satisfaction
to all its members. The anarchists, both Marxist and non-Marxist,
pushed this reasoning to its logical extreme.[5] It matters little for this
discussion whether the extremists on both sides meant their doctrines
to be taken literally or as analogies for the sake of clarity and vigor

---

[4] For a brief summary of his logic, see G. H. Sabine, *A History of Political Theory*
(New York, 3d ed., 1961), pp. 167–69.
[5] For an outline of recent anarchist thought (which is an updated version of
anarchist philosophics of ancient times), see F. W. Coker, *Recent Political Thought*
(New York, 1934), ch. VII. Also relevant are chs. VIII (on syndicalism), IX (on
guild socialism), and XVIII (on pluralism).

of statement. They bracketed the range of possibilities. In the history of political thought, not only the extremes, but virtually all conceivable intermediate positions, have at some time or other been advanced or defended.

During most of the short history of organization theory, few theorists seriously questioned the premise that central direction (expressed structurally as a hierarchy of authority because of the need of leaders to delegate formal powers and because of the assumed inability of men to supervise directly more than a small number of colleagues) is the primary method of achieving coordination; indeed, hierarchy and organization were sometimes treated as almost synonymous.[6] Yet very early some questioning voices were heard, particularly after experimental studies in the sociology of industry drew attention to the responsiveness of workers to cues and signals emanating from sources other than (and sometimes hostile to) the designated managers of the firms examined. Mary Parker Follett, a political scientist of Pluralist persuasion, became well known to students of organization for her advocacy of "power with rather than power over" and for her criticism of "the illusion of final responsibility."[7] Later on, Argyris[8] and Thompson and others[9] would search explicitly for a pattern of organization that is non-hierarchical. An electronics firm on the West Coast recently

[6] *E.g.*, J. O. Mooney, *The Principles of Organization* (New York, 1947), pp. 14–15: "The scalar principle is the same form in organization that is sometimes called hierarchical. ... The common impression regards this scale or chain merely as a 'type' of organization, characteristic only of the vaster institutions of government, army, church, and industry. This impression is erroneous. It is likewise misleading, for it seems to imply that the scalar chain in organization lacks universality. These great organizations differ from others only in that the chain is longer. The truth is that wherever we find an organization even of two people, related as superior and subordinate, we have the scalar principle. This chain constitutes the universal process of coordination, through which the supreme coordinating authority becomes effective throughout the entire structure." See also, M. G. Weiner, "Observations on the Growth of Information-Processing Centers," in A. H. Rubenstein and C. J. Haberstroh, eds., *Some Theories of Organization* (Homewood: Dorsey and Irwin, 1960), p. 150: "The transition from individuality to division of labor and the acceptance of hierarchy in the form of a leadership structure ... represents the point at which an 'organization' can be said to exist."
[7] H. C. Metcalf and L. Urwick, eds., *Dynamic Administration: The Collected Papers of Mary Parker Follett* (New York, 1941), especially pp. 101 ff. and ch. VII.
[8] C. Argyris, *Personality and Organization* (New York, 1957).
[9] V. A. Thompson, *Modern Organizations* (New York, 1961); G. G. Fisch, "Line-Staff is Obsolete," *Harvard Business Review*, Vol. 39, pp. 67–79 (1961); B. M. Bass, "Industrial Organization for the Space Age," unpublished manuscript, Graduate School of Business Administration, University of Pittsburgh, 1963. See also the query of W. M. Evan, "Indices of the Hierarchical Structure of Industrial Organizations," 9 *Management Science*, Vol. 9, pp 468–77 (1963), regarding the validity of the "iron law of hierarchy."

reorganized itself on what are alleged to be non-hierarchical lines.[10]
It would be grossly inaccurate to equate these organizational analysts
with the anarchists, but there can be no question that organization
theory has begun to display an awareness of a range of positions on the
central-reciprocal scale that political philosophers have explored extensively for centuries.

I do not intend to imply that political philosophy is somehow superior to organization theory, or that organization theory is a mere
branch of the history of political thought. My object in pointing out
similarities between their treatments of coordination is simply to demonstrate that these seemingly unrelated disciplines confront common
problems in common ways.

III

Another such problem is the reconciliation of individual or other
narrow objectives with the objectives of the collectivity. Political
theorists discuss it in terms of special interests as against the general
or public interest. Organization theorists speak of personal or subgroup goals *vis-à-vis* organizational goals. But the issues are the same.

In both fields, the dominant opinion seems to be that every collectivity is in some sense goal-seeking, or purposive. That is, there is some
general interest or organizational goal shared or at least acknowledged
by nearly all the participants in the system, and although the over-
arching purpose is accomplished by the labor of individuals, it is
distinct from the goals or interests of individuals; rather, it is viewed
as an attribute of the system as a whole. There is little agreement on
the specifics of the general interest, and even a given commentator may
switch from one to another interpretation as conditions change. (Implicitly, however, one goal can be discerned in every interpretation:
the survival of the system.) Yet, although students of states and of
organizations may never arrive at a consensus on exactly what the
shared interests of human associations are, many of them tend to take
it for granted that one exists for every human association.[11]

---

[10] The firm is Non-Linear Systems, Inc., of Del Mar, California. Its structure and
procedures are described by A. H. Kuriloff, "Management by Integration and
Self-Control," *Proceedings of the Industrial Engineering Institute*, Febraury, 1963.
[11] Plato and Aristototle, for example, saw as the purpose of the city-state the
promotion of the highest moral development of its citizens. For Hobbes, the end
of government was the preservation of order. For Locke, it was the protection of
"natural rights," such as the right to private property. For the Utilitarians, it was
to produce the greatest good for the greatest number. For the early liberal
economists, it was to furnish just enough service and regulation to permit the

A substantial number of political theorists, on the other hand, have taken the view that virtually every definition of the public interest is but a reflection of the personal interests of the definer, and consequently, the only realistic way to understand the performance of a system is to construe its output (or its policies) as nothing more than the resultant of the interplay of many special interests. The representatives of each interest may invoke the symbol of the public interest as an honorific, perhaps even with sincere conviction that the actions they espouse *are* better for the system and all the members of the system, but what is actually decided and done is the product of negotiations and understandings among specialized groups and individuals.[12]

Among organization theorists, the counterpart to this point of view is seldom advanced even tacitly, let alone explicitly; it is distinctly a minority position. Barnard, however, comes close to it. Although he discusses organizational purposes at length, and attributes great importance to them, they are not central to his analysis. He defines formal organizations without referring to goals, and he describes them largely in terms of individual motivations and objectives coordinated with each other through an "economy of incentives." The "absolute test" of efficiency is survival of the organization. An organization is thus por-

---

reciprocal processes of the market place to operate effectively. In all these instances, selected haphazardly from the broad array of goals postulated in political thought, the existence of a common purpose and interest is axiomatic.

The same is true of most contemporary organization theory, although the specification of common interests is rarely articulated as explicitly as in political philosophy. Rather, it is assumed that every human association has *some* goals shared by all its members, and can be understood only in terms of those common purposes, *E.g.*, in H. S. Simon, D. W. Smithburg, and V. A. Thompson, *op. cit.*, at p. 3, purpose and cooperative action are described as the "two basic processes of what has come to be called administration. ... Administration can be defined as the activities of groups cooperating to accomplish common goals." Similarly, P. M. Blau and W. R. Scott, *op. cit.*, at p. 1, declare that what organizations "all have in common is that a number of men have become organized into a social unit —an organization—that has been established for the explicit purpose of achieving certain goals." And C. Argyris, *Understanding Organizational Behavior* (Homewood: Dorsey, 1960) hypothesizes, at pp. 10–11, "that organizations are intricate human strategies designed to achieve certain objectives," and that the objectives of any organization include "achieving its goals (intended consequences)."

[12] Bentham, for instance, defined the interest of any community as the sum of the interests of those who compose it (H. M. Magid, *op. cit.*, p. 622). A. F. Bentley, in *The Process of Government* (Bloomington: Principia, 1935), said (at p. 269), "All phenomena of government are phenomena of groups pressing one another, forming one another, and pushing out new groups and group representatives (the organs and agencies of government) to mediate the adjustments." D. B. Truman, using a similar framework of analysis in *The Governmental Process* (New York, 1953), added (at p. 51), "In developing a group interpretation of politics, ... we do not need to account for a totally inclusive interest, because one does not exist." See also, E. P. Herring, *The Politics of Democracy* (New York, 1940), ch 30.

trayed as a kind of marketplace in which each man pursues his own goals by offering a contribution in return for those inducements (selected from the range of inducements provided, consciously or unwittingly, by the system) that appeal to him. The enterprise is an arena in which each participant offers his wares and services in exchange for what he can get. From the elaborate network of agreements, accommodations, and behaviors come products, wages, salaries, profits, prices, dividends, interest, taxes, working conditions, and all the other outputs of a complex system. Managers, workers, suppliers, customers, stockholders, creditors, competitors, government regulators, consultants, academics, and others may all see different transcendent purposes in the undertaking, so that its ends are in a sense the sum of all the special purposes.[13] To this extent, this view resembles in many respects the view of the state espoused by the political theorists mentioned above. What is sometimes referred to as a collective purpose is merely the resultant of a constantly shifting adjustment among individual and subgroup purposes.

Over the relationship of private interests to the general interest, organization theorists and political theorists have divided into similar camps. Again, the resemblances between the fields are impressive.

IV

The foregoing illustrations do not exhaust the parallels between organization theory and political theory.[14] But they are probably sufficient to establish the point of departure for this discussion, namely, that striking similarities have developed in two disciplines that seem to be quite different in their interests and methods.

Why should this occur? Why should two fields of study with such discrepant premises and perspectives converge?

Perhaps it is because the discrepancies are, after all, merely the distinctions between different species of the same genus. When all is said and done, they both treat of phenomena that encompass vast areas, if not all, of human life. We are all members of at least several organi-

---

[13] C. I. Barnard, *The Functions of the Executive* (Cambridge: Harvard University Press, 1938), pp. 73 ("a formal organization ... [is] a system of consciously coordinated activities or forces of two or more persons"), 93, 137 ("The individual is always the basic strategic factor in organization."), ch. XI, and pp. 161–75. See also, H. A. Simon, *Administrative Behavior* (New York, 1947), pp. 103–07; Simon describes coordination in terms of adjustments among individuals' behaviors. But he does observe that the individuals must find one plan agreeable to all participants if they are to cooperate, thus introducing the equivalent of common purpose.

[14] For an exploration of the political theory implicit in the writings of organization theorists, see D. Waldo, *The Administrative State* (New York, 1948).

zations, and organizations give characteristic content and general form to our lives. Moreover, states, governments, the branches and agencies of governments, political parties, and interest groups are organizations like other organizations even though they have their unique attributes. What aspect of civilized existence then lies outside the scope of organization theory?

At the same time, every organization is sometimes construed as a political system, with all the problems of leadership, policy formation, succession, strategy, rivalry, resistance, revolution, and influence that this implies.[15] If organizations are an all-embracing subject of inquiry, politics is an equally comprehensive theme. To be sure, organization theorists tend to avoid political institutions in searching for data, and political philosophers tend to concentrate on those institutions immediately associated with public governments. But they may end with strong similarities because they are both addressed to phenomena permeating the whole of human affairs. Fields that take so much for their province must have far more overlap than is immediately obvious.

Furthermore, they both start from normative bases. Political theorists were historically engaged in a quest for the ideal political system; organization theorists began by seeking "the one best way"—*i.e.*, the most efficient way—to organize production and distribution. There are probably some in both disciplines who still believe such ideal arrangements, superior to all alternatives under any conditions and at any time, are attainable; most contemporary theorists, I believe, now adopt a relativist position, holding that the definition of the ideal changes as circumstances change, and perhaps even that a wide variety of organizational and political patterns may satisfy equally well the requirements of any particular definition. At any rate, men in both fields set out to discover the "laws" or "principles" governing social behavior so as to formulate proposals for improvement consonant with the constraints imposed by reality. Sometimes they try to sharpen their thinking by reasoning from admittedly over-simplified hypotheses, such as man in a state of nature or completely rational man. Eventually, however, they complicate their models by adding variables that render the hypotheses better approximations of the real world. (Such variables are more often discovered by non-normative research of an historical or experimental kind than by intuition.) Conceivably, the fields may come to resemble each other because they have parallel normative underpinnings.

---

[15] *E.g.*, N. Long, "The Administrative Organization as a Political System," in S. Mailick and E. H. Van Ness, *op. cit.*

But the explanation of the resemblances may not lie in the character of the disciplines at all; perhaps it is to be found rather in the nature of the world the disciplines purport to describe. The convergence *could* result from the existence of such pronounced and persistent regularities in large-scale human associations that no matter which such associations one examines and what approach one adopts, the sum of the findings of each set of observers will inevitably be much the same as those of any other set. When all the blind men compare their notes, they *do* end up with a description of an elephant, and the description by each team of blind men will not differ materially from the description produced by any other team, because, after all, it *is* an elephant they are studying. The consensus of two relatively insulated fields, when the whole range of their content is reviewed, lends corroboration to the impression that our ideas about organizations and politics have a substantial degree of validity.

V

Whatever the explanation of the similarities between organization theory and political theory, one obvious implication of the similarities is that the two fields can probably learn a great deal from each other. In the literature on organizations, political theorists will find reports on experiments and rigorous logical analyses bearing heavily on the concerns of political philosophy. In the history of political thought, which may be regarded as a collection of descriptive models of social behavior or a series of tentative propositions about the ways men act in organized groups, organization theorists will find a rich store of ideas they seem to be toiling to reproduce independently.

But my purpose in writing this piece is not merely to labor the obvious point that scholars in two disciplines stand to gain by sharing their materials more extensively in the future than they have in the past. More important are the indications that theory in both areas is to a large extent imprisoned by the premises and perspectives and reasoning of an earlier day, trapped into recapitulating and refining familiar concepts instead of developing new approaches and assumptions that might free theory from the cycling loop into which it has fallen. Although there are important exceptions, it appears that much modern writing in both fields tends to retrace established paths instead of finding new ones. Those who are not conversant with the history of thought often devote their energies to rediscovering triumphantly old and even ancient ideas, and to reviving traditional controversies. Those who have mastered the history of thought often apply themselves to proving there is nothing new under the sun. Each for his own reasons ends up operating within confines identified with prior generations. Each for his own reasons fetters his imagination.

To be sure, the exceptions are notable. Some strikingly original recent approaches to the study of human behavior, such as computer simulation of individual thought processes and social situations, may well have dramatic consequences for the viewpoints and findings of the social sciences. By and large, however, it is the *scarcity* of unconventional ideas rather than the problems of choosing among them that impresses the observer. Even sophisticated methods of research and analysis, bound by the outlooks and assumptions of earlier times, add only a little to our knowledge and insight.

This is hardly surprising; we are all products of our heritage, and it is not easy to conceive of altogether new ways of looking at things, however urgent may be the need for novel ideas. That is why it is important to try not only to invent new concepts, but also to seek them out in our current environment by borrowing from seemingly unrelated disciplines, and by picking up the threads of inquiry previously explored and prematurely dropped. One such concept seems to me to hold particularly great promise of putting organization behavior in a perspective quite unlike the one from which we seem unable to escape, and thus to provide stimuli and generate perceptions which apparently lie beyond the scope of our ordinary frame of reference. I refer to what in its broadest terms may be described as the treatment of human organizations as a form of life rather than as an artifact designed, created, and directed exclusively by the human intellect.

Such a biological analogy in political theory was drawn in classical antiquity and occasionally in later periods of Western history,[16] and it has even appeared in the writings of one or two contemporary organization theorists.[17] But the logic of it has never been rigorously followed out in the light of modern knowledge and, perhaps even more perti-

---

[16] Plato, for instance, drew a parallel between the body and the city, and Hegel also turned to the metaphor of the organism. *Cf.* L. Strauss and J. Cropsey, *op. cit.*, pp. 16, 25, 630. And after Darwin, comparisons between social and biological evolution were commonly employed, though usually in a fashion that did violence to the biological theory.

[17] See C. Barnard, *op. cit.*, p. 79: "Systems of cooperation which we call organizations I regard as social creatures, 'alive,' just as I regard an individual human being ..." (His argument that an organization is more than the sum of its parts, as a person is more than the sum of his parts, is almost identical with that of Aristotle; *cf.* H. V. Jaffa, *op. cit.*, p. 66.) See also M. Haire, "Biological Models and Empirical Histories of the Growth of Organizations," in M. Haire, ed., *Modern Organization Theory* (New York, 1959), pp. 272–306; and P. Selznick, "Foundations of the Theory of Organization," *American Sociological Review*, Vol. 13, pp. 25–35 (1948), and *Leadership in Administration* (New York, 1957).

nently, in the light of the growth and evolution of organizational forms in recent times. Currently out of fashion in political science, and in the social sciences generally,[18] this now neglected tradition strikes me as more likely to improve our understanding of human associations than it ever could before. And it probably requires a discipline as boldly inclusive, as young and therefore as flexible and open-minded, and as vigorous as organization theory, to dare to reopen this approach and to employ it successfully.

VI

Seen from this angle, what would the world of organizations look like? Probably crowded, continually changing, difficult to analyze, viscous. For compared to an individual organism, organizations do not display a notably high level of integration most of the time; the responsiveness of their components to each other is relatively slow and uncertain. Their boundaries are often loosely defined, easily changed, and permeable. Most organizations contain, are contained by, and overlap other organizations; they are unusual among the forms of life in that they can share constituent elements with each other. They interact with their surroundings, usually exchanging something (either acquired or produced) from inside their boundaries for something beyond their boundaries. Generally, there are subsets of elements within them that exercise greater influence over the other elements with respect to certain processes than the other elements exercise over these subsets; and some subsets interact extensively with the environment beyond the boundaries as well as with elements within the boundaries. There are reasons to suspect that organizations have a high rate of mortality, and though one can point to many individual cases of long-lived organizations, the number that disappear every year is probably staggering.[19]

Yet the number of human organizations in the world at any given

---

[18] But see D. T. Campbell, "Evolutionary Theory in Social Science: A Reappraisal," unpublished paper, Northwestern University, 1961, and the references cited therein. See also R. Redfield, ed., *Levels of Integration in Biological and Social Systems* (Lancaster: Jacques Cattell Press, 1942).

[19] The impression that large numbers of organizational fatalities occur is suggested in part by the frequency of business failures. Barnard, for example (*op. cit.*, p. 5), comments, "successful cooperation in or by formal organizations is the abnormal, not the normal, condition. What are observed from day to day are the successful survivors among innumerable failures. . . . Failure to cooperate, failure of cooperation, failure of organization, disorganization, disintegration, destruction of organization—and reorganization—are characteristic facts of human history."

moment is also probably enormous. Virtually every individual is a member of at least several organizations, and while this does not mean there are necessarily more organizations in the world than there are people, it indicates that the ratio of organizations to people is quite substantial. Consequently, with so many organizational claims on the resources at the disposal of human beings, including time and obedience, some organizations lose out in the competition for these resources. (In part, the shortage results from a highly unbalanced distribution of claims and resources. But it is also plausible that the number of organizations making claims on resources increases more rapidly than the volume of available resources—by a kind of Malthusian law—so that the possible ways of allocating resources are likely always to exceed the reservoir of resources available.) That is, as is true with other forms of life, organizations make upon the resources essential to their survival demands that tend to press beyond the limit of supply, and the demands are kept more or less in check by the demise of organizations or declines in the rate at which new ones form. It should be noted, incidentally, that from this standpoint, an employer, a veterans association, a trade union, a political party, a neighborhood civic group, a bowling club, a church, and a government agency, and other groups, though superficially unconnected, may all be in competition with one another, for they may all be rivals for the resources (again including the time and obedience) of the same persons.[20]

Under these circumstances, what determines which organizations will survive? One possible determinant is the deliberate strategy of organizations to adapt to conditions; those making the appropriate choices will continue. Much of organization theory, economic theory, and political theory is devoted to the analysis of this sort of rationality.

But it is also conceivable that the biologist's approach could be useful here. When conditions prove fatal to some members of a population while other members survive and even flourish, biologists tend to ascribe the good fortune of the survivors to chance variations in their make-up that protect or even favor them under prevailing conditions. May we not also postulate that in the world population of organizations—those comparatively poorly integrated, sluggish, fragile entities—random variations occur which may make no difference under one set of circumstances, but which may favor or impede some organizations when circumstances change? Admittedly, the calculated strategies may in the end turn out to *be* the critical factor; the bio-

---

[20] In this connection see P. M. Blau and W. R. Scott, *op. cit.*, pp. 215–17.

logical analogy does not preclude this possibility. But it directs attention also to other factors that may be important, factors easily neglected if we concentrate exclusively on rationality.

For example, size may be more important in survival than anything an organization *does* in response to a challenge; all organizations of a greater than given size may endure even though they all respond differently, while smaller organizations may disappear no matter what they do. (By the same token, of course, a change of conditions may wipe out the giants and multiply the pygmies.) Or a substantial measure of self-containment may characterize all the organizations that persist after a drastic modification of the environment (though another environmental shift may favor organizations highly dependent on outside sources). Or in one context, all surviving organizations may exhibit extreme centralization; in another, only the decentralized ones may remain. Sometimes, highly specialized organizations may be the only ones to come through; at other times, only diversified ones may weather a new situation. Those attributes an organization happens to have when changes occur may be more significant than the course of action its leaders elect to pursue; indeed, the paths of action themselves may be determined as much by organizational characteristics as by human intellect.

Now, it is true that an organization can take steps to increase or decrease its size or its self-containment or its centralization or its specialization; these do not lie beyond the scope of manipulation. Thus, organizational *characteristics* as well as organizational *policies* are subject to rational adjustment. Nevertheless, at any given time, any population of organizations will include exceedingly diverse members. For there will be many different judgments as to what adjustments will be advantageous, what adjustments dysfunctional; all organizations will not estimate the future in the same way, and even those that do will differ about the appropriate preparations for that future. Moreover, fortuitous elements, such as personality, the unique history of an organization, tradition, acts of nature, and unplanned internal developments, will produce different consequences in different organizations. So even if all relevant organizational attributes could be rationally controlled, organizations would vary, and every environmental change would benefit some organizations and injure others. But there is no obvious reason to assume that all such attributes are rationally planned; many seem quite accidental, and the selective process is thus intensified.

But human organizations enjoy an advantage that their biological counterparts do not: they have the capacity, at least theoretically, to observe and imitate their more successful fellow-organizations. Logically, then, when conditions change, can they not wait to see the effects and follow the lead of the flourishing ones? In this way, it would seem, most could survive any challenge. In fact, however, organizations can rarely adjust very swiftly. To maintain flexibility for speedy transformation may require the sacrifice of other advantages. Furthermore, every organization contains equilibrium-maintaining mechanisms that resist and moderate change; stability cannot be thrown to the winds. Most organizations therefore cannot alter themselves instantaneously, and differences among them will remain even after the initial impact of environmental changes has indicated which forms are favored.

For these reasons, then, organizational forms may play no less a part in organizational survival than do organizational policies, and we may anticipate that environmental variations will always wipe out some organizations and improve the fortunes of others. A kind of "natural selection" is taking place; in other words, an evolutionary process going on continuously.

Even if this could be demonstrated, what difference would it make? What contribution could it make to the development of organization theory? Where does it lead?

Since we have hardly explored the process, it would be rash to venture a prediction. We can only hope it may prove as useful to the study of organizations as it did to the study of biology. And we can only speculate on what the nature of its utility might be. For example, it might stimulate comparisons of long-lived organizations that give us a better understanding of their longevity. It might facilitate evaluation of allegedly consistent and widespread trends toward specific patterns of organization, and explanation of those trends that do in fact occur.[21] It could encourage a more sophisticated typology of organizations than any we now have, and a better catalogue of relevant environmental conditions and their effects on each category. It might even improve our assessment of organizational survival strategies. But while no one can say exactly what will be uncovered by research based on a theory of organizational evolution, it is a line of inquiry, not well investigated up to now, that has a potential for illuminating regularities hitherto unperceived, or at least unarticulated, in the social sciences. And organization theorists are in the best position to conduct

---

[21] For illustrations of the impression that there is a secular trend toward increasing centralization in modern life, see H. A. Simon, D. W. Smithburg, and V. A. Thompson, *op. cit.*, pp. 272 ff.; R. Redfield, *op. cit.*; R. Seidenberg, *Post-Historic Man* (Boston: Beacon, 1957).

the inquiry because they do not limit themselves to any particular type or aspect of organization.

VII

I am not here proposing a simple return to Social Darwinism—which, in fact, is an egregious misnomer, since the doctrines thus alluded to have little to do with principles of natural selection described by Darwin and other biologists. Nor do I intend to suggest that organizations should be regarded as identical with organisms; on the contrary, it is their unique character as life-forms that I would emphasize. Nor, finally, do I consider this approach a substitute for others; if it has any value, it will be as an addition to our other instruments of analysis, not as a replacement for them. I am arguing only that the possibilities of employing this method rigorously have not been fully realized, and that it seems especially applicable to the study of organizational behavior.

The biological analogy is disturbing to many modern political theorists and organization theorists because it appears to many of them to downgrade human beings, to deny the importance of the gift of thought, to reduce persons to the level of social insects or of cells in a living system. Even if this were the case, it would not justify refusal to consider this frame of reference. When the people of the Western world were compelled by the findings of modern astronomers to abandon the belief that they were at the center of the universe (and thus to recognize what many of the ancients knew), when they were taught by modern biology that they are part of nature (which was also the ancient view), and when they were reminded by modern psychologists that they are something less than wholly rational creatures, the demotions were painful and met with resistance. Yet they added to man's intellectual stature by giving him a fuller and more accurate picture of the world in which he lives, and liberated him from flattering myths and misconceptions, in many ways more degrading than the truth. Men may conceivably become more godlike by accepting their own limitations than by refusing to envisage them at all. There can be excesses in individual-centered philosophies as well as in community-centered doctrines.

But the lesson from early political philosophy is that it is by no means necessary to deny the distinctively human qualities of mankind in order to treat human associations as natural phenomena. On the contrary, the classical opinion was that men fulfilled their potentialities as human beings *only* in the associations as natural to them as the air they breathe. For organization theorists to regard organizations as living forms, then, is not to equate human society with an anthill and people with ants. It may simply be a path to observations and to speculative and empirical inquiries to which our prevailing biases and preoccupations now blind us.

Chapter 1
Managing by Ones and Twos:
Freeing-up Relations Between Individuals

No manager is a social island. Whatever his level, therefore, every manager faces difficult problems of freeing-up the relations between individuals in ways that permit effective and purposive interaction. We shall focus on three such problem areas: that of facilitating effective communication between the supervisor and another individual; that of the manager motivating other individuals or himself; and that of the manager helping to change his behavior or that of other individuals.

If these problem areas are boldly set forth, beyond them no simple statements are possible. Thus such supervisory efforts may be necessary going "up" the hierarchy to superiors, "across" the functional departments to peers, or "down" the chain of command to subordinates. Moreover, these efforts may involve individuals or groups. Such supervisory efforts to free-up relations also must be "directionally" sensitive. For example, sometimes the need is simply for "more communication." Typically, however, the problem is qualitative as well as quantitative. Thus even an inept supervisor can increase the motivation of his employees to resist his authority, and easily. The typical managerial challenge is to control the direction as well as to increase the volume.

Our approach to the complexities of freeing-up the relations between individuals in organizations explores three emphases. In turn, specific attention will focus on communicating, motivating, and changing behavior. The distinctions in foci should not be taken literally. Thus they comprise only avenues of approach to the same phenomena. The relevance of these foci is not restricted to managing by ones and twos, of course, but they do have their analytical uses, if their tentative status is recognized.

If Chris Argyris is anywhere near the mark, freeing-up the relations between individuals in organizations has a high priority indeed. The multiple foci of his "T-Groups for Organizational Effectiveness" make the point impressively. Thus the article isolates a set of compelling and widespread organizational demands that distort or freeze communication between individuals, and this includes costs measured in terms of motivational difficulties and behavioral rigidities. Moreover, the article also sketches the properties of a new technique—laboratory training or T-grouping. Analysis of the technique has multiple payoffs. It illustrates the cost of freezing or stereotyping; it suggests the value in organizations of more "open" patterns of interacting; and it permits the relatively safe practice of "new behaviors" possible in T-groups.

More specifically, Argyris sees massive forces in organizational life that encourage nonauthentic communicating. These forces have a perverse thrust, for nonauthentic communications induce significant problems of motivation and behavior. For example, a commonly held organizational value sanctions only expression that is "rational, logical, and clearly communicated." Other expressive modes—emotional and interpersonal—are treated in the breech. Thus "emotional" and "personal" references commonly are heavily censored. Repressing their expression is a core element of what Argyris calls the "pyramidal values" that underlie much organizational theory and practice. But the piper demands his pay, and Argyris sees such censoring and repression at the heart of many organization problems.

The significant difficulties induced by the fixation of the pyramidal values on rational and technical aspects are numerous. Let us trace one typical problem sequence. Individual A does not acknowledge his feelings about B, B experiences A as not "open", and consequently B will be "closed" and leery of taking risks in interacting with A. Consequently, A may have even greater difficulty acknowledging his feelings about B, so the cycle spirals viciously to more dangerous levels. The process, patently, has consequences as narrow as the relations of two individuals and potentially as wide as the total organization of which they are members. At its worst, the process can degenerate into a personal and organizational standstill compounded of an acute and unrealistic need to avoid "rocking the boat."

Fortunately man can cope with the forces which encourage nonauthentic communication. That is, different demands than those of the pyramidal values can be acted upon. The essential goal is integrating the rational and the emotional, the technical and the social elements. Argyris goes into considerable detail about how T-grouping can help organization members with this basic integrative problem. He also stresses the advantages—both organizational and personal—of interaction that is characterized by acknowledging, being open and taking risks. In their absence, communications in an organization are liable to degenerate into formalized defensiveness with all the attendant costs of not talking. Resulting defensiveness often will be complemented by a cross-examination style of questioning which makes communication more difficult although the purpose is to gain information.

There is no easy cataloging of Argyris' "T-Groups for Organizational Effectiveness." Perhaps its unifying theme is an optimism that individuals in organizations can undo what they have wrought, if given an appropriate setting. Thus Argyris stresses the role of "feedback" in authentic communicating, he details the various barriers that exist in traditionally structured organizations, and he explores the ways in which laboratory techniques that facilitate feedback can be transferred to the work setting. In providing authentic feedback, the individual can serve himself and his organization. Moreover, Argyris stresses that traditional views of organization restrict—often at significant cost—man's opportunity to express himself. The "pyramidal values" suppressing emotional content are in the latter category, for example. Here again Argyris is optimistic. He also emphasizes the central and constructive role of the emotional component of man in communicating.

We can reinforce and deepen Argyris' approach by a brief reference to material, not reprinted here, concerning communication. In one of the better books on oral communication, to introduce our point broadly, Irving Lee analyzes the many potential obstacles that intervene between the sender and the receiver in oral communication.[1] The list of these obstacles is formidable. It includes semantic, psychological and sociological elements. Given the potential obstacles, perhaps the major wonder is that communication breakdowns do not occur more often.

Any coping with the problems of oral communication must be based on an understanding of the stages or sequences in communication, and it must cope with such problems as Argyris manifestly proposes to do. We can rely on one of Wendell Johnson's contributions to supply some preliminary understanding of communication stages.

Usefully, the contrasts and similarities between Johnson and Argyris may be sketched. To begin, consider their focus for inquiry. Argyris ranges over the broad spectrum of a technique in all its ramifications for individuals, groups and large organizations. In contrast, Johnson's focus is microscopic. He focuses attention on the several stages of the intrapersonal and interpersonal act of communicating between two individuals. This focus is dramatically spotlighted by the title of Johnson's piece, "The Fateful Process of Mr. A Talking to Mr. B."[2] In

---

[1] Irving Lee, *How to Talk With People* (New York: Harper & Bros., 1962).
[2] Wendell Johnson, "The Fateful Process of Mr. A. Talking to Mr. B," *Harvard Business Review*, Vol. 31 (January-February, 1953), pp. 49–56.

contrast to Argyris, then, Johnson looks sharply and narrowly at the microprocesses of communication, marvels at their delicate complexity, and provides useful guidelines for making the best of a difficult set of conditions. More specifically, the flavor and considerable substance of Johnson's contribution may be presented diagramatically below.

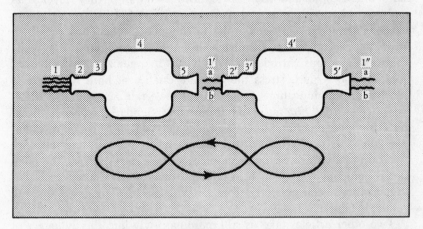

Key: Stage 1, event, or source of stimulation, external to the sensory end organs of the speaker; Stage 2, sensory stimulation; Stage 3, pre-verbal neurophysiological state; Stage 4, transformation of pre-verbal into symbolic forms; Stage 5, verbal formulations in "final draft" for overt expression; Stage 1', transformation of verbal formulations into (a) air waves and (b) light waves, which serve as sources of stimulation for the listener (who may be either the speaker himself or another person); Stages 2' through 1" correspond, in the listener, to Stages 2 through 1'. The arrowed loops represent the functional inter-relationships of the stages in the process as a whole. Source: Johnson, *op. cit.*, p. 50.

Figure 1   Stages in the Process of Communication.

Briefly, Johnson breaks down a communication sequence. That sequence is affected by the following.

1. Sensory limitations of both sender and receiver which are relevant to Stages 1 and 2 for the sender and which are relevant to Stages 1' and 2' for the receiver in Figure 1.
2. Pre-verbal stages of sender's nervous system or noiseless bodily states that are transformed into words, relevant to Stages 3 (for the sender) and 3' (for the receiver).
3. Filters in both sender and receiver that pick and choose what is communicated overtly and what is heard and which intervene between Stages 3 and 4 as well as between Stages 3' and 4'.
4. Symbolizations which select from an abundance of possible verbalizations in Stages 4 and 4'. Selections may be influenced by:
   a. for Freudians, the unconscious;
   b. for semanticists, the impositions of culture and usage;

c. for Pavlovians, the individual's learning experiences.
5. The "final draft" at Stage 5 and 5' is the result of those limitations of symbolic forms imposed in Stages 4 and 4'.

This welter of detail cannot hide the essential similarities of Johnson's microscopic and Argyris' telescopic views. If they diverge in emphases, both Johnson and Argyris converge toward common conclusions about the manager's roles in communicating. Thus both men stress the central role of "feedback" in authentic communication while they detail various barriers to it which exist in organizations. Moreover, Johnson and Argyris stress the intimate duality of both sending and receiving communications. That is, when we *tell something to somebody* we also *tell him much about ourselves.* Similarly, what we "hear" tells us *about something* but it also tells us *about ourselves.* For example, Johnson's pre-verbal states influence what we "tell" and what we "hear." Finally, both students emphasize the central role of the emotional component of man in communication. Neither individuals nor organizations, consequently, can safely avoid dealing with the full rational-emotional range.

Two other articles take us still more narrowly into the dynamics of relations between ones and twos while they also introduce us to factors that are as broad as life. Argyris' "Basic Self-Actualization Trends of the Human Personality" tentatively lists various dimensions along which individuals move toward personal maturity. This brief piece has profound implications for individuals and organizations. For example, individuals will be both more personally satisfied and more motivated toward outstanding performance as they are placed under structural arrangements and supervisory techniques that permit or encourage them "to grow." This brief notice suggests it all.

The revolutionary challenge in Argyris' formulation merely requires stating. Traditionally, the individual was chosen for employment as he fitted the organization. Thus the purpose of personality testing generally has been to cull rejects.[3] The concept of dimensions of personal growth oppositely implies that "the organization" also must be judged in terms of the degree to which it permits meeting the needs of its members. Altruism supplies only part of the explanation. For to the degree that organizations chronically fail the latter test, individuals can and will commit less of themselves to organizational purposes.

These suggested dimensions for personal growth should be applied as well as understood. Let us give an example of what we mean. An increasingly sophisticated research literature supports the broad conclusion that the management of men can consistently disregard man's

---

[3] See Robert T. Golembiewski, *Men, Management, and Morality* (New York: McGraw-Hill, 1965), esp. chapter 4.

need for personal growth only by despoiling man and usually only by reducing his effectiveness in organizations.[4] The reader consequently should find it profitable to continually apply the dimensions for personal growth as a standard against which to test what passes for managerial wisdom about how men must be managed. For example, consider the "pyramidal values" that prescribe what should be communicated in organizations. Does respect of these pyramidal values help the individual organization member "to grow," that is to move along the several dimensions of personal growth from the infant state toward mature, healthy adulthood? In this case, as in many others, conventional managerial wisdom does not measure up to the standard.

Further, Argyris' dimensions for personal growth also imply significant questions about motivation. These motivational questions demand explicit attention. William Scott's contribution "Attitudes, Motives, and Behaviors" provides just this attention in useful ways. Thus Scott conceives of motivation as behavioral movement by an individual to satisfy his own needs. These needs create a state of tension, tension which the individual can extinguish or reduce only by satisfying his needs. Man is motivated to scratch, in a crude sense, because he itches.

Scott is concerned with how man in an organization can be motivated to act in ways that are useful to him and to his organization. Scott's reprinted piece makes two particularly useful contributions to dealing with these two problems. Thus he presents a schema encompassing "primary drives," "basic motives" and "derived work motives." These concepts help us intellectually to bridge the gap between "natural man" and man in organizations. These descriptive categories also spotlight the complexity and multiplicity of the levels at which ones and twos must be managed. In addition, Scott describes an interesting approach to estimating motivational strength. The approach provides a useful standard against which many organizational practices and procedures designed to motivate performance can be judged.

Communicating and motivating are complex and subtle matters, particularly because increasing the sheer volume of one or the other typically is the least of the matter. That is to say, communicating and motivating commonly imply change to "new behaviors" rather than mere intensification of "old behaviors." Indeed, no little part of freeing-up the relations between individuals is oriented toward creating the kind of climate in which defensiveness for its own sake is minimized, in which the "noisy feedback" of distorted cues is reduced, and in which necessary behavioral adaptations can be made more freely.

There are no simple guidelines for encouraging behavioral change

---

[4] A number of supporting studies are reviewed in Chris Argyris, *Integrating the Individual and the Organization* (New York: Wiley, 1964), esp. pp. 35–112.

in self or in others, but a number of straightforward techniques can play important roles in clarifying the involved dynamics. The summary statement,[5] "A Way of Analyzing Change," sketches a technique termed "force-field analysis." The technique is rooted in sound theoretical notions that conceive any persisting behavior as a quasi-stationary equilibrium point, a balance of "driving forces" and "restraining forces." Useful guidelines for analyzing behavioral change are derived from this concept of behavior as a field of forces. Thus one can estimate the intensity of individual forces as well as determine their direction. The relative lengths of the "tails" of individual vectors of force then can indicate major targets for change. The ideal change strategy is to convert powerful restraining forces into driving forces. The effects of this change strategy on inducing movement to a new behavioral equilibrium point can be marked. Force-field analysis does not fail managers if they must settle for less than the ideal. For example, the technique suggests the particular usefulness of the strategy of removing restraining forces.

Ample evidence suggests that managerial action commonly neglects the change strategies suggested by force-field analysis. Thus, management generally resorts to adding driving forces in attempting to induce some desired change in behavior. Such driving forces—"artificial pressure," for example—commonly induce the emergence of new restraining forces, however. The result can be little or no behavioral change: the old equilibrium point can be maintained, more or less, because approximately equivalent but opposing forces have been induced. Paradoxically, this may be the best of this family of worlds. Thus some favored driving forces of management—e.g., "artificial pressure" —can induce significant defensive behaviors on the part of the employees. Such a reaction can overbalance the driving force added by management and, particularly in the long run, can result in less of the behavior that management hoped to increase. Certainly Argyris' piece suggests just such an unintended outcome.

If force-field analysis has its attractions, however, its limitations also are patent. We will stress two of these limitations. Analysis is but a prelude to action, and the problems of executing are formidable indeed. Few changes are minor, that is, and any change is likely to imply big risks for someone.

Relatedly, force-field analysis stops short of describing specific ways in which the motivational force-fields of individuals can be influenced. Recent research does not shrink from the task. Indeed, the

---

[5] The material is summarized from National Training Laboratories, *Reading Book: Nineteenth Annual Summer Laboratories In Human Relations Training* (mimeographed, 1965).

bulk of the applicable literature is great and growing. We can only sample that literature here, but we feel we are sampling from a rich vein indeed. Two articles—Herzberg's "The Motivation–Hygiene Concept and Problems of Manpower" and Homme and Tosti's "Contingency Management and Motivation"—provide the specificity which force-field analysis lacks.

Herzberg undoubtedly has created one of the most massive contemporary waves of interest in contrasting "motivating" and "hygiene" factors.[6] And that interest is not some speculative fly of a research summer. Practical applications—most prominent in Texas Instruments[7] —constitute substantial evidence that Herzberg has touched a vital nerve in administrative reality. Basically, Herzberg argues that those things which positively motivate tend to be distinct from those things that merely prevent a person from being actively dissatisfied. The latter are "hygiene" factors and include elements like good working conditions or competent technical supervision. "Motivators" oppositely cluster around the work itself, the responsibility it carries, and the achievement it permits. As Herzberg notes: "The motivator factors ... make people happy with their jobs because they serve man's basic and human need for psychological growth; a need to become more competent."[8]

With little simplification, the burden of Herzberg's demonstration may be summarized tersely. What people want is what motivates them; and what people at work generally want is "motivators" more than "hygiene" factors. Concretely, the presence of "hygiene" factors guarantees only that the worker will not be dissatisfied. In contrast, the presence of "motivators" can lead to superior performance even in the absence of positive "hygiene" factors. The coexistence of "motivators" and "hygiene" factors at work presumes close identification with work and deep absorption in it.

This generalization of Herzberg's research contains two major implications, one stressing neglect and the other significant attention. First, management action often has neglected the value of "motivators." Given the exquisite concern over the years with the panoply of "hygiene" factors—wages, pensions, insurance and the like—"motivators" have suffered from neglect. Few firms have attempted to motivate their employees by changing the design of work to make it

---

[6] See particularly Frederick Herzberg, Bernard Mausner, and Barbara Bloch Snyderman, *The Motivation to Work* (New York: John Wiley, 1959).

[7] M. Scott Myers, "Who Are Your Motivated Workers?," *Harvard Business Review*, Vol. 42 (January-February, 1964), pp. 73–88.

[8] Frederick Herzberg, "The Motivation-Hygiene Concept and Problems of Manpower," *Personnel Administration*, Vol. 27 (January-February, 1964), p. 5.

more of a "motivator."[9] Rather, we are told that work is commonly and deliberately organized to despoil it as a growth opportunity for the individual. In return, wages are kept high and the workpace is set to make light demands on the worker.[10] These "hygiene" factors are intended to prevent active dissatisfaction and to induce the worker to accept the infrahuman burdens of work.

Second, Herzberg's research is part of a growing tradition of research in a number of contexts ranging from the treatment of various emotional symptomologies to the job of getting high school dropouts to finish a programmed learning course. We may call this full gamut of work "conditioning learning" or "conditioning therapies," taken in the broad meaning of the term therapy.

Broadly speaking, "conditioning learning" uses an individual's own high-preference behaviors to motivate him. The general idea may be illustrated. Consider the case of a nonpsychotic patient who was growing weaker because of insufficient food intake. Eating was a low-preference behavior for her. Traditional therapy would have probed for deep causal events and would have provided often elaborate interpretations. In short, the woman would have been told what would help her or she would have gained insight about it in terms of some therapist's interpretive framework. Conditioning therapy utilized the patient first and foremost, in sharp contrast. Thus her high-preference behaviors were ascertained, to wit, talking with people and watching television. The derived therapy was tailored to these needs, and the woman was allowed to watch TV and converse with others only while she was eating. The results were gratifying in this case as in others.[11] The original low-preference behavior was changed by associating it closely and continuously with higher preference behaviors.

Conditioning learning suggests that one can get the proverbial horse to drink water as well as lead him to it, and that suggestion contains a vigorous germ of truth. Homme and Tosti introduce us to that germ of truth in their article "Contingency Management and Motivation." They review some of Premack's innovating work while discussing and illustrating the use of high-preference behaviors to reinforce

---

[9] There are some such firms, however. Golembiewski's *Men, Management, and Morality* reflects a wide variety of such efforts to build "motivators" into work.

[10] George Strauss, "Some Notes On Power-Equalization," pp. 39–84, in Harold J. Leavitt, editor, *The Social Science of Organizations* (Englewood Cliffs, N. J.: Prentice-Hall, 1963) takes such a position, for example.

[11] Joseph Wolpe, "The Comparative Clinical Status of Conditioning Therapies and Psychoanalysis," pp. 5–20, in Joseph Wolpe, Andrew Salter, and L. J. Reyna, editors, *The Conditioning Therapies: The Challenge In Psychotherapy* (New York: Holt, Rinehart and Winston, 1964).

lower-preference behaviors with the intent of making them more probable.

Herzberg's results find a direct interpretation in the work of Premack and others on conditioning learning. What Herzberg's workers told him was that "motivators" built into work permitted high-preference behaviors on their part. The performance of that work—even if working were generally a lower preference behavior for employees—consequently became rewarding because it permitted individual growth. The definition of a "good day's work" is likely to have an upward bias under this condition. "Hygiene" factors added to a job that required low-preference behaviors are attractive in themselves, but the job still requires only low-preference behaviors. Work is consequently suffered for the "hygiene" rewards which, in turn, permit high-preference behaviors only off the job. Work thus reasonably becomes something one does enough of to maintain the "hygiene" rewards, but usually no more. With the availability of labor unions or various formal and informal ways of restricting output, the working definition of "enough" commonly has a lower common denominator.[12]

The other selections in this chapter permit similar interpretations in terms of Premack's work with "reinforcing responses." Thus the "pyramidal values" sketched by Argyris in "T-Groups for Organizational Effectiveness" force the organizational member to provide low-preference behaviors with the predictable consequence that work will engage only some smaller part of the individual's talents and efforts. Since work so poorly serves man, in turn, so also does man poorly serve his work.

Whatever the illustration, the consequences of emphasizing low-preference behaviors are significant. Management thus deprives itself of the opportunity to utilize effective "reinforcing responses" to encourage desired behaviors. From the employee's point of view, moreover, management's neglect prevents the individual from serving his own deeper needs as he serves the organization. The dual loss is doubly lamentable.

---

[12] Illustrative of the available research, see Louis E. Davis, "Job Design and Productivity: A New Approach," *Personnel*, Vol. 33 (March, 1957), esp. pp. 419–27.

T-Groups for Organizational Effectiveness*

Chris Argyris

• What causes dynamic, flexible, and enthusiastically committed executive teams to become sluggish and inflexible as time goes by? Why do they no longer enjoy the intrinsic challenge of their work, but become motivated largely by wages and executive bonus plans?

• Why do executives become conformists as a company becomes older and bigger? Why do they resist saying what they truly believe—even when it is in the best interests of the company?

• How is it possible to develop a top-management team that is constantly innovating and taking risks?

• Is it inevitable that we get things done only when we create crises, check details, arouse fears, and penalize and reward in ways that inadvertently create "heroes" and "bums" among our executive group?

Ask managers why such problems as these exist and their answers typically will be abstract and fatalistic:
—"It's inevitable in a big business."
—"Because of human nature."
—"I'll be damned if I know, but every firm has these problems."
—"They are part of the bone and fabric of the company."
Statements like these *are* true. Such problems *are* ingrained into corporate life. But in recent years there has evolved a new way of helping executives develop new inner resources which enable them to mitigate these organizational ills. I am referring to *laboratory education*—or "sensitivity training" as it is sometimes called. Particularly in the form of "T-groups," it has rapidly become one of the most controversial educational experiences now available to management. Yet, as I will advocate in this article, if laboratory education is conducted competently, and if the right people attend, it can be a very powerful educational experience.

How does laboratory education remedy the problems I have mentioned? By striving to expose and modify certain values held by typical executives, values which, unless modified and added to, serve to impair interpersonal effectiveness. As Exhibit i explains, these values are ingrained in the pyramidal structure of the business enterprise. The exhibit summarizes several basic causes of management ineffectiveness

* Reprinted with permission of author and publisher from *Harvard Business Review,* Vol. 42 (March, 1964), pp. 60–74.

as isolated by three studies: (1) in a large corporate division—30,000 employees, grossing $500 million per year; (2) a medium-size company —5,000 employees, grossing in excess of $50 million per year; and (3) a small company—300 employees. The results of these studies are reported in detail elsewhere.[1]

Exhibit I. The Pyramidal Values

There are certain values about effective human relationships that are inherent in the pyramidal structure of the business organization and which successful executives (understandably) seem to hold. Values are learned commands which, once internalized, coerce human behavior in specific directions. This is why an appreciation of these values is basic in understanding behavior.

⟶ What are these "pyramidal" values? I would explain them this way.

1. The important human relationships—the crucial ones—are those which are related to achieving the organization's objective, i.e., getting the job done, as for example:

> We are here to manufacture shoes, that is our business, those are the important human relationships; if you have anything that can influence those human relationships, fine.

2. Effectiveness in human relationships increases as behavior becomes more rational, logical, and clearly communicated; but effectiveness decreases as behavior becomes more emotional. Let me illustrate by citing a typical conversation:

> "Have you ever been in a meeting where there is a lot of disagreement?"
> "All the time."
> "Have you ever been in a meeting when the disagreement got quite personal?"
> "Well, yes I have, but not very often."
> "What would you do if you were the leader of this group?"
> "I would say, 'Gentlemen, let's get back to the fact,' or I would say, 'Gentlemen, let's keep personalities out of this.' If it really got bad, I would wish it were five o'clock so I could call it off, and then I would talk to the men individually."

3. Human relationships are most effectively motivated by carefully

---

[1] Chris Argyris, *Interpersonal Competence and Organizational Effectiveness* (Homewood, Illinois, Richard D. Irwin, Inc., 1962); *Understanding Organizational Behavior* (Homewood, Illinois, The Dorsey Press, Inc., 1960); and *Explorations in Human Competence* (manuscript, Department of Industrial Administration, Yale University, New Haven, 1964).

defined direction, authority, and control, as well as appropriate rewards and penalties that emphasize rational behavior and achievement of the objective.

If these are the values held by most executives, what are the consequences? To the extent that executives believe in these organizational values, the following changes have been found to happen.

(1) There is a *decrease* in receiving and giving information about executives' interpersonal impact on each other. Their interpersonal difficulties tend to be either suppressed or disguised and brought up as rational, technical, intellectual problems. As a result, they may find it difficult to develop competence in dealing with feelings and interpersonal relations. There is a corresponding decrease in their ability to own up to or be responsible for their ideas, feelings, and values. Similarly there is a dropping off of experimentation and risk-taking with new ideas and values.

(2) Along with the decrease in owning,* openness, risk-taking, there is an *increase* in the denial of feelings, in closeness to new ideas, and in need for stability (i.e., "don't rock the boat"). As a result, executives tend to find themselves in situations where they are not adequately aware of the human problems, where they do not solve them in such a way that they remain solved without deteriorating the problem-solving process. Thus, if we define interpersonal competence as (a) being aware of human problems, (b) solving them in such a way that they remain solved, without deteriorating the problem-solving process, these values serve to decrease interpersonal competence.

(3) As the executives' interpersonal competence decreases, conformity, mistrust, and dependence, especially on those who are in power, increase. Decision making becomes *less effective,* because people withhold many of their ideas, especially those that are innovative and risky, and organizational defenses (such as management by crisis, management by detail, and through fear) *increase.* So do such "protective" activities as "JIC" files (just in case the president asks), "information" meetings (to find out what the opposition is planning), and executive politicking.

If this analysis is valid, then we must alter executives' values if we are to make the system more effective. The question arises as to what changes can and *should* be made in these values.

But since executives are far from unknowledgeable, why have they clung to these pyramidal values? First, because they are *not necessarily wrong.* Indeed, they are a necessary part of effective human relationships. The difficulty is that alone they are not enough. By themselves they tend to lead to the above consequence. What is

---

*Defined in text.

needed is an additional set of values for the executives to hold. Specifically there are three.

1. The important human relationships are not only those related to achieving the organization's objectives but those related to maintaining the organization's internal system and adapting to the environment, as well.

2. Human relationships increase in effectiveness as *all* the relevant behavior (rational and interpersonal) becomes conscious, discussable, and controllable. (The rationality of feelings is as crucial as that of the mind.)

3. In addition to direction, controls, and rewards and penalties, human relationships are most effectively influenced through authentic relationships, internal commitment, psychological success, and the process of confirmation. (These terms are clarified in the body of the article.)

Change Through Education

But how does one change an executive's values? One way is by a process of re-education. First there is an unfreezing of the old values, next the development of the new values, and finally a freezing of the new ones.

In order to begin the unfreezing process, the executives must experience the true ineffectiveness of the old values. This means they must have a "gut" experience of how incomplete the old values are. One way to achieve this is to give them a task to accomplish in situations where their power, control, and organizational influences are minimized. The ineffectiveness of the old values, if our analysis is correct, should then become apparent.

A second requirement of re-education arises from the fact that the overwhelming number of educational processes available (e.g., lecture, group discussion, and the like) are based on the pyramidal values. Each lecture or seminar at a university has clearly defined objectives and is hopefully staffed by a rational, articulate teacher who is capable of controlling, directing, and appropriately rewarding and penalizing the students. But, as I have just suggested, these represent some of the basic causes of the problems under study. The educator is in a bind. If he teaches by the traditional methods, he is utilizing the very values that he is holding up to be incomplete and ineffective.

To make matters more difficult, if the re-educational process is to be effective, it is necessary to create a *culture* in which the new values can be learned, practiced, and protected until the executives feel confident in using them. Such a culture would be one which is composed of people striving to develop authentic relationships and psychological success. Briefly, *authentic relationships* exist when an individual can behave in such a way as to increase his self-awareness and esteem and, at the same time, provide an opportunity for others to do the same. *Psychological success* is the experience of realistically challenging situations that tax one's capacities. Both are key components of executive competence.

The creation of a re-educational process where the unfreezing of the old values, relearning of the new values, and refreezing of the new values under primary control of the students, embedded in a culture that is rarely found in our society, is an extremely difficult task. Yet an approach to fulfilling these requirements is offered by laboratory education.

Probably because of its novelty, laboratory education has become one of the most talked about, experimented with, lauded, and questioned educational experiences for top executives. The interest of top executives has been so great that the National Training Laboratories (a nonprofit educational organization which administers most of the laboratories) has had to increase the programs many fold in the past ten years.[2]

Any educational experience that is as novel as laboratory education is destined to be controversial. And this is good because reasoned controversy can be the basis for corrections, refinements, and expansions of the process. Research (unfortunately not enough) is being conducted under the auspices of the National Training Laboratories and at various universities such as the University of California, Case Institute of Technology, Columbia, George Washington, Harvard, M.I.T., Michigan, Texas, and Yale, to name a few.

Aims of Program

The first step in a laboratory program is to help the executives teach themselves as much about their behavior as possible. To do so they create their own laboratory in which to experiment. This is why the educational process has been called "laboratory education." The strategy of an experiment begins with a dilemma. A dilemma occurs when, for a given situation, there is no sound basis for selecting among alternatives, or there is no satisfactory alternative to select, or when habitual actions are no longer effective.

---

[2] For information regarding the training laboratories that are available, one may write to Dr. Leland P. Bradford, National Training Laboratories, National Education Association, 1201 16th Street, Northwest, Washington 6, D.C.

What do people do when confronted with a dilemma? Their immediate reaction is to try out older methods of behaving with which they
are secure, or else to seek guidance from an "expert." In this way, the
anxiety so invariably associated with not knowing what to do can be
avoided. In the laboratory, then, the anticipated first reactions by participants to a dilemma are to try traditional ways of responding.

Only when conventional or traditional ways of dealing with a dilemma have been tried—unsuccessfully—are conditions ripe for inventive action. Now people are ready to think, to shed old notions because they have not worked, to experiment, and to explore new ways
of reacting to see if they will work. The period when old behavior is
being abandoned and when new behavior has yet to be invented to
replace it is an "unfrozen" period, at times having some of the aspects
of a crisis. It is surrounded by uncertainty and confusion.[3]

Fullest learning from the dilemma-invention situation occurs when
two additional types of action are taken:

❑ One is feedback, the process by which members acquaint one
another with their own characteristic ways of feeling and reacting in
a dilemma-invention situation. Feedback aids in evaluating the consequences of actions that have been taken as a result of the dilemma
situation. By "effective" feedback I mean the kind of feedback which
minimizes the probability of the receiver or sender becoming defensive
and maximizes his opportunity to "own" values, feelings, and attitudes.
By "own" I mean being aware of and accepting responsibility for one's
behavior.

❑ The final step in the dilemma-invention cycle is generalizing
about the total sequence to get a comprehensive picture of the "common case." When this is done, people are searching to see to what
extent behavior observed under laboratory conditions fits outside situations. If generalization is not attempted, the richness of dilemma-
invention learning is "lost."

T for Training

The core of most laboratories is the T (for training) group.[4] This
is most difficult to describe in a few words. Basically it is a group

---

[3] See Robert K. Blake and Jane S. Mouton, *The Managerial Grid* (Houston, Texas,
Gulf Publishing Co., 1963).

[4] For a detailed summary of research related to laboratory education, see Dorothy
Stock, "A Summary of Research on Training Groups," in *T-Group Theory and
Laboratory Method; Innovation in Education*, edited by Leland Bradford, Kenneth
Benne, and Jack Gibb (New York, John Wiley & Sons, Inc., 1964).

experience designed to provide maximum possible opportunity for the individuals to expose their behavior, give and receive feedback, experiment with new behavior, and develop everlasting awareness and acceptance of self and others. The T-group, when effective, also provides individuals with the opportunity to learn the nature of effective group functioning. They are able to learn how to develop a group that achieves specific goals with minimum possible human cost.

The T-group becomes a learning experience that most closely approximates the values of the laboratory regarding the use of leadership, rewards, penalties, and information in the development of effective groups. It is in the T-group that one learns how to diagnose his own behavior, to develop effective leadership behavior and norms for decision making that truly protect the "wild duck."

Role of Educator

In these groups, some of the learning comes from the educator, but most of it from the members interacting with each other. The "ground rules" the group establishes for feedback are important. With the help of the educator, the group usually comes to see the difference between providing help and attempting to control or punish a member; between analyzing and interpreting a member's adjustment (which is not helpful) and informing him of the impact it has on others. Typically, certain features of everyday group activity are blurred or removed. The educator, for example, does not provide the leadership which a group of "students" would normally expect. This produces a kind of "power vacuum" and a great deal of behavior which, in time, becomes the basis of learning.

There is no agenda, except as the group provides it. There are no norms of group operation (such as *Robert's Rules of Order*) except as the group decides to adopt them. For some time the experience is confusing, tension-laden, frustrating for most participants. But these conditions have been found to be conducive to learning. Naturally, some individuals learn a great deal, while others resist the whole process. It is rare, however, for an individual to end a two-week experience feeling that he has learned nothing.

Usually the T-group begins with the educator making explicit that it is designed to help human beings to—

    ... explore their values and their impact on others,

    ... determine if they wish to modify their old values and develop new ones,

... develop awareness of how groups can inhibit as well as facilitate human growth and decision making.

Thus a T-group does not begin without an objective, as far as the educator is concerned. It has a purpose, and this purpose, for the educator, is emotionally and intellectually clear.

However, the educator realizes that the purpose is, at the moment, only intellectually clear to the members. Thus, to begin, the educator will probably state that he has no specific goals in mind for the group. Moreover, he offers no specific agenda, no regulations, no rules, and so on. The group is created so its members can determine their own leadership, goals, and rules.

There is very little that is nondirective about a T-group educator's role. He is highly concerned with growth, and he acts in ways that he hopes will enhance development. He is nondirective, however, in the sense that he does not require others to accept these conditions. As one member of the T-group, he will strive sincerely and openly to help establish a culture that can lead to increased authentic relationships and interpersonal competence.

However, he realizes that he can push those in the group just so far. If he goes too far, he will fall into the trap of masterminding their education. This is a trap in which group members might like to see him fall, since it would decrease their uncomfortableness and place him in a social system similar (in values) to their own. In other words, his silence, the lack of predefined objectives, leadership, agenda, rules, and so on, are not designed to be malicious or hurt people. True, these experiences may hurt somewhat, but the hypothesis is that the pain is "in the service of growth."

At this point, let me assume that you are a member of such a T-group, so that I can tell you what you are likely to experience.

Action & Reaction

At the outset you are likely to expect that the educator will lead you. This expectation is understandable for several reasons:

1. An educator in our culture tends to do precisely this.
2. Because of the newness of the situation, the members may also fear that they are not competent to deal with it effectively. They naturally turn to the educator for assistance. It is common in our culture that when one member of a group has more information than the others as to how to cope with the new, difficult situation, he is expected by the others, *if he cares for them,* to help them cope with the

new situation. For example, if I am in a cave with ten other people who are lost and I know how to get out, it would be from their viewpoint the height of noncaring for me to fail to help them get out.

3. Finally, the members may turn to the educator because they have not as yet developed much trust for each other.

The educator may believe it is helpful, during the early stages of a T-group, to tell you that he understands why you feel dependent on him. But he will also add that he believes that learning can take place more effectively if you first develop an increasing sense of trust of one another and a feeling that you can learn from one another.

In my case, when I act as the educator for a T-group, I freely admit that silence is not typical of me and that I need to talk, to be active, to participate. In fact, I may even feel a mild hostility if I am in a situation in which I cannot participate in the way that I desire. Thus, anything you (members) can do to help me "unfreeze" by decreasing your dependence on me would be deeply appreciated. I add that I realize that this is not easy and that I will do my share.

Typically, the members begin to realize that the educator supports those individuals who show early signs of attempting to learn. This is especially true for those who show signs of being open, experimentally minded, and willing to take risks by exposing their behavior. How are these qualities recognized?

There are several cues that are helpful. First, there is the individual who is not highly upset by the initial ambiguity of the situation and who is ready to begin to learn. One sign of such an individual is one who can be open about the confusion that he is experiencing. He is able to own up to his feelings of being confused, without becoming hostile toward the educator or the others. Such an individual is willing to look at his and others' behavior under stress, diagnose it, and attempt to learn from it. Some of these individuals even raise questions about other members' insistence that the educator should get them out of the ambiguous situation.

Some members, on the other hand, react by insisting that the educator has created the ambiguity just to be hostile. You will find that the educator will encourage them to express their concern and hostility as well as help them to see the impact that this behavior (i.e., hostility) is having on him. There are two reasons for the educator's intervention: (1) to reinforce (with feelings) the fact that he is not callous about their feelings and that he is not consciously attempting to be hostile; and (2) to unfreeze others to explore their hostility toward him or toward each other. Such explorations can provide rich data for the group to diagnose and from which to learn.

Problem of Mimicking

As the group continues, some members begin to realize that the educator's behavior now may serve for what it is. That is, it may be as valid a model as the educator can manifest of how he would attempt (a) to help create an effective group, and (b) to integrate himself into that group so that he becomes as fully functioning a member as possible. The model is his; he admits owning it, but he is *not* attempting to "sell" it to others or in any way to coerce them to own it.

You may wonder if viewing the educator as a source of "model behavior" would not lead you simply to *mimic* him. (In the technical literature this is discussed as "identification with the leader," or "leader modeling behavior.") Although this may be the case, we should not forget that as you begin to "unfreeze" your previous values and behavior, you will find yourself in the situation of throwing away the old and having nothing new that is concrete and workable. This tends to create states of vacillation, confusion, anxiety, ambivalence, and so on.[5] These states in turn may induce you to "hang on" to the old with even greater tenacity. To begin to substitute the new behavior for the old, you will feel a need to see (1) that you can carry out the new behavior effectively and (2) that the new behavior leads to the desired results.[6]

Under these conditions the members usually try out any bit of behavior that represents the "new." Experimentation not only is sanctioned; it is rewarded. One relatively safe way to experiment is to "try out the educator's behavior." It is at this point that the individual is mimicking. And he should feel free to mimic and *to talk about the mimicking and explore it openly*. Mimicking is helpful if you are aware of and accept the fact that you do not *own* the behavior, for the behavior with which you are experimenting is the educator's. If the educator is not anxious about the mimicking, the member may begin safely to explore the limits of the new behavior. He may also begin to see whether or not the educator's behavior is, for him, realistic.

Individual vs. Group

At the outset the educator tends to provide that assistance which is designed to help the members to—

---

[5] Roger Barker, Beatrice A. Wright, and Mollie R. Gonick, "Adjustment to Physical Handicap and Illness," *Social Science Research Council Bulletin 55*, 1946, pp. 19–54.

[6] Ronald Lippitt, Jeanne Watson, and Bruce Westley, *The Dynamics of Planned Change* (New York, Harcourt, Brace & World, Inc., 1958).

. . . become aware of their present (usually) low potential for establishing authentic relationships,

. . . become more skillful in providing and receiving nonevaluative descriptive feedback,

. . . minimize their own and others' defensiveness,

. . . become increasingly able to experience and own up to their feelings.

Although interpersonal assistance is crucial, it is also important that the T-group not be limited to such interventions. After the members receive adequate feedback from one another as to their inability to create authentic relationships, they will tend to want to become more effective in their interpersonal relationships. It is at this point that they will need to learn that group structure and dynamics deeply influence the probability of increasing the authenticity of their interpersonal relations. For example:

> As soon as the members realize that they must become more open with those feelings that typically they have learned to hide, they will need to establish group norms to sanction the expression of these feelings. Also, if members find it difficult in the group to express their important feelings, this difficulty will tend to be compounded if they feel they must "rush" their contribution and "say something quick," lest someone else take over the communication channels. Ways must be developed by which members are able to use their share of the communication channels. Also, group norms are required that sanction silence and thought, so that members do not feel coerced to say something, before they have thought it through, out of fear that they will not have an opportunity to say anything later.

An example of the interrelationship between interpersonal and group factors may be seen in the problems of developing leadership in a group. One of the recurring problems in the early stages of a T-group is the apparent need on the part of members to appoint a leader or a chairman. Typically, this need is rationalized as a group need because "without an appointed leader a group cannot be effective." For example, one member said, "Look, I think the first thing we need is to elect a leader. Without a leader we are going to get nowhere fast." Another added, "Brother, you are right. Without leadership, there is chaos. People hate to take responsibility and without a leader they will goof off."

There are several ways that your group might consider for coping with this problem, each of which provides important but different kinds of learning:

¶ One approach is to see this as a group problem. How does leadership arise and remain helpful in a group? This level of learning is important and needs to be achieved.

¶ Another possibility is for the group members to explore the underlying assumptions expressed by those individuals who want to appoint leaders. For example, in the case illustrated above, both men began to realize that they were assuming that people "need" appointed leadership because, if left alone, they will not tend to accept responsibility. This implies a lack of confidence in and trust of people. It also implies mistrust of the people around the table. These men were suggesting that without an appointed leader the group will flounder and become chaotic. Someone then took the initiative and suggested that their comments implied a lack of trust of the people around the table. Another individual suggested that another dimension of mistrust might also be operating. He was concerned how he would decide if he could trust the man who might be appointed as the leader. The discussion that followed illustrated to the group the double direction of the problem of trust. Not only do superiors have feelings of mistrust of subordinates, but the latter may also mistrust the former.

One of the defendants of the need for leadership then said, "Look, Mr. B. over there has been trying to say something for half an hour, and hasn't succeeded. If we had a leader, or if he himself were appointed leader temporarily, then he might get his point of view across." Several agreed with the observation. However, two added some further insightful comments. One said, "If we give Mr. B. authority, he will never have to develop his internal strength so that he can get his point across without power behind him." "Moreover," the other added, "if he does get appointed leader, the group will never have to face the problem of how it can help to create the conditions for Mr. B. to express his point of view." Thus we see that attempting to cope with the basic problems of group membership can lead to an exploration of problems of group membership as well as requirements of effectively functioning groups.

The question of trust, therefore, is a central problem in a T-group, indeed, as it is in any group organization. If this can be resolved, then the group has taken an important step in developing authentic relationships. As the degree of trust increases, "functional leadership" will tend to arise spontaneously because individuals in a climate of mutual trust will tend to delegate leadership to those who are most competent for the subject being discussed. In doing so, they also learn an important lesson about effective leadership.

⟨ Another kind of learning that usually develops clearly is that the group will not tend to become an effective task-oriented unit without having established effective means to diagnose problems, make decisions, and so on. It is as the group becomes a decision-making unit that the members can "test" the strength and depth of their learning. The pressure and stress of decision making can help to show the degree to which authenticity is apparent rather than real. It can also provide opportunity for further learning, because the members will tend to experience new aspects of themselves as they attempt to solve problems and make decisions.

Further Components

Laboratory education has other components. I have focused in detail on T-groups because of their central role. This by no means describes the total laboratory experience. For example, laboratory education is helpful in diagnosing one's organizational problems.

Diagnosing Problems. When a laboratory program is composed of a group of executives who work in the same firm, the organizational diagnostic experiences are very important. Each executive is asked to come to the laboratory with any agenda or topic that is important to him and to the organization. During the laboratory, he is asked to lead the group in a discussion of the topic. The discussion is taped and observed by the staff (with the knowledge of the members).

Who Learns From T-Group Experiences?

People who learn in T-groups seem to possess at least three attributes:

1. A relatively strong ego that is not overwhelmed by internal conflicts.

2. Defenses which are sufficiently low to allow the individual to hear what others say to him (accurately and with minimal threat to his self), without the aid of a professional scanning and filtering system (that is, the therapist, the educator).

3. The ability to communicate thoughts and feelings with minimal distortion. In other words, the operational criterion of minimal threat is that the individual does not tend to distort greatly what he or others say, nor does he tend to condemn others or himself.

This last criterion can be used in helping to select individuals for the T-group experience. *If the individual must distort or condemn himself or others to the point that he is unable to do anything but to continue to distort the feedback that he gives and receives, then he ought not to be admitted to a T-group.*

To put this another way, T-groups, compared to therapy groups, assume a higher degree of health—not illness—that is, a higher degree of self-awareness and acceptance. This is an important point. *Individuals should not be sent to the laboratory if they are highly defensive.* Rather, the relatively healthy individuals capable of learning from others to enhance their degree of effectiveness are the kinds of individuals to be selected to attend.

Once the discussion is completed, the group members listen to themselves on the tape. They analyze the interpersonal and group dynamics that occurred in the making of the decision and study how these factors influenced their decision making. Usually, they hear how they cut each other off, did not listen, manipulated, pressured, created win-lose alternatives, and so on.

Such an analysis typically leads the executives to ask such questions as: Why do we do this to each other? What do we wish to do about it, if anything?

On the basis of my experience, executives become highly involved in answering these questions. Few hold back from citing interpersonal and organizational reasons why they feel they have to behave as they do. Most deplore the fact that time must be wasted and much energy utilized in this "windmilling" behavior. It is quite frequent for someone to ask, "But if we don't like this, why don't we do something about it?"

Under these conditions, the things learned in the laboratory are intimately interrelated with the everyday "real" problems of the organization. Where this has occurred, the members do not return to the organization with the same degree of bewilderment that executives show who have gone to laboratories full of strangers. In the latter case, it is quite common for the executive to be puzzled as to how he will use what he has learned about human competence when he returns home.[7]

Consultation Groups. Another learning experience frequently used is to break down the participants into groups of four. Sessions are held where each individual has the opportunity both to act as a consultant giving help and as an individual receiving help. The nature of help

---

[7] For an example, see Argyris, *Interpersonal Competence and Organizational Effectiveness,* op. cit., Chapter 9.

is usually related to increasing self-awareness and self-acceptance with the view of enhancing interpersonal competence.

Lectures. As I pointed out above, research information and theories designed to help organizational learning are presented in lectures—typically at a time when it is most clearly related to the learnings that the participants are experiencing in a laboratory.

Role-Playing of "Real" Situations. As a result of the discussions at the laboratory program, many data are collected illustrating situations in which poor communications exist, objectives are not being achieved as intended, and so on. It is possible in a laboratory to role-play many of these situations, to diagnose them, to obtain new insights regarding the difficulties, as well as to develop more effective action possibilities. These can be role-played by asking the executives to play their back-home role. For other problems, however, important learnings are gained by asking the superiors to take the subordinates' role.

Developing and Testing Recommendations. In most organizations, executives acknowledge that there are long-range problems that plague an organization, but that they do not have time to analyze them thoroughly in the back-home situation (for example, effectiveness of decentralization). In a laboratory, however, time is available for them to discuss these problems thoroughly. More important, as a result of their laboratory learnings and with the assistance of the educators, they could develop new action recommendations. They could diagnose their effectiveness as a group in developing these recommendations—have they really changed; have they really enhanced their effectiveness?

Intergroup Problems. One of the central problems of organizations is the intergroup rivalries that exist among departments. If there is time in a laboratory, this topic should be dealt with. Again, it is best introduced by creating the situation where the executives compete against one another in groups under "win-lose" conditions (i.e., where only one can win and someone must lose).

Correcting Misunderstandings

Any educational activity that is as new and controversial as laboratory education is bound to have misconceptions and misunderstandings built around it. Therefore, I should like to attempt briefly to correct a few of the more commonly heard misunderstandings about laboratory education.

(1) *Laboratory methods in general, and T-groups in particular, are not a set of hidden, manipulative processes by which individuals can*

be "brainwashed" into thinking, believing, and feeling the way some-one might want them to without realizing what is happening to them.

Central to a laboratory is openness and flexibility in the educational process. It is open in that it is continually described and discussed with the participants as well as constantly open to modification by them.

Along with the de-emphasis of rigidity and emphasis on flexibility, the emphasis is on teaching that kind of knowledge and helping the participants develop those kinds of skills which increase the strength and competence to question, to examine, and to modify. The objectives of a laboratory are to help an individual learn to be able to reject that which he deeply believes is inimical to his self-esteem and to his growth—and this would include, if necessary, the rejection of the laboratory experience.

(2) *A laboratory is not an educational process guided by a staff leader who is covertly in control and by some magic hides this fact from the participants.*

A laboratory means that people come together and create a setting where (as is the case in any laboratory) they generate their own data for learning. This means that they are in control and that any behavior in the laboratory, including the staff member's, is fair game for analysis.

I should like to suggest the hypothesis that if anything is a threat to the participants, it is not the so-called covert control. The experience becomes painful when the participants begin to realize the scope and depth to which the staff is ready "to turn things over to them." Initially this is seen by many participants as the staff abdicating leadership. Those who truly learn come to realize that in doing this the staff is expressing, in a most genuine way, their faith in the potentiality of the participants to develop increasing competence in controlling more of their learning. As this awareness increases, the participants usually begin to see that their cry of "abdication of leadership" is more of a camouflage that hides from them how little they trusted each other and themselves and how over-protected they were in the past from being made to assume some responsibility for their learning.

(3) *The objective of laboratory education is not to suppress conflict and to get everyone to like one another.*

The idea that this is the objective is so patently untrue that I am beginning to wonder if those who use it do not betray their own anxiety more than they describe what goes on in a laboratory. There is no other educational process that I am aware of in which conflict is generated, respected, and cherished. Here conflict, hostility, and frustration become motivations for growth as well as food for learning. It is with these kinds of experiences that participants learn to take risks—the kinds of risks that can lead to an increase in self-esteem. As these experiences are "worked through" and the learnings internalized, participants soon begin to experience a deeper sense of self-awarness and acceptance. These, in turn, lead to an increased awareness and acceptance of others.

And this does *not* necessarily mean liking people. Self-acceptance means that individuals are aware of themselves and care so much about themselves that they open themselves to receiving and giving information (sometimes painful) about their impact on others and others' impact on them, so that they can grow and become more competent.

(4) *Laboratory education does not attempt to teach people to be callous, disrespectful of society, and to dislike those who live a less open life.*

If one truly begins to accept himself, he will be less inclined to condemn nongenuineness in others, but to see it for what it is, a way of coping with a nongenuine world by a person who is (understandably) a nongenuine individual.

(5) *Laboratory education is neither psychoanalysis nor intensive group therapy.*

During the past several years I have been meeting with a group of psychiatrists and clinical psychologists who are trying to differentiate between group therapy and everything else. One problem we discovered is that therapists define therapy as any change. The difficulty with this definition is that it means any change is therapy.

We have concluded that it may be best to conceive of a continuum of "more" or "less" therapy. The more the group deals with unconscious motivations, uses clinical constructs, focuses on "personal past history," and is guided in these activities by the leader, the more it is therapy. Therapy is usually characterized by high proportions of these activities because the individuals who are participating are so conflicted or defensive that they are not able to learn from each other without these activities.

In my view, a T-group is—or should be—a group that contains individuals whose internal conflicts are low enough to learn by:

• Dealing with "here and now" behavior (what is going on in the room).

• Using relatively nonclinical concepts and nonclinical theory.

• Focusing on relatively conscious (or at most preconscious) material.

• Being guided increasingly less by the leader and increasingly more by each other.

• Accomplishing this in a relatively (to therapy) short time (at the moment, no more than three weeks).

This does not mean that T-groups do not, at times, get into deeper and less conscious problems. They do; and, again, they vary primarily with the staff member's biases. Usually most educators warn the group members against striving to become "two bit" psychologists.

(6) *Laboratory education does not have to be dangerous, but it must focus on feelings.*

Interpersonal problems and personal feelings exist at all levels of the organization, serving to inhibit and decrease the effectiveness of the system. Does it seem to be logical (in fact, moral) for a company to say that it is not going to focus on something that people are already experiencing and feeling? The truth is that people *do* focus on interpersonal problems every hour of the day. They simply do not do it openly.

Now for the argument that the laboratory program can hurt people and is, therefore, dangerous. The facts of life are that people are being hurt every day. I do not know of any laboratory program that did, or could, create for people as much tension as they are experiencing in their everyday work relationships.

It is true that laboratory education does require people to take risks. But does anyone know of any learning that truly leads to growth which does not involve some pain and cost? The value of laboratory education is that it keeps out the people who want to learn "cheaply" and it provides the others with control over how much they wish to learn and what they want to pay for it.

(7) *The objective of laboratory education is to develop effective reality-centered leaders.*

Some people have expressed concern that if an executive goes through such a learning experience, he might somehow become a weak leader. Much depends on how one defines strong leadership. If strong leadership means unilateral domination and directiveness, then the individual will tend to become "weaker." But why is such leadership strong? Indeed, as I have suggested, it may be weak. Also it tends to develop subordinates who conform, fear to take risks, and are not open, and an organization that becomes increasingly rigid and has less vitality.[8]

Nor can one use the argument that directive leadership has worked and that is why it should remain. There are data to suggest that directive leadership can help an organization under certain conditions (e.g., for routine decisions and under extreme emergencies). But these

---

[8] Ibid.

conditions are limited. If directive leadership is effective beyond these relatively narrow conditions, it may be because of a self-fulfilling prophecy. Directive leadership creates dependence, submissiveness, and conformity. Under these conditions subordinates will tend to be afraid to use their initiative. Consequently, the superior will tend to fill in the vacuum with directive leadership. We now have a closed cycle.

The fact is that directive leaders who learn at a laboratory do not tend to throw away their directive skills. Rather, they seem to use directive leadership where and when it is appropriate. It cannot be emphasized too strongly that there is nothing in laboratory education which requires an individual to throw away a particular leadership pattern. The most laboratory education can do is help the individual see certain unintended consequences and costs of his leadership, and help him to develop other leadership styles *if* he wishes.

(8) *Change is not guaranteed as a result of attendance.*

Sometimes I hear it said that laboratory education is not worthwhile, because some individuals who have attended do not change, or if they do change, it is only for a relatively short period of time.

Let me acknowledge that there is an immense gap in our knowledge about the effectiveness of a laboratory. Much research needs to be done before we know exactly what the payoff is in laboratory education. However, there are a few statements that can be made partially on the basis of research and experience and partially on the basis of theory.

One of the crucial learnings of a laboratory is related to the development of openness and trust in human relationships. These factors are not generated easily in a group. It takes much effort and risk. Those who develop trust in a group learn something very important about it. Trust cannot be issued, inspired, delegated, and transferred. It is an interpersonal factor which has to be *earned* in each relationship. This is what makes trust difficult to develop and precious to have.

Thus, it does not make very much sense to expect that suddenly an individual will act as if he can trust and can be trusted in a setting where this was never true. One executive was needled by the corporate president, who observed that he had not seen any change in the former's behavior. The executive responded: "What makes you think I feel free to change my behavior in front of you?"

This remark points up the possibility that if there is not any observable change, it could mean that the individual has not learned much. But is could also mean that he has learned a great deal, *including* the fact that he ought not to behave differently when he returns. For, it must be emphasized, laboratory education is only a partial attack on the problem of organizational effectiveness. If the changes are to become permanent, one must also change the nature of the organizational structure, managerial controls, incentive systems, reward and penalty systems, and job designs.[9]

Impact on Organization

The impact of laboratory education on the effectiveness of an organization is extremely difficult to isolate and measure.[10] Organizations are so complex, and their activities influenced by so many factors, that it is difficult to be precise in specifying the causes of the impact.

In one study that I conducted of the 20 top executives of a large corporate division, I did find a significant shift on the part of the experimental group toward a set of values that encouraged the executives to handle feelings and emotions, deal with problems of group maintenance, and develop greater feelings of responsibility on the part of their subordinates for the effectiveness of the organization. This shift is quantified in EXHIBIT II.

As the exhibit shows, the impact of laboratory education continued at a high level for a period in excess of six months. However, during the tenth month a fade-out began to appear. *This was studied and data were obtained to suggest that the executives had not lost their capacity to behave in a more open and trustful manner, but they had to suppress some of this learning because the corporate president and the other divisional presidents, who were not participants in the laboratory, did not understand them.*

This finding points up two important problems. Change is not going to be effective and permanent *until the total organization* accepts the new values. Also, effective change does *not* mean that the executives must lose their capacity to behave according to the pyramidal values. They do so whenever it is necessary. However, now they have an additional way to behave, and they use it whenever possible. They report that irrespective of the problem of acceptance by others, they find the pyramidal values are effective when they are dealing primarily

---

[9] For a more theoretical discussion of this matter, see Chris Argyris, *Integrating the Individual and the Organization* (New York, John Wiley & Sons, Inc., 1964).

[10] Robert K. Blake and Jane S. Mouton, "Toward Achieving Organization Excellence," in *Organizational Change*, edited by Warren Bennis (New York, John Wiley & Sons, Inc., 1964). As this article went to press, I read an excellent manuscript of a speech evaluating the effectiveness of laboratory education, "The Effect of Laboratory Education Upon Individual Behavior," given by Douglas R. Bunker before the Industrial Relations Research Association in Boston on December 28, 1963.

EXHIBIT II. BEFORE AND AFTER VALUES OF 11 EXECUTIVES
WHO EXPERIENCED LABORATORY ECUCATION

In an administrative situation, whenever possible . . .	Before T-group	Six months after
1a. The leader should translate interpersonal problems into rational intellective ones	100%	10%
1b. The leader should deal with the interpersonal problems	0	81
2a. The leader should stop emotional disagreement by redefining the rational purpose of the meeting	90	10
2b. The leader should bring out emotional disagreements and help them to be understood and resolved	6	81
3a. When strong emotions erupt, the leader should require himself and others to leave them alone and not deal with them	100	18
3b. When strong emotions erupt, the leader should require himself and offer others the opportunity to deal with them	0	82
4a. If it becomes necessary to deal with feelings, the leader should do it even if he feels he is not the best qualified	100	9
4b. The leader should encourage the most competent members	0	90
5a. The leader is completely responsible for keeping the group "on the track" during a meeting	100	0
5b. The group members as well as the leader are responsible for keeping the group "on the track"	0	100

with *routine, programmed* decisions. The new values and manner of leadership seem to be best suited for decisions that are *unprogrammed, innovative,* and require high commitment.

It is important to emphasize that laboratory education does *not* tell anyone what type of leadership to select. It does not urge him always to be more "democratic" or "collaborative." A successful laboratory helps the executives realize the unintended costs of the "old," develop "new" leadership behavior and philosophies, and become competent in utilizing whatever leadership style is appropriate in a given situation. A laboratory helps an individual increase his repertory of leadership skills and his freedom to choose how he will behave. If it coerces the executive, it is for him to become more *reality-centered.*

Another way of describing the impact of a laboratory program on an organization is for me to offer you excerpts from a tape of a meeting where the executives discussed the difficulties as well as successes that they were having 30 days after the program. The first part of the tape contains a discussion of examples of concrete changes which the members felt were a result of the laboratory. Here is a sample of the changes reported:

(1) Executives reported the development of a new program for certain pricing policies that could not be agreed

upon before, and laid part of the success to their new ability to sense feelings.

(2) One executive stated, "We are consciously trying to change our memos. For example, we found a way to decrease the 'win-lose' feelings and 'rivalries.'"

(3) The personnel director reported a distinct improvement in the sensitivity of the line managers to the importance of personnel problems, which before the laboratory seemed to have a second-class status. He said he was especially pleased with the line executives' new awareness of the complexity of personnel problems and their willingness to spend more time on solving them.

The rest of the tape is excerpted and presented in EXHIBIT III.

Exhibit III. Discussion of Attitude Changes by T-Group Members·

The excerpt presented here mirrors the tone of the entire meeting. I have not purposely selected only that section in which the men praised the laboratory. If the men had criticized the laboratory, such criticism would have been included. As you may see, the researcher actually pushed the group for more negative comments.

Except for minor editing, these are direct quotes:

No. 4 [after reporting that his superior, a member of the experimental group, had made a decision which should have been left to him]: I was really fuming. I was angry as hell. I walked into his office and I said to myself, "No matter what the hell happens, I'm going to tell him that he cannot do that any more." Well, I told him so. I was quite emotional. You know it floored me. He looked at me and said, "You're right; I made a mistake, and I won't do that again." Well I just don't think he would have done that before.

No. 7: The most important factor in motivating people is not what you say or do; it's giving a person the opportunity to express his views and the feeling that one is seriously interested in his views. I do much less selling but it sure takes longer.

No. 2: I've had a problem. I now have a greater need for feedback than before, and I find it difficult to get. The discussion on internal commitment made much sense to me, and I try to see if I can create conditions for it.

The thing that bothers me is that I try to handle it correctly, but I don't get feedback or cues as to how well I'm doing, as I used to at the lab. The meeting is over, and you don't know whether you've scored or not. So after each meeting I've got 10 question marks. The things that before were never questions are now question marks.

You don't get feedback. You ask for something and they respond, "I know what you're trying to do." They think I've something up my sleeve. All I want is to get feedback. It was obvious to me they were all waiting for me to make the decision. But I wanted them to make it. This was their baby, and I wanted them to make it. Two days later they made it. Fine, in this case I got feedback. The point was that their decision was a severe reversal, and I realize it was difficult for them to make. But they made it. Before, I simply would have pointed out the facts, and they would have "agreed" with the reversal, but down deep inside they would have felt that they could have continued on. As it is now, it's their decision. I think they now have a greater sense of internal commitment. People are now freer to disagree.

No. 11: My list of decisions to be made is longer. I am hoping that they will make some decisions. I now know how much they wait for me.

No. 11 [after telling how he wrote a note which in effect damned No. 2 and maintained his own correctness, then reread it and realized how defensive he was]: Before I wouldn't have even seen this.

No. 2: One of our most difficult jobs will be to write our feelings and to write in such a way that others can express their feelings.

No. 3: I have some difficulties in evaluating this program. What have we gotten out of this? What are we able to verbalize about what we got out of this? Do others of you have difficulty in verbalizing it?

No. 2: I have the same difficulty. I have been totally ineffective describing the experience.

No. 8: Each time I try I give a different answer.

No. 1: I don't have too much difficulty. One thing that I am certain of is that I see people more as total human beings. I see aspects of them that I had never seen before.

No. 9: I'm frustrated because I now realize the importance of face-to-face communication. I'm so far from the general managers that it is not so hot. Has anyone tried to write memos that really get feelings brought out?

I find myself questioning much more than I ever did before. I have a more questioning attitude. I take into account more factors.

No. 4: We've been talking about things as if we've slowed down a bit. We haven't. For example, remember you [No. 1] and I had a problem? I'm sure Arden House was very helpful. If I hadn't been there, my reaction to you would have been different. I would have fought you for hours.

No. 1: I know we can talk to each other more clearly. It's not a conscious way. It's spontaneous.

No. 3: I have to agree we can make some decisions much faster. For example, with No. 2 I simply used to shut up. But now I can be more open. Before the laboratory, if I had an intuitive feeling that something was wrong, but I wasn't sure, I'd keep quiet until things got so bad that then I'd have a case to go to the boss. Now I feel freer to talk about it sooner and with No. 2.

I now feel that we are going to say exactly how we feel to anyone. You [the president], for example, don't have to worry, and, therefore, question, probe, and draw us out.

President: Yes, and today I found No. 1, who told me that he simply would not agree with me. And I said to myself, "God bless you. He really is open now."

No. 1: I agree. I would not have expressed this feeling before being in this group. It's obvious that one should but I didn't.

[No. 2 and No. 1 show real insight into how they are being manipulated by people outside and above the group. They are much more aware of the manipulative process. "This kind of manipulation is dynamite. It burns me up."]

No. 1: Yes, it's really horrible to see it and not be able to do anything about it.

No. 7: In this case it seems to me you've got to really hit hard, because you're dealing with an untrained man [laughter]. . . . I think I now have a new understanding of decision making. I am now more keenly aware of the importance of getting a consensus so that the *implementation* is effective. I am not trying to say that I do this in every meeting. But I do strive more to give opportunity for consensus.

No. 1: One of the problems that I feel is that the "initiated" get confused so they don't play the game correctly. Sometimes I feel walked upon, so I get sore. This is difficult. [Many others expressed agreement.]

No. 6: Does it help to say, "I trust you?" I think it does.

No. 11: For example, No. 2, you went to a meeting where you admitted you had made a mistake. Boy, you should have heard the reaction. Boy, Mr.——— admitted a mistake. Well, wonderful; it helped to get these guys to really feel motivated to get the job done.

No. 9: Yes, I heard that many took on a deeper feeling

of responsibility to get the program on the right track.

No. 7: I'd like to come back to what No. 6 said. I used to say to people that I trusted them, that I was honest, and so on. But now I wonder if people really believe me, or if they don't begin to think if I'm not covering that I'm not honest.

No. 3: Another example which I am now aware of is the typical way we write memos. We start off: "I have confidence in your judgment to handle this question," and so on. Few more paragraphs. Then fifth paragraph reads: "Please confirm by return mail exactly what you have done and what controls have been set up."

No. 2: I agree. We do an awful lot to control people. Although I think that we're trying.

[No. 7 gave examples of how he stopped making a few phone calls to exert pressure. Others agreed.]

The Researcher: Aren't there negative comments?

No. 11: We have one man who has chosen not to be here. I wonder why?

No. 3: Well, really, to me that is a sign of health in the group. He feels he would still be accepted even if he didn't come. It certainly would be easy for him to come and just sit here.

No. 1: Yes, he wouldn't go to the trouble of avoiding a meeting that you didn't think was important.

No. 3: The only negative that I can think is: "What can you tell me that actually increases effectiveness?" I am not sure, but I must agree that there is a whale of a different climate.

No. 7: Well, I'd like to develop a list of things that we feel we have gotten out of this program so far. How do others of you feel? [All agreed, "Let's try."]

[All group members reporting they reached the following conclusions]:

(a) All of us begin to see ourselves as others see us . . . a real plus.
(b) A degree of greater confidence in oneself in meetings and in interviews. Beginning to be more comfortable with self.
(c) Greater confidence in associates. We feel more secure that you're telling what you think. . . . Greater feeling of freedom of expression to say what you really think.
(d) Individuals have a greater understanding and appreciation of viewpoint of associates.

(e) Greater appreciation of the opposite viewpoint.

(f) An awareness of what we do and others do that inhibits discussion.

(g) More effective use of our resources . . . getting more from them, and they feel this . . . patient to listen more.

(h) Meetings do not take longer and implementation is more effective. Internal commitment is greater.

(i) We have had a great realization that being only task-oriented, we will not get the best results. We must not forget worrying about the organization and the people.

(j) We get more irritated to infringement of our jobs and unique contributions.

(k) Fewer homemade crises.

No. 6: One of the difficult things about the list is that when you look at it, you wake up to the fact that you haven't really been using these principles. When you tell someone else who doesn't realize the gap between knowing something and actually doing it, he doesn't realize.

No. 7: But I think I really did learn and do care. Now when I think what I used to do, because that was the way. Today I realize that I could have had three times as much if I had known what I know now.

Conclusion

While I do not hold up laboratory education as a panacea to remedy all organizational problems, I do feel six conclusions can fairly be drawn:

(1) Laboratory education is a very promising educational process. Experience to date suggests that it can help some organizations to *begin* to overcome some of their problems.

(2) Laboratory education is *not* a panacea, nor is it a process that can help every organization. Furthermore, it must be followed by changes in the organization, its policies, managerial controls, and even technology. Not all organizations can profit from it; nor do all organizations need similar amounts of it. All these factors should be carefully explored before becoming involved.

(3) Not all laboratory programs are alike. Some focus more on interpersonal learning, some on intellectual problem solving, some on small groups, some on intergroups, and some on varying combinations of all of these. Again a careful diagnosis can help one to choose the right combination for the organization, as well as the appropriate educators. Nor are all laboratory programs equally effective. The competence of the educators can vary tremendously,

as well as the receptivity of those who attend. The best thing to do is to attempt to attend a laboratory program conducted by competent professionals.

(4) Openness, trust, commitment, and risk-taking grow only where the climate is supportive. A one-shot program, even at its best, can only begin the process of unfreezing the executive system. For optimum results, repeat or "booster" programs will be necessary.

(5) Although I personally believe that a laboratory program with the "natural" or actual working groups has the greatest probable payoff, it also has the greatest risk. However, one does not have to begin the process this way. There are many different ways to "seed" an organization, hoping to develop increasing trust and risk-taking. The way that will be most effective can best be ascertained by appropriate study of the executive system.

(6) Finally, if you ever talk to an individual who has had a successful experience in a laboratory, you may wonder why he seems to have difficulty in describing the experience. I know I still have difficulty describing this type of education to a person who is a stranger to it.

I am beginning to realize that one reason for the difficulty in communication is that the meaningfulness of a laboratory experience varies enormously with each person. Some learn much; some learn little. I find that my learning has varied with the success of the laboratory. Some can hardly wait until it is over; others wish that it would never end. Anyone who understands a laboratory realizes that all these feelings can be real and valid. Consequently, to attempt to describe a laboratory (especially a T-group) to an individual who has never experienced one is difficult because he may be one of those persons who would not have enjoyed the process at all. Therefore, an enthusiastic description may sound hollow.

Another reason why it is difficult to communicate is that the same words can have different meanings to different people. Thus one of the learnings consistently reported by people who have completed a laboratory is that the trust, openness, leveling, risk-taking (and others) take on a new meaning — a meaning that they had not appreciated before the laboratory. This makes it difficult for a person who found laboratory education meaningful to describe it to another. He may want very much to communicate the new meanings of trust, risk-taking, and so on, but he knows, from his own skepticism before the laboratory, that this is a difficult undertaking and that it is not likely to succeed.

The point to all this is that the results of laboratory education are always individualistic; they reflect the individual and the organization. The best way to learn about it is to experience it for one's self.

Basic Self-Actualization Trends
of the Human Personality*

Chris Argyris

All organizations may be said to strive to achieve their objectives, maintain themselves internally, and adapt to their external environment. This multidimensional process may be called self-actualization. In order to make more precise predictions about the problems involved when human beings are considered for employment by the formal organization, it is necessary to be more explicit, if possible, about the demands the former will tend to make upon the latter. Since the human personality is a developing organism, one way to become more precise is to define the basic growth or development trends "inherent" in it (so long as it remains in the same culture). One can then logically assume that, at any given moment in time, the human personality will be predisposed to find expression for these developmental trends. Such an assumption implies another, namely, that there are basic development trends characteristic of a relatively large majority of the population being considered. This assumption might seem strained, especially to the psychologists inclined to stress individual differences. However, individual differences need not necessarily be ignored. As Kluckhohn and Murray point out,[1] people tend to have some similar basic psychological characteristics because of their biological inheritance and the socio-cultural matrix within which they develop. This does not preclude the possibility that each individual can express these basic characteristics in his own idiosyncratic manner. Thus the concept of individual differences is still held.

So much for the logic behind the developmental trends listed below. It is assumed that human beings in our culture:

1. Tend to develop from a state of passivity as infants to a state of increasing activity as adults. (This is what Erikson[2] has called self-initiative and Bronfenbrenner[3] has called self-determination.)

---

* Reprinted with permission of author and publisher from Argyris, *Personality and Organization* (New York: Harper & Brothers, 1957), pp. 49–52. Copyright © 1957 by Harper and Brothers. (Footnotes have been renumbered.)
[1] Kluckhohn, Clyde, and Murray, H. A., "Personality Formation: The Determinants," in *Personality*, (ed.) by above authors (New York: Knopf, 1949), pp. 35–37.
[2] Erikson, E. H., *Childhood and Society* (New York: Norton, 1950). See also Kotinsky, R., *Personality in the Making* (New York: Harper, 1952), pp. 8–25.
[3] Bronfenbrenner, Urie, "Toward an Integrated Theory of Personality," in *Perception*, by Robert R. Blake and Glen B. Ramsey (New York: Ronald Press, 1951), pp. 206–257.

2. Tend to develop from a state of dependence upon others as infants to a state of relative independence as adults. Relative independence is the ability to "stand on one's own two feet" and simultaneously to acknowledge healthy dependencies.[4] It is characterized by the liberation of the individual from his childhood determiners of behavior (e.g., family) and developing his own set of behavioral determiners. This individual does not tend to react to others (e.g., the boss) in terms of patterns learned during childhood.[5]

3. Tend to develop from being capable of behaving only in a few ways as an infant to being capable of behaving in many different ways as an adult.[6]

4. Tend to develop from having erratic, casual, shallow, quickly-dropped interests as an infant to having deeper interests as an adult. The mature state is characterized by an endless series of challenges, where the reward comes from doing something for its own sake. The tendency is to analyze and study phenomena in their full-blown wholeness, complexity, and depth.[7]

5. Tend to develop from having a short time perspective (i.e., the present largely determines behavior) as an infant to a much longer time perspective as an adult (i.e., where the behavior is more affected by the past and the future).[8] Bakke cogently describes the importance of time perspective in the lives of workers and their families and the variety of foresight practices by means of which they seek to secure the future.[9]

6. Tend to develop from being in a subordinate position in the family and society as an infant to aspiring to occupy an equal and/or superordinate position relative to their peers.

7. Tend to develop from a lack of awareness of self as an infant to an awareness of and control over self as an adult. The adult who tends to experience adequate and successful control over his own behavior

---

[4] This is similar to Erikson's "sense of autonomy" and Bronfenbrenner's "state of creative interdependence."

[5] White, Robert W., *Lives in Progress,* (New York: Dryden Press, 1952), pp. 339 ff.

[6] Lewin and Kounin believe that, as the individual develops needs and abilities, the boundaries between them become more rigid. This explains why an adult is better able than a child to be frustrated in one activity and behave constructively in another. See Lewin, Kurt, *A Dynamic Theory of Personality* (New York: McGraw-Hill, 1935); and Kounin, Jacob S., "Intellectual Development and Rigidity," in *Child Behavior and Development* (ed.) Barker, R., Kounin, J., and Wright, H. R. (New York: McGraw-Hill, 1943), pp. 179–198.

[7] White, Robert W., *op. cit.,* pp. 347ff.

[8] Lewin also cites the billions of dollars that are invested in insurance policies. Lewin, Kurt, "Time Perspective and Morale," in *Resolving Social Conflicts* (New York: Harper, 1948), p. 105.

[9] Bakke, E. W., *The Unemployed Worker* (New Haven: Yale University Press, 1940), pp. 23–24.

tends to develop a sense of integrity (Erikson) and feelings of self-worth.[10] Bakke, [11, 12] shows that one of the most important needs of workers is to enlarge those areas of their lives in which their own decisions determine the outcome of their efforts.

These dimensions are postulated as being descriptive of a basic multidimensional developmental process along which the growth of individuals in our culture may be measured. Presumably, every individual, at any given moment in time, can have his degree of development plotted along these dimensions. The exact location on each dimension will probably vary with each individual, and even within the same individual at different times. Self-actualization may now be defined more precisely as the individual's plotted scores (or profile) along the above dimensions.

It may be helpful to add a few words of explanation concerning these dimensions of personality development.

1. They comprise only one aspect of the total personality. All the properties of personality described previously must be used in trying to understand the behavior of a particular individual. Much depends upon the individual's self-concept, his degree of adaptation and adjustment, and the way in which he perceives his private world.

2. The dimensions are continua where the growth to be measured is assumed to be continuously changing in degree. An individual is presumed to develop continuously in degree, from the infant end to the adult end of each continuum.

3. The only characteristic assumed to hold for all individuals is that, barring unhealthy personality development, they will be predisposed toward moving from the infant end to the adult end of each continuum. This is a model (a construct) describing the basic growth trends. As such, it does not make any predictions about any specific individual. It *does*, however, presume to supply the researcher with basic developmental continua along which the growth of any individual in our culture may be described and measured.

4. So long as one develops in a particular culture one will never obtain maximum expression of these developmental trends. Clearly, all individuals cannot be maximally independent, active, and so forth all the time and still maintain an organized society. It is the function of culture (e.g., norms and mores) and society (e.g., family, friends, schools, churches, and laws) to inhibit maximum expression and to help an individual adjust and adapt by finding his optimum expression.

A second factor that prevents maximum expression and fosters opti-

---

[10] Rogers, Carl R., *Client-Centered Therapy* (Boston: Houghton Mifflin, 1951).
[11] Bakke, E. W., *op. cit.*, p. 247.
[12] Bakke, E. W., *op cit.*, p. 29.

mum expression is the individual's own finite limits set by his personality. Some people fear the same amount of independence and activity that others desire. Also, it is common-place to find some people who do not have the necessary abilities to perform specific tasks. No given individual is known to have developed all known abilities to their full maturity.

Finally, defense mechanisms also are important factors operating to help an individual to deviate from the basic developmental trends.

5. The dimensions described above are constructed in terms of latent or genotypical characteristics. If one states that an individual needs to be dependent, this need will probably be ascertained by clinical inference because it is one that individuals are not usually aware of. Thus, if one observes an employee acting as though he were independent, it is possible that if one goes below the behavioral surface, the individual may be quite dependent. The obvious example is the employee who always seems to behave in a contrary manner to that desired by management. Although his behavior may give the appearance that he is independent, his contrariness may be due to his great need to be dependent upon management, which he dislikes to admit to himself and to others.

Attitudes, Motives, and Behaviors[*]

William G. Scott

Thus, attitudes are first in a series of steps which precede overt human behavior. They are prejudices, predilections, habits of thought, or mental dispositions. Further, attitudes are intimately associated with human motives, which are eventually manifested in behavior directed toward a goal. For example, a person might have a fear of financial insecurity in old age which would motivate him in a quest for security. Overt behavior in this regard could be frugality in his younger years, coupled with employment by a company with an adequate pension program.

Figure 5-2 The relation of attitudes to behavior

Attitudes and their ultimate effect on behavior can be visualized by Figure 5–2.

Work Motives

Man is not born with a desire to make money, any more than he is born with a love of liberty or a sense of responsibility and justice. Motives are learned. Work motives also are learned, but they constitute only a small segment in a very broad range of human motives. Therefore, any analysis of work motives must follow a more general discussion of motives viewed in the larger sense.

Referring back to Figure 5–2, it is seen that motives appear between attitudes and response. At the risk of repeating, attitudes pave the way for the development of motives, and then, depending on the particular motive, a certain response is chosen.

The pure meaning of motive is associated with *directed behavior*. That is, an individual perceives a goal and responds with a form of behavior directed toward obtaining it. This treatment specifically excludes physiological needs, such as hunger, thirst, and fatigue, from the category of motives. Most basic biological needs are automatically,

[*] Reprinted with permission of author and publisher from *Human Relations in Management* (Homewood, Ill.: Irwin, 1962), pp. 77, 79–84.

or at least partially automatically, satisfied. The key point is that the satisfaction of physiological needs is not completely a matter of individual will, whereas the satisfaction of motives is a matter of individual volition. Again, *motives imply that resulting behavior will be consciously directed toward a goal.*[6] The goal may be viewed as a specific satisfaction for a specific motive.

Motives can be satisfied through numerous forms of activities including religion, education, social service, family life, and many more. Of course, work is a channel of satisfaction for a number of learned human motives.

Figure 5–3 shows a system of classification of work motives illustrating their relationship to primary drives, basic motives, and their ultimate requirement of satisfaction.[7] Figure 5–3 is interpreted as follows:

Primary drive. The biological drive, already mentioned, requires the satisfaction of those basic needs essential to maintain physiological integrity—organic survival. The nature of satisfaction for this drive is specifiable. The need for food, water, rest, air, and elimination is necessary for the survival of the human organism, even though the level of satisfaction of these biological requirements differs from person to person.

Basic motives. There are two basic motives—psychological and social. The psychological motive results in a quest by an individual to maintain his mental integrity or balance. The social motive stems from the natural gregariousness of man, and his need to associate with his fellow man.

Unlike the biological drive, it is impossible to generalize and predict the specific routes individuals will follow to satisfy these motives. Further, the satisfaction of basic motives is volitional. Although it was said that the social motive is basic for man in general, the example of a hermit or recluse comes to mind immediately to demonstrate the volitional character of this category of motives.

Derived (work) motives. This last category provides the richest source of motives underlying human behavior. The ten derived work motives are only a few of many possible reasons why people work. These motives are derived from the basic social and psychological motives. But they are not connected in a specific way to one or the other basic motives. Who can say with any degree of certainty that the recognition motive is social or psychological in origin? The

---

[6] For a general discussion of motives see Morris S. Viteles, *Motivation and Morale In Industry* (New York: Norton, 1953), pp. 69–71.

[7] Kornhauser observes that the classification of motives has become unpopular among social psychologists, but he does defend and use such classifications in his work. See Arthur Kornhauser, Robert Dubin, and Arthur M. Ross (eds.), *Industrial Conflict* (New York: McGraw-Hill Book Co., 1954), pp. 67–72.

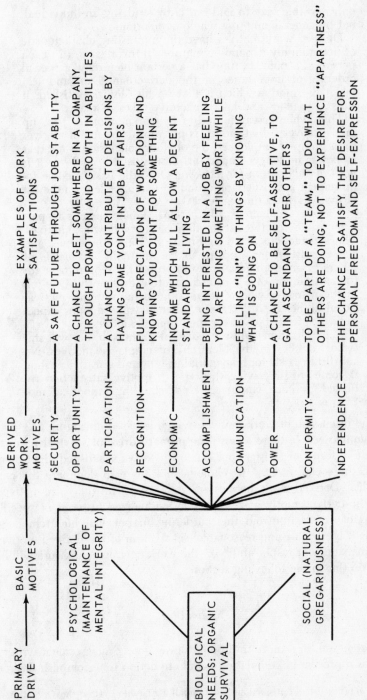

Figure 5-3 Basic and derived work motives and their satisfaction

only possible way to find out is by studying an individual, not by generalizing to a whole population.

Derived work motives have the interesting characteristic of being highly dynamic in nature. In this regard, (1) each person at a point in time has a certain hierarchy, a special ordering of importance of the derived motives; and (2) when the motive which is first on his "list" is satisfied, it slips in urgency and another motive takes its place.

Thus when research studies in worker motives turn up the "discovery" that money is not top of the list of motives for a group of employees, the obvious conclusion is *not* that money is no longer important. Money is still vital *but it is not the only reason for working.* Once the basic income requirement is satisfied, other motives supercede it on the list of motives, for a time at least.

The requirement of satisfaction. Management is in part responsible for the satisfaction of derived work motives. The satisfactions listed in Figure 5–3 are suggestive; and some satisfactions appear to be mutually exclusive of others.[8] Each individual may interpret his requirement for the satisfaction of a particular motive differently. One job of the manager who is attempting to improve his motivational ability is to determine what his subordinates expect in terms of satisfaction for their unique motives.

Generalizations will not accomplish this job, nor will statistical studies of the hierarchy of employee motives. No substitute exists for managerial insight and sensitivity when it comes to perceiving the type of motive satisfaction required by each employee. Understanding individual motives is a day-to-day task.

The discussion of work motives, which is based on Figure 5–3, may be summarized in these terms. The primary drive of survival requires primitive forms of satisfaction. When this drive is satisfied higher motives, the social and the psychological, emerge to dominate the personality. Derived work motives are associated with the basic motives; but the derived motives are highly individualized in terms of specific forms of satisfaction and their ordering in personal hierarchies. So far as it is possible and reasonable, satisfaction of the derived motives is a management responsibility in the work environment. More will be said on this in the following section.

Motivation

Motivation, in a more traditional sense among management writers, means a process of stimulating people to action to accomplish desired

---

[8] For another list of satisfactions see Lyndall F. Urwick, "How the Organization Affects the Man," *Management Review*, July, 1957, pp. 54–61.

goals. Although many words are substituted for motivation (such as "actuating" and "directing") the meaning of the process is reasonably clear. Motivation is a function which a manager performs in order to get his subordinates to achieve job objectives.

While this point of view is valid and useful, there is another side of the coin of motivation. Instead of viewing motivation as a management process it is profitable to look at it from the standpoint of the individual who is motivated. Psychologists call individual motivation a *state of tension*.

Motivation, so considered, represents an unsatisfied need which creates a condition of tension or disequilibrium causing the individual to move in a goal-directed pattern toward restoring a state of equilibrium by satisfying the need.[9]

Management should be aware that the strength of tensions, and therefore the strength of motivations, vary. Atkinson[10] views motivation strength in the form of an equation—motivation = f(motive × expectancy × incentive). The strength of motivation to perform some act is a function of:

1. *The strength of the motive* which is the position of a motive in the individual's hierarchy of motives, representing a level of urgency for fulfillment.
2. *Expectancy* which is the probability that the act will obtain the goal.[11]
3. *The value of the incentive* which is the rewards hoped for by obtaining the goal. The greater the rewards, the greater will be the motivational strength, providing the other two factors remain equal.[12]

---

[9] Viteles, *op. cit.*, p. 73.
[10] John W. Atkinson, "Motivational Determinants of Risk Taking Behavior," *Psychological Review*, 1957, pp. 360–61.
[11] Deutsch reports, for example, that highest individual motivation would be found among individuals in highly motivated groups where the probability for success in achieving a goal was low. In these experiments, however, the authors focus on the degree of group integration (solidarity) which is achieved under varying stress situations. They conclude that groups which are highly motivated and which also perceive a small chance of obtaining a valuable goal will react by forming a greater degree of interdependency among themselves. See Morton Deutsch, "Some Factors Affecting Membership Motivation and Achievement Motivation in a Group," *Human Relations*, 1959, pp. 81–95. For similar conclusions, see Leonard Berkowitz, Bernard I. Levy, and Arthur R. Harvey, "Effects of Performance Evaluations on Group Integration and Motivation," *Human Relations*, 1957, pp. 195–208.
[12] In an earlier study, Kahn and Morse pointed out that motivational strength was dependent upon (1) the strength of the need served by the behavior, (2) availability of alternative behaviors to meet the need, (3) the extent to which behavior sets up opposing tensions to interfere with the satisfaction of other needs, and (4) the ratio of need satisfaction to required energy input—pleasure-pain. R. L. Kahn and N. C. Morse, "The Relationship of Morale to Productivity," *Journal of Social Issues*, 1951, p. 12.

The equation can be portrayed as follows to give an example of motivational strength in several situations.

$$+ \text{ high}$$
Assume: A = Motive strength which can be
$$- \text{ low}$$
$$+ \text{ high}$$
B = Expectancy which can be
$$- \text{ low}$$
$$+ \text{ high}$$
C = Incentive value which can be
$$- \text{ low}$$

Eight possible states of motivational strength can be illustrated from this simplified situation.

FIGURE 5-4 VARYING DEGREES OF MOTIVATIONAL STRENGTH

	A	B	C			A	B	C
1.	+	+	+		5.	−	−	+
2.	+	+	−		6.	−	+	−
3.	+	−	+		7.	+	−	−
4.	−	+	+		8.	−	−	−

The left side of Figure 5–4 shows degrees of relatively high states of motivational strength; the right side indicates various degrees of low motivational strength.

Again, it is the individual who perceives and assigns actual values to the plus and minus signs in the motivational equation. Naturally, management would prefer to see evidence of plus rather than minus signs of individual motivational strength toward company and job objectives. Such a situation would indicate individual tensions which could be satisfied by the pursuit of company established goals. However, as Ginsberg says, management has difficulty appreciating that organizational goals and the goals of employees are not the same.[13] Shades of mutuality of interests!

Motivation is not an automatic nor is it a one-sided management process. Individual motivational tensions are social, psychological, as well as economic in origin. Knowing the unmet motives, expectancies, and value systems of individuals provides management with the concrete information necessary to perform the *process* of motivation considered in the more traditional sense.

---

[13] Eli Ginsberg, "Perspectives on Work Motivation," *Personnel*, July, 1954, pp. 43–44.

A Way of Analyzing Change:
Force-Field Analysis*

No individual or organization has ever been exempt from change, but it is unlikely that either individuals or organizations have ever been challenged more by the need to change than they are today. The management of change is a major part of the responsibility of managers everywhere, whether the organization is concerned with health, education, or the production of goods or services.

This article is a modest contribution to successful coping with the ubiquituous problems of change. Let us sketch the personal and organizational challenges of change while we also outline our strategy for helping meet the challenge. Increasingly, managers in today's organizations must analyze change as it takes place, they must attempt to predict what changes will occur and what these changes imply, and they must plan to take deliberate action to induce desired changes. There is no magical way of doing the total job, and this is an awesome datum.

There is a second way of viewing the challenges of change. That is, any help in doing the job must be welcome. The present approach to providing such help is to introduce a simple but useful conceptual way for considering change. This aids in filling a critical need, for the diversity of behaviors involved in any process of change requires some conceptual tool to permit the ordering of complex reality. Without such conceptual "handles" reality too easily slips out of our grasp.

The conceptual tool introduced here—force-field analysis—derives from the pioneering work of the psychologist Kurt Lewin. He conceived of man in terms consistent with those of modern science. The behavior of man derives not from his "nature," for example, as it exists independently. Rather, man exists within a total field of forces, and his behavioral position at any point in time reflects the resultant balance of the forces acting upon him at that moment. Until that balance of forces is changed, the behavior persists. This condition is called "quasi-stationary equilibrium." More traditional approaches would despair of changing behavior unless man's "nature" were changed first. *[otherwise called "inertia"!!]*

Consider a typical profile of the production record of a work unit in some organization, to illustrate the general sense of Lewin's concept. Let us assume that production varies only within a narrow range, approximating a so-called "straight-line production norm." Why does this profile of productivity persist? An explanation consistent with

---

* Based on National Training Laboratories, *Reading Book* (1965).

Lewin's concept of behavior as a resultant of opposing forces within an individual's life-space takes this form:[1]

> [The pattern persists] because the forces that tend to raise the level of production are equal to the forces that tend to depress it. Among the forces tending to raise the level of production might be: (a) the pressures of supervisors on the work team to produce more; (b) the desire of at least some team members to attract favorable attention from supervisors in order to get ahead individually; (c) the desire of team members to earn more under the incentive plan of the plant. Such forces Lewin called "driving forces." Among the forces tending to lower the level of production might be: (a') a group standard in the production team against "rate busting" or "eager beavering" by individual workers; (b') resistance of team members to accepting training and supervision from management; (c') feelings by workers that the product they are producing is not important. Granted the goal of increased productivity, these forces are "restraining forces." The balance between the two sets of forces, which defines the established level of production, Lewin called a "quasi-stationary equilibrium."

The verbal illustration of the notion of a field of forces also may be presented graphically. That is, we can depict the driving and restraining forces that peg our hypothetical straight-line production profile as in Figure 1. Essentially, the graphical representation facilitates description. Thus it enables us to "see" the pushes and pulls of the forces in opposition, holding productivity at a stable level. The figure also includes a further visual advantage. Thus both the driving and the restraining forces in Figure 1 are distinguished in terms of their (hypothetical) relative strengths. The force a' is a more powerful restraining force than b', for example, as is represented by the longer vector arrow for a'. Judgments about such relative strengths cannot always be accurately made in practice, of course, but we often have a strong intuitive idea about which forces in a particular situation are "stronger," and we do act on these ideas. Force-field analysis requires that we recognize and consciously manipulate these intuitive estimates. The results of the exercise are often surprising. Thus a force we originally thought to be significant may become less so as the detailed forces are set down and compared with one another; that once potent force may have to be decomposed into several component forces which in turn derive from an entirely unexpected source. At the very least, the use of the force-field notion helps clarify the relevant aspects of a

---

[1] "Change Does Not Have to be Haphazard," p. 58, from National Training Laboratories, *Reading Book, Nineteenth Annual Summer Laboratories In Human Relations Training, 1965* (mimeographed).

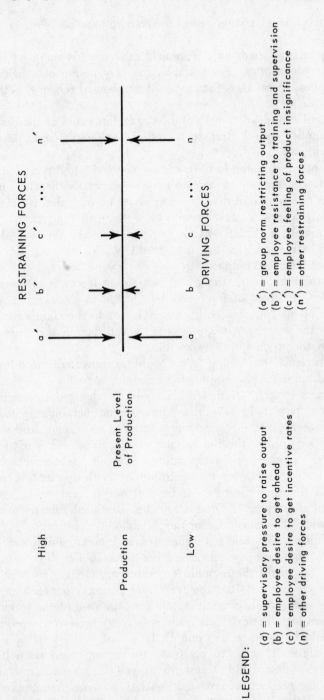

Figure 1 Illustrative analysis of the field of forces freezing a stable level of output.

LEGEND:

(a) = supervisory pressure to raise output
(b) = employee desire to get ahead
(c) = employee desire to get incentive rates
(n) = other driving forces

(a´) = group norm restricting output
(b´) = employee resistance to training and supervision
(c´) = employee feeling of product insignificance
(n´) = other restraining forces

program of planned change even if serendipitous benefits do not result.

The approach to change via force-field analysis aids action as well as facilitates description. For example, the very notion of a field of forces implies three basic strategies for planned change. These strategies are:

1. the number and/or strength of driving factors could be increased;
2. the number and/or strength of restraining factors could be decreased; and
3. previously restraining forces could be changed into driving forces.

These three strategies for change may be illustrated briefly. First, the number or strength of driving forces could be increased variously, as by adding a new supervisor who gains the trust and respect of work-unit members. A derivative new desire to make the well-liked supervisor "look good," for example, might be a substantial driving force toward increased output.

Second, the number or strength of restraining forces could be decreased. For example, attempts could be made to demonstrate the importance of the contribution of the work unit to the commendable purposes of the parent organization or to the satisfaction of consumers provided by the product of the work unit.

Third, previously restraining forces could be converted into driving forces. The norm of low output, for example, suggests a particular target for this strategy. If that norm could be changed to sanction higher output, patently, a new driving force of considerable magnitude would replace a previously restraining force of some magnitude. As this description implies, this third strategy has high payoffs. Variations of the third strategy are correspondingly difficult to bring off, but despair is not in order. Several contributions in the present volume demonstrate that the effort is not beyond our present capabilities. These include: Argyris, "T-Groups for Organizational Effectiveness"; Golembiewski, "The Small Group and Public Administration"; Van Zelst, "Sociometrically Selected Work Teams Increase Productivity."

Because of its simplicity—and despite it—force-field analysis can be enormously useful for the administrative analyst. Of particular note, for example, is the fact that the technique permits and encourages several successive levels of analysis. Thus, in the case of the productivity of our hypothetical work unit, a second level of force-field analysis could be done on any one of the forces isolated at the first level of analysis. That is, to illustrate, the group norm restricting output might be described in terms of its specific driving and restraining forces. The products of force-field analysis at more than one level are various. Patently, increasingly fine and detailed analysis is possible. Moreover, force-field analysis at the second level and beyond may suggest ways of unfreezing attitudes that were not clear at the first level. Or, successive applications of force-field analysis may require reformulating what was thought to be the original change-problem.

Of course, a technique is only a technique. Together with the following useful guidelines for instituting planned change, however, force-field analysis acquits itself well. Useful guidelines include the following:[2]

1. to change any sub-system, relevant aspects of the total environment also must be changed;
2. to change behavior at any one level of a hierarchical organization often requires complementary and reinforcing change at levels above and below the target level;
3. to begin change, the target should usually be a point at which stresses exist, for these stresses can help motivate change in the system;
4. to work toward thoroughgoing changes in a hierarchical structure often implies starting at the policy-making level;
5. to plan any process of change, both the formal and informal organizations must be considered; and
6. to encourage the effectiveness and smoothness of change, individuals at many levels of an organization should participate in fact-finding, in diagnosing needed changes, in formulating goals and programs for change, and in reality-testing those goals and programs.

---

[2] *Ibid.*, pp. 60–64.

The Motivation-Hygiene Concept and Problems of Manpower*

Frederick Herzberg

I wish to preface my remarks in this article with a disclaimer of competence in the field of manpower. My research and contemplative efforts are more directly related to an equally large and protean problem, that of industrial mental health. From my investigations in the latter area, I have formulated a general theory of mental health, and a specific application to job attitudes that may have bearing on certain aspects of "manpower" questions.

I apologize to the reader who already has familiarity with the Motivation-Hygiene theory of job attitudes for occupying the next few pages with a repetition of data and comments which have appeared a number of times elsewhere. I must lay the groundwork for my thoughts on "manpower" by first presenting my theory of job attitudes, without which I have very little excuse for accepting the invitation to contribute to this issue.

The Motivation-Hygiene theory of job attitudes began with a depth interview study of over 200 engineers and accountants representing Pittsburgh industry. (10) These interviews probed sequences of events in the work lives of the respondents to determine the factors that were involved in their feeling exceptionally happy and conversely exceptionally unhappy with their jobs. From a review and an analysis of previous publications in the general area of job attitudes, a two-factor hypothesis was formulated to guide the original investigation. This hypothesis suggested that the factors involved in producing job satisfaction were separate and distinct from the factors that led to job dissatisfaction. Since separate factors needed to be considered depending on whether job satisfaction or job dissatisfaction was involved, it followed that these two feelings were not the obverse of each other. The opposite of job satisfaction would not be job dissatisfaction, but rather *no* job satisfaction; and similarly the opposite of job dissatisfaction is *no* job dissatisfaction—not job satisfaction. The statement of the concept is awkward and may appear at first to be a semantic ruse, but there is more than a play with words when it comes to understanding the behavior of people on jobs. The fact that job satisfaction is made up of two unipolar traits is not a unique occurrence. The

* Reprinted with permission of author and publisher from *Personnel Administration* (National Press Bldg., Washington, D.C.), Vol. 27 (January-February, 1964), pp. 3–7.

difficulty of establishing a zero point in psychology with the procedural necessity of using instead a bench mark (mean of a population) from which to start our measurement, has led to the conception that psychological traits are bipolar. Empirical investigations, however, have cast some shadows on the assumptions of bipolarity; one timely example is a study of conformity and non-conformity, where they were shown not to be opposites, but rather two separate unipolar traits (3).

Methodology

Before proceeding to the major results of the original study, three comments on methodology are in order. The investigation of attitudes is plagued with many problems, least of which is the measurement phase; although, it is measurement to which psychologists have hitched their scientific integrity. First of all, if I am to assess a person's feeling about something, how do I know he has a feeling? Too often we rely on his say so, even though opinion polling is replete with instances in which respondents gladly respond with all shades of feeling when in reality they have never thought of the issue and are devoid of any practical affect. They respond to respond and we become deceived into believing that they are revealing feelings or attitudes. Secondly, assuming the respondent does have genuine feelings regarding the subject under investigation, are his answers indicative of his feelings; or are they rationalizations, displacements from other factors which are for many reasons less easy to express, coin of the realm expressions for his particular job classification, etc.? Those who have had experience with job morale surveys recognize these ghosts and unfortunately some have contributed to the haunting of companies. Thirdly, how do you equate feelings? If two persons state that they are happy with their jobs, how do you know they are equally happy? We can develop scales, but in truth we are only satisfying our penchant for rulers which do not get inside the experience and measure the phenomenological reality, but rather have significance wholly within our devices.

To meet these objections, the methodology of the original study was formulated. It included a study of changes in job attitudes in the hope that if attitudes change there is more likelihood that an attitude exists. Further, it focused on experiences in the lives of the respondents which contained substantive data that could be analyzed apart from the interpretations of the respondents. Finally, rather than attempt to measure degree of feeling, it focused on peak experiences and contrasted negative peaks with positive peaks; without being concerned with the equality of the peaks. Briefly, we asked our respondents to describe periods in their lives when they were exceedingly happy and unhappy with their jobs. Each respondent gave as many "sequences of events" as he could which met certain criteria including a marked change in feeling, a beginning and an end, and contained some substantive description other than feelings and interpretations.

A rational analysis of the "sequences of events" led to the results shown in the accompanying chart. For a more complete description of the methodology as well as the results, see *The Motivation to Work.* (10)

The proposed hypothesis appears verified. The factors on the right that led to satisfaction (achievement, recognition for achievement, intrinsic interest in the work, responsibility, and advancement) are mostly unipolar; that is, they contribute very little to job dissatisfaction. Conversely, the dissatisfiers (company policy and administrative practices, supervision, interpersonal relationships, working conditions, and salary) contribute very little to job satisfaction.

Satisfiers and Dissatisfiers

What is the explanation for such results? Do the two sets of factors have two separate themes? It appears so, for the factors on the right all seem to describe man's relationship to what he does, to his job content, achievement on a task, recognition for task achievement, the nature of the task, responsibility for a task, and professional advancement or growth in task capability.

What is the central theme for the dissatisfiers? Restating the factors as the kind of administration and supervision received in doing the job, the nature of interpersonal relationships and working conditions that surround the job, and the amount of salary that accrues to the individual for doing his job, suggest the distinction with the "satisfier" factors. Rather than describing man's relationship to what he does, the "dissatisfier" factors describe his relationship to the context or environment in which he does his job. One cluster of factors relates to what the person does and the other to the situation in which he does it.

As usual with any new theory, a new jargon is invented, perhaps to add some fictitious uniqueness to the theory, although I prefer to think that these new terms better convey the meaning of the theory. Because the factors on the left serve primarily as preventatives, that is to prevent job dissatisfaction, and because they also deal with the environment, I have named these factors "the hygiene" factors in a poor

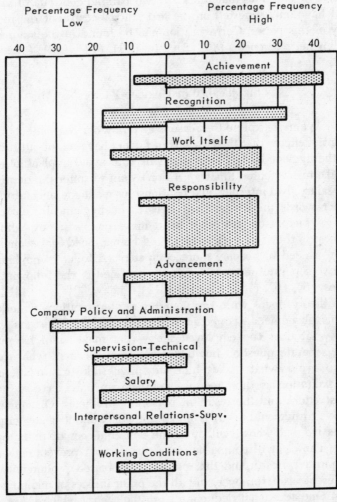

Figure 1 Comparison of satisfiers and dissatisfiers

The wider the box the longer the duration of the attitude. Reproduced from *The Motivation to Work*, Frederick Herzberg, et. al. (New York: John Wiley and Sons, 1959).

analogy with the way the term is used in preventive medicine. The factors on the right I call the "motivators" because other results indicate they are necessary for improvement in performance beyond that pseudo improvement which in substance amounts to coming up to a "fair day's work."

In these terms we can recapitulate the major findings of the original study by stating that it is the hygiene factors that affect job dissatisfaction and the motivator factors that affect job satisfaction; with the further understanding that there are two parallel continua of satisfactions. I have only reported on the first study because of the required brevity of this paper. Corroboration can be found in the studies with the following references, (1), (2), (4), (13), (14), (15), (16).

Significance of Hygiene Factors

Why? We next explore the reasons given by our respondents for the differential effects that the two sets of factors have on job attitudes. In brief, the hygiene factors meet man's need to avoid unpleasantness. "I don't like to be treated this way; I don't want to suffer the deprivation of low salary; bad interpersonal relationships make me uncomfortable." In other words they want their lives to be hygienically clean. The motivator factors on the other hand make people happy with their jobs because they serve man's basic and human need for psychological growth; a need to become more competent. A fuller commentary on these two separate needs of man are contained in the following publications, (5), (6), (7), (8), (10), (11), (12).

This theory opens wide the door for reinterpretations of industrial relations phenomena. To begin with, job attitudes must be viewed twice; what does the employee seek—what makes him happy; and then a separate question not deducible from the first, what does he wish to avoid—what makes him unhappy? Industrial relations that stress sanitation as their modus operandi can only serve to prevent dissatisfactions and the resultant personnel problems. Of course such attention to hygienic needs is important, for without it any organization, as we well know, will reap the consequences of unhappy personnel. The error of course lies in assuming that prevention will unleash positive health and the returns of increased productivity, lowered absenteeism, turnover, and all the other indices of manpower efficiency. One additional deduction from the theory which is supported by empirical findings should be added. The effect of improved hygiene lasts for only a short time. In fact man's avoidance needs are recurrent and of an infinite variety, and as such we will find that demands for improved salary, working conditions, interpersonal relations and so on will continue to occupy the personnel administrator without any hope of escaping the "what have you done for me lately."

There is nothing wrong with providing the maximum of hygienic benefits to the employee, as much as the society can afford (which appears to be more than the historic cries of anguish which have always accompanied the amelioration of work hygiene would indicate). What is wrong is the summation of human needs in totally hygienic terms. The consequences of this onesided view of man's nature has led to untoward consequences of much greater import than the direct monetary costs of these programs to our organizations. The more pertinent effect has been on the psychological premises of industrial relations and its effect in turn on the self concepts of the employees.

Since hygiene is the apparent key to industrial success, the motivators are given but lip service, and attention to the challenge and meaningfulness of jobs is satisfied via the pious espousal of cultural noises. We are today familiar with the industrial engineering principle of leveling jobs down to the lowest common talent as it applies to the rank and file assembly operation. The same denigration of human talent at the managerial and professional level, the sacrificing of human performance and potentiality to insure that no one will fail or make for unpleasantness, is obscured by referring to the rank and file when acknowledging the lack of meaning in work. At these higher levels, the effects of the assembly line are accomplished by the overuse of rules and regulations, rational organizational principles and the insidious use of interpersonal *skills*. We find that more and more training and education is required to do less and less; more and more effort on surround and less and less substance on accomplishment. Pride in work, in successful accomplishment, in maximizing one's talent is becoming socially gauche or more tragically a victim of progress. We cry for nurturance of human talent and find that we have no place for most of it; human talent on the job has become as much of a surplus commodity as our wheat. And where are our personnel managers? Their problem is hygiene, not the creative function of maximizing human resources.

Significance of Motivators

The Protestant Ethic is being replaced by an Avoidance Ethic in our world of work, and those in charge of personnel utilization have almost totally directed their efforts to maintenance procedures. This is seen from the very beginning of employment in the practice of college recruitment on the campus, where each company sets up its own enticing tent, and selection is transformed into public relations, luring of candidates, and in fact the incredible situation of the candidate interviewing the interviewer.

Job attitude data suggest that after the glow of the initial year on the job, job satisfaction plummets to its lowest level in the work life of individuals (9). From a life time of diverse learning, successive accomplishment through the various academic stages, and periodic reinforcement of efforts, the entrant to our modern companies finds, that rather than work providing an expanding psychological existence, the opposite occurs; and successive amputations of his self-conceptions, aspirations, learning, and talent are the consequence of earning a living. Of course as the needs and values of our industrial enterprises have become the template for all aspects of our lives, the university is preparing many young people by performing the amputations early, and they enter already primed for work as only a means of hygienic improvement; or for those still capable of enjoying the exercise of their human talents, as means of affording off the job satisfactions. If the number of management development programs is a valid sign, the educational system has done its job too well.

A reaction to retirement policies is beginning to set in as the personal consequences of organizational definitions of human obsolescence are being told. Prior to retirement, however, are 30 to 40 years of partial retirement and partial commitment to work for the too many who have not "succeeded" in terms of organizational advancement. From the first orientation to the farewell party, the history of work careers is a history of human waste. What a paradox we face. There is a shortage of talent in the country at a time when our problems are defined in planetary dimensions and to meet these circumstances we have evolved a system and a philosophy to use and motivate our talent that serves to decrease further this precious resource.

What alternatives are there? A spate of new research and literature is becoming available that is reacting to personnel and managerial psychology that has too long tried to emulate the vast and short term goals of the military. The new literature while encompassing diverse problems, exhortations, solutions and conceptions, seems to have the common theme of emphasizing the motivator needs of man and the necessity for the personnel function of industry to pause in its search for the Holy Grail of instruments, to become creative in finding ways to meet the motivator needs. Man is distinguished from all other animals in that he alone is a determiner. How strange that when it comes to the satisfactions of his special psychological growth needs he finds himself a victim of outside determinisms and helpless in affecting the way he is utilized in work. The short term economic "necessities" cannot justify the larger economic loss and the denial of human satisfaction that the restriction of human talent inevitably costs. I might add that many of the barriers to fuller utilization of manpower that are "justified" by economic reasons, are in reality, devices of fearful and inadequate managers who are not prepared to meet the challenge of managing adults. The philosophy of management which prizes such men is changeable. We need a goal of industry which includes the expansion of manpower utilization in addition to the expansion of productivity and profit. The acceptance of such a goal as basic will lead to the means for its implementation. Personnel cannot remain the one management function that only establishes objectives for which techniques and procedures are available.

References

1. Fantz, R. Motivation factors in rehabilitation. *Unpublished doctoral dissertation, Western Reserve University Library,* Cleveland, 1961.

2. Gibson, J. Sources of job satisfaction and job dissatisfaction. *Unpublished doctoral dissertation, Western Reserve University Library,* Cleveland, 1961.

3. Guilford, J. P.; Christensen, P. R., Bond, N. and Sutton, M. A factor analysis study of human interests. *Res. Bull.,* 53–11, Human Resources Research Center, San Antonio, 1953.

4. Hamlin, R. and Nemo, R. Self-actualization in choice scores of improved schizophrenics. *J. Clin. Psychol.,* 18, 1962.

5. Herzberg, F. New approaches in management organization and job design. *Industrial Med. and Surgery,* November, 1962.

6. Herzberg, F. Basic needs and satisfactions of individuals. *Industrial Relations Monograph,* No. 21, Industrial Relations Counselors, Inc., New York: 1962.

7. Herzberg, F. Comment on the Meaning of Work. Proceedings of symposium of the worker in the new industrial environment. *Industrial Med. and Surgery,* June, 1963.

8. Herzberg, F. The meaning of work to the individual. In, *Basic psychology and physiology of work,* edited by H. Hellerstein, C. C. Thomas Press, Ft. Lauderdale, In Press.

9. Herzberg, F. et al. Job attitudes: Research, and opinion. Psychological Service of Pittsburgh, 1957.

10. Herzberg, F., Mausner, B., and Snyderman, B. *The motivation to work.* John Wiley and Sons, New York: 1959.

11. Herszberg, F., and Hamlin, R. A motivation-hygiene concept of mental health. *Mental Hygiene,* July, 1961.

12. Herzberg, F., and Hamlin, R. Motivation-hygiene concept and psychotherapy. *Mental Hygiene,* July, 1961.
13. Lodahl, T. Patterns of job attitudes in two assembly technologies. *Graduate School of Business and Public Administration, Cornell University,* Ithaca, New York, 1963.
14. Saleh, S. Attitude change and its effect on the pre-retirement period. *Unpublished doctoral dissertation, Western Reserve University Library,* Cleveland, 1962.
15. Schwarz, P. *Attitudes of middle management personnel.* American Institute for Research, Pittsburgh, 1961.
16. Schwartz, M., Jenusaitis, E. and Stark, H. Motivation factors among supervisors in the utility industry. *Personnel Psychology,* 16, 1963.

Contingency Management and Motivation*

L. E. Homme and D. T. Tosti

There is a growing technology concerning the application of the laws of behavior. In the application of the laws of behavior to practical affairs, the most important factor is motivation. Although motivation is widely held to be a complex phenomenon—many books have been written explaining how complicated it is—the practical problem of motivation is reduced to this simple question: What reinforcers are available? With control of reinforcing events, one can produce a motivated organism, that is, an organism which will respond under the circumstances specified. Without such control, only the accidental contingencies of the environment operate. While psychologists agree that a reinforcing event is necessary to increase or maintain response strength, it is only when we ask, "What is the nature of reinforcement?" that we encounter disagreement. Because of the overwhelming importance of reinforcers, existing motivational constructs must be examined to see whether they can be of help in finding reinforcers.

Some Explanations for the Effects of Reinforcement

Perhaps the most popular approach to theory building is to lean heavily on intervening variables. One such explanation of reinforcement offers the use of the drive construct; reinforcement is explained in terms of drive reduction. In drive reduction theory, reinforcement is said to reduce drive stimuli, to reduce or satisfy a need. Although this explanation has been widely applied, it has not been wholly satisfactory, both for theoretical and practical considerations. The drive theorists claim that most human behavior is controlled by secondary drives, but, in these pronouncements, they have not always specified the antecedent conditions, and thus their intervening variable is reduced to a mere renaming explanation of behavior. Even as a classification system, the drive construct has not been especially useful in determining effective reinforcing events in normal human behavior. Drive constructs have proven worthless in the application of the laws of behavior, except, of course, to comfort the explainer by permitting him to name a new drive whenever he discovers a new reinforcer.

* Reprinted with permission of authors and publisher from *NSPI Journal*, Vol. 4 (September, 1965). The *Journal* is published by the National Society for Programmed Instruction.

Two other explanations of reinforcement have gained attention. One of these states that reinforcement is a change in stimulation; the other maintains that reinforcement is the opportunity to emit a high probability response. In operant responding, some behavior leads to a reinforcing event. It has generally been overlooked that this event consists of two independently observable occurrences, the introduction of a food pellet and the subsequent eating of it. Traditionally, emphasis has been placed on the reinforcing stimulus, the presentation of the pellet. It may be, however, equally as important to emphasize the reinforcing response.

In an important series of papers beginning in 1959, Premack, D., (1959, 1961, 1963, 1963, 1963) has been saying, and finding evidence in support, that there is no need to invoke a drive concept in explaining why water, say, functions as a reinforcer. It water functions as a reinforcer, it does so simply because the experimenter has arranged matters (by deprivation) so that drinking has a higher probability than the response to be strengthened. As further support for this formulation, he has shown that, under appropriate conditions, drinking can be reinforced by the opportunity to run. In Premack's experiments, it is the reinforcing response which is emphasized, not the reinforcing stimulus. Extending this conceptualization, it may be possible to predispose a human S so that, momentarily at least, a given behavior is at a higher probability than one we are attempting to strengthen.

In the case of an experimental animal, the same response, eating, for example, continues to be a high probability behavior throughout the experiment. In the case of the non-experimental animal or the non-deprived human, on the contrary, behavior probabilities vary from moment to moment. What is a high probability behavior at one moment will get executed and instantly become a low probability behavior the next. Moreover, it may remain a low probability behavior for a long interval. For example, when the pet cat awakens, eating and whatever preceded eating on prior occasions are high probability behaviors. Once eating has occurred, its probability is near zero, and getting out of the house may now be a high probability behavior. Once out, this, of course, is a near zero probability response, and some time later getting in is a high probability behavior, and so it goes. Similarly, with a human, smoking may be a high probability behavior at one instant. A minute or two later, it may have a probability close to zero. "Getting a glass of water" may be an extremely high probability behavior at one instant; after drinking it may be close to zero, and so on.

When we think of a reinforcer, we are inclined to think of something with rather stable properties. Food for a food-deprived organism, water for a water-deprived organism, evoke the same behavior from one reinforcement to the next. Premack's analysis of what the sufficient properties of a reinforcing response are, however, imposes no such constraints. If we take the Premack data seriously, we will not ask, "What is the reinforcer for this session?" We will ask, rather, "What is the reinforcer at this instant in time?"

The notion of a reinforcing response has led to the discovery of many "new" reinforcers. It is difficult to classify all these as being high probability behaviors because they may not be emitted more than once in any session. The term "reinforcing responses" is useful to designate these behaviors.

In a recent experiment with nursery school children, high probability behaviors were used to reinforce lower probability behaviors (Homme, L. E., C. deBaca, P., Devine, J. V., Steinhorst, R., and Rickert, E. J., 1963). It is doubtful that a drive reduction position would have led us to suspect that having the opportunity to run down the hall could be classified as a reinforcing event. Notice that in the case of their reinforcing event there is no clearly identifiable reinforcing stimulus, unless it is the verbal instruction, "Run down the hall." Nevertheless, when he made the behavior of running down the hall contingent upon the emission of counting, we could, and did, shape counting behavior. This example illustrates the advantage of speaking of a reinforcing event, a concept which includes both the reinforcing response and the discriminative stimulus which sets it off.

Factors Involved in the Management of Contingencies

The application of contingency management has been much more straightforward than might be expected. One simply takes notice of which behaviors are reinforcing responses, then permits this behavior to occur only after behavior one wishes to reinforce. Interestingly enough, there is very little problem in finding things which may act as reinforcing responses. The difficulty in everyday manipulation involves the arrangement of the appropriate contingencies, that is, arranging these behaviors so that the reinforcing response occurs immediately after the behavior one wishes to reinforce. There is also some difficulty, when one is learning to manage motivation, in taking advantage of the high probability behaviors that do exist. For example, suppose a student is scribbling, and looking-at-the-blackboard is the response desired. Notice that here is a very clear-cut case of two behaviors: one of high probability (scribbling) and one of low probability (looking-at-the-blackboard). If a plan can be devised to make the scribbling depend upon having looked at the blackboard, then the problem is solved. With most children, a verbal instruction like this will do: "Look at the blackboard while I write a word; then scribble some more."

The rule for this example can be summarized in this way: Notice what behavior is at a high probability at the moment, then instruct S (the student) that he can execute more of it if he will do a small amount of lower probability behavior first.

Humans signal in a variety of ways when certain behaviors may be reinforcing ones. When eating ice cream is such a behavior, a child may signal this by saying, "I want an ice cream cone," may run for the freezer, or do whatever produced the opportunity to engage in ice cream eating the last time. Another signal of a reinforcing behavior, as Premack points out, is its frequency. As a matter of fact, S may give this signal often enough and intensely enough for it to be distinctly annoying. The adaptive thing to do is to use, rather than be annoyed by, high probability behaviors. Use them to reinforce other behaviors of lower probability in need of strengthening.

For example. A child is seated at the dinner table. Dinner is served. The other members of the family are eating. The child, however, does not eat. She plays with her shoes. The usual way to solve this problem is obvious: "Stop playing with your shoes! Eat your dinner!" The other way is to notice that "playing with shoes" is a high frequency behavior and eating is a low one. When the problem is viewed this way, the contingency manager says, "Eat one bite of potatoes, then play with your shoes some more." It may be startling to spectators, but the latter method works. Instead of having an emotional scene with both parent and child upset, the manager has a child cooperating in a game-like atmosphere. What stimulus set off the playing-with-shoes operant in the first place? It is impossible to say, but it does not matter. If this higher frequency operant follows a lower frequency one, the latter will get strengthened.

Reinforcing Events

As was previously stated, there are two discriminable divisions of the reinforcing event. Under certain conditions, the reinforcing stimulus is the most appropriate consideration, while under others, it is the reinforcing response, without reference to any stimulus conditions, which is the most useful. In practical situations, members of the first class are: compliments, verbal encouragements, thanks, gold stars, good grades, movies, and so on. It is true that such events are not without response components of viewing or hearing, but it is primarily the stimulus attributes which make them easy to identify.

Other reinforcing events can best be characterized by their response characteristics and little emphasis need be placed on the stimulus properties. In every repertoire, there are apparently hundreds of such responses which may fit this class. With such a large supply of reinforcers to draw from, control over behavior should not only be precise but relatively effortless.

Difficulties in the Control of Behavior

It is a strange fact of life that often control of behavior is not effortless. Parents, teachers, and others have tremendous struggles in attempting to control behavior. Children have screaming tantrums in supermarkets, refuse to eat at mealtime, won't go to bed at bedtime, hate school, won't learn, and so forth. Not all children, certainly not all the time—but some children, some of the time. Usually unwanted behaviors are kept suppressed by punishment, but like most suppressed behaviors, they pop up occasionally. Often enough to be , troublesome.

If it is not the lack of reinforcers which makes behavioral control difficult, one might reason, it must be the lack of knowledge of the principles of behavioral control. If one attempts to verify this, he will find that this, too, is incorrect. If given a test on the principles of behavior so far discussed, most people would score very high. It is not a lack of reinforcers or a lack of knowledge about how to use them. The difficulty can be primarily traced to a failure to systematically apply what is known. It is not only that reinforcement principles are not systematically applied, they are, if applied at all, only sporadically applied.

Father, for example, returning home after a hard day at the office, seems to expect that the laws of behavior can be suspended for a time while he catches his breath. Mother, busy with her work, seems to feel the same way. For the time being, at least, she thinks she is too busy to pay attention to those psychological laws and wants them suspended until she has more time.

The likelihood of doing this—suspending the laws of behavior temporarily—is roughly the same as suspending the laws of gravity. The laws work all the time. One may not notice them or do anything but struggle with them, but they are working. A behavior which doesn't get followed by a reinforcer will decrease in probability whether things are planned that way or not. Whenever a low strength behavior gets followed by a reinforcer, it will increase in strength, whether the contingency is deliberately arranged or not.

There is a choice, then. Either one manages the contingencies or they get managed by accident. Either way, there will be contingencies, and they will have their effect. That is a sobering thought—that these laws of behavior, which we have to assume are as powerful as any other laws of nature, are usually ignored and left to chance. A visitor from another planet who knew about the laws of behavior would probably assume that this leaving contingencies to chance might result in a great deal of improper behavior and even mental illness.

The Mismanagement of Contingencies

Several unusual reinforcers have been under discussion, such as playing with shoes. There are more conventional reinforcers with which almost everyone is familiar, such as giving attention to a child or rewarding him with candy. When these conventional reinforcements are used, more often than not they get administered exactly at the wrong time. Sometimes it is nearly impossible not to reinforce at the wrong time.

For example, suppose a child is playing quietly in a roomful of adults. His play is constructive, and he is bothering no one. Nobody pays attention to him. But let him "act up." Suddenly he is the center of attention. This is incredibly bad behavioral engineering, but very difficult to avoid. It is difficult in the sense that it is difficult to remember to reinforce while desirable behavior is occurring, before the undesirable behavior occurs.

It is an interesting intellectual exercise to specify how one would go about it if he deliberately set out to shape up some misbehavior. How would one arrange matters, for example, so he would end up with a child who is motivated to whine loud and persistently?

The behavior wanted is whining. Therefore, one ought to wait until a little whining occurred, then reinforce. For the reinforcer, attention alone will do. If one wants to administer a better-than-average reinforcer, he would make the attention emotional. Scream at the child, "Will you stop that whining!!" This will more than likely constitute a better reinforcer than most. If that is too much trouble and one still wants whining strongly reinforced, something else can be found to add to attention. Ice cream, soda pop, candy, or the opportunity to engage in some high probability behavior ought to do it. Notice that the rule about reinforcing a first approximation has been obeyed. Any sort of whine will do for the first trial. Even an inadequate whine will do at first. Next time reinforcement will be withheld until the whining gets a little louder. The time after that the whining must be still louder before it is reinforced. One can anticipate in this hypothetical example that whining will soon be loud and strong. Further, not every response has been reinforced—only occasional ones. This means that whining will be extremely difficult to get rid of. Another way of saying this is that the response will be very persistent. There you have it. Through the reinforcement of successive approximations, you have shaped up, theoretically, a strong, persistent whining response. Theoretically?

Implications

Considerations of the management of motivation through the use of reinforcing responses not only has practical implications, as we've discussed here, it also has theoretical implications. Just as the concept of operant behavior eliminated the need for specifying an eliciting stimulus for every response, so the concept of the reinforcing response eliminates the need for specifying a reinforcing stimulus for every reinforcing event, while emphasizing the need for the precise control of contingencies between two responses.

The authors wish to thank Professor Henry C. Ellis for his helpful comments during the preparation of this paper.
Paper presented at the Third National Convention of the National Society for Programmed Instruction, Philadelphia, May 1965.

References

1. Homme, L. E., C. deBaca, P., Devine, J. V., Steinhorst, R., and Rickert, E. J. "Use of the Premack principle in controlling the behavior of nursery school children," *J. exp. Anal. Behav.*, 4: 544 (1963).
2. Premack, D. "Toward empirical behavior laws: I. positive reinforcement," *Psycol. Rev.*, 66: 219–33 (1959).
3. Premack, D. "Predicting instrumental performance from the independent rate of the contingent response," *J. exp. Psychol.*, 61: 163–71 (1961).

4. Premack, D. "Rate differential reinforcement in monkey manipulation," *J. exp. Anal. Behav.*, 6: 81–9 (1963).
5. Premack, D. "Prediction of the comparative reinforcement values of running and drinking," *Science* 139: 1062–63 (1963).
6. Premack, D. "Running as both a positive and negative reinforcer," *Science*, 142: 1087–88 (1963).

Chapter 2
Managing by Tens and Twenties: Supervising Immediate Work Units

Most managers in organizations are pulled in two directions, whether they are first-level supervisors or middle managers or high-level executives. That is, managers as superiors often directly monitor the activities of relatively few people immediately "below" them. These managers at the same time respond as subordinates to one or a few individuals immediately "above" them in the hierarchy.

This duality has a simple consequence: most managers have big troubles in their immediate supervision of small work units. For under the glare of face-to-face conditions and without the protection of greatly superior formal status, matters of consequence must be worked out in the heat of action rather than in cool logic. Policies and procedures must be shaped with people rather than with paper. Any failure in working things out implies a breakdown in the crucial process of linking the efforts of one level of organization with those levels near it. Consequently, managers must be sensitive to the desires of "their men."[1] At the same time, there are those higher in the hierarchy who monitor action attentively with a particular eye for any supervisor who too ardently serves the needs of subordinates. Suspended in this dynamic web of often conflicting interests, the manager struggles with his direct supervision of tens and twenties.

The stresses placed on immediate supervisory relations in organizations are significant, and they often are crucial. Indeed, the simultaneous pressures from "immediately below" and from "on high" have long been cited as especial sources of difficulty in organizations, and par-

---

[1] The general point is perhaps made most sharply by the degree to which the jailors in a maximum-security prison are dependent upon the goodwill of the prisoners. See Gresham Sykes, *The Society of Captives* (Princeton, N. J.: Princeton University Press, 1958).

ticularly so at the first level of supervision. The image of the "man in the middle" is consequently now a familiar one in the management literature. Many men in organizations at all levels know the feeling personally.

An influential version of the portrait-in-tension of immediate supervision is Fritz Roethlisberger's "The Foreman: Master and Victim of Double Talk." The article is a classic statement of conflicting organizational demands in the management of tens and twenties, whether those tens or twenties are at the very highest or the very lowest levels of organization. Despite Roethlisberger's use of the term "foreman," the relations he describes obtain whether the superior is a first-line supervisor in industry or government, and they apply whether he is a vice-president in a business firm or bureau or a departmental head in the federal government. Roethlisberger is firmly unequivocal in his judgment of the importance of these ubiquitous relations. "In the modern business structure," he put it, "there is probably no relation more important than that of the subordinate to his immediate superior."[2]

The picture of immediate supervisory relations is not a monolith, of course. Many of the details of supervisory in-betweenness will vary at different levels of organization and in different kinds of organizations. Thus unions have been far less influential in complicating immediate supervisory relations in business than in government, although this is subject to probable change over the next few years. The impact of line-staff dynamics is likely to influence immediate supervisory relations as much at high as at low levels, in addition, although many important differences in style will exist. Language at the operating level, for example, is likely to be more exotic and uninhibited.

Variations on the theme notwithstanding, similarities in the causes and the consequences of the typical dynamics of supervising immediate work units are striking. Thus Roethlisberger stresses two common factors that complicate such relations. First, he sees management generally overloading an inherently delicate set of relations without giving corresponding attention to strengthening the supervisor's position. Second and relatedly, Roethlisberger sees much mischief for immediate supervisory relations deriving from management's general failure to take account of "informal organization" in ways that serve both individual and organizational needs.

That Roethlisberger took a solid bite out of reality can be demonstrated variously. Consider, for example, that managers do not merely

---

[2] Fritz J. Roethlisberger, "The Foreman: Master and Victim of Double Talk," *Harvard Business Review*, Vol. 23 (Spring, 1945), p. 286.

absorb the pressures of being "in the middle." They cope on their own with the organizational pressures they feel. That their coping so commonly implies personal and organizational costs makes it clear that the problems are beyond tidy resolution by individuals. These problems of organization must be solved systematically.

Peter Blau outlines one of these double-edged adaptations to the conflicting demands imposed on immediate supervisors in his "Strategic Leniency and Authority." Blau describes immediate supervisors as typically bargaining their discrete neglect of violations of organizational policies to increase their influence with their immediate subordinates. In this variation, then, only cheaters prosper. More seriously, the resort to such surreptitious supervisory greasing-of-the-ways starkly reflects the ill-resolved managerial problems that organizations thrust into the unwilling hands of immediate supervisors. These ill-resolved problems force jerry-built supervisory adaptations that raise significant organizational issues related to authority and discipline. These issues also may have moral implications for the individual.

Argyris' "Three Supervisory Adaptations to 'Artificial Pressure'" sketches yet another set of common supervisory reactions to the pressure of being "in the middle," and they have more narrowly personal implications. Briefly, Argyris develops a picture of top-level management's keeping supervisors at lower levels "on their toes" by "putting on the pressure" through the use of "staff" personnel handling budget matters. In the largest part, this managerial strategy seems a counsel of despair. The strategy is compounded of top management's knowledge of the difficulty of controlling work at a distance in their concept of "organization" and of management's fear that if it were not for "artificial pressure" supervisors would indulge in an orgy of serving the selfish interests of their own work units and consequently would sacrifice production. Even granting that the strategy of top management achieved its ends—and that is doubtful—Argyris demonstrates that supervisors in the plants he studied adopted behaviors that over the long run could hardly serve their needs or those of their organization. Supervisors "handled" managerial pressure in one or more of these ways:

1. "passing on" the pressure in the form of heightened conflict between departments;
2. acting out the conflict in line-staff conflicts; and
3. internalizing the pressure by being over-controlled or over-controlling.

The mixed consequences of such managerial pressure can be suggested variously. For example, as Argyris notes, "artificial pressure" often encourages the development of groups among employees who use their social power for self-protection. Consequently, a supervisor often will be placed in an uncomfortable position by managerial action designed to reduce the power of informal groups. He can join informal groups of employees protecting themselves from perceived arbitrary managerial action; or he can oppose such groups, thereby risking further loss of already weakened supervisory influence.

Managerial "pressure" seems ill-advised, whatever the outcome. Whether the supervisor fights or joins the informal group, the organization stands to lose. In either case, also, the supervisor's position must be an uncomfortable one. This double-bind illustrates those unfortunate products attributed by Roethlisberger to management's awkward handling of informal organizations among its employees.

References like that above to the requirement that management treat groups in useful ways need not remain at a general level. Indeed, three contributions reprinted in this volume permit a considerable specificity about ways informal organizations among employees can be managed to serve the needs of group members as well as the interests of the formal organizations in which the groups exist. The range over which greater specificity is possible may be outlined. The three pieces respectively deal with: (1) the description of types of groups encountered in organizations, the description of which emphasizes the forces that underlie group development; (2) an introduction to some dimensions for specifically characterizing small groups in ways that have managerial relevance; and (3) a survey of the leadership dynamics necessary to take advantage of what is presently known about small groups in organizations.

The task of describing some important types of groups is accomplished by Leonard R. Sayles in "Work Group Behavior and the Larger Organization." Sayles focuses on three types of groups—friendship cliques, task groups, and interest groups—which may or may not overlap in organizations. Each of these types of groups is shown to have an important impact on performance and satisfaction, particularly as they tie individuals to organizational purposes or as they bind individuals together in resistance to formal authorities. Reciprocally, the organization of work is shown to help determine the kinds of groups that will develop. The two generalizations preoccupy Sayles. Throughout, consequently, he searches for ways of integrating the demands of work and of social relations to serve both individual and organizational needs.

Since knowledge is in important senses an infinite regression, we must press toward even more specific group differentiation. That is, it is patently important to isolate (for example) friendship cliques. But it is then necessary to specify differentiating characteristics of the subspecies "friendship cliques," and the scientific cycle is thereby triggered to repeat itself. This recycling has a serious purpose. For only to the degree that we can increasingly specify group properties will it become increasingly possible to integrate the demands of work and the demands of man's social relations. Only thus will it become increasingly possible to serve both individual and organizational interests.

"The Small Group and Public Administration" by Robert T. Golembiewski carries us further toward the goal of the specification of group properties necessary to permit refined predictions and useful applications of knowledge. Golembiewski roughly distinguishes three categories of dimensions necessary for group description: a structural panel; a style panel; and a population panel. Results of a number of studies are reviewed to illustrate dimensions in each of the panels, and the studies converge to two common points. Knowledge of small-group properties is managerially significant. Moreover, in some cases, relatively simple techniques have been developed to permit applied use of this significance.

Several reservations must hedge this strong conclusion. The article treats individual group properties and individually relates them to organizational performance, in the main. This reflects convenience rather than the power of any few variables to predict or describe behavior, however. Prediction and description will be more powerful when families of properties of groups are determined. For example, the article stresses the particular significance for analysis and application of certain clusters of group properties such as high cohesiveness, high consensus about leadership and norms, and so on. Moreover, although written for an audience interested primarily in public administration, the argument applies to groups in all contexts.

Knowledge of group properties is not the end of the line. For example, some of our knowledge about group properties can be extended conveniently to that most popular of managerial topics, leadership. "Three Styles of Leadership" by Robert T. Golembiewski illustrates the possible. The article's strategy is plain. Differences in group norms and in member personality characteristics in one work unit, for example, are shown to be important conditions that will influence the choice of an appropriate style of leadership for the supervisor of that unit. Three styles of leadership are considered, and the available research literature is sampled to illustrate how one style or another is more or less appropriate as conditions vary. "Appropriate" here refers to the increased probability of high production and high satisfaction.

Several possible stumbling blocks in the article require brief notice. First, a supervisor's style of leadership is usually a matter of more or less rather than of either/or. Their styles, in short, are defined in terms of the relative incidence of various behaviors. For example, most individuals are complex enough that they normally perform some behaviors that can be considered "group-centered" even though their style is basically "leader-centered." The three gross leadership styles in the article are not up to the task of providing the specificity required for the full range of such differences in degree as they exist in nature. The general distinctions are useful for our analytical purposes, however, as they do highlight important consequences of differences in supervisory styles.

Second, and also related to man's complexity, most supervisors at least in the short run have wide enough response repertoires to honestly supply behaviors appropriate to most individual and group conditions. Over the long run, however, the performance of low-preference behaviors has many undesirable consequences for all concerned. The long-run implication of the present argument recommends the placement of individuals in conditions demanding behaviors from them which are high-preference behaviors in their response repertoires. Some research has in fact gone a considerable distance down this particular road.[3] In any case, the argument of the article certainly is not for dishonest role-playing by individuals who are "not really that way."

The charge of personal phoniness by supervisors for organization purposes could not be wider of the present mark. Indeed, the long-run implication of the last three previewed articles is for increasingly genuine relations as both supervisor and employees are assigned to work units in such ways that they can employ high-preference behaviors while they serve organizational purposes. Individuals scoring high on "authoritarianism," for example, might be assigned to the same work unit, and their supervisor also might be chosen for his tendency to provide behaviors which members of his specific work unit are predisposed to accept. Present random methods of assignment encourage more cat-and-mousing. That is, both supervisor and supervised attempt to play nonauthentic games in providing behaviors that at once seem culturally correct but which often are inappropriate because they require individuals to supply behaviors which they consider relatively undesirable. The general prescription of an authoritarian style of supervision, and its general failure to provide superior results, adequately illustrates the present casual approach to assignment as well as one of its common products.

The day of truly scientific assignments on a mass scale in terms of

---

[3] William C. Schutz, *FIRO-B* (New York: Rinehart, 1958).

personality characteristics is still some time away, to be sure, but there are ways of taking managerial advantage of the dynamics of the assignment of "compatible" members to work units. "Self-choice" is one such technique. It may be characterized as a poor man's approach to scientific assignment in terms of the personality characteristics of work unit members.

"Self-choice" refers to the use of organization members as resources in matters of assignment. Thus employees might be allowed to choose their workmates on a team project. "Above-choice" is more typical. Here management makes assignments on whatever criteria are convenient.

Available evidence demonstrates that self-choice commonly "works." Van Zelst's "Sociometrically Selected Work Teams Increase Productivity," for example, presents very attractive results from one application of the technique on a construction project. Above-choice prevailed in the pre-experimental period of nine months. The attractiveness of self-choice is dramatically reflected in the data presented below. Whatever dynamics employees tapped in their process of choice, those dynamics were beyond management's reach. Moreover, the results of self-choice were appealing to both the individual and organization. That is, not only did costs go down, but employee satisfaction increased and personnel turnover rates fell sharply following the use of self-choice. These dual consequences are the ideal products of any manager's efforts to cope with the demands placed upon him in his supervision of tens and twenties.

Like all managerial techniques, self-choice yields not only "positive" results. Thus a work group composed of individuals who chose one another should be better able to reduce output as well as better able to increase it.[4] Sometimes, in fact, self-choice has contributed to the development of groups with anti-management norms and attitudes. Although such outcomes are apparently not common, the aware manager should be prepared to act quickly when they do occur.

---

[4] For a summary treatment consult Robert T. Golembiewski, *Men, Management, and Morality* (New York: McGraw-Hill, 1965), esp. pp. 110–14. For a technical description of the probable dynamics tapped by self-choice see Golembiewski, "Small Groups and Large Organizations," in James March, editor, *Handbook of Organizations* (Chicago: Rand McNally, 1965), pp. 87–141.

The Foreman: Master and Victim of Double Talk*

Fritz J. Roethlisberger

The increasing dissatisfaction of foremen in mass production industries, as evidenced by the rise of foremen's unions, calls for more human understanding of the foreman's situation. This dissatisfaction of foremen is no new, nor static, problem. It arises from the dynamic interaction of many social forces and is part and parcel of the structure of modern industrial organization. In its present manifestation it is merely a new form and outbreak of an old disease, which management has repeatedly failed to recognize, let alone diagnose or treat correctly. Master and victim of double talk, the foreman is management's contribution to the social pathology of American culture.

Some of the reasons cited in the current situation for the increasing receptiveness of foremen to unionization in mass production industries are:

(1) The weekly take-home pay of many foremen is less than that of the men working under them; this condition has been aggravated under war conditions in those factories where foremen do not receive extra compensation for working overtime.

(2) The influx of inexperienced workers, under war demands, has made the foremen's jobs more difficult.

(3) The rise of industrial unions has stripped the foremen of most of their authority.

(4) Many union-minded workers have been upgraded to supervisory positions.

(5) Many production workers promoted to the rank of foreman during the war expansion face the possibility of demotion after the war and the sacrifice of seniority credits in the unions from which they came for the period spent as foremen.

It would be absurd to argue that these factors, particularly as they are aggravated by war conditions, have not contributed to the grievances which foremen hope to correct by unionization. In a number of companies it is only fair to say that management has recognized some of these grievances and, when possible, has taken corrective steps. But is the correction of these grievances alone enough? Unfortunately, the possibility still exists that too little attention will be given to the

* Reprinted with permission of author and publisher from *Harvard Business Review*, Vol. 23 (Spring, 1945), pp. 283–298, and republished in Vol. 43 (September-October, 1965), pp. 22–6+.

underlying situation. The symptom-by-symptom attack that management is prone to take in solving its human affairs will fail to go below the surface. Failing to recognize the hydra-headed character of the social situation with which it is faced, management will cut off one head, only to have two new heads appear.

The major thesis of this article therefore will be that once again "management's chickens have come home to roost."[1] And this question is raised: Can management afford not to take responsibility for its own social creations—one of which is the situation in which foremen find themselves?

The Position of the Foreman

Nowhere in the industrial structure more than at the foremen level is there so great a discrepancy between what a position ought to be and what a position is. This may account in part for the wide range of names which foremen have been called—shall we say "informally"?— and the equally great variety of definitions which have been applied to them in a more strictly formal and legal sense. Some managements have been eloquent in citing the foremen's importance with such phrases as: "arms of management," "grass-roots level of management," "key men in production," "front-line personnel men," and the like. Not so definite is the status of foremen under the National Labor Relations Act, since they can be included under the definitions given both for "employers" and "employees." To many foremen themselves they are merely the "go-betweeners," the "forgotten men," the "stepchildren" of industry. And what some employees call some foremen we shall leave to the reader's imagination.

But even without this diversity of names, it is clear that from the point of view of the individual foreman the discrepancy between what he should be and what he is cannot fail to be disconcerting. At times it is likely to influence adversely what he actually does or does not do, communicates or does not communicate to his superiors, his associates, and his subordinates. For this reason let us try to understand better the foreman's position in the modern industrial scene.

It is in his new streamlined social setting, far different from the "good old days," that we must learn to understand the modern foreman's anomalous position. The modern foreman has to get results— turn out production, maintain quality, hold costs down, keep his em-

---

[1] See Clinton S. Golden and Harold J. Ruttenberg, *The Dynamics of Industrial Democracy* (New York, Harper & Brothers, 1942).

ployees satisfied—under a set of technical conditions, social relations, and logical abstractions far different from those which existed 25 years ago.

More Knowledge Required

For one thing, he has to "know" more than his old-time counterpart. Any cursory examination of modern foreman training programs will reveal that the modern foreman has to know (and understand) not only (1) the company's policies, rules, and regulations and (2) the company's cost system, payment system, manufacturing methods, and inspection regulations, in particular, but also frequently (3) something about the theories of production control, cost control, quality control, and time and motion study, in general. He also has to know (4) the labor laws of the United States, (5) the labor laws of the state in which the company operates, and (6) the specific labor contract which exists between his company and the local union. He has to know (7) how to induct, instruct, and train new workers; (8) how to handle and, where possible, prevent grievances; (9) how to improve conditions of safety; (10) how to correct workers and maintain discipline; (11) how never to lose his temper and always to be "fair"; (12) how to get and obtain cooperation from the wide assortment of people with whom he has to deal; and, especially, (13) how to get along with the shop steward. And in some companies he is supposed to know (14) how to do the jobs he supervises better than the employees themselves. Indeed, as some foreman training programs seem to conceive the foreman's job, he has to be a manager, a cost accountant, an engineer, a lawyer, a teacher, a leader, an inspector, a disciplinarian, a counselor, a friend, and, above all, an "example."

One might expect that this superior knowledge would tend to make the modern foreman feel more secure as well as be more effective. But unfortunately some things do not work out the way they are intended. Quite naturally the foreman is bewildered by the many different roles and functions he is supposed to fulfill. He is worried in particular by what the boss will think if he takes the time to do the many things his many training courses tell him to do. And in 99 cases out of 100 what the boss thinks, or what the foreman thinks the boss thinks, will determine what the foreman does. As a result, the foreman gives lip service in his courses to things which in the concrete shop situation he feels it would be suicidal to practice. In the shop, for the most part, he does his best to perform by hook or by crook the one function clearly left him, the one function for which there is no definite staff counterpart, the one function for which the boss is sure to hold him responsible; namely, getting the workers to turn the work out on time. And about this function he feels his courses do not say enough—given the particular conditions, technical, human, and organizational, under which he has to operate.

Freedom of Action Restricted

Curiously enough, knowledge is not power for the modern foreman. Although he has to know a great deal about many things, he is no longer "the cock of the walk" he once was. Under modern conditions of operation, for example, there seems to be always somebody in the organization in a staff capacity who is supposed to know more than he does, and generally has more say, about almost every matter that comes up; somebody, in addition to his boss, with whom he is supposed to consult and sometimes to share responsibility; somebody by whom he is constantly advised and often even ordered.

To the foreman it seems as if he is being held responsible for functions over which he no longer has any real authority. For some time he has not been able to hire and fire and set production standards. And now he cannot even transfer employees, adjust the wage inequalities of his men, promote deserving men, develop better machines, methods, and processes, or plan the work of his department, with anything approaching complete freedom of action. All these matters for which he is completely or partially responsible have now become involved with other persons and groups, or they have become matters of company policy and union agreement. He is hedged in on all sides with cost standards, production standards, quality standards, standard methods and procedures, specifications, rules, regulations, policies, laws, contracts, and agreements; and most of them are formulated without his participation.

Far better than the old-timer of 25 years ago the modern foreman knows how much work should be done in what length of time; how much it is worth; what the best methods to be used are; what his material, labor, and burden costs should be; and what the tolerances are that his product should meet. But in the acquisition of all this untold wealth of knowledge, somehow something is missing. In some sense, not too clearly defined, he feels he has become less rather than more effective, less rather than more secure, less rather than more important, and has received less rather than more recognition.

Interactions With Many People

Let us explore further this feeling of the modern foreman. Not only does he have to know more than his old-time counterpart about the "logics" of management, but also he has to relate himself to a wider range of people. In any mass production industry the foreman each day is likely to be interacting (1) with his boss, the man to whom he formally reports in the line organization; (2) with certain staff specialists, varying from one to a dozen people depending on the size and kind of organization—production control men, inspectors, standards men, efficiency engineers, safety engineers, maintenance and repair men, methods men, personnel men, counselors; (3) with the heads of other departments to which his department relates; (4) with his subordinates—subforemen, straw bosses, leadmen, group leaders, section chiefs; (5) with the workers directly, numbering anywhere from 10 to 300 people; and (6), in a union-organized plant, with the shop steward. Exploring the interdependence of each of these relationships as they impinge in toto upon the foreman makes it easier to understand how the modern foreman may feel in his everyday life. A diagram may help to make this clear (see Exhibit 1). [Note: This diagram shows only those forces impinging upon the foreman through the actions of other people. It is not designed to show the reaction of the foreman to these actions, in terms of either feelings or overt behavior; or to show the reactions of the workers to management's actions, which in turn become one of the chief forces acting upon the foreman. These reactions will be considered below.]

Foreman-Superior. In the modern business structure there is probably no relation more important than that of the subordinate to his immediate superior.[2] This statement applies straight up the line from worker to president. It is in the relation between a subordinate and his immediate superior that most breakdowns of coordination and communication between various parts of the industrial structure finally show up. It is here that distortions of personal attitude and emotional disturbances become more pronounced. Why this relation is so important could be indicated in any number of ways. But it is clear that any adequate analysis would go far beyond the confines of this article, since it would involve a critique of modern business organization and the individual's relation to authority and, in part, an examination of the ideologies held by the leaders and executives of business.[3] It is

---

[2] See B. B. Gardner, *Human Relations in Industry* (Chicago, Richard D. Irwin, Inc., 1945).

[3] See Chester I. Barnard, *The Functions of the Executive* (Cambridge, Harvard University Press, 1938), pp. 161–184.

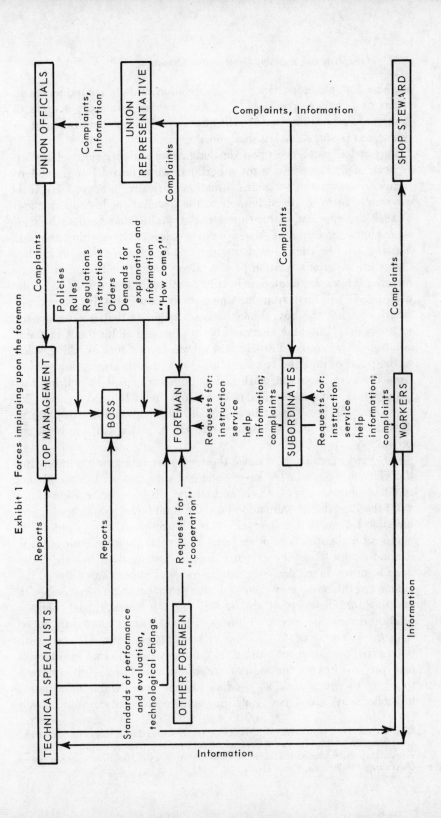

Exhibit 1 Forces impinging upon the foreman

enough that the importance of this relation and its consequences in terms of behavior, particularly at the foreman level, are matters of common observation; and it will be at this level of behavior and its associated *feelings* that we shall remain.

Personal dependence upon the judgments and decisions of his superiors, so characteristic of the subordinate-superior relation in modern industry, makes the foreman's situation basically insecure.[4] He feels a constant need to adjust himself to the demands of his superior and to seek the approval of his superior. Everything that he does he tries to evaluate in terms of his superior's reaction. Everything that his superior does he tries to evaluate in terms of what it means or implies about his superior's relation to him. Everything that his subordinates and workers do he immediately tries to evaluate in terms of the criticism it may call forth from his superior. In some cases this preoccupation with what the boss thinks becomes so acute that it accounts for virtually everything the foreman says or does and all his thinking about what goes on around him. He will refrain from doing anything, even to the point of dodging responsibility, for fear of bringing disapproval from the boss. Hours at work and at home are spent in figuring and anticipating what explanations or reasons he will need to give the boss. And the boss's most innocent and unintentional acts—failure to say "good morning," for instance—are taken perhaps to imply disapproval.

It is hard to realize how much those who are interested in improving the efficiency of industry have neglected this area. If the man-hours spent by subordinates both on and off the job in preoccupation about what the boss thinks were added up, the total hours would be staggering—not to mention the results this phenomenon has produced in nervous breakdowns and other forms of mental anguish. Stranger still, it almost appears as if modern industrial organization, which prides itself so much on its efficiency, has aggravated rather than reduced the amount of this preoccupation, with disastrous consequences for health and thus for efficiency. All this applies to the foreman in particular.

The crux of the foreman's problem is that he is constantly faced with the dilemma of (1) having to keep his superior informed with what is happening at the work level (in many cases so that his superior may prepare in turn for the unfavorable reaction of his superior and so on up the line) and (2) needing to communicate this information in such a way that it does not bring unfavorable criticism on himself

---

[4] For an excellent statement on this point, see Douglas McGregor, "Conditions of Effective Leadership in the Industrial Organization," *Massachusetts Institute of Technology Publications in Social Science*, Series 2, No. 16 (from the *Journal of Consulting Psychology*, Vol. VIII, No. 2, 1944).

for not doing his job correctly or adequately. Discrepancies between the way things are at the work level and the way they are represented to be by management cannot be overlooked, and yet the foreman feels obliged to overlook them when talking to his boss. This makes the foreman's job particularly "tough" and encourages him to talk out of both sides of his mouth at the same time—to become a master of double talk.

Each foreman, of course, resolves the conflict in terms of his own personal history, personality, and temperament. Some foremen become voluble in the face of this situation; others are reduced to stony silence, feeling that anything they say will be held against them. Some keep out of the boss's way, while others devise all sorts of ways for approaching him and trying to direct attention to certain things they have accomplished. And extraordinary are the skills which some more verbally articulate foremen develop in translating *what is* into a semblance of *the way it ought to be* in order to appease their superiors and keep them happy.

But, for the most part, the foreman, being loyal and above all wanting to be secure, resolves the conflict and maintains good relations with his superiors by acting strictly in accordance with his functional relations and the logics of management. In spite of what this may lead to in his relations to workers and other groups, his relations with his superiors at least are not jeopardized.

Thus the foreman, like each individual in the modern industrial structure, is in effect painfully tutored to focus his attention upward to his immediate superiors and the logics of evaluation they represent, rather than downward to his subordinates and the feelings they have. So rigid does the conditioning of supervisors and executives in the industrial structure become in this respect that it is almost impossible for them to pay attention to the concrete human situations below them, rich in sentiments and feelings. For them, this world of feeling does not exist; the territory is merely populated with the abstractions which they have been taught to see and the terms in which they communicate—"base rates," "manhours," "budgets," "cost curves," "production schedules," and so on.

Foreman-Specialist. Also of extreme importance are the foreman's relations to the technical specialists who *originate* the standards of performance which he must *uphold* and to which his subordinates and workers must *conform.* This experimentally minded group of engineers, accountants, and technologists can become one of the chief sources of change, and rapid change, at the work level; through them changes can be introduced at the work level at a more rapid rate than they can be assimilated by customary shop codes and practices.

Through them, also, "controls" can be exercised far more precisely than heretofore. It is one thing for a foreman to know what his cost performance has been; it is another matter to know what his actual costs should be in relation to a standard. What was heretofore a matter of experiential judgment after the fact becomes now a matter of projective evaluation and of constantly shooting at a target—a target whose outlines become increasingly more clear-cut and demanding, at least in one area of his job.

It is little wonder that this group can become (although it does not need to become, as we shall discuss later) a constant source of threat to the foreman's feelings of security. These men of course affect and often make more difficult his relations to workers. They also provide reports to management which can make his relations to his boss exceedingly uncomfortable. The result: more double talk.

It is well to note that these control groups can (as can the union) short-circuit foremen and levels of supervision lower in the line by providing information direct to higher levels of supervision.[5] Whatever the value of this information in evaluating the foreman's performance, it results in certain pressures upon him. Each superior can request explanations from, or give orders to, his foreman based on such information; yet the foreman cannot control it and indeed may be unaware of it until his superior initiates action. Information flowing through the line the foreman can censor before it reaches the boss; but this way the boss can get information at the same time he does, or even before, and the foreman is no longer able to foresee or to gauge the boss's reaction. The results of this in mental anguish, in preoccupations, in worries about what the boss may think or do, in preparation of explanations, "good reasons," and alibis, are tremendous. Because of the subjective nature of the data, the technologists of industry have not as yet decided to study this area or even to give it much attention. But the modern foreman, from the point of view of both his effectiveness and his satisfaction at work, finds the actual phenomena only too real.

Foreman-Foreman. By the very nature of the closely knit technological processes of a manufacturing organization, the foreman of one department often has to work very closely with a foreman of another department. These lateral relations are not formally defined, and their functioning depends largely upon the informal understandings which exist between foremen. Thus, the kind and amount of cooperation which one foreman is likely to obtain from another foreman is in good

---

[5] Discussed more fully by B. B. Gardner, *op. cit.*

part determined by their interpersonal relations. Here again, the boss comes in, because the preoccupation with what the boss thinks may also affect the foreman's relation to his colleagues at the same level.

Although all foremen have equal formal status, they do not, as everyone in a shop situation knows, enjoy equal informal status. The individual foreman's relative status is determined by such factors as age, sex, service, earnings, and social symbols of one sort or another. But the chief determining factor is his direct relation to the boss, i.e., how close he is to the boss. Not only the foreman's need for security but also the closely allied strivings for status and recognition are therefore directed to his superior. He needs to feel "close" to him. Thus he may constantly be comparing his relation to the boss with that of his colleagues. If this comparison indicates his position to be weak, he may enter into competition with his colleagues for recognition from the boss. As can be imagined, such emotional disturbances in the work situation may impede rather than facilitate cooperation among foremen, and they constitute a peculiar kind of "headache" for the superior.

Foreman-Worker. It is in his relation to the workers, however, with the rise of "scientific" management and with the growth of industrial unions, that the modern foreman's position becomes especially difficult. Here "the straw that breaks the camel's back" is finally reached. Here the problem of getting smooth operation becomes acute because, as we have seen, the foreman according to the logic of industrial organization must (1) *uphold* at the work level the standards, policies, rules, and regulations which have been *originated* by other groups and see to it that the workers *conform* to them and, at the same time, (2) obtain if possible the workers' spontaneous *cooperation* to this way of doing business. As anyone who has been in such a position knows, this is not a very easy task. As a rule, people do not like to conform to matters when they have no say in them, when they do not participate or feel that their point of view is taken into account. This is not a popular way of evoking spontaneity of cooperation; it is not consistent with our basic social values. Yet over and over again both foremen and workers are told, merely told, to conform to conditions over which they have very little or no say—conditions, moreover, which shockingly fail at times to take into account what is of vital importance to them in their work situations.

This state of affairs affects the foreman's personal situation: his strivings to satisfy his needs for security, personal integrity, and recognition in the work situation. Further, it makes his job in relation to his workers very difficult. Again and again, he is put in a position either of getting the workers' cooperation and being "disloyal" to management or of being "loyal" to management and incurring the resentment and overt opposition of his subordinates.

For those who do not fully appreciate the conflicting position in which the foreman is placed, it may be desirable to show the nature of the two constrasting worlds in the middle of which the foreman stands and spends his workaday life. In business, as in any organized human activity, there are two sets of social processes going on:

> (1) There are those social processes which are directly related to the achievement of purpose and which result in "formal organization." In business, for example, formal organization leads to such things as practices established by legal enactment or policy, specifications, standard methods, standard procedures, standards of time, output, quality, cost, and so on. They are concerned with those means most appropriate to achieve certain ends. And as such they can be changed rapidly.

> It should be noted that these manifestations of formal organization are essentially logical in character. Through formal organization man expresses his logical capacities; in fact, it is one of the chief outlets for the expression of man's logical capacities. It should also be noted that in the past 25 years there has been a tremendous amount of attention given to this aspect of business organization. It is in part because of this that, as we tried to show, the modern foreman's environment is so radically different from the good old days. And yet the foreman, unlike some higher executives, cannot stay only in this logically sheltered atmosphere.

> (2) There are those spontaneous social processes going on in any organized human activity which have no specific, conscious common purpose and which result in "informal organization." Informal organization leads to such things as custom, mores, folkway, tradition, social norms, and ideals. In business, for example, it expresses itself at the work level in such things as what constitutes fair wages, decent conditions of work, fair treatment, a fair day's work, and traditions of the craft. It takes the form of different status systems: e.g., old-timers should get preferential treatment; supervisors should get more money than their subordinates; and office workers are superior to shop workers. These are attitudes and understandings based on feeling and sentiment. They are manifestations of "belonging," and they do not change rapidly.

It should be especially noted that these manifestations of informal organization are not logical in character. They are concerned with values, ways of life, and ends in themselves—those aspects of social life which people strive to protect and preserve and for which at times they are willing to fight and even die. It should also be noted that a cursory examination of the periodicals, books, formal statements, and speeches of business executives and business experts shows that little systematic attention has been given to this aspect of business organization. This is indeed a curious state of affairs since, as every foreman intuitively knows, it is only through informal organization and its manifestations that he can secure spontaneity of cooperation at the work level.

Informal organization in any organized human activity serves a very healthy function. It binds people together in routine activity. It gives people a social place and feeling of belonging. It provides the framework for the fulfillment of human satisfaction. It gives people a feeling of self-respect, of independent choice, of not being just cogs in a machine. Far from being a hindrance to greater effectiveness, informal organization provides the setting which makes men willing to contribute their services.

Yet what is management's attitude toward these informal groups which form at the work level? Curiously enough, their appearance makes management uneasy. And sometimes management willfully tries to break them up. Such ill-conceived attempts inevitably produce open hostility to the aims of management. For informal organization cannot be prevented; it is a spontaneous phenomenon necessary wherever coordinated human activities exist.

More important still—for it is more often the case—these informal groups are ignored and not even recognized. Having no representation in the formal organization, which to many an executive is by definition the "reality," they just do not exist. As a result—not from malicious design but from sheer oversight born of overlogicized training—these informal groups at the work level become inadvertently the victims of change, disruption, and dislocation. Technical changes are introduced without any attention to what is happening to the members of these groups in terms of their group associations. New methods of work and new standards are initiated, newcomers are added, someone is transferred, upgraded, or promoted, and all as if this group life did not exist. What happens? There develops a feeling of being "pushed around"—a very uncomfortable feeling which most people dislike and which often provokes the reaction of trying to push the pusher with equal intensity in the opposite direction.

Because their way of life is constantly in jeopardy from technological changes, new methods, raised standards, and constant manipulation of one kind or another by logically minded individuals, these groups in industry take on a highly defensive and protective character. Their major function becomes, unfortunately, the resistance to change and innovation, and their codes and practices develop at variance with the economic purpose of the enterprise. Much pegging of output at a certain level by employees is an expression of this need to protect their ways of life, as well as their livelihood, from too rapid change.

As might be expected, these defensive and protective characteristics of many informal groups at the work level—and they exist full blown in many factories even before any formal union appears—have serious consequences for foremen (not to mention new workers and other individuals). Any supervisor or foreman in charge of such groups has two, if not three, strikes against him to begin with. Anything he does in relation to them is likely to be "wrong." To ignore them completely would be to invite overt hostility; to accept them completely would be to fail in fulfilling his responsibilities to management. Yet the foreman is the key man of management in administering technical changes. He often has the impossible task of taking plans made by the specialists without thought of the realities of human situations and relating them to just such situations.

Foreman-Union. Once these patterns of behavior become formalized in a union, the foreman's debacle becomes complete. Into this situation, now, is introduced a new set of logics, verbal definitions, rules, and regulations, by means of which he is supposed to set his conduct toward the workers. The last vestiges of initiative, of judgment, and, what is perhaps more important, of personal relations with his subordinates are taken away from him. Literally the foreman is left "holding the bag"—a bag containing (1) the maximum of exquisitely logical rules, definitions, procedures, policies, standards that the human mind can devise, by means of which he is now supposed to do his job, and (2) the minimum of those relationships and their associated feelings through which he can obtain the wholehearted cooperation of people. Standing in the middle of a now formally bifurcated situation, where one half is trying to introduce changes and improvements into the factory situation and the other half by habit and conditioning is trying to prevent or resist them, the modern foreman is expected to "cooperate."

The Foreman's Situation Summarized

The salient features of the foreman's situation should now be clear. In very broad outline—tentatively and approximately formulated—the failure on the part of top management, in mass production industries in particular, to understand the social implications of its way of doing "business" has resulted in the development of certain rigidities which do not make for cooperation in the industrial structure:

> (1) At the bottom of the organization there are people called *employees* who are in general merely supposed to *conform* to changes which they do not originate. Too often the attitude is that employees are merely supposed to do what they are told and get paid for it. Directing them there is—
> (2) A group of *supervivsors* who again are merely supposed to *uphold*—"administer" is the popular word—the standards of performance and policies determined by other groups, one of which is—
> (3) A group of *technical specialists* who are supposed to *originate* better ways and better standards through which the economic purpose of the organization can be better secured and more effectively controlled by—
> (4) A group of *top management* men who in their *evaluation* of the workers' behavior assume that the major inducement they can offer to people to cooperate is financial (i.e., that they are merely providing a livelihood, rather than a way of life); that informal organization is either "bad" or not "present"; and that authority comes from the top, so that no attention has to be given to that authority which is a matter of individual decision and comes from the bottom. This group's whole explicit theory of human cooperation—but not necessarily the practice of it—dates back to the eighteenth century: (a) society is composed of a rabble of unorganized individuals; (b) these individuals are only interested in the pursuit of profit and pleasure; and (c) in the pursuit of these ends the individual is essentially logical.[6]

These rigidities in operation make people in one group feel that they are excluded from the activities of other groups and prevent the wholehearted participation of all groups in the full attainment of the organization's objectives.

These rigidities in the industrial structure also have serious consequences for the satisfactions of individuals. Man's desire to belong, to be a part of a group, is constantly being frustrated. Things that are important to him seem to be disregarded. Opportunities for personal and social satisfaction seem to be denied. Yet, contrary to the assumptions made by management, all the evidence of modern investigation shows:

> (1) Society is composed of people related to each other in terms of group associations.

---

[6] These assumptions are taken from Elton Mayo, *The Social Problems of an Industrial Civilization* (Boston, Division of Research, Harvard Business School, 1945).

(2) The desire to belong, to be a part, the desire for continuous and intimate association at work with other human beings, remains a strong, possibly the strongest, desire of man.

(3) In the pursuit of these ends man is essentially non-logical and at times irrational, i.e., willing to die or, as management should know only too well, to "cut off his nose to spite his face."

As a result of being constantly deprived of real social (not logical) interrelationship and of those basic human satisfactions which come from it, the worker becomes restless and dissatisfied, if not openly resentful and hostile. And like any human being he expresses his dissatisfaction in a number of ways: by being absent, by quitting, by pegging output, and by joining a union where he hopes to satisfy the needs for self-expression that his job no longer provides.

In this environment the foreman stands—victim, not monarch, of all he surveys. And what does he survey? On the one hand, a monument of technical achievement such as no civilization has seen before, and, on the other hand, what Elton Mayo likes to refer to as "the seamy side of progress," a bleak and arid human scene scorched dry by the babel of words and logics which have long ceased to have any power to motivate or fill with renewed hope and vigor the hearts of men. Separated from management and separated from his men, dependent and insecure in his relation to his superiors and uncertain in his relations to his men, asked to give cooperation but in turn receiving none, expected to be friendly but provided with tools which only allow him to be "fair"—in this situation of social deprivation our modern foreman is asked to deliver the goods.

One only needs to add to this picture the more recent complications of expanded war industries, the influx of new workers—some of them women, untutored and inexperienced in the ways of the factory; some of them Negroes, equally inexperienced and untutored but also apprehensive of their place in this "white man's heaven"—and we have the picture of the social environment of our modern foreman.

In this predicament, how does this foreman feel and behave? In one of three ways:

(1) He "stews in his own juice" and, like Sir Hudibras's rusty sword, "he eats into himself for lack of something else to hew and hack," i.e., becomes obsessive.

(2) Or as current newspapers and periodicals have kept us informed, he joins a union, i.e., becomes aggressive.

(3) Or he too—who knows?—may go to Washington to be delivered from his social isolation and logocentric predicament, i.e., may seek a political solution for his social void.

So at the foreman level do the "mills of God" grind out the three major ills of our industrial civilization.

The Administrative Process

The purpose of the article thus far has not been to prove a thesis; it has been to present and interpret as vividly as possible—*from the point of view of feelings and relationships*—the foreman's situation in mass production industry. No examples have been given, but countless could be cited by any person who has had intimate contact with a war plant during the past five years. The final evidence, however, it is well to remember, exists in the minds of foremen and in their behavior, not in this article; and for those who doubt, let them go out and look and listen for themselves.

But a "distortion" has crept into our discussion, and it needs to be clarified. In dealing with the nuances of social relationship existing in a factory situation, the author has preforce been generalizing at a level somewhat removed from but not unrelated to the concrete and the particular. And although concerned with "a moving equilibrium" and the social forces working both for and against it, nevertheless up to now he has paid almost exclusive attention to those social forces operating to upset stability—simply in order to bring out inescapably the fact that the forces making for unbalance do exist, in latent if not in active form, in *every* mass production industry. The picture presented thus far has been therefore a picture of the inexorable grinding out of the social forces and logics that modern technology has unleashed—in the raw, so to speak, and uncontrolled by the "administrative process." But we must not forget that there is, often equally present and equally strong, the compensatory function of the "administrator."

In the last analysis the forces acting upon the foreman, as upon any other individual in the industrial structure, are the actions of other people. It was for this reason that the actions of the principal people with whom the foreman has relations in his working environment were examined. It should be clear, however, that the actions of these different characters are not always the same. Bosses, technical specialists, foremen, workers, and shop stewards differ in their behavior, sometimes very radically. This fact cannot be ignored; indeed, its implications are tremendous. And if *management's* actions are different, foremen's reactions are likely to be different.

In business (and in unions too) there are not only "men of goodwill" but also men with extraordinary skill in the direction of securing cooperative effort. These men, at all levels, perform an "administrative" function the importance of which is too little recognized. Much of their time is spent in facilitating the process of communication and in gaining the wholehearted cooperation of men. Many of them are not too logically articulate, but they have appreciation for a point of view different from their own. Not only can they appreciate the fact that a person can be different from themselves but, more important still, they can accept his right to be different. They always seem to have the time to listen to the problems and difficulties of others. They do not pose as "experts"; they know when to secure the appropriate aid from others.

Such "administrators," selfless and sometimes acting in a way which appears to be lacking in ambition, understand the importance of achieving group solidarity—the importance of "getting along," rather than of "getting ahead." They take personal responsibility for the mixed situations, both technical and human, that they administer. They see to it that the newcomer has an effective and happy relationship with his fellow workers, as well as gets the work out. Accomplishing their results through leisurely social interaction rather than vigorous formal action, more interested in getting their human relationships straight than in getting their words and logics straight, more interested in being "friendly" to their fellow men than in being abstractly "fair," and never allowing their "paper work" to interfere with this process of friendliness, they offer a healthy antidote to the formal logics of the modern factory organization previously described.

The importance of the "administrative" functions these men perform for the smooth running of any organization is incalculable, and fortunately industry has its fair share of such men. It is the author's impression that a greater proportion of them are found at the lower levels of management, because the logics of promotion in business organization seldom recognize their skills. Were it not for them, it is the author's opinion that the unleashed forces of modern technology would spin themselves out to doom and destruction. Aware of the twofold function of industrial leadership, i.e., the social organization of teamwork and the logical organization of operations, they maintain that healthy balance which makes for individual growth and development and, ultimately, for survival of the organization.

Yet, curiously enough, the theories of administration, as frequently expressed by business leaders, experts, and teachers, bear little resemblance to the functions these men actually perform and give little justification to their actions. As a result, they sometimes suffer from feelings of inferiority and lose confidence in themselves, an unfortunate consequence for them as individuals and also for the organization they serve. It is not comfortable to think that industry may depend for its stability on the personal and intuitive skills of a few such gifted people. Can the "administrative" skills they practice, the skills of getting action through social interaction, be made explicit and communicated?

What Is the Solution?

In the author's opinion, the foreman's dissatisfaction in large part results from actions of management. These actions of management are not the expression of maliciousness, bad faith, or lack of goodwill on the part of business executives. Far from it; they are merely the inexorable working out of the social forces which modern technology has produced and which we have not learned to recognize or control. They are the result of our ignorance and of our failure to pay as much explicit attention to the social organization of teamwork as to the logical organization of operations in our modern industrial enterprises.

The solution of the problem, therefore, seems to depend on a better realization of the "administrative process" as it operates to secure the cooperation of people in the furtherance of the economic objectives of business organizations. More than anything else, the modern world needs men who understand better the nature of, and give more explicit attention to, the social systems they administer. This is the challenge the modern world presents to business leadership; this is the great adventure for the coming generation. The business leaders of today and tomorrow, like the foremen, are facing a new "society," a streamlined "adaptive" society, a world which modern technology has produced and which is far different from the "established" society of their forefathers.[7] For their effectiveness, as well as for their survival, the coming "administrators" must be given new skills and new insights.

Can this job be done? The signs of the times are promising. In all quarters of business there are resolute young men who "when hope is dead will hope by faith," who will build the new world. In this connection it is well to remember that man's enormous capacity for adaptation, readjustment, and growth is his most striking characteristic, and it is upon this strength that we can hopefully rely.[8] In business and educational institutions, a fresh breath of life is beginning to stir. The possibilities of new courses and new methods of teaching and training are being explored.

---

[7] For an elaboration of this distinction between an "established" and an "adaptive" society, see Elton Mayo, *op. cit.*
[8] On this point, see Carl R. Rogers, *Counseling and Psychotherapy* (Boston, Houghton Mifflin Company, 1942).

A New Concept of Administration

Can the outlines of this new "administration" be even dimly envisaged? What will these new "administrators" be like, and in what skills will they be trained? Here we can only guess and express some personal opinions and hopes.

(1) The new "administrator" will need to know and understand better the nature of "organization"—its structure and dynamic interrelations. It is indeed a strange remark to make, in the year 1945, that an executive will have to know something about "organization," the very phenomenon with which he daily deals. But strange as the remark may seem, the average executive knows little or nothing, except for what is implicitly registered in his nervous system, about the "social organization" of his business. Most of his explicit concern, most of his logical thinking, is only about "formal organization." About the other aspects of organization, he only stews, frets, and gets stomach ulcers.

(2) "Administrators" of the future, to do their new jobs effectively, will have to develop a common language structure which represents accurately the interdependent realities of the phenomena with which they deal—technical, economic, organizational, social, and human. Too many different and often times conflicting "languages" riddle present business. No longer can the human beings who contribute their services to a business organization be regarded as "so many beads on a string." For the new world a new language has to be created which will keep together in words, rather than keep separate by words, those things that are together in the territory. This will be a language of mutually interdependent relations, of togetherness, of equilibrium, of adaptation, and of growth.

(3) The new "administrator" will have to understand better the problem of communication—and not only the aspect of communication which by persuasion attempts to sell one's own point of view, but that which tries to understand and has respect for another's point of view. In the systematic practice of taking into account another person's point of view as the first step in obtaining that person's cooperation—a most difficult skill—he should have daily and continuous drill. He should be taught to listen, in addition to being logically lucid and clear. He should learn to practice the "democratic method" *at the level of daily interaction* in the work situation.

(4) New methods and new skills will have to be developed whereby change can be introduced into the work situation without provoking resistance. About no urgent and pressing problem of modern industry is there so little systematic knowledge—so little understanding and so much misunderstanding. In no area has it been so convincingly demon-

strated, again and again and again, that people refuse to cooperate in meeting a standard of performance when they have not been allowed to participate in setting it up or, many times, even to "understand" it. In no area are the ordinary methods of "salesmanship" so woefully lacking.

For this particular aspect of "administration," the introduction of changes into the shop, we shall need to exercise and practice new insights regarding human motivation. These insights will have to envisage how technological progress and improvement can go hand in hand with individual and social development. Technological change will have to be introduced at the work level so that the group affected will see it, in North Whitehead's phrase, as "enlargement of its own way of life rather than as an interruption to it." And for the working out of these new methods and skills, more time and more effort will have to be given, more ingenuity and more understanding will have to be exercised.

(5) The new "administrator" will have to understand better the dependent relation of the subordinate to the superior in business organizations and the feelings of insecurity this dependence arouses. He will have to learn new methods and techniques of assuring his subordinate of those minimum conditions of security, not merely financial, without which the subordinate's position becomes intolerable. For this he will have to learn something about the principles of individual growth and development through active participation and assumption of responsibility, and these principles he will have to learn to practice in relation to his subordinates in an atmosphere of approval. He will have to learn to be responsible for people, not merely responsible for abstract and logical categories.

We will not obtain this type of "administrator" merely through verbal definition, i.e., by defining what his formal responsibilities and duties are. He has to be fostered and made to feel secure, allowed to grow and, occasionally, to make mistakes and thereby learn. He has to be nurtured like a plant; and, like a plant, the environment in which he grows, the care and human understanding he gets, will determine whether he flourishes or withers, gets bugs, and so on. Unlike our present foremen, who have suffered from too many logical definitions and too little human understanding, he must not be allowed to "wither" and be forced to join a union in order to recapture the zest of growth and life again.

(6) The new "administrator" will have to learn to distinguish the world of feelings from the world of facts and logic. And for dealing effectively with this world of feelings, he will have to learn new techniques—which at first may seem strange, after having been ignored and

misunderstood for so long. Particularly, of course, he will have to learn about "informal organization," that aspect of organization which is the manifestation of feeling and sentiment. Only by paying as much attention to informal organization as to formal organization will he become aware of what can and cannot be accomplished by policy formulation at the concrete level of behavior. He will have to learn new techniques of "control." He will see clearly that "feelings" cannot be verbally legislated out of existence; that, as a first step in their "control," they need to be expressed and recognized.

These and many other new methods and skills the new "administrator" will have to learn. He will have to learn to "control" the future by first learning to "control" the present. He will have to learn to formulate goals and ideals which make the present in which we live more, rather than less, meaningful. And to achieve these new levels of insight and practice, he will have to throw overboard completely, finally, and irrevocably—this will be difficult—the ideologies of the "established society" of the eighteenth and nineteenth centuries. This new representative of a new "adaptive society" at all cost must not be the representative of an "ism." For he does not represent any particular way of life: he is only the guarantor of the "ways of life"—plural—that are important to many different people. In this task he can only represent what Elton Mayo calls "polyphasic methods" of dealing with the complex human, social, economic, and organizational problems of our industrial civilization.

Can we develop a group of such "administrators"? This of course is a matter of opinion. To the author it seems that, if only ½ of 1% of the time, effort, and money that have been spent in the direction of technological improvement were to be devoted to seeking better and improved methods of securing cooperation, the accomplishment would be considerable—and that is an intentional understatement. It just does not seem sensible to suppose that man's ingenuity, if given free scope, would fail in this undertaking. The task is tremendous; the challenge is great; the stakes are high; but only by traveling some such arduous road, in the author's opinion, can business leadership face up to its real social responsibilities.

Retrospective Commentary

Today's HBR readers are probably most interested in two questions. *First,* from an overall point of view, what in this article is most relevant today? *Second,* more specifically, what is the foreman's situation today compared with what it was 20 years ago?

Relevance

In my opinion, the most significant element of the article resides in the method of analysis. Twenty years ago I made what today would be called a "role analysis" of the foreman's job. I looked at his relationships to the other members of his "role set," that is, to the other groups with whom he had to interact and who had something to say about what his role should be. Within these groups, I not only found no consensus but also discovered *conflicting expectations* about what the foreman was supposed to be doing. He suffered seriously from what today would be called "role conflict and ambiguity." He was "the man in the middle"—what I called then, "Master and Victim of Double Talk."

During the past two decades, continued researches from this point of view have shown that the foreman's dilemma is merely a "special case" of a more general problem. In modern industry the foreman is not the only man or position suffering from this "disease." Some of his colleagues on the staff and superiors in the line seem to have caught it too. As a result of the advance of science and technology, the acceleration of change, and the introduction of many new roles, modern industry seems to be riddled with role conflict and ambiguity. A recent study would seem to indicate that about 80% of the work force, from worker to president, may be suffering from some such strains, and that role conflict increases with supervisory rank in a curvilinear relationship "in which the maximum of conflict occurs at what might be called the upper middle levels of management."[*]

Role analysis, like any other method, is a useful but limited tool. Applied to the diagnosis of a particular situation, it can reveal some of the factors that may be making for trouble. Applied as a general model for the analysis of organizational behavior, it may find only what it is looking for. As the authors of the above-mentioned study cautioned, if one focuses too much on disease rather than on health, one can find only too easily that the whole world is ridden with disease.

So I too should like to warn my new readers to treat "role conflict" not as a disease to be eliminated but, rather, as something that needs to be better understood and managed. This is the difficult lesson to learn from the many disease-sounding syndromes, typologies, concepts, and words that the behavioral sciences have generated. The trick is how to use them—as Adlai Stevenson would have said—"without inhaling."

---

[*] Robert L. Kahn et al., *Organizational Stress: Studies in Role Conflict and Ambiguity* (New York, John Wiley & Sons, Inc., 1964), p. 382.

Foreman's Situation Today

Having made these preliminary remarks, I am now prepared to entertain the question, "Is there more or less role conflict at the foreman level in 1965 than in 1945?" My first, honest answer is "I don't know," but I realize this may be unsatisfactory, so let me give you my second-best answer, which is closer to a guess.

In my judgment, the chances are better than even (say, 60%) that there is more conflict at the foreman level now than there was 20 years ago, but the conflict is probably being better managed, both by the foreman himself and by his boss and his boss's bosses. In 1945, the foreman seldom talked freely with other members of his "role set"; in 1965, he can be found more often meeting with them in "natural groups." The manager of 1945 spent more of his time bossing the individual foremen; the manager of 1965 is spending more time managing "role sets." If the human relations movement in industry has made any difference, it is along these dimensions that I would be looking for it to show up. Otherwise, I fear that once again the experts in communication have failed to communicate. If so, I fear that we may have been spending too much time inhaling a new vocabulary and not enough time with the phenomena.

Strategic Leniency and Authority[*]

Peter M. Blau

The hierarchy of authority in a bureaucracy, essential for coordination, often produces among its lower echelons profound feelings of inequality and apathy that impede identification with the organization's objectives. The initiation of needed adjustments by the operating members of the organization presupposes, in addition to the five conditions already discussed, a method of hierarchical coordination that minimizes these harmful consequences for work motivation. After analyzing the ways in which bureaucratic authority is exercised, we shall return to this problem at the end of this chapter.

To start with, let us consider another paradox between official requirements and actual practice. In theory, bureaucratic superiors are expected to exert strict and impersonal control over subordinates. But in fact, immediate supervisors and foremen frequently "play ball" with their subordinates and let them "get away with" infractions of many rules. What accounts for this leniency?

Strategic Leniency and Authority

A psychological explanation of the failure to enforce strict discipline among subordinates might attribute it to poor leadership. Some supervisors are overly lenient, it could be held, because inborn or acquired personality traits prevent them from asserting their authority over others and maintaining effective leadership. Note that this explanation assumes as a matter of course that the bureaucratic superior who appears lenient merely indulges his subordinates and is less effective than the disciplinarian in discharging his supervisory responsibilities. Empirical evidence, however, indicates that the very opposite is the case.

A study of twenty-four clerical sections in an insurance company analyzed the relationship between method of supervision and productive efficiency.[1] In closely supervised sections, whose heads gave clerks detailed instructions and frequently checked up on them, productivity was usually lower than in sections where employees were given more

---

[*] Reprinted with permission of author and publisher from *Bureaucracy In Modern Society* (New York: Random House, 1956), pp. 69–74.
[1] Daniel Katz, Nathan MacCoby, and Nancy C. Morse, *Productivity, Supervision and Morale in an Office Situation*, Ann Arbor: Institute for Social Research, University of Michigan, 1950, especially pp. 17, 21, 29.

freedom to do the work in their own way. Moreover, supervisors who were primarily concerned with maintaining a high level of production, interestingly enough, were less successful in meeting this goal than those supervisors who were more interested in the welfare of their subordinates than in sheer production; in the latter case, productivity was generally higher. Finally, groups who worked under more authoritarian supervisors were, on the whole, less productive than those supervised in a relatively democratic fashion. Other studies have also found that disciplinarian supervisors are less effective than more liberal ones.[2]

Such findings are often misinterpreted as signifying that democratic ways are superior to authoritarian ones. But this is a rather loose use of the term "democratic," the exact meaning of which is worth preserving. Since "democracy" denotes rule from below (literally, "people's rule") and not from above, one person's supervision of others can, by definition, not be democratic. This is not the place for a discussion of the relation between democracy and bureaucracy; the final chapter is reserved for this purpose. But here it should be noted that tolerant supervisory practices, in contrast to disciplinarian ones, are neither democratic nor an indication that controlling power over subordinates has been surrendered. On the contrary, leniency in supervision is a potent strategy, consciously or unconsciously employed, for establishing authority over subordinates, and this is why the liberal supervisor is particularly effective.

Let us clarify the concept of authority. First, it refers to a relationship between persons and not to an attribute of one individual. Second, authority involves exercise of social control which rests on the *willing* compliance of subordinates with certain directives of the superior. He need not coerce or persuade subordinates in order to influence them, because they have accepted as legitimate the principle that some of their actions should be governed by his decisions. Third, authority is an observable pattern of interaction and not an official definition of a social relationship. If a mutinous crew refuses to obey the captain's orders, he does not in fact have authority over his men. Whatever the superior's official rights to command obedience and the subordinates' official duties to obey him, his authority over them extends only to conduct that they voluntarily permit to be governed by his directives. Actual authority, consequently, is not granted by the formal organizational chart, but must be established in the course of social interaction, although the official bureaucratic structure, as we shall see presently, facilitates its establishment.

---

[2] See, for instance, F. J. Roethlisberger and William J. Dickson, *Management and the Worker*, Cambridge: Harvard University Press, 1946, pp. 452–53.

What are some of the practices of a lenient foreman or supervisor? Above all, he allows subordinates to violate minor rules, to smoke or talk, for example, despite the fact that it is prohibited by management. This permissiveness often increases his power over them by furnishing him with legitimate sanctions that he can use as he sees fit. If an action of his subordinates displeases him, the supervisor can punish them by commanding: "Cut out the smoking! Can't you read the sign?" Had he always enforced the rule, this penalty would not have been available to him. Indeed, so crude a use of sanctions is rarely necessary. The mere knowledge that the rule exists and, possibly, that it is enforced elsewhere, instills a sense of obligation to liberal superiors and induces subordinates more readily to comply with their requests.

Whereas the disciplinarian supervisor generally asserts his official prerogatives, the lenient and relaxed one does not. The latter attempts to take the wishes of his subordinates into account in arranging their work schedule, although he has the right to assign their work at his own discretion. Sometimes he goes to special trouble to accommodate a subordinate. Instead of issuing curt commands, he usually explains the reasons for his directives. He calls his subordinates by their first names and encourages their use of his first name (especially in democratically minded American organizations). When one of his subordinates gets into difficulties with management, he is apt to speak up for him and to defend him. These different actions have two things in common: the superior is not required to do them, and his subordinates greatly welcome his doing them. Such conduct therefore creates social obligations. To repay the supervisor for past favors, and not risk the cessation of similar favors in the future, subordinates voluntarily comply with many of his requests, including some they are not officially required to obey. By refraining from exercising his power of control whenever it is legitimate to do so, the bureaucratic superior establishes effective authority over subordinates, which enables him to control them much more effectively than otherwise would be possible.

Complementary role expectations arise in the course of interaction between superior and subordinates and become crystallized in the course of interaction among subordinates. As the superior permits subordinates to violate some rules and to make certain decisions themselves, and as they grow accustomed to conform with many of his directives, they learn to expect to exercise discretion in some areas and to follow supervisory directives in others, and he learns to expect this pattern of conduct from them. The members of the work group, by watching one another at work and talking among themselves about the manner in which they perform their duties, develop social consensus about these role expectations and thereby reinforce them. The newcomer to the group, who must be taught "how things are done around here" as distinguished from "what's in the book," provides an opportunity for further affirming this consensus by making it explicit.

The resulting common role expectations are often so fully internalized that employees are hardly aware of being governed by them. The members of one department might find it natural for their supervisor to interrupt their work and tell them to start on a new task. The members of another department in the same organization might consider such a supervisory order as gross interference with their work, since they had become accustomed to using their discretion about the sequence of their tasks, yet readily comply with other directives of the supervision. These role expectations of independence from the supervisor in some areas and unquestioning obedience in others define the limits of his authority over subordinates.

Three Supervisory Adaptations to "Artificial Pressure"*

Chris Argyris

One of the most common of the factory supervisors' attitudes about budgets was that budgets were used as a pressure device to increase production efficiency. Many cases were cited to support this point. Finance people also admitted that budgets helped "keep people on the ball" by raising their goals and increasing their motivation. The problem of the effects of pressure applied through budgets seems to be the core of the budget problem.

The Causes of Pressure

Employees and front-line supervisors believe that the cause for pressure from the top is due to top management's belief that most employees are basically or inherently lazy. Employees and front-line supervisors also feel that top management believes that employees do not have enough motivation of their own to do the best possible job.

The interviews with top management officials revealed that the employees' beliefs were not totally unfounded, as a few quotations from some of the top management (both line and finance) make clear:

> I'll tell you my honest opinion. Five per cent of the people work, ten per cent of the people think they work. And the other eighty-five per cent would rather die than work.
>
> I think there is a need for more pressure. People need to be needled a bit. I think man is inherently lazy and if we could only increase the pressure, I think the budget system would be more effective.

Such feelings, even if they are never overtly expressed toward employees, filter through to the employees in very subtle ways. Budgets represent one of the more subtle ways. Once the employees sense these feelings exist in top management, they may become very resentful.

The Effects of Pressure

How do people react to pressure? In three of the plants studied factory supervisors felt they were working under pressure and that the budget was the principal instrument of pressure. Management exerts

---

* Reprinted with permission of author and publisher from *What Budgets Mean to People* (New York: Controllership Foundation, 1952).

pressure on the work force in many ways, of which budgets is but one. Budgets, being concrete, seem to serve as a medium through which the total effects of management pressure are best expressed. As such they become an excellent point of focus for studying the effect of pressure on people in a working organization.

The Creation of Groups

An increase in tension, resentment, suspicion, fear and mistrust may not be the only result of ever stronger management pressures transmitted to supervisors, and in turn, to employees. We know, from psychological research, that people can stand a certain amount of pressure. After this point is passed, it becomes intolerable to an individual. We also know that one method people have to reduce the effect of the pressure (assuming that the employees cannot reduce the pressure itself) is to join groups. These groups then help absorb much of the pressure and the individual is personally relieved.

The process of individuals joining groups to relieve themselves of pressure is not an easy one. It does not occur overnight. The development of a group on such a basis seems to have the following general stages of growth.

> First, the individuals "feel" the pressure. They are not certain, but they sense an increase in pressure.
> Second, they begin to see definite evidences of the pressure. They not only feel it, they can point to it.
> Since they feel this pressure is on them personally, they begin to experience tension and general uneasiness.
> Next, the people usually "feel out" their fellow workers to see if they sense the pressure.
> Finding out that others have noted the pressure, the people begin to feel more at ease. It helps to be able to say, "I'm not the only one."
> Finally, they realize that they can acquire emotional support from each other by becoming a group. Furthermore, they can "blow their top" about this pressure in front of their group. Gradually therefore, the individuals become a group because in becoming a group they are able to satisfy these needs:
> 1. A need to reduce the pressure on each individual
> 2. A need to get rid of tension
> 3. A need to feel more secure by belonging to a group which can counteract the pressure.

In short, a new, cohesive group has developed to combat management pressure. In a sense, the people have learned that they can be happier if they combine against this management pressure.

Suppose now that top management, aware of the tensions which have been generated and the groups which have been formed, seeks to reduce the pressure. The emphasis on budgets is relaxed. Perhaps even the standards are "loosened." Does this then destroy the group? After all, its primary reason for existence was to combat the pressure. Now, the pressure is gone. The group should eventually disintegrate.

The answer seems to be that the group continues to exist!

The evidence for this is not as conclusive as it should be. Therefore, the following explanation should be considered primarily in the realm of inference and conjecture rather than scientific fact.

These factors seem to operate to keep the group in existence:

1. There is a "time lag" between the moment management announced the new policy and the time the workers put it into effect.
2. The individuals have made a new and satisfactory adjustment with each other. They have helped to satisfy each other's needs. They are, as the social scientist would say, "in equilibrium" with each other. Any attempt to destroy this balance will tend to be resisted even if the attempt represents an elimination of a "bad" or unheathly set of conditions. People have created a stable pattern of life and they will resist a change in this pattern.
3. The individuals fear pressure will come again in the future. Because of this feeling, they will tend to create unreal conditions or to exaggerate existing conditions so that they can rationalize to themselves that pressure still exists and, therefore, the need for the group also exists.

Pressure on Front-Line Supervisors

But what about the foreman? Strong pressures converge upon him. How does he protect himself from these pressures?

He cannot join a group against management, as his work force does. For one reason, he probably has at least partially identified himself with management. For another reason, he may be trying to advance in the hierarchy. Naturally, he would not help his chances for advancement if he joined a group against management.

The evidence of the previous chapters seems to indicate that the line supervisor cannot pass all the pressure he receives to his employees. Time and time again the factory supervisors stated that passing the pressure down would only create conflict and trouble which would lead to a decrease in production.

The question arises, where does the pressure go? How do the supervisors relieve themselves of at least some of the pressure? There is evidence to suggest at least three ways in which pressure is handled by the supervisors:

1. Interdepartmental strife. The foremen release some of the pressure by continuously trying to blame fellow foremen for the troubles that exist. "They are," as one foreman expressed it, "trying to throw the dead cat in each other's backyard."

   In three plants observed, much time was spent by certain factory supervisors in trying to lay the blame for errors and problems on some other department.

2. Staff versus factory strife. The foremen released much of the pressure by blaming the budget people, production control people and salesmen for their problems. The data already presented concerning factory supervisors' attitudes toward budget people substantiate this point.

3. "Internalizing" pressure. Many supervisors who do not express their feelings about the pressure have in reality "internalized" it and, in a sense, made it a part of themselves. Such damming up of pressure seemed to be expressed in the following ways:

   (i) Supervisor A is quiet, relatively nonemotional, seldom expresses his negative feelings to anyone, but at the same time he works excessively, Supervisor A can be found working at his desk long after the others have gone home. As one supervisor expressed it, "That guy works himself to death."

   (ii) Supervisor B is nervous, always running around "checking up" on all his employees. He usually talks fast, gives one the impression that he is "selling" himself and his job when interviewed. He is forever picking up the phone, barking commands and requesting prompt action.

Both of these types (or a combination of these types) are expressions of much tension and pent up emotions that have been internalized. People working under such conditions finally are forced to "take it easy," or they find themselves with ulcers or a nervous breakdown.

But that is not the end of the problem. Constant tension leads to frustration. A frustrated person no longer operates as effectively as he was accustomed. He finds that he tends to forget things he used to remember. Work that he used to do with pleasure, he now delegates to someone else. He is no longer able to make decisions as fast as he did months ago. Now he finds he has to take a walk or get a cup of coffee—anything to get "away from it all."

Work Group Behavior and the Larger Organization[*]

Leonard R. Sayles See - phy.

The individual's most immediate and meaningful experiences of work
are obtained in the context of the work group and his work associates.
The larger organization is experienced by indirection, but membership
in the small group contributes directly to the shaping of attitudes and
behavior toward the entire world of work. For this reason of potency,
therefore, the contribution of the small group to the total organization
has been a subject of substantial research by those interested in human
relations in industry.

Conceptions of the Work Group

As Whyte observes, the individual is *not* a member of a single group
within a larger structure.[1] Rather, he typically interacts in a variety of
settings within the organization. It is the task of the researcher to
identify those interaction patterns which are focused and concentrated
so that it is reasonable to speak of a "group."

If we follow all the members of the organization through their hours
on the job, or find some "high" vantage point and observe the total of
all interactions, we are likely to be impressed with this proliferation
of memberships. Most apparent is membership, except for that unique
individual, the president, in some *command group;* that is, the employee shares a common supervisor with a number of colleagues. Dis-
tinguishable from this group, but closely related, is a *functional* or
task group—those employees who must collaborate in some fashion if
the work task defined by the organization is to be accomplished. In
fact, both of these groups are rather well defined by the larger organization, and the group typically retains those boundaries.

However, there are two other kinds of clusterings that tend to over-

---

[*] Reprinted with permission of author and publisher from *Research In Industrial
Relations* (New York: Harper and Bros., 1957), pp. 131–145. Copyright © 1957
by Harper & Brothers.

A substantial portion of the material included is from a study by the author
sponsored by the Bureau of Industrial Relations of the University of Michigan
on the relationship of work group behavior to technological and organizational
factors. Our major emphasis is on industrial work groups, although examples will
be drawn from other work settings.

[1] William F. Whyte, "Small Groups in Large Organizations," in *Social Psychology
at the Crossroads*, John Rohrer and Muzafer Sherif, eds. (New York: Harper,
1951), pp. 303–304.

lap and penetrate the organization in unexpected ways. They are not defined by the formal organization and are often included under the general term, informal organization. One has received much attention from researchers: the *friendship clique*. The other is less well studied, but equally important. That is the *interest group*. This is comprised of those employees who share a common economic interest and seek to gain some objective relating to the larger organization.

Memberships in these groups are not exclusive; often they will overlap considerably. However, the motivations of the members, and, more important, their behavior, are distinctive; and we have no reason to believe that the boundaries will be perfectly coincident.

The Command Group. Perhaps the most obvious kind of small group in the large organization is composed of the supervisor and his immediate subordinates. As Jacques observes, the entire organization is composed of interconnected *command groups,* the subordinates in one group being superiors in their own command group, with the exception of the first level.[2] While we might expect that research would have emphasized this unit of the organization, if we exclude the manifold studies of leadership styles dealt with elsewhere in this volume, there are relatively few systematic explorations of the relationship between the leader and his subordinates as a group, as individuals, and among the subordinates themselves. Jacques' volume is a notable exception.[3] His examination of the command group has a strong psychiatric flavor. He stresses the leader's ambivalence: his *authority* over his subordinates and *dependence* upon them, his sense of isolation, the problem of integrating pair relationships (leader and individual subordinates) with cohesiveness among subordinates, and the mixed feelings of the subordinates as a group who find the leader both expendable and indispensable (one to be protected or exposed?).

The Friendship Clique. This has been conceived as the elementary building block of human organization. As Mayo writes, "Man's desire to be continuously associated with his fellows is a strong, if not the strongest human characteristic."[4]

At the workplace we find a multitude of friendship groups repre-

---

[2] Elliot Jacques, *The Changing Culture of a Factory* (New York: Dryden Press, 1952), pp. 273–297.

[3] There are two other noteworthy recent exceptions. Argyris devotes a small volume to the relationship between a plant manager in a medium-sized factory and his immediate subordinates. (Chris Argyris, *Executive Leadership* [New York: Harper, 1954]). Two researchers at the Harvard Business School provide us with a very revealing study of the day-to-day changes in the relationship between a first-line supervisor and assembly-line girls during a period of technological changes —Harriet Ronken and Paul Lawrence, *Administering Changes* (Boston: Graduate School of Business Administration, Harvard University, 1952).

[4] Elton Mayo, *Social Problems of an Industrial Civilization* (Boston: Graduate School of Business Administration, Harvard University, 1945), p. 111.

senting the diverse interests of the workers placed there by the organization. The boundaries of these clusterings appear to reflect the employees' off-the-job interests and associations or previous work experience. Age, ethnic background, outside activities, sex, marital status, and so on, comprise the mortar that binds the clique together.

The friendship group has emerged as the agency which welds the individual to the organization. Loyalty, even attachment, to the total organization with its impersonality, extended hierarchy, and social distance becomes ambiguous. However, attachment to the immediate and easily perceived face-to-face group is the predominant reality of organization experience. For the individual it provides a source of personal security in an impersonal environment.

Where cliques are largely nonexistent, as in the rapidly expanding aircraft plants of California, turnover can be enormous. The presumption is that stable social groups take time to crystallize; during the period of formation many potential members will leave voluntarily because they do not find an established unit with which they can affiliate. This in turn inhibits the formation of permanent groups; the process is self-defeating.

Thus Lombard and Mayo conclude that the naive administrator who seeks to break up these cliques because of the inefficiency and wasted motion of the purely social activities involved is actually doing a disservice to the organization.[5] In fact, they find that it takes skillful leadership to encourage their formation, at least in organizations undergoing rapid expansion. A recent well-received text[6] in the field of public administration comes out strongly on the side of encouraging on-the-job social life, concluding that production increased when social conversation was allowed. However, a study employing methods of precise interaction observation is unique in casting some doubts as to the positive correlation between social interaction and productivity.[7]

More serious criticism of the universal efficacy of friendship cliques, however, involves considerations of personality and work structure differences. A study of "rate busters" disclosed a significant majority who were indifferent to, if not hostile to, the social groupings they found on the job.[8]

---

[5] Elton Mayo and George F. Lombard, *Teamwork and Labor Turnover in the Aircraft Industry of Southern California* (Boston: Graduate School of Business Administration, Harvard University, 1940).
[6] Herbert Simon, Donald Smithburg, and Victor Thompson, *Public Administration* (New York: Knopf, 1950), pp. 113–114.
[7] A. B. Horsfall and Conard Arensberg, "Teamwork and Productivity in a Shoe Factory," *Human Organization*, VIII (Winter 1949), pp. 21 ff.
[8] These men tended to have a rural background emphasizing individualism. Orvis Collins and Donald Roy, "Restriction of Output and Social Cleavage in Industry," *Applied Anthropology*, V (Summer 1946), pp. 1–14.

A recent examination of British longshoremen finds that approximately half of the longshoremen on the docks studied have consciously avoided social entanglements of work group membership. Given an opportunity to join semipermanent gangs, they prefer random work assignments that leave them free to come and go at will, with no group responsibility.[9]

Formation of social groups also appears to be a function of the structure of the work situation itself. Argyris, in his Bank study, finds that incidence of informal social groupings among tellers is less than for bank employees who have less interaction with customers.[10] This conclusion would confirm a basic hypothesis of Chapple, that individuals seek some equilibrium in their rate and range of interaction.[11]

From this theoretical approach, we would expect that the whole range of group activities, not just social life, would be influenced by the interaction pattern fostered by the job. The previously cited study by the University of Liverpool researchers, for example, notes that dockworkers who were members of semipermanent crews were rarely found among the informal leaders of the longshoremen or among the active participants in the union.[12] Moving in the other direction, Lipset concludes that because some jobs handicap workers in maintaining adequate off-the-job relations with other friends (e.g., unusual working hours as among printers, actors, and policemen), they tend to form more closely knit "fellow worker" groups, as evidenced by their record of high participation in local union activities.[13]

Similarly, George Strauss has observed an unusually high degree of membership participation in certain occupational groups involving relative isolation from fellow workers, like insurance salesmen, utility meter readers and substation operators.[14]

Such studies add to the trend toward considering the *need for social relations* as a variable worth studying in itself. It would be interesting to know, for example, whether industrial occupations in which there is high inter-worker dependence in the work process, such that almost

---

[9] University of Liverpool, *The Dock Worker* (Liverpool: University Press of Liverpool, 1954), pp. 61 ff.

[10] Chris Argyis, *Organization of a Bank* (New Haven: Labor and Management Center, Yale University, 1954), p. 129.

[11] Eliot D. Chapple, "Applied Anthropology in Industry," in *Anthropology Today*, A. L. Kroeber, ed. (Chicago: University of Chicago Press, 1953), pp. 819–831. Many of the observations in this section are based on the theoretical work of Chapple.

[12] University of Liverpool, *op. cit.*, p. 72.

[13] Seymour M. Lipset, "The Political Process in Trade Unions: A Theoretical Statement," in *Freedom and Control in Modern Society*, Monroe Berger, Theodore Abel, and Charles Page, eds. (New York: Van Nostrand, 1954), pp. 101–102.

[14] Personal correspondence, Professor Strauss, University of Buffalo.

constant interaction is required, show less social life than groups characterized by relatively independent operations.

The Task Group. Perhaps one of the most important aspects of small group behavior in large organizations is their relation to the work process itself. The formally designated task builds a group structure, just as do individual social needs and the organizational authority structure.

More specifically, the work process stimulates group controls of (1) work method, (2) output standards of productivity, and (3) relative compensation and prestige relationships.

1. Impact on Work Method. The experience of working in close proximity on a day-to-day basis induces methods that may depart from the organization's original conception of the job, or at least "fills in" the specific details of the operation not specified in the formal work plan. Thus, employees may exchange repetitive jobs, although such trading is illegal; one worker may do two jobs while a colleague rests; or, as Whyte[15] found, they may change the sequence of the operations to reduce tensions and provide short cuts. Roy observed similar "adjustments" in relations among tool room clerks, job sellers, and machinists where the objective was maximizing piece rate earnings.[16]

Some of these informal, or unplanned for, work methods may decrease worker output. For example, workers' machinations in Roy's machine shop tended to overstate make-ready time during job changes. However, other worker innovations, such as those described by Whyte, undoubtedly increase the total product. Gross found that radar teams, through communication circuits set up during off-the-job social periods, were compensating for deficiencies in the information provided by the formal organization.[17]

Similarly researchers have analyzed the initiative exhibited by a group of department store salesmen in evolving a new work pattern that solved a serious internal morale problem created by a new incentive system.[18]

However, the work structure can be designed so that elaborations of the informal group necessarily work in opposition to the major objectives of the organization. Recent studies of changes in the method

[15] William F. Whyte, "The Social Structure of the Restaurant," *The American Journal of Sociology*, LIV (January 1949), pp. 306–307.

[16] Donald Roy, "Quota Restriction and Goldbricking in a Machine Shop," *The American Journal of Sociology*, LVII (March 1952), pp. 427–442.

[17] Edward Gross, "Some Functional Consequences of Primary Controls in Formal Work Organizations," *American Sociological Review*, XVIII (August 1953), pp. 370–371.

[18] Nicholas Babchuck and William Goode, "Work Incentives in a Self-Determined Group," *American Sociological Review*, XVI (October 1951), p. 686.

of mining coal, conducted by the Tavistock Institute in Great Britain, illustrate such organization.[19] The change from jobs completed by small groups of miners in one shift to successive operations carried out by three shifts resulted in reduction of interaction and communication and a consequent decrease in the miners' recognition of their total responsibility for the operation.[20]

Thus the Tavistock studies suggest that the goal of the engineer in designing the technological organization is to provide the work group with a relatively autonomous task so that responsible *internal* leadership can develop. This kind of organizational structure is, in fact, the very essence of decentralization:

> A primary work organization of this type has the advantage of placing responsibility for the complete . . . task squarely on the shoulders of a single, small, face-to-face group which experiences the entire cycle of operations within the compass of its membership. For each participant the task has total significance and dynamic closure.[21]

The development of mutually convenient methods of conducting the work process can extend to the "job" of collective bargaining. We have ample evidence that union-management relationships at the work group level often depart radically from established practices and attitudes prevailing at higher levels, and may in fact contradict these other, more "formal" relationships.[22]

Aside from evolving methods which seem most convenient to work group members, the pattern of doing the job is fitted to the status system of the group. Those members with most prestige, if at all possible, receive the best jobs. Where possible, working location and equipment are similarly "assigned." And where these are not under group control, helping and trading can be adjusted to the status system. The exchange-of-favors system readily responds to the prestige hierarchy. Of course, the evaluation placed on jobs is itself a product of group interaction.

The methods evolved within the group for task completion become firmly established. Where outside forces (e.g., technological change) threaten to induce changes, the ranks close and resistance is applied.

---

[19] E. Trist and K. Bamforth, "Some Social and Psychological Consequences of the Longwall Method of Coal-Getting," *Human Relations,* IV, No. 1 (1951).

[20] The same problem can arise even though the employees are not separated into different time shifts. A study of a textile mill provides us with an example of the impact of worker-machine allocations. Cf. A. K. Rice, "Productivity and Social Organization in an Indian Weaving Shed," *Human Relations,* VI, No. 4 (1953).

[21] Trist and Bamforth, *op. cit.,* p. 6.

[22] Cf. Melville Dalton, "Unofficial Union-Management Relations," *American Sociological Review,* XV (October 1950), pp. 611–619.

In part, of course, this may be the natural reaction of the culprit fearing punishment for rule infractions. A more reasonable explanation of the informal group's resistance to change, however, is the intimate relationship between the task group as an entity and the work methods they have evolved. A threat to one is a real threat to the other.

2. Impact on Output Standards. Probably more attention has been given to this aspect of task group behavior than to any other. Starting with the work of Mathewson, and extending through the Western Electric studies, a long and distinguished line of studies indicate that work groups often formulate quite specific output standards and obtain close conformity from their members in *maintaining* these standards. Productivity itself is increasingly conceived of as a group phenomenon.

Several reasons have been advanced as to why output control occupies a place of such importance in the life of the group. Work standards are one of the most important aspects of the job, which can in some fashion be influenced by worker action. The energy expenditure required by the job is largely determined by the number of units required, rather than by the nature of the job itself. Presumably without group control management would be able to utilize individual differences, and competition for promotion and greater earnings, to obtain higher and higher standards. This would penalize particularly the slower worker and the older employee. It might, however, penalize all workers by cutting piece rates, where such exist, and/or reducing the number of employees required by the operation. "Run away" output might have internal ramifications. We have observed situations where group controls were weak, and younger, low-prestige employees exceeded the production and earnings records of their "betters." The results were calamitous for the status hierarchy of the department and ultimately for the effectiveness of the formal organization.

Output control is a basic objective of group action as well as an essential element in maintaining group stability. Not only the relationship of the members to one another, but the durability of the worker relationship to his job depends on the efficacy of this process. Again we need to note that the resultant is not always unfavorable to management. We have many instances on record where the group has sanctioned increasingly high productivity,[23] rejected fellow workers who could not maintain high output, and resisted threats to existing high quality standards.

Evidently a great deal of the interest in "informal group relations"

---

[23] Cf. George Strauss, "Group Dynamics and Intergroup Relations," in William F. Whyte and others, *Money and Motivation* (New York: Harper, 1955), pp. 90–96.

is the result of this presumed relationship between output standards evolving within the group and actual worker productivity. Wilensky in an earlier chapter [of *Research in Industrial Human Relations*] reviews some of the efforts to find the magic formula to convert group norms from "low" to "high."

Some of the earliest research on productivity was based on the assumption that internal harmony in the work group would produce higher performance records. Increasingly researchers have become disillusioned with the relationship between social satisfaction and worker effort. Perhaps one of the most telling blows to the impetus to devote substantial energies to building work groups that are "sociometrically sound" is the provocative study by Good and Fowler in a low morale plant. They found "the informal relationships which developed were such as to maintain pressures toward high production in the face of considerable *animosity* toward the owners and *among the workers themselves*."[24] While their findings are severely limited by the somewhat unique environment they chose, it has become recognized that the relationship between friendship and output is a complex one.

More recently, Seashore finds in a study in a large "heavy equipment manufacturing company" that highly "cohesive" work groups are more likely to have output records that diverge *in either direction* from plant averages.[25] By implication, then, tightly knit work groups are almost as likely to have notably *poor* production records as outstandingly *good* ones.

The present author is inclined to believe that these inconsistencies in research results are due to an overemphasis on output as a part of informal group equilibrium. Control over output is also a major weapon in the arsenal of the group engaging in conflict with management, other work groups, and even the local union. We need to know more about the *total situation* facing a given work group, including these external factors, before predicting its work performance.

The evolution of the method of *group decision* for gaining acceptance for changes in production methods and output standards is recognition of the potency of group standards. The theory presumes that leadership methods that involve the entire work group in the change process have two major advantages:

(*a*) They can eliminate the major barrier of existing group standards which militate against any change, per se.

---

[24] William Goode and Irving Fowler, "Incentive Factors in a Low Morale Plant," *American Sociological Review*, XIV (October 1949), p. 624; italics added by author.
[25] Stanley Seashore, *Group Cohesiveness in the Industrial Work Group* (Ann Arbor: Institute for Social Research, University of Michigan, 1954), p. 98.

(*b*) More positively, they commit the individual to new efforts in the context of his group membership. In a sense, the individual "promises" his fellows to accomplish some change in his behavior. Valuing the opinions of his associates, he feels bound to maintain his agreement.

Ideally the "decision" itself becomes the new standard or norm of conduct for the task group. Similarly efforts to develop plant-wide incentive systems are premised on the assumption that output and effort are dependent on the relation of the work group to the total social system of the plant.[26]

3. Impact on Relative Compensation and Prestige Relationships. The fact that jobs take on a significant social meaning can be seen in the importance attached to wage differentials within the group itself. For example, we have many instances on record when management assigned an equal value to each job and the group found significant distinguishing characteristics. Jobs ranked by employees as *more important or desirable* are expected to have higher earnings than jobs ranked below. The established hierarchy is reinforced over time by the gradual perfection of the correlation between esteem accorded particular workers and prestige accorded to their jobs. The "more important" workers have moved to the "more important" jobs. (The importance attached to the job is not only a function of the earning capacity but also the quality of the surroundings, equipment, the tempo of the work required, etc.) Problems occur only when changes are introduced which violate the established hierarchy.

A persistent problem has been that jobs which the group evaluates as relatively undesirable may need to be compensated at a higher rate than the "desirable" jobs, in order to attract adequate personnel. However, this differential may be contrary to the status system of the work group. Similarly, jobs evaluated (by the group) as desirable may lack characteristics which would bring them a high rating under the organization's formal ranking plan. These contradictions between the group and the organization's ranking system become more important during periods of relative labor shortage, when new recruits are difficult to obtain and when the group undergoes aging.

While these several concepts of the "informal group" are not identical, and in some cases not even complementary in their basic dimensions, they do have one common feature. All stress equilibrium, the development of a system of interpersonal relations which stabilizes the work situation (among subordinates and between superior and subordinates), an interconnected series of friendship linkages, work

---

[26] Cf. William F. Whyte and others, *Money and Motivation, op. cit.,* p. 225.

flow relationships, output levels, and status-income relations. The objectives are the maintenance of individual and group stability by insuring a predictability of day-to-day events and effecting a *modus vivendi* as between individual on-the-job needs and the requirements of the formal organization.

As such, the *informal group* in any and all of its meanings is serving well-recognized and accepted human needs. Its existence and continued preservation are hardly matters for surprise. The building up of routines, of established methods of accomplishing tasks, of predictable social relationships, of group roles—these are all elements of structuring which social scientists have found typical of the human group. In fact, the elements define the group.

Particularly through the setting and maintenance of group standards, informal groups have protected their memberships from possible indiscretions that might reflect adversely on them all; also they have provided support for the individual, by acting as a buffer to outside organizations and by sustaining him through the provision of *known and acceptable* routines of behaving within the face-to-face work group.

Thus the informal group, as perceived in such studies, *reacts to* the initiations of other organizations, particularly management. Being defined in equilibrium terms, the reaction is always an attempt to *regain* the previous undisturbed state—to protect work methods, social relationships, and output levels incorporated in the norms of the group.

Concerted Interest as the Focus. Workers also band together into *interest groups*. These are formed not only to protect their members but also to exploit *opportunities* to improve their relative position. Improvements can take the form of "looser standards," a preferred seniority position, more overtime, more sympathetic supervision, correction of "inequities," better equipment, and countless other less tangible goals that make the job a better one and that often serve to substitute for the more traditional kinds of promotions and mobility.

Distribution of these benefits may be much influenced by pressures of united and determined informal groups. What management feels is "equitable," just as what the union determines is in the "members' interest," is determined to a large extent by attitudes expressed by those individuals who can support their demands by group reinforcements. Those work groups which for one reason or another are unable to exercise similar power in the market place of the plant are penalized.

This is not the traditional concept of the informal group seeking conformity with established norms of conduct. These are much more "free enterprise" units, interacting in a struggle for maximization of utility. All are not equally aggressive in the struggle for self-improvement or equally well equipped with the wherewithal to do battle via the grievance procedure and the more direct pressure tactics on union and management. Some lack the spirit of combat, others the means, while only a restricted few are endowed with the characteristics associated with sustained "activity" and progress toward the goals they seek.

Much of what we say implies a degree of dual or even treble *disloyalty*. Other groups, management, the union, and fellow workers, are perceived as either barriers or sources of assistance. From the point of view of the interest group, it is not high identification or loyalty that counts, but rather the right tactics in using or ignoring these other aggregations.

Thus, management is neither "good" nor "bad," liked or disliked as such. In fact, this approach suggests that it may not always be fruitful to think in pro-management and pro-union terms. It may well be that a group which is satsified with *itself*, with its ability to protect and improve its own interests, is more favorable to *both* union and management.[27]

The results for the larger plant may not be a system tending toward equilibrium at all. We might expect that certain combinations of pressure groups actually involve the organization in increasing instability —a trend toward disequilibrium. We have observed plants where the interaction of these groups involves increasingly greater discontent, turmoil, and nonadaptive behavior. That is, their behavior tends to reinforce the very problems it was designed to solve.

Similarly, the internal structure of these groups is much more responsive to changes in its external environment than is often implied in the concept of the informal work group as a relatively durable, impervious entity. Literally overnight, technical changes introduced by management can convert a cohesive task force into a disunited, apathetic "rabble," squabbling over internal differences. Similarly, we have observed a group of weakly-united employees become a force of some magnitude in the social system of the plant within a brief period, with no changes in personnel.

The existence of these *interest group* types suggests that greater attention should be given to matching supervisory "types" with group "types." We have tended to think of effective supervision as being the product of a relationship between a good leader and his group, on the assumption that the group of subordinates was a constant. In fact,

---

[27] These areas ... [are] further elaborated in the author's ... study, *Technology and Work Group Behavior* (Ann Arbor: Bureau of Industrial Relations, University of Michigan, 1956).

variations in the effectiveness of supervision may be as much due to inherent differences in the group itself as to the leadership practices exhibited by the supervisor.

The Internal Dynamics of the Work Group

We have concentrated primarily on the relationship of the small group to the larger organization, the functions served, the "compatibilities" and "incompatibilities." Therefore, we have failed to explore much of the research that stresses the intriguing inner processes of these groups, as semiautonomous organizations. This means neglecting the processes of self-selection and exclusion developed in the work of Moreno and his colleagues in the field of sociometry. We have also omitted the prolific findings of the "group dynamics school" with its emphasis on leadership patterns and role differentiation, factors contributing to cohesiveness, and the impact of the group itself on membership perceptions and attitudes. Bales and his associates at Harvard have probed deeply into the "ebb and flow" of the problem-solving process within the group. The sequential member roles have been analyzed effectively.

For our purposes it would seem appropriate at least to make specific reference to the work of George Homans. His work places substantial emphasis on the relationship of the internal life of the group to the outside environment (primarily the attitudes, organizational structure, and work method induced by management).[28] "Elaborations" of behavior and sentiment induced in the small group in turn modify the larger organization. While we believe an overemphasis on the concept of *equilibrium* may be misleading, Homans' theorizing does provide a framework within which to relate the small group to the larger organization of which it is a part.

Conclusion

Clusterings of workers-on-the-job all have these characteristics: They stem from the uniqueness of individual personality, which refuses to combine into larger "wholes" without changing those entities. The sum of a group of individuals is something more than the total of the constituents; it is a new organization, because most of the members (there are significant exceptions as we have noted) obtain satisfaction in gaining acceptance as a part of the group, and the

[28] George Homans, *The Human Group* (New York: Harcourt Brace, 1950).

group itself wields an influence over its members. Put in another way, there are pressures toward *conformity* within the group. These pressures result in the establishment of accepted ways of living together. The way of life of the group includes a complex system of customs and rules, vested interests, and interaction patterns which govern the relationship of members of the group to one another and to the larger environment of which it is a part.

This observance of group-sanctioned behavior and attitudes "fills out" the rationally conceived organization. What is on paper an organization becomes a "living, breathing" social organism, with all the intricacies, emotions, and contradictions we associate with human relations. While no organization would long persist which did not provide its members with this opportunity for spontaneous "human relations," a major problem of the larger organization becomes one of successfully incorporating the small group.

The Small Group and Public Administration[*]

Robert T. Golembiewski

Outstanding even among the bullish research upturns in the social sciences has been the attention devoted to the small group.[1] This emphasis does not reflect a passing scholarly fancy. There has been sufficient research progress and sufficient demonstration that striking changes can be wrought in group achievement to warrant continued attention to the way people behave in small groups.[2] One graphic example is illustrated [in Figure 1]. It records the average hourly pro-

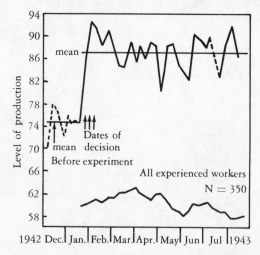

Figure 1 The Effects of "Group Decision Making" versus Management Exhortation in Increasing Production[3]

[*] Reprinted with permission of author and publisher from *Public Administration Review,* 19 Summer, 1959), pp. 149–156.
[1] This article is based upon the author's 1958 doctoral dissertation at Yale University, *The Small Group, Public Administration, and Organization: An Analysis of Small Group Research Concepts and Operations.*
[2] For a summary of a wide variety of such descriptive studies, see Muzafer Sherif and Carolyn Sherif, *Groups In Harmony and Tension: An Integration of Studies On Intergroup Relations* (Harper and Brothers, 1953).
[3] The figure is reproduced from Kurt Lewin, "Group Decision and Social Change," in Theodore M. Newcomb and Eugene L. Hartley, editors, *Readings In Social Psychology* (Holt, 1947), p. 343. The job in question had been set by time and motion analysis. Sixty units per hour were considered standard and seventy-five units per hour were considered the job ceiling. The "group decision-making" work unit was able to surpass this ceiling—around which it had produced—and sustain the higher level of production. The increase is more striking than a similar increase by lower productivity workers.

duction of a group of workers allowed to come to their own decisions about work goals and processes (top line), compared to other workers in the plant who were exhorted by management to increase output (lower line).

To permit detailed descriptions of such cases of small group change, much recent study has been devoted to the relations of persons in *ad hoc* groups in social laboratories. Such work does not yet permit the construction of a theory which allows us to understand small groups, that is, to predict their behavior and prescribe for their ills. For theory development requires the ability to identify for small groups the characteristics most relevant to their behavior and it also requires the ability to measure differences in these characteristics. Now only a few characteristics have been isolated. Thus research results are fragmentary and may even be inaccurate. Furthermore, several different measurement techniques have been used to study most group characteristics. Thus comparability of the studies made is uncertain.

Nevertheless, a research base has been constructed and some insights can be offered the administrator about small group behavior and significant ways in which groups differ. The administrator of course must be concerned about small groups since any organization contains many. Moreover, the administrator is directly involved with several of them. The concept of informal organization, now familiar to many administrators, also is being illumined by small-group studies.

What we are learning about the properties of small groups might be classified in three categories:

1. group structure, i.e., the way members generally are related to each other—as by rank or personal affinity or specific job assignment.

2. group style, e.g., the values the group gives to the different functions of leadership.

3. individual member characteristics as related to group performance.

Group Structure

Studies have revealed the strong tendency for groups to develop structural characteristics such as an internal communications system and a "pecking order." Especial attention has been focused upon the important structural characteristic, leadership. Several useful operations for identifying individuals ranked high on leadership have been developed. Moreover, research has demonstrated the important influence of leaders on the group, particularly on its internal communication, as well as their importance as representatives of the group to the outside.

These structural characteristics are relevant to administration. Formal organization prescribes a hierarchy of authority and channels of communication, but the psychological unity of the small group cuts across the boundaries of the formal system of organization and procedures. Moreover, the group tries to stabilize its environment. The group thus exerts a continuing pressure on methods, on the degree of formal delegation to it, and on attempts to control it.

Uses in research and administration are obvious. Thus students like the sociologists Selznick and Blau have attempted the general description of organizations through the interaction of these alternative structures of authority and communication—the formal organization and the small groups within it. Moreover, the successful administrator who has learned to use informal relationships among his subordinates as communication channels (who might, in fact, even develop such channels) will find research attempts to identify both small-group leaders and information pathways a potentially important applied product. Informal rankings (i.e., the way group members would rank each other as opposed to the official rank) have proven extremely important in administration. There is substantial evidence, for example, that instability in informal rankings and/or sharp differences in formal and informal rankings are major causes of group friction and low productivity. Data on informal leaders that have been sifted out of small group studies could be considered, then, in selecting supervisors (with formal authority) who also would have actual (informal) authority. This would contribute to gearing into the organization's purposes[4] the small group's potential for controlling its own behavior.

Study of structure properties has also had important broader consequences for research and practice in administration. Primarily, such work has diverted effort from the search for the supposedly universal "traits of leaders." Small group studies were unsuccessful in isolating such general traits. We therefore no longer think of leadership as a bundle of personality traits in a particular individual but rather as a *function,* and as a function whose specific characteristics vary from situation to situation.

These are subtle but pervasive changes in our understanding. The

---

[4] The idea is not novel. Experiments along these lines were performed with successful results in the military. See, for example, Robert J. Wherry and Douglas H. Fryer, "Buddy Ratings: Popularity Contest or Leadership Criteria?," 12 *Sociometry* 179–90 (February-August, 1949). A specific applied experiment compared self-chosen construction work teams with those chosen by supervisors. Self-chosen teams proved more effective as measured by four criteria—job satisfaction, turnover rate, an index of labor cost, and an index of material cost. Raymond H. Van Zelst, "Validation of a Sociometric Regrouping Procedure," 47 *Journal of Abnormal and Social Psychology* 299–301 (April, 1952). See also the section on style properties in this article, however.

emphasis on small group leadership as a function has precipitated a search for broad classes of leadership behavior. Sophisticated statistical techniques have isolated three broad functions of leadership from a wide range of specific actions of persons labelled leaders by members and observers of small groups: "group task facilitation," "sociability," "individual prominence."[5] Such findings increase our understanding of groups. For example, in conferences and on railroad work gangs, the failure of the formal superior to perform one or more of the three leadership functions was a precondition to the development of informal leaders.[6] Such findings, also, have potentially important applied uses. These three functions of leadership thus might comprise the skeleton of a check list of actions to be performed by formally-designated superiors intent on being informal leaders as well.

The fact that groups value the performance of the three leadership functions in different degrees also emphasizes the situational nature of leadership. This bare finding contributes to research and practice in administration, for the contrary emphasis—that the same leadership traits are transferable to all situations—has long been current. The new problem is: What are the relevant differences between situations? In group situations, one of the differences isolated was the structural characteristic "cohesiveness." Cohesiveness is conceived as the resultant of the forces to remain in a group and those to leave it. Investigations of cohesiveness, then, attempt to estimate the "social gravitational field" of the small group. The conception has proved strategic for research and application. For example, the degree of group influence on members varies with cohesiveness. This means that highly cohesive groups find it possible to maintain higher (or lower) levels of productivity than groups of lower cohesiveness in the same situations. (Differences tend to be statistically significant.) This curvilinear relationship has been observed in *ad hoc* laboratory groups, work units in a manufacturing plant, and conference groups.[7] Thus the situationally-oriented research on cohesiveness taps a vital area unknown

---

[5] Group task facilitation has been described in terms of behavior such as "enforces operating procedures"; sociability in terms such as "socially acceptable to group members and sensitive to what goes on in the group"; and individual prominence in terms such as "forceful" and "quick to take the lead." Relevant studies have developed elaborate systems for observing and classifying such behavior. Administrative case studies have yet to provide the basis for such an analytical step beyond the well-documented findings that formally-designated authorities are not the only elements in policy-making.

[6] Consult, for example, Walter H. Crockett, "Emergent Leadership In Small Decision-Making Groups," 51 *Journal of Abnormal and Social Psychology* 378–83 (November, 1955).

[7] An interesting relevant study is provided by Stanley E. Seashore, *Group Cohesiveness in the Industrial Work Group* (Survey Research Center, University of Michigan, 1954).

to traditional organization theory. Cohesiveness research promises to improve the judgments of administrators and researchers about small groups, both by increasing the accuracy and scope of predictions based upon cohesiveness and also by reducing the possibility of inconsistent observations of the same group by different persons.

Style Properties

Since findings consistently show that small groups weigh the performance of the three major functions of leadership differently, the reasons that different weights are given these functions are as important as the group's structural properties. This is often overlooked. Thus predictions have been made that productivity in a work situation will be higher in those cases in which the formal supervisor also is ranked highest on informal leadership. But this does not always appear true.[8] An approximate explanation may be outlined. One work unit, as a matter of style, may emphasize sociability in bestowing informal leadership and may undervalue task facilitation. In that situation, the formal superior who succeeds also in being the informal leader would not be likely to achieve high production. Contrarily, units with high production records would probably emphasize the "task facilitation" function in according informal leadership. In the same way, it is necessary to know the group's "style" to predict its productivity from a measure of its cohesiveness. The implied warning is a general one for small group analysis: predictions based upon a single property are suspect because of the possible important influence of unspecified properties.

Group norms are an important property of small group style. "Norm" has several incompletely overlapping meanings, but in general it refers to ways of looking at reality and of behaving that are shared by group members. Norms are reflected in production curves that constantly remain flat, reflecting informal restrictions on output, or, if the admin-

---

[8] A study of the congruence of informal rank (set by the group) and formal rank in flight crews isolated such a general pattern. The study concluded that the crews under study behaved in an increasingly harmonious, trusting, and cooperative manner as crew status congruency increased. Technical productivity, however, first showed improvement, then underwent some deterioration as congruency moved from minimum to maximum. Two reasons were offered: with increasing congruency, formal crew leaders become more considerate and thus lose willingness to organize and structure activity; and high congruency is associated with the close integration of the crew which provides security against the pressures of the larger organization, hence, fear of external authority is lessened. Stuart Adams, "Status Congruency As A Variable In Small Group Performance," 32 *Social Forces* 18, 19, 21 (October, 1953).

istrator is fortunate, in steadily increasing production.[9] But these are only the more obvious reflections of norms. There is significant evidence that much organization behavior reflects the influence of small norms in more subtle but no less substantial ways.[10]

Small-group analysis provides such important insights into the development and influence of norms as:

1. Norm formation is a very common phenomenon in small groups. It occurs even in experimental groups brought together for a very brief time.[11]

2. Group norms often are *the* standards for behavior evaluation, even when contradictory norms are prescribed by a formal organization or by "society." Thus it was found that a criminal gang[12]

> not only has its own code which governs the conduct of its members, but it even goes so far as to impose it upon outside society ... in terrorizing witnesses and in exacting the death penalties upon them and upon members of the gang who are suspected of having given information to the police ... [This] shows how a closely knit group develops its own standards and is outraged and puzzled by the attempts to deal with them according to law.

3. The small-group member is not necessarily aware that his behavior is influenced by group norms. Nor are the controlling norms always explicit.

4. The importance of norms to small groups is reflected in the sanctions which they mobilize against violators. Thus the "binging" reported in the Hawthorne studies was a form of physical punishment for norm violations. Such sanctions have been observed not only in natural state small groups, but also in *ad hoc* groups assembled for research.

---

[9] The Bank Wiring Test Room and the Relay Assembly Test Room experiments, respectively, illustrate these norm directions in the well-known Hawthorne studies. See Fritz J. Roethlisberger and William J. Dickson, *Management and the Worker* (Harvard University Press, 1939).

[10] Peter M. Blau, *The Dynamics of Bureaucracy: A Study of Interpersonal Relations In Two Government Agencies* (University of Chicago Press, 1955), for example, discusses the impact of informal norms about bribery which were contrary to agency policy.

[11] The classic study is that of Sherif with autokinesis. He demonstrated that individuals tended to converge toward a norm-like shared estimate of the distance that a light in a dark room moved during brief exposures. These estimates tended to be the basis of estimates later made by individuals in an "alone" situation. The light in the experiment does not move, although it seems to do so. The unstructured situation seems to induce group development, albeit for limited purposes only. M. Sherif, "A Study of Some Social Factors In Perception," 28 *Archives of Psychology* No. 187 (1935).

[12] J. Landesco, *Organized Crime In Chicago,* Part 3 in the Illinois Association for Criminal Justice, *Illinois Crime Survey* (Blakely, 1929), p. 1055.

5. As expected, the degree of norm influence on behavior is a direct function of cohesiveness, indicating both the importance of cohesiveness and the interrelation of structure and style properties.

The importance of norms for the small group is plausibly explained. They seem to be related to two important general classes of human needs: (1) some basis for evaluating opinions and abilities; (2) a sense of intimate belonging. The small group is a convenient but not exclusive medium for providing such need satisfaction. It offers the individual the warmth of friendship, the nod of approval, and the strength of reinforcement. These constitute sufficient motives for norm observance. Moreover, small groups often stabilize the environment in ways beyond the capacity of single individuals, as in maintaining output limits. The starch of this stability is the inviolability of small group norms. Thus norm violations threaten the small group as a system for the provision of member satisfactions.

This does not do justice to norm research, but it does suggest the importance of norms in administration. For norms are the gateways (or the roadblocks) to the attainment of organization objectives. Both students and practitioners of administration thus must recognize and respect norms. In a prescriptive sense, organizers of human effort have an even greater stake in such research. For they are daily engaged in inducing norms that are consistent, and/or in changing norms that are inconsistent, with formal organization demands. Existing research on small group norms, which has experimentally tested some of the suggestions of the early descriptive literature on the group, provides some basis for understanding and controlling norms relevant to administration.

A second line of research on group style characteristics—on small group atmosphere—also has important implications for administration. This research derives from the experiments of Lewin, Lippitt, and White on the effects on children's behavior of such styles of adult supervision as "authoritarian" and "democratic."[13] In general, the authoritarian supervisor emphasized unilateral decision-making by self and obedience by the children; the democratic supervisor emphasized collective decision-making. The dramatic impact of supervisory style and group atmosphere on member behavior was demonstrated by shifting individuals between groups; and the effects of supervisory behavior on group atmosphere were demonstrated by periodic supervisory style changes. Groups with democratic atmospheres tended to

---

[13] For a convenient summary, see Ralph White and Ronald Lippitt, "Leader Behavior and Member Reaction In Three 'Social Climates,'" in Dorwin Cartwright and Alvin Zander, eds., *Group Dynamics: Research and Theory* (Row, Peterson, 1953), pp. 585–611.

perform effectively and to be cooperatively task-oriented even when the adult supervisor was absent. Authoritarian groups, however, tended to disintegrate in the absence of the supervisor and to engage in non-task and especially aggressive behavior.

The findings have tenable explanations. Permissive may be compared to authoritarian supervisory style in terms of the wide or narrow distribution of leadership functions. In permissive situations, then, groups are more likely to develop and enforce work norms. In authoritarian situations, the supervisor might exercise significant control over group members under certain conditions, e.g., physical presence. The development of group-centered influence, however, might be inhibited by the supervisor's attempts to perform all leadership functions. In other cases, such attempts might induce the development of a group, but existing research suggests that it often would be a group mobilized in opposition to the supervisor.[14]

Research with permissive and authoritarian styles of supervision also tends to verify such findings. Under permissive supervision, therapy for the mentally disturbed was more effective; productivity and/or participant satisfaction was greater in research laboratories, in clerical divisions, and in college classrooms; and so on.[15] But only the tendency has been demonstrated, for there also are opposed results. This is expected. In the first place, permissive supervisory style may encourage group norm formation more than an authoritarian style. But the norms need not be consistent with such external expectations as higher therapy effectiveness or higher productivity. Group pressure might be mobilized in a contrary direction. Moreover, the mixed results may be due to differences in supervisory techniques (generally unspecified), in the tasks performed, or in the types of persons in the group.

Despite the gaps, research on small group style is administratively relevant. Style differences, however, are often overlooked. For example, it seems likely that the neglect of style properties of a task unit limits the usefulness of typical job analyses and typical methods of personnel selection at all levels. Moreover, organization theory and

---

[14] The difference, in essence, is between a cohesiveness based on member-to-member attachments and one based on member-to-leader attachments. Interest in the group as a locus of control has been great for at least two reasons related to this difference. First, more or less constant surveillance of the members of even small work units is difficult, even if the supervisor has no other responsibilities. Second, the personality talents necessary to exert leader-to-member control without negative reactions are probably rare. This is especially the case in the absence of a strong generalized respect for formal authority.

[15] See, especially, Howard Baumgartel, "Leadership Style As A Variable In Research Administration," 2 *Administrative Science Quarterly* 344–60 (December, 1957).

(probably to a lesser extent) practice are analogous to the authoritarian style. This probably induces much nonproductivity in the many situations in which task units have formal supervisors. Existing small group results suggest that a re-evaluation of prescription and practice is advisable,[16] at least for small units.

Individual Member Characteristics

Differences in the characteristics of individual members (i.e., the properties of group members as opposed to the style and structure of the group as a whole) also explain why no direct relation need exist between group style and such external measures as high productivity or even such internal measures as participant satisfaction. Thus in the Lewin experiments, most children preferred the permissive condition. But as one child, perhaps significantly the son of an army officer, noted: "[The authoritarian supervisor] was best ... [he] was strictest and I liked that a lot ... he decided what we were to do." This interaction of population and style properties is illustrated by an experiment with college students using the "Twenty Questions" parlor game.[17] By asking questions of a moderator, the subjects attempted within a time limit to identify unknown items without any information beyond the fact that the item is an animal, vegetable, or mineral. The pattern of results may be briefly suggested.

TABLE I

GROUP PERFORMANCE UNDER VARYING ATMOSPHERE
AND INTELLIGENCE COMPOSITION

| | Efficiency Criterion | |
Condition	Questions Per Problem	Per Cent Problems Solved
Permissive Atmosphere—Bright Subjects	15.5	100.0
Authoritarian—Bright	18.5	87.5
Authoritarian—Dull	24.5	75.0
Permissive—Dull	31.0	37.5

Roughly, there is consistent evidence of the greater efficiency of the bright children under permissive conditions and of the dull under

[16] For some of the reworking of traditional organization concepts precipitated by such work, see the interesting recent article by Morris Janowitz, "Changing Patterns of Organizational Authority: The Military Establishment," 3 *Administrative Science Quarterly* 473–93 (March, 1959).

[17] Allen D. Calvin, Frederick K. Hoffman, and Edgar L. Harden, "The Effect of Intelligence and Social Atmosphere On Group Problem Solving Behavior," 45 *Journal of Social Psychology* 61–74 (February, 1957).

authoritarian conditions.[18] The moral of the illustration is patent: population as well as group structure and style properties must be specified in small group analysis.

Work with population properties, in general, has advanced less than research with small group structure and style properties. Two lines of investigation, however, do give promise of substantial analytical and applied payoffs: study of the personality characteristic, authoritarianism, and the compatibility of the personalities of members of small groups.

There has been considerable recent study of the authoritarian personality, the inflexible, anxiety-ridden, impulsive conformist who must wield authority and/or surrender to an authority figure. Existing measures of authoritarianism leave room for improvement.[19] Significantly, however, when extreme scorers on an authoritarianism measure were used to compose two sets of experimental groups (one of high scorers on the test, the other of low scorers), two distinct group atmospheres developed.[20] Thus groups of high authoritarianism scorers, compared to low scorers, were more aggressive, more concerned with status and striving for individual prominence, less apt to develop warm interpersonal relations, and less effective (according to observers) on cooperative problem solving. The individuals designated by participants in high authoritarian groups as best performers of leadership functions had different behavior styles than those designated by the low authoritarian groups. Designated leaders in high authoritarian groups were more interested in monopolizing the performance of leadership behaviors, less sensitive to others, less friendly, and so on.

The social engineering implications of work with population prop-

---

[18] The relationships showed up prominently even though problem difficulty was not controlled. Differences between the bright subjects and the dull ones are predictably greatest on complex problems. The dulls might be more efficient than brights on simple problems because of a higher boredom effect among the brights. Existing work suggests that adequate description of the characteristics of tasks will require a great deal of research. This work is of relevance to personnel administration. See, generally, Research and Development Board, *Symposium On Techniques For the Measurement of Group Performance* (Panel On Human Relations and Morale, Committee On Human Resources, Department of Defense, 1952).

[19] Richard Christie and Marie Jahoda, eds., *Studies In the Scope and Method of "The Authoritarian Personality"* (Free Press, 1954).

[20] William Haythorn, Arthur Couch, Peter Langham, and Launor F. Carter, "The Behavior of Authoritarian and Equalitarian Personalities in Groups," 9 *Human Relations* 57–74 (February, 1956); and Haythorn, Couch, Donald Haefner, Langham, and Carter, "The Effects of Varying Combination of Authoritarian and Equalitarian Leaders and Followers," 53 *Journal of Abnormal and Social Psychology* 210–19 (September, 1956).

erties has been carried further by Schutz,[21] who underscores the importance of population properties in small group studies. Schutz composed compatible and incompatible groups using measures of intelligence and of three other population properties—dependence on authority symbols, personalness, and assertiveness. A compatible group— to illustrate with a single criterion—had members all ranked high on personalness while an incompatible group had some members ranked high and some low on personalness. Schutz held that "the dominant reason for a group's productivity depends on the extent to which the members can get along together." Schutz' general success in verifying hypotheses derived from this major premise and from the manipulation of group population properties suggests the utility of the approach. Thus, as predicted, compatible groups tended to be more productive on cooperative tasks, their member satisfaction was higher, and they were rated significantly higher on a generalized "goodness" criterion by both members and observers. It was also possible to predict leadership and personal liking choices from a knowledge of member personalities. However, Schutz neglects style differences. For a compatible group would seem more able to enforce low as well as high productivity, even though the compatible groups studied by Schutz all seemed to be high producers.

It is premature to judge the utility of either the authoritarianism or compatibility approach to population properties. Moreover, there are formidable research obstacles to such work.[22] But the research has a patent relevance for administration. In the field of personnel administration, for example, such work indicates that physiological and intellectual population measures are necessary—but not sufficient—to under-

---

[21] William C. Schutz, "What Makes Groups Productive?" 8 *Human Relations* 429–66 (No. 4, 1955).

[22] One of the research difficulties—a significant finding in itself—is that probably four-fifths or more of the individuals tested are not extreme scorers on any personality property. That is, individuals have wide "response repertoires." Such repertoires are rank-orders of the probabilities that various behaviors will occur. Thus authoritarian behavior by an individual may have a low probability. But many individuals have such behaviors in their repertoire and may invoke them when the situation warrants. This makes prediction difficult. For some interesting evidence, see Leonard Berkowitz, "Personality and Group Position," 19 *Sociometry* 210–22 (December, 1956).

The fact that individuals are behaviorally flexible, however, does not eliminate the importance of such style properties as group atmosphere. For group style determines for many people the specific behaviors which will be activated from their response repertoires. If group style elicits behaviors which are low-probability behaviors in the individual's response repertoire, however, negative tensions are likely to be mobilized in the individual. Findings indicating that many individuals prefer permissive atmospheres are thus very important for personnel administration. For organization theory and practice often tend toward inducing a directive atmosphere.

stand and prescribe patterns of human relations in organizations. Moreover, traditional methods of promotion also cause significant productivity losses by failing to suit the personality of supervisors to task unit members. Thus the opportunity of reinforcing formal authority with informal sanctions often is lost.[23]

Research-wise, then, population properties cannot be neglected. Application-wise, the work with population properties in small group analysis is one of the lines of effort which promises to conserve productive energies now dissipated because of our imprecise knowledge.

Future Research and Application

Handsome dividends have accrued from small group research and it is reasonable to expect greater future returns. Perhaps more important is the transferability of the method of study to other branches of social science. The relationship is not necessarily one-way. Thus students and practitioners of public administration familiar with the approach can contribute to research by describing the structural, style, and population characteristics of groups with which they work, comparing different groups in these terms, and even arranging groups in such a way as to test hypotheses.

But group study is no panacea. Primarily, this review should suggest the enormous efforts necessary to insure, in Gulick's words, that in "the next decade, nothing, nothing must take second place to our effort to understand the patterns of human awareness and how men who are working together in teams can find release for their energies."[24] Properties in all three small group categories must be specified more definitely for useful description and for prediction. Moreover, there are also important value questions associated with *the use* of the

---

[23] The point is important because superiors and subordinates tend to use different ranking criteria, e.g., "standard operating procedures" versus "social consideration." Provision for such differences is made, for example, in Hypothesis I in Milton Mandell, "Hypotheses On Administrative Selection," 19 *Public Administration Review* 13 (Winter, 1959).

Moreover, high work unit performance often has been related to the degree to which a formal superior meets the criteria of his subordinates. See, for example, Cecil A. Gibb, "Leadership," in Gardner Lindzey, ed., *Handbook of Social Psychology* (Addison-Wesley Publishing Co., 1954), Vol. II, pp. 892–93. Consistent with the discussion above, however, a curvilinear relation probably exists between the fit of supervisor characteristics and subordinate ranking criteria and productivity. In a psychological group, such ranking criteria will be group norms. Supervisory failure to fit them, then, will induce negative group sanctions and thus significant loss of productive energies.

[24] Luther Gulick, "Next Steps In Public Administration," 15 *Public Administration Review* 76 (Spring, 1955).

results of small group analysis, questions which become more pressing as knowledge advances. (Experience with scientific management, which seemed to its early enthusiasts to be free of values but is in fact fraught with value questions, should have made the point.) Further, the results of small group analysis are not applicable to public administration as a whole. Small groups may not be miniatures of larger and more complex organizations,[25] for example. In fact, findings of the physical and life sciences suggest that it is necessary to study levels of organization (e.g., atoms, molecules, mass) as well as level integration (e.g., the concept of valence and the combination of atoms into molecules).[26] Laws applicable at one level of organization are not sufficient to account for occurrences at other levels of organization of a class of phenomena. At least temporarily, then, extensions of small group results ought to be made with caution. Finally, one can almost hear the first anguished cry of protest by an operating official that the agency small group analyst is limiting his program control.

---

[25] Nicholas J. Demerath and John W. Thibaut, "Small Groups and Administrative Organizations," 1 *Administrative Science Quarterly* 139–54 (September, 1956), however, have argued that small groups are usefully considered as "miniatures" of large organizations.

[26] Alex B. Novikoff, "The Concept of Integrative Levels In Biology," 101 *Science* 209–15 (March 2, 1945).

Three Styles of Leadership and Their Uses*

Robert T. Golembiewski

Managers who have tried to keep track of research and thinking on the subject of leadership may well sympathize with the centipede that was asked how it managed its legs, for this innocent question, the limerick tells us, reduced the unfortunate creature to lying "distracted in a ditch considering how to run."

The question asked in the leadership literature—"How does one lead men?"—is every bit as disconcerting as the one put to the centipede. Nevertheless, the parallel between them is not quite exact. The centipede, until he had to think about it, was only doing what came naturally and doing it well. Leadership in the work situation, however, does not belong to the order of instinctive behavior. Doing what comes naturally in striving for leadership often leaves much to be desired.

Though management has tended to be all too receptive to endorsements for this, that, or the other leadership approach, its interest has sound foundations. In the first place, a considerable body of evidence shows that the productivity of a work unit is affected by the kind of leadership the unit receives. In the second, decisions about what style of leadership to adopt must to some extent be made for the company as a whole rather than being left to the intuitions of individual managers. Still, management's interest has not been satisfied, for the evidence supporting any one leadership style can always be countered, and frequently is, by evidence supporting its precise opposite. The bewildered organization that has tried and abandoned one style after another may well be pardoned for asking, "Where do we go from here?"

Fortunately, it is beginning to look as if a theory based on empirical findings is at last in the making. No one yet knows exactly what its ultimate content will be, but its outlines can now be perceived and—even more important—can be put to use to improve managerial practice.

At this point, it may be useful, therefore, to review the research findings that form the skeleton of this theory and to examine their practical implications. But before doing so, it is necessary to define the term "leadership"—though this in itself is a question that has stirred up endless controversy. For the purposes of this article, however, "leadership" will be taken to mean the consistent ability to influence people in desired ways.

* Reprinted with permission of author and publisher from *Personnel*, 38 (July-August, 1961), pp. 34–45.

On the classification of leadership styles, fortunately, there is more agreement. Most authorities recognize three basic types: "leader-centered," or "autocratic"; "group-centered," or "democratic"; and "individual-centered," or "free-rein."[1] The supposedly modern view, of course, is that the group-centered style is the most conducive to productivity. By contrast, the traditional view admits only the leader-centered style, regards the group-centered style as a plaything of psychologists, and dismisses the free-rein style as constituting not leadership, but rather its surrender.

Each in Its Place

Supporters of any all-or-nothing view have one thing in common: they will often be surprised to find that the research literature does not consistently support any one leadership style. The reason for this lies not in any failing of the research itself but in the simple fact that there is no "best" style. Indeed, the question "Which kind of leadership should we use?" prevents any useful answer. The question should be, rather, "Which kind of leadership *when?*"

This "when," it is worth pointing out, constitutes an integral part of the question, for every scientific formulation must at some point specify the conditions it covers. Even the well-tested law explaining what happens when objects are dropped holds true only for objects that are heavier than air. If the objects are dropped at certain points in space, moreover, they will "fall up," or float.

This approach provides a partial explanation of the apparent chaos of the research literature. Many studies that seem to contradict each other are simply accounts of leadership phenomena under different conditions. Studies based upon observation of similar conditions, on the other hand, have yielded a pattern of consistent results.

Fortunately, leadership study has now taken on a "situational" approach. The main point of this approach has been well expressed in popular terms by Auren Uris, who advises the would-be leader as follows: "The skill with which you apply the three basic tools of leadership—autocratic, democratic, and free-rein techniques—determines your personal success as a leader."[2]

What, then, are the conditions that should be taken into account in the choice of a leadership style? There are many. Four among them, however—personality, task characteristics, task roles, and group characteristics—are particularly important and have been explored in a

---

[1] For a typical treatment, see A. Uris, *How to Be a Successful Leader.* McGraw-Hill Book Company, Inc., New York, 1953, pp. 32–39.
[2] *Ibid.*, p. 31.

number of research studies. A separate examination of each of these conditions should provide some guidelines for translating such advice as Uris' into action.

Personality. As the advocates of group-centered leadership often fail to realize, not all people can function well under the same kind of leadership. There are, for example, many people whose personalities make them unfitted for a group- or individual-centered style.[3] Such a person was Administrator H, described in Harold Lasswell's *Psychopathology and Politics.*[4] A childhood marked by unfortunate sexual experiences and domination by an overbearing, prudish father had left him sharply, though unconsciously, ambivalent toward authority. Consequently, he worked well under supervision but invariably became careless when he was given substantial freedom on the job.

Needless to say, giving free rein to a subordinate like H would bring nothing but trouble, though over the long run his personality might possibly change enough to permit a looser kind of supervision. Studies of "authoritarianism" confirm these common-sense conclusions about how to deal with men like Administrator H. Authoritarians behave in ways that reveal compulsive conformity based upon a view of the world as menacing and unfriendly. Though they are not necessarily people of low intelligence, they think in relatively few channels, from which they cannot be moved. In addition, they seek security through the exercise of authority or, better still, through surrender to some powerful authority figure.

Studying authoritarianism in military groups, Medalia formulated and tested the following two hypotheses:[5]

1. People with strong authoritarian tendencies will be more likely to accept formal military leaders with the conventional traits of the "good officer" than will people with weak authoritarian tendencies.

2. People with strong authoritarian tendencies will be more likely to re-enlist than will people with weak authoritarian tendencies.

The data that emerged from his study are shown in Table 1. Not only do these findings support both hypotheses but, when one takes into account certain technical factors in the study that tended to obscure any relations, they suggest a very strong relation between personality and leadership style.

---

[3] Many personnel men are aware of these personality effects and therefore recruit only from those groups of people whose general social training seems likely to produce the personality characteristics appropriate to the organization's leadership style. Thus some companies seek out rural workers because of their alleged amenability to formal discipline.

[4] *The Political Writings of Harold D. Lasswell.* The Free Press, Glencoe, Ill., 1951, pp. 127–35.

[5] N. Z. Medalia, "Authoritarianism, Leader Acceptance, and Group Cohesion," *Journal of Abnormal and Social Psychology,* LI, No. 2 (1955), pp. 207–13.

TABLE 1

RELATION OF AUTHORITARIANISM IN MEMBERS OF A MILITARY GROUP TO
ACCEPTANCE OF FORMAL HEADS AND INTENT TO RE-ENLIST

| | | Authoritarianism | | | Difference Between High and Low |
		High	Medium	Low	
Leader Acceptance					
Above Median		59%	52%	36%	+23
Below Median		41	48	64	−23
	Total	100%	100%	100%	
Intent to Re-enlist					
Yes or Undecided		38%	34%	24%	+14
No		62	66	76	−14
	Total	100%	100%	100%	

The practical advantages of adapting leadership style to personality characteristics seem clear from this study. In the groups analyzed, it could mean a 23 per cent increase in the acceptance of the formal leader by his subordinates and a 14 per cent increase in the intent to reenlist. These figures indicate the need for developing a valid diagnostic indicator of the leadership style to which an individual will respond best. Comparable changes in a business organization would certainly prove well worth the cost of meshing leadership style and personality factors.

A word of qualification must, however, be inserted here. Most people have wide "response repertoires." That is, they are able to perform the wide range of behaviors required by the various styles of leadership despite their personal preference for a particular style.

This adaptability was demonstrated by Berkowitz in an experiment with a communication network that channeled a great deal of information to some positions and very little to others.[6] Half the subjects were assigned to communication positions in which they would have to act in ways that were not congruent with their personalities: submissive people were placed in central positions, dominant people in peripheral positions. The other half were assigned to the positions appropriate to their personalities. Though the two kinds of subjects at first performed quite differently, Berkowitz found, the "misplaced" subjects generally managed to adjust to the demands of their positions by the last of the three trials in the experiment.

Berkowitz' experiment, however, was brief. The findings of other research projects indicate that if it had continued, the subjects in the first group would ultimately have displayed reactions ranging from

---

[6] L. Berkowitz, "Personality and Group Position," *Sociometry*, XIX, No. 4 (1956), pp. 210–22.

dissatisfaction to attempts at sabotaging the work process. Just when it is that such reactions begin to appear will be determined by circumstances and personalities. But when they do hit, they hit hard.

A manager, then, may vary his style of leadership, but he cannot force people to act forever in ways that are uncongenial to their personalities. This imposes a difficult task upon the manager and the organization—ascertaining the behavior preferences of the individual subordinates and then arranging the work so as to allow them to carry out their tasks in the manner they prefer. Unless this is done, the formal head will remain just that, rather than being accepted by his men as their leader.

Task Characteristics. The second major condition affecting the usefulness of any given leadership style is the nature of the task to be performed. Though little work has so far been done in classifying tasks, it should be adequate here to note that tasks may be distinguished in terms of (1) the obviousness of the solution to the problem or of the work itself and (2) the amount of cooperation the task requires.

Unfortunately, research to date has for the most part assumed that all tasks are quite complex and require a great deal of interpersonal cooperation. Because socioemotional factors affect performance most strongly when the task is of this kind, the leader-centered style, which tends to generate emotional flareups, usually shows up poorly under these circumstances, while the group-centered style shows up well.

Many tasks, however, do not have these assumed characteristics. One of Deutsch's experiments illustrates the value of distinguishing between kinds of tasks.[7] The prediction to be tested was that internally cooperative groups would be more effective than internally competitive groups. When groups of both kinds attempted to solve human relations and puzzle problems, it was found, the "cooperative" groups did indeed perform better on a number of measures of effectiveness, including quantitative and qualitative output, member satisfaction with group functioning and output, and amount of aggressive behavior. But on several measures the differences between the two kinds of groups were more marked for the human relations problem than for the puzzle problem. It seems as if the objectively demonstrable nature of the puzzle solution made it difficult for members of the "competitive" groups to block each other in subtle ways. (Certainly, the nature of the task would have made direct blocking seem ridicu-

---

[7] M. Deutsch, "The Effects of Cooperation and Competition upon Group Process," in *Group Dynamics: Research and Theory*, ed. D. Cartwright and A. Zander. Row, Peterson and Company, Evanston, Ill., 1953, pp. 319–53. See especially tables 23.5, 23.7, 23.9, and 23.11.

lous.) The open-endedness of the human relations problem, on the other hand, gave them ample opportunity to run each other ragged.

In terms of leadership style, these data suggest that the leader-centered style is particularly inappropriate to tasks that have more than one possible solution and that require a considerable amount of interpersonal cooperation. More important still, the data seem to leave little room for the leader-centered style even on tasks with just the opposite characteristics, for, as has already been noted, the group-centered style generally proved the more effective not only for the human relations problem but for the puzzle problem as well. In actual business and industrial situations, it should also be pointed out, emotional tensions can affect performance adversely at any number of points in the operation—at far more points than in Deutsch's experimental situation. Moreover, the marked preference most people show for the group-centered style furthers its claim to being the more useful of the two.

This does not mean, however, that the leader-centered style should be rejected out of hand. A situation in which most of the operators are strongly authoritarian and the task is a simple one requiring little cooperation is obviously tailor-made for authoritarian leadership.

The Role of Intelligence

Calling a task "simple" of course implies some relation between the task itself and the intelligence of the people who are to perform it. The importance of taking this relation into account in deciding upon a leadership style has been demonstrated by a simple experiment with a game based on "Twenty Questions."[8] As Table 2 indicates, though all the subjects worked on essentially the same task, the "Brights" did

TABLE 2

EFFECTS OF LEADERSHIP STYLE AND MEMBERS' INTELLIGENCE UPON GROUP PERFORMANCE IN "TWENTY QUESTIONS" GAME

Members' Intelligence and Leadership Style		Measures of Performance	
		Median No. of Questions Asked Per Problem	Per Cent of Problems Solved
Bright	Group-centered	15.5	100.0
	Leader-centered	18.5	87.5
Dull	Group-centered	31.0	37.5
	Leader-centered	24.5	75.0

[8] A. D. Calvin *et al.*, "The Effect of Intelligence and Social Atmosphere on Group Problem-Solving Behavior," *Journal of Social Psychology*, XLV, First Half (1957), pp. 61–74.

their best under a group-centered style, and the "Dulls" under a leader-centered style. The relation was especially marked for the "Dulls," whose problem-solving efficiency was only half as high under group-centered leadership as under authoritarian leadership.

Regulating work assignments by task and personality characteristics may seem like a great deal of bother, but the 100 per cent performance difference for the "Dulls" suggests that the extra bother will more than pay its own way. Indeed, business would most likely find it profitable to subsidize the research necessary for the development of even more precise ways of differentiating people than those now available. The "Brights" in this experiment—to give just one illustration of the value of this greater precision—probably included some authoritarian subjects. (Though low intelligence is frequently accompanied by high authoritarianism, high intelligence is not so frequently accompanied by low authoritarianism.) Excluding the authoritarians from the "Bright" sample would probably have had two effects: the performance of the remaining "Brights" under group-centered conditions would have improved, and that of the "Brights" under leader-centered conditions would have deteriorated. In the industrial situation, both the individual and management could profit from a more comfortable "fit" of employees to their tasks.

Task Roles. Still another question to be considered in choosing a leadership style is "Who does what?"—that is, "What are the roles of the leaders and followers?" Though the very notion of leadership implies a set of roles different from those of followership, just what functions are covered by each set cannot be rigidly prescribed. Indeed, the distribution of functions is often the product of social consensus, and may vary even among work teams performing the same operation in the same organization.

Roles do, however, fall into three broad categories: roles peculiar to the superior, roles peculiar to the subordinate, and "mixed" roles, whose functions are performed by either or both. The general argument here, by way of preview, is that each of these three classes implies a different leadership style.

Evidence indicates that supervisors who are successful in influencing their subordinates' behavior in the desired directions—that is, supervisors who are leaders—work at sharpening these differences in roles. In a study by Kahn and Katz, supervisors of section gangs on a railroad and supervisors of clerical sections in an insurance company were asked how much of their time was usually spent in supervisory matters, and how much in other matters.[9] Their answers, shown in Table

---

[9] R. L. Kahn and D. Katz, "Leadership Practices in Relation to Productivity and Morale," in Cartwright and Zander, *op. cit.*, p. 615.

3, revealed that the supervisors with low-producing sections were two or three times more likely to perform the same duties as their men, or to perform the paperwork aspects of their jobs, than the supervisors with high-producing sections.

TABLE 3 TIME SPENT IN SUPERVISING
IN RELATION TO SECTION PRODUCTIVITY

Section Productivity	50% or More of Time Spent in Supervising %	Less Than 50% of Time Spent in Supervising %	Not Ascertained %	Total %
Insurance company				
High	75	17	8	100
Low	33	59	8	100
Railroad				
High	55	31	14	100
Low	25	61	14	100

These findings can be explained by a little common-sense reasoning: The behavior of the low-producing supervisors reflects either a lack of consensus about roles in their work groups or their own failure to respect an existing consensus. Whatever the case, conflict is likely, and must inevitably result in productivity losses.

Not only should the superior differentiate his functions from those of his subordinates, but he should, of course, perform certain *specific* functions. The amount of planning he does, for example, is directly related to the productivity of his section. Some interesting data on this score were obtained by asking foremen in a tractor factory whether they were able to plan their work ahead as much as they liked.[10] Though their answers, given in Table 4, suggest that the high-producing foremen actually did more planning than the low-producing fore-

TABLE 4 FOREMEN'S PERCEPTION OF
OPPORTUNITY FOR PLANNING IN
RELATION TO SECTION PRODUCTIVITY

Section Productivity* %	Foremen's Responses			
	Can Plan Ahead As Much as Needed %	Sometimes Have Trouble Planning Far Enough Ahead %	Can Seldom or Never Plan Ahead %	Total %
97-101	37	42	21	100
91-96	51	32	17	100
86-90	29	41	30	100
80-85	29	46	25	100
50-79	14	40	46	100

* Productivity is expressed as per cent of standard.

[10] *Ibid.*, p. 619.

men, it should be noted that the foremen were talking about the fulfillment of their planning expectations, not about how much planning they actually did or how much they thought necessary. It seems reasonable to assume that high-producing foremen were more aware of the importance of planning than the others. Thus their less-than-complete satisfaction may reflect high hopes rather than low accomplishment. If this is so, then they must have been even more active in planning their work than the table suggests.

Tables 3 and 4 deal with but two of the three categories of roles outlined above: roles peculiar to the subordinate and roles peculiar to the superior. There is, however, substantial evidence of the harm that superiors do in failing to respect the third category of roles: those whose performance is "mixed." The conflict generated by supervisory insensitivity to this third category is, of course, the subject of much of the human relations literature.

But what leadership styles do these three categories demand? As the provisional model in Table 5 shows, it seems likely that the su-

TABLE 5   A PROVISIONAL MODEL OF
ROLES AND APPROPRIATE LEADERSHIP STYLES

Category of Roles	Typical Function	Generally Appropriate Leadership Style
1. Roles peculiar to the superior	Setting general goals	Leader-centered
2. "Mixed" roles	Relocating machines on which individuals have worked for many years	Group-centered
3. Roles peculiar to the subordinate	Deciding how to use a tool	Free-rein

perior's roles are best handled with a leader-centered style, "mixed" roles with a group-centered style, and the subordinate's roles with a free-rein style. This does not, however, mean that the superior should surrender all his power over certain functions. On the contrary, every role assumes a set of guidelines for behavior, and the three leadership styles are merely different techniques for developing and enforcing them. When the guidelines are violated—whatever the leadership style under which they were developed—the supervisor is put into a decisive position.

If, for example, a worker insisted on tightening bolts with his teeth, his fellow workers and his supervisor would undoubtedly be scandalized and would agree that the worker's freedom in deciding how to perform this operation did not extend quite so far as all that. Group pressure—especially in a work unit operating under group-centered leadership—might encourage him to change his ways. But the supervisor would still be on the spot, formally and socially. He would have to supplement this pressure and perhaps take formal action. When violations of the behavioral guidelines are winked at, the supervisor invariably comes off a loser.

The supervisor who would be a leader, then, must have a deft touch. A useful criterion for determining when to step in can be found in the concept of "relevance," that is, in how the issue ranks in terms of its importance to, say, the employees, the organization as a whole, or the boss.

The more relevant an issue is to the group, experimental evidence shows, the more willing the group is to accept a relatively authoritarian way of dealing with it. Thus a leader who is strongly supported by his group may depend primarily on free-rein and group-centered styles, which encourage member involvement. When a relevant issue arises, however, he will exercise substantial influence, and, in fact, the group will expect him to do so. (The leader-centered superior with a work unit of authoritarians will, of course, hold a tight rein on most matters and therefore need not have such a delicate touch. But such situations are rare.)

An issue may, of course, be relevant to the formal organization but not to the group. If, for example, the work unit neglects its responsibilities to the company on the question of the level of production, the superior may have to use a leader-centered style despite the group's reluctance to have him do so. On less relevant matters, however, he would do well to balance it with a group-centered or free-rein style, which would reduce any tension generated by the leader-centered style. The "relevance" concept, in other words, supplements the model in Table 5, for an unanticipated relevant item may appear in any one of the three categories. The handling of such items will in the long run determine whether the formal head continues to function as a leader or loses his control over the group.

Group Characteristics.   Discussing the relevance of an issue for a work group implies that the group has developed certain common standards *of* its own and *on* its own. This characteristic of groups—the tendency to develop group norms and group goals—may be accompanied by fairly powerful mechanisms for imposing the group's will upon its members and upon the outside world. The group therefore plays a large part in determining the success of the various leadership styles. Group properties have, of course, been examined at length in the social science literature, and this author has sketched their broad implications for organization performance elsewhere.[11]

---

[11] R. T. Golembiewski, "The Small Group and Public Administration," *Public Administration Review*, XIX, No. 3 (1959), pp. 149–56.

One aspect worth considering here is the degree to which the group *as a group* accepts its formal head. If the group feels that its supervisor is not fulfilling its needs, it may find itself a more satisfactory leader from within its own ranks. This should not be a matter of indifference to industrial managers, for the emergence of an informal leader who acts as spokesman for a work unit is often associated with low productivity. In the Kahn and Katz study, workers in railroad section gangs were asked, "Is there some one man in the section who speaks up for the men when they want something?" Fewer than one in six respondents in the high-producing sections answered *yes*, while over half the respondents in the low-producing sections did so.[12]

Must the Leader Be Liked?

Such data as these, however, should not be taken as an endorsement of group-centered leadership. All three styles are equal to the task of winning informal acceptance for the formal head, though under different conditions. Moreover, the supervisor is not always well advised to try to raise his informal status to the level of his formal status. He must consider, among other things, the nature of his group's norms, which he will have to respect if he is to gain informal acceptance. If, as is by no means uncommon, the norms favor low output, his attempt to gain high informal status may force him to compromise his formal position.

The dangers of such an attempt are illustrated in a study of aerial bombardment crews by Adams.[13] Each member of each crew was ranked on several measures of status within the crew—formal rank, popularity, reputed flying ability, and so on. When the formal ranks of the members of any crew were quite similar to their ranks on the other measures, Adams found, the crew as a whole did well on "social performance" (harmony, intimacy, and the like). The crews that showed up best in these two respects, however, were not the best in "technical performance" (e.g., bombing accuracy). These findings seem reasonable. The popularity of the formal leaders of these crews was probably based in part upon their respect of a norm opposed to outstanding technical performance. Obviously, it did not make them particularly effective in their formal position. On the contrary, their closeness with their men helped the crews resist the demands of the "outside" organization.

A supervisor inheriting a work unit with a low-output norm faces a

---

[12] Kahn and Katz, *op. cit.*, p. 616.
[13] S. Adams, "Status Congruency as a Variable in Small Group Performance," *Social Forces*, XXXII, No. 1 (1953), pp. 16–22.

difficult task in choosing a style of leadership. If he employs a free-rein style, he will most likely succeed only in supporting the group norm. At the other extreme, the use of a leader-centered style may well harden the group's resistance to the formal organization. Even if the supervisor succeeds in breaking the group norm, he will most likely arouse antagonisms bound to affect the work process sooner or later.[14] (One major exception must be noted here: Groups of authoritarians, as has already been pointed out, will generally respond well to a leader-centered style. But this offers little practical consolation, given the apparent rarity of such groups.) Finally, it is the group-centered style, paradoxical though it may seem, that offers the best chance of success in changing a low-output norm, and group-centered leadership has actually proved useful in a number of instances. The reason for this seems to be that low output is a means by which the members of a work unit protect themselves against some perceived threat. A group-centered style often acts to make the group members feels less threatened and thus reduces their need for the low-output norm. But this is not inevitable.

In sum, every leadership style stands liable to failure in the attempt to develop and enforce a more acceptable output norm. If none of them works, the supervisor has no choice but to stop being a practicing psychologist and recommend that the unit be broken up.

Concluding Notes

The difficulties of choosing a leadership style, then, are great even if only a single condition is considered. From the two preceding paragraphs alone it should be clear that the question of how to lead any given work group is far more complex than is recognized by any existing generalizations, all of which call for a single leadership style. To compound this complexity, however, the four sets of conditions discussed in this article always appear in combination, so that some elements in a situation may favor one style while some elements favor another.

In fact, our increasing knowledge of the complexity of the question has outmoded the traditional designations of leadership styles. These designations, which suggest exclusive categories, ought to be modified so as to express the ways in which leadership styles continuously change in response to changing situations. The suggestions presented

---

[14] Such a situation is analyzed in R. T. Golembiewski, "O & M and the Small Group," *Public Administration Review*, XX, No. 4 (1960), pp. 205–12.

above outline the nature of the necessary changes. Needless to say, though these suggestions are consistent with the available research findings, they will need further verification before they can be considered rules for action.

Finally, it must be noted that the foregoing discussion has centered on the question "What are the conditions under which various leadership styles are most useful?" and has, in effect, neglected the question "What *should be* the dominant leadership style?" This neglect should not be taken as indicating that the question of value is unimportant. Rather, it recognizes that in practice the choice of a leadership style implies, and is preceded by, a value choice. In the field of leadership, as in every other, the use of empirical regularities must always be guided by considerations of what ought to be.

A Note on Van Zelst's "Sociometrically Selected Work Teams Increase Productivity"

Based on Raymond H. Van Zelst

Many managerially relevant techniques have come from the burgeoning social sciences. Consider "sociometry." J. L. Moreno defines sociometry as: "A process of classification which is calculated to bring individuals together who are capable of harmonious interpersonal relationships, and so create a social group which can function at the maximum efficiency and with a minimum of disruptive tendencies and processes."[1] As one of a growing number of scholars interested in the intricacies of interpersonal relations in small group situations, Raymond Van Zelst applied the sociometric technique to the assignment of members of work groups. Workers made choices of preferred work partners, and Van Zelst was able to test the hypotheses that such sociometrically selected groups would be superior in quantity and quality of output and that they would also maintain a higher group morale.[2]

The subjects in the Van Zelst study were carpenters and bricklayers in the Chicago area. All workers involved were skilled craftsmen who had worked together at least five months, and thus had some knowledge of each other's personalities and skills. Each worker was asked to make three choices for a perferred partner. Where possible, each worker was given first choice.

Criteria used for ascertaining the effectiveness of the sociometric procedure were labor costs, materials costs and personnel turnover over an eleven-month period. The results of the study appear in the table and appear to validate the major hypothesis of sociometric regrouping. We may briefly review these findings. Significant improvements were noted on all three critical factors, e.g., turnover, labor costs, and materials costs. Turnover was reduced to a point of insignificance; labor costs were not only lower than engineering estimates, but, more important, also were considerably less than comparable costs for a preexperimental group; and materials costs were lower at statistically significant levels than in the preexperimental group and in engineering estimates.

While reductions in turnover and labor cost are important findings

---

[1] Moreno, James L., *Who Shall Survive* (Washington: Nervous and Mental Disease Publishing Company, 1937), p. 2.
[2] Van Zelst, Raymond, "Sociometrically Selected Work Teams Increase Production," *Personnel Psychology* Vol. 5 (Autumn, 1952), pp. 175–87.

TABLE 1 COMPARATIVE CRITERIA PERFORMANCE DATA OF
GROUPS AND ENGINEERS' ESTIMATES OF
ANTICIPATED PERFORMANCE

Variable	Mean	S.D.	Critical Ratio
1. Turnover			3.69
(a) before experimental period	3.11	1.03	
(b) during experimental period	.27	.23	
2. Labor cost—per row of units			27.75
(a) engineers' estimate	37.20		
(b) before experimental period	36.66	.52	
(c) during experimental period	32.22	.67	
3. Materials Cost—per row of units			13.16
(a) engineers' estimate	33.50		
(b) before experimental period	33.00	.57	
(c) during experimental period	31.00	.56	

in the Van Zelst study, the reduction in materials costs is probably more significant. High morale in a small group environment almost inevitably reduces turnover rates. All other things being equal, high-morale workers do not leave their jobs. Production rates, measured on a quantitative base, also often can be expected to increase along a line paralleling an ascending morale curve. Such "improvements," however, are at times achieved only by sacrificing quality. Low concern with quality can be measured, in part at least, in terms of materials costs. High materials costs often can be traced to a feeling of frustration on the part of workers. Such attitudes reveal themselves in excess breakage, damage or loss of tools and equipment, sloppy workmanship and the like. Lowered materials costs, on the other hand, are primarily due to an involvement of the worker in the quality of the finished product.

Van Zelst did not inquire into such matters as incidence of grievances, absenteeism, worker-supervisory relations, competition between teams, union-management relations and other qualitative indices of improvements in the work environment. His data do, however, suggest the efficacy of further studies along the lines he has laid out.

A word of warning must be raised here about the danger of generalizing on the efficacy of buddy teams. Sociometric selection of co-workers need not yield attractive consequences under all conditions. For example, permitting workers to choose their coworkers could be expensive if such selections required extensive retraining of some workers. Additionally, the sociometric approach seems most applicable when subjects have had an opportunity to know each other, to gain a modicum of mutual trust and respect, and to define their own needs and aspirations.

Chapter 3

Managing by Hundreds:
Middle Management and Departmental Dynamics

The management of hundreds may be circumscribed as a specific area of concern, but only roughly. Thus we may boldly designate the management of hundreds as within the province of the middle manager, but only if we do not press for the meaning of "middle manager." Without pretending to cope with the designational issues involved, we settle here for describing a "middle manager" as one of a large and variegated class of managers whose field of activity lies between that of the first-line supervisor and of those realms presided over by managers who can truly be labelled "executives."

However tentative it is, the rough circumscription of the province of the middle manager permits several rough but useful distinctions. Executives formulate and monitor policy; middle management provides advice on which policy is based and develops the procedures and personnel capable of making that policy "go"; and first-level supervisors oversee the actual performance of work. In the federal service, more specifically, middle management may be bounded roughly by unit supervisors on the low side and by bureau officialdom on the high side. Typically, middle managers head organizational cadres of hundreds, although larger and smaller exceptions abound.

Middle managers may be either "line" or "staff," but the demands made upon them come from a similar mold. Importuning from above to follow "policy" and pleas from below to "be realistic" make the role of middle management difficult and often uninviting.

Some of the difficult and uninviting demands made upon the middle manager may be boldly set down. Consider his linking of policy and procedure. Thus the middle manager does not make policy. However he is often cast in the role of advisor concerning policy, and he almost always is responsible for implementing policy. Being an "organizational engineer" has its advantages, no doubt, but the role has many difficult aspects. For example, middle managers must tailor procedures and work flow to policies decided upon by others. These policies often are expressed in archaic terms, reflect subtle compromises and imply interests often indifferent about or opposed to the immediate interests of the middle manager. Yet he must take much of the "heat" from both "above" and "below" if the policies, when they are put into practice, sit poorly with operating personnel.

Other difficult and uninviting demands made of middle managers abound. For example, the middle manager does not usually directly supervise large numbers of employees, yet he is responsible in diverse ways for the oversight of hundreds of employees subdivided into immediate work units of tens or twenties under first-line supervisors. To a similar point, although the middle manager typically is not involved in collective bargaining with employee representatives, he frequently is the target of employee representatives when grievances occur or are imagined.

Problems also derive from the middle manager's commonly having risen to his level by demonstrating unusual competence in a narrow specialty. Unfortunately, the criterion of choice often is beside-the-point of the challenges facing the middle manager. The point cannot be done justice here, but we can outline a case. That is, the middle manager constantly faces problems that require a sophisticated knowledge about many fields, problems that require a particular ability to integrate knowledge in action. In other terms, it is middle management's challenge to integrate diverse "staff" contributions into the "line" effort.

The task of integrating line and staff contributions is a mammoth one, whatever a middle manager's qualifications. Thus two seasoned observers conclude that: "There is probably no other single area of management which in practice causes more difficulties, more friction, and more loss of time and effectiveness."[1] Their judgment is comparatively mild, in fact. In any case, their summary judgment seems appropriate. Consider only that "staff" typically is "not in the chain of command" and consequently may not be directly "responsible for performance." In addition, the "line" often views "staff" as "interfering outsiders" with little knowledge of and less sympathy for the "real go-go-go" of an organization. These few observations indicate the kinds of dross out of which the middle manager must make organizational gold.

---

[1] Harold Koontz and Cyril O'Donnell, *Principles of Management* (New York: McGraw-Hill, 1959), p. 135.

A summary may be hazarded. At his best, the middle manager can be a crucial and creative link between high levels and low. He can compress the data bubbling up to him in forms useful for upper-level decision making, and he can give practical life to executive philosophy and policies as they are applied "downward." At his worst, the middle manager can be a kind of well-paid cattle prod for top management, attempting to shock first-level supervisors into a frenzy of activity. As one middle manager complained: "We sit here all day pushing papers from top to bottom and back again. All the while we are left out of the actual operations at the bottom, and we don't take part in decisions at the top. We just push."[2]

Nor do these conflicting demands imply it all. The threat of imminent obsolescence also contributes to the great and probably growing discomfiture of the middle manager. At worst, the prophets of gloom maintain, electronic data processing (EDP) means the disappearance of vast numbers of middle management jobs. At best, others argue, the manager's power and status will be reduced drastically in our increasingly automated world. Neither alternative inspires the confidence of middle managers.[3]

This chapter, consequently, has dual emphases. It focuses on the organizational demands that will increasingly challenge the "new" middle manager, and it also reflects the demands long felt by the "old" middle manager.

Donald R. Shaul's "What's Ahead for Middle Management" looks directly at both the old demands and the new. His benchmarks for judging the probable changes in the job of the middle manager due to automation are these five aspects of the managerial job: planning, organizing, staffing, directing, and controlling. His conclusion, if anything, implies a new significance for middle management in an automated society. Shaul sees important changes in the middle manager's participation in control. Aside from that, he sees new demands being made on the middle manager while the old demands refuse to wither away. In contrast to being a threat, Shaul sees EDP as raising the status of the middle manager. New problems certainly will be created, and the middle manager's job will be more complex, but he will have a greatly increased volume of information to analyze, evaluate and apply. Moreover—since time-consuming clerical work and "guesstimates" that once were the hallmark of middle management can be made faster and better by machines—the middle manager will be in-

---

[2] Keith Davis, *Human Relations At Work* (New York: McGraw-Hill, 1962), p. 195.
[3] Herbert A. Simon, *The New Science of Management* (New York: Harper & Bros., 1960), for example, reflects both emphases.

creasingly free to concentrate on the nonroutine. The nonroutine substance that can receive attention may be suggested by this list: motivating, leading, training, coordinating and advising. The middle manager may assume many of the functions commonly considered to be in the province of executives.

To be sure, the issues which Shaul confronts are still in the complex processes of resolution. Consequently, no one can reasonably argue without reservations. Indeed, the most popular expressions[4] of the impact of automation on management challenge Shaul at almost all significant points. And little hard research exists, in any case. What direct research has been accumulated,[5] however, strongly suggests that Shaul's summary statement is a close approximation of managerial reality under the impact of automation.

Some tentativeness is in order about the specifics of the impact of automation on middle management, that is, but Shaul's argument cannot be taken lightly. In striking close to the sense of direct studies of applications of the new information technology, Shaul's argument implies profound managerial consequences. Even if Shaul is only more or less correct, for example, the middle manager's span of control will increase radically. Faced with the need to coordinate a multiplicity of specialized staff services, the middle manager must break through the numbers barrier of five or six that orthodox opinion has usually represented as the maximum number of subordinates that can be effectively supervised.

Gerald G. Fisch's "Stretching the Span of Management" provides great insight on an important theme. He argues not only that tomorrow's middle managers will be faced with an increased span of control, but he also maintains that the traditional notion has always been inappropriate. The traditional notion of a narrow span of control, Fisch argues, sinks or swims on the appropriateness of such assumptions as the following: that supervisors have similar personal qualifications; that managerial jobs are essentially homogeneous; and that all types of subordinates require the same kind of supervision. Students of management have long conceded these assumptions were fallacious, and Fisch builds on this agreement to develop the notion of a "span of management." He analyzes various factors that may affect a desirable span of management and concludes that as many as fifty middle man-

[4] *Ibid.* See also Harold J. Leavitt and Thomas L. Whisler, "Management In the 1980's," *Harvard Business Review,* Vol. 36 (November-December, 1958), pp. 13–27.

[5] Dominic G. Parisi, "The Impact of A Change In Information Technology on Management Organization Structure . . . ." (Unpublished Ph.D. Dissertation, Northwestern University, June 1966.)

agers might be supervised by one executive. Similarly, middle managers can have large numbers of individuals reporting to them. The implied role for middle management has dual components, greater freedom and greater responsibility.

The arguments of Fisch and Shaul require a new intensity and seriousness in approaching an old question: What type of person is required to fill positions in middle management? The required profile seems clear enough. The new middle manager must be well-versed in modern computational and behavioral techniques; he must be able to utilize machines to help solve problems related to people; and he must be able to converse meaningfully with staff personnel in their own tongues. The new middle manager, therefore, must be a "professional generalist." That is, he must be an expert in the integration of many fields and in the considerable substance of each. The new middle manager is sharply distinguished in the latter sense from the "amateur generalist" of broad classical training patterned on the British model. Fritz Morstein-Marx's warning of some years ago about the narrow specialist consequently has a contemporary immediacy. "But it is in the nature of the expert to cherish what he knows," Morstein-Marx noted, "to worship at the altar of his own knowledge, and to smite both ignorance and heresy with inspired zeal."[6]

That modern technology permits less and less room for the "narrow specialist" is implied by a wide range of evidence. For example, most available evidence suggests that the massive adoptions of the computer imply either greater decentralization or at least no significant reversal of the trend toward decentralization. The available evidence deals with the opinions of managers about what the computer implies for management[7] as well as with actual longish experiences with computer installations.[8] Directly, the overall trend to decentralization implies that more and more decisions will be made at lower levels of organization, thereby robbing the "narrow specialist" of places to hide. Lipstreu sees the computer as having such an impact on the supervisor's job, for example. He concludes that: "The supervisor will surely

---

[6] Fritz Morstein-Marx, "The Mind of the Career Man," *Public Administration Review*, Vol. 21 (Winter, 1961), pp. 8–15.

[7] Thus fewer than one in ten executives of some 200 major American corporations felt that electronic data processing would reverse the trend of the past several decades toward decentralization. "Will New Methods of Data Processing Affect Organization Planning?," *American Business*, Vol. 25 (November, 1955), pp. 9ff.

[8] Considering only firms having five to ten years of experience with computers, the Canadian Civil Service Commission found no modifications of organization structure like those predicted by observers who felt recentralization was an inevitable consequence of the introduction of modern data-processing tools. See "The Impact of A.D.P. On Organization Structure," *O & M Bulletin*, Vol. 17 (August, 1962), pp. 124–32.

regain some of his lost discretionary authority. Automaticity of work requires that he make decisions at the work level quickly, decisions which formerly were made at higher levels in the hierarchy. His work will increasingly resemble that of present middle management. . . ."[9] And compelling evidence suggests that the computer will require *better* middle managers and may also create a need for *more of* them.[10]

There will be be difficulties aplenty in recruiting the new middle managers, from all indications, whether we will only need to upgrade their skills or whether we will also have to increase their numbers. William C. Thomas, Jr. provides evidence suggesting the point in his "Generalist vs. Specialist," a study of career personnel in the public bureaucracies of New York City. Thomas found only limited mobility across departmental lines at the lower bureaucratic levels, one proving ground for the professional generalist, but even this puny well runs dry as one rises through middle levels of management. Thomas paints a picture of narrow specialization as the dominant career, of the individual becoming habituated to the ways of one department, of the individual developing vested interests in that department, and of the individual opposing any efforts to increase interdepartmental mobility for himself or for others. It is in such terms that Thomas explains the rejection of a program aimed at permitting the "lateral entry" of college graduates as municipal interns in New York City. A similar explanation applies to failures on the federal level to develop a "senior civil service."[11]

The prospects for providing the "new" middle managers are not uniformly dismal, of course. The burgeoning graduate schools of administration and management on the business side reflect an aggressive effort to meet the growing demand for "professional middle managers." And the increasing resort to a wide variety of executive development experiences also reflects a general desire to impart appropriate skills and attitudes to those already in business and government organizations. However, it is still a matter of running fast enough to stand still.

There also are glimmers of hope that structural rearrangements can help save organizations that require generalists from molding specialists. Harry R. Knudson's "Enter the Personnel Generalist" illustrates the

[9] Otis Lipstreu, "Organizational Implications of Automation," *Journal of the Academy of Management*, Vol. 3 (August, 1960), p. 123. See also Otis Lipstreu and Kenneth A. Reed, "A New Look at the Organizational Implications of Automation," *Journal of the Academy of Management*, Vol. 8 (March, 1965), pp. 24–31.

[10] John F. Burlingame, "Information Technology and Decentralization," *Harvard Business Review*, Vol. 38 (Nov.-Dec., 1961), pp. 121–26.

[11] Paul Van Riper, "The Senior Civil Service and the Career System," *Public Administration Review*, Vol. 18 (Summer, 1958), pp. 192–200.

possible. On the basis of experience in Raytheon Laboratories, Knudson agrees with Thomas that the liabilities of the specialist commonly outweigh his advantages. Knudson sees the specialist as remote from the actual work, and he sees him as having insufficient involvement in the complex lateral negotiations concerning goods and services that characterize the environment of today's middle manager. Moreover, Knudson describes actual organizational arrangements that permit cultivating the generalist. Knudson's contribution is particularly useful because he deals primarily with line-staff relations which increasingly constitute a major tension point for middle managers.

One particular disadvantage of the specialist is his narrow preoccupation with hierarchical relations. Here organizational history decidedly walks—if indeed it is not running—away from the specialist. The new middle manager must be sensitive to vertical relations, but lateral or horizontal relations are increasingly relevant for him. In modern organizations the manager rarely controls all of the resources necessary to carry out his organizational activities. He must, therefore, engage in a constantly changing set of relations with superiors and subordinates, staff personnel, and his own peers in order to get the goods and services he needs.

Leonard R. Sayles's "Lateral Relations in Work" provides insight into the "horizontal" dimensions of the managerial job and at their implications for managerial behavior. His argument may be illustrated briefly. For example, Sayles distinguishes three types of lateral relations. "Trading relations" comprise those processes by which the terms of future relations are established. Here the manager is a vendor or a customer in a selling situation with another manager, and each side bargains for gain. "Work-flow relations" involve activities that must be performed by different individuals or groups in a relatively fixed sequence. Failure to meet deadlines in such relations can cause a total breakdown. "Service relations" often are significant in determining whether deadlines are met, referring as they do to various supporting activities that from time to time are crucial to work-flow relations. Service relations consequently imply the maximum potential for intraorganizational conflict. Service relations imply these and other sources of conflict: they lack the regularity of work-flow relations; they are more likely to carry incompatible demands; and they encourage temporary alliances between organizational units based on reciprocity.

Sayles's piece implies the great and growing importance of line-staff integration in lateral relations. All of Sayles's types of lateral relations intimately (if differentially) involve staff activities, thus underscoring their importance for the middle manager. Unfortunately, the traditional notion of "staff" is rooted in a concern with vertical relations only. That is, "staff" is defined residually in the traditional concept as "outside the line of command," "advisory only" or "as thinking rather than acting." By implication, in the traditional view, vertical relations are sufficient to define the role of staff. As Sayles shows, the orthodox view is myopic.[12] For example, staff officials will be deeply involved in service relations which (as Sayles shows) have very significant lateral components that escape the vertical chain of command.

We cannot avoid the challenge to management raised by lateral relations. Our approach has two orientations. First, we can seek some help in meeting the challenge from the previously mentioned articles. Great optimism is not in order. Thus Knudson does describe one approach to line-staff relations that promises to ease the difficulties of managing lateral relations in organizations. That is, Raytheon's experiment with the "personnel generalist" is an attempt to cope with the difficulties of lateral relations traceable to subspecialization of staff services. But the negatives have it, on balance. Basically, the successful middle manager in a line or staff unit must negotiate the complex crosscurrents of the various kinds of lateral relations and he must initiate trading relations before crises and stoppages occur. Training and long indoctrination in a narrow specialty are poor preparations for these freewheeling dynamics, however. These data highlight the disadvantages of the career patterns sketched by Thomas. Such career patterns do not contribute to a pool of Knudson's "generalists."

Second, we will seek aid in managing lateral relations in two final selections. The two pieces come from the same mold. Both selections deal with alternative models for organizing work. One deals with two generalized comparative models, and the second selection focuses on two alternative models for line-staff relations. But the two pieces imply similar conclusions. Thus traditional notions about organizing work are poorly adapted to the challenge of usefully managing lateral relations in organizations. In addition both selections outline alternative models and sketch their probable consequences.

The two concluding selections of this chapter help in managing lateral relations in another sense. Directly, they reflect a common rationale. Thus mere critical carping provides no answer to the difficulties of managing lateral relations in organizations. Structural redesign alone can accomplish the job. And structural redesign, in turn, depends upon subtle but significant changes in the attitudes and concepts about organizing held by both managers and the managed in public and business organizations. The two selections aim at just such attitudinal and conceptual changes.

---

[12] See also Robert H. Guest, *Organizational Change: The Effect of Successful Leadership* (Homewood, Ill.: Irwin-Dorsey, 1962), esp. pp. 9–81.

Let us introduce the general alternative models first. Directly, orthodox theory about organizing provides an ill-equipped ballpark for playing out the complex dynamics of lateral relations. Similarly, that theory is ill-suited for the training of generalists. Innovation in ways of thinking about organization is necessary to improve matters and this is the dominant theme of Robert T. Golembiewski in his "Civil Service and Managing Work," which emphasizes lower and middle levels of management. In sum, the original goals of our public personnel systems have worked themselves out to inhibit effective management. No significant modifications are necessary to apply the argument to business and industry. Particular difficulties derive from the fact that most public agencies, like business organizations, are organized in terms of functions or processes. Departmentation around functions or processes is prescribed by scientific management dogma, but so much the worse for the dogma. Such departmentation invariably results in a limited span of control, an unwieldly "managerial entity," and diminished managerial control over the work environment. Golembiewski sketches the senses in which product-oriented structure removes many blocks to "effective management," roughly defined as high productivity and high participant satisfaction. The article also details structural arrangements and managerial techniques necessary to develop generalists at relatively low levels of organizations, and thus it directly helps meet the new demands facing the middle manager.

The unorthodox model for organizing developed in Golembiewski's paper not only facilitates the management of hundreds, be it noted. The senses in which that model eases the problems of managing tens and twenties, for example, may be sketched briefly. Recall Roethlisberger's conclusion that top management must shoulder the responsibility for overloading the inherently difficult relations of direct supervision without adding to the stature of the supervisory position. This reflects the grip of the orthodox theory of organization, which implies that top management's control can be increased only by despoiling the supervisory job. The supervisor's job is increasingly narrowed, for example, as management respects the "principle of specialization" and spins off more and more activities to "staff" units which dilute the supervisor's control over the work environment. Thus the first-level supervisor usually is "responsible for production." But significant aspects of hiring, firing, rewarding and punishing typically are influenced if not directly controlled by such staff units as Personnel. The unorthodox model provides one avenue of escape from such dreary consequences of the traditional pattern for organizing work. The discussion of enhanced supervisory "power" under the unorthodox model, for example, illustrates the values of such escape.

Similarly, the unorthodox model for organizing also facilitates the management of ones and twos in complex ways. For example, "job enlargement" and "job rotation" are more simply administered under that model. The full argument cannot be detailed here, but economical illustration should suggest the advantages of the unorthodox model in moderating difficulties involved in trying to meet the needs of individuals at work. Thus employees in an "unorthodox" organization need not experience the psychological and sociological problems of switching their immediate unit of organization to participate in a program of job rotation. For that unit of organization contains multiple specialties. In contrast, the traditional theory of organization departmentizes around processes at lower levels. A program of job rotation thus is likely to require movement between immediate units of organization.

The advantages of the unorthodox model for organizing work seem substantial. Illustratively, independent research demonstrates the common attractive payoffs in productivity and satisfaction of such techniques as job rotation and job enlargement.[13] Some of the readings above provide us with the theory capable of explaining why individuals in organizations tend to respond positively to such techniques. For example, as jobs are enlarged most individuals will experience an enhanced opportunity to move toward greater personal growth along the dimensions suggested by Argyris. Obviously, to illustrate the point, the individual can utilize a wider range of his capabilities on an enlarged job than on a routine job. The positive effects of such growth possibilities appear even when the job enlargement seems minor. This suggests the enormous latent energies that can be unleashed when individuals are allowed the opportunity to move along the dimensions of personal growth.[14] For example, such positive effects were striking in comparisons of the behaviors of operators performing ten simple mechanical operations with the behaviors of operators performing five.

These details of the complex mutual advantages of the unorthodox model for organizing at the several levels of organization might be

---

[13] See particularly on job enlargement, Chris Argyris *Personality and Organization* (New York: Harper and Bros., 1957), pp. 177–187. Interesting insights into job rotation are provided by James R. Norris, "Human Aspects of Management," *Journal of Business,* Vol. 29 (October, 1956), pp. 268–73.

[14] Impressive substantiation of the positive effects of even minor enlargement of jobs is presented by Charles Walker and Robert H. Guest, *Man On the Assembly Line* (Cambridge, Mass.: Harvard University Press, 1952), esp. p. 54. The positive results of a more ambitious enlargement of supervisory jobs are detailed in J. Douglas Elliott, "Increasing Office Productivity Through Job Enlargement," *Office Management Series,* No. 134 (New York: American Management Association, 1953) and Dause L. Bibby, "An Enlargement of the Job of the Worked," in *Proceedings of the 17th Conference Texas Personnel and Management Association* (Austin, Texas: University of Texas, 1955).

elaborated into very long descriptive chains, but our goal is more to outline than detail. Specifically, we seek to suggest the variegated analysis that is possible and we seek to motivate the reader to accept the full challenge. And what we have done thus far should economically serve to meet our interests. Hence we leave the further details of developing such interrelations—as well as the joy of the necessary discoveries—to the reader.

Let us not exaggerate our case in the name of brevity, however. Of course, job enlargement does not always have positive consequences. Indeed, we now know quite a bit about the conditions under which job enlargement will "work" and those under which it has not,[15] but our argument here is more gross. If managers do bet—and they must— the probabilities are that job enlargement will prove useful.

Again our argument turns into itself. Job enlargement will require new managerial attention to training and development, and this necessity suggests one important component of what the new job of the middle manager may become.

Much the same story of the inadequacy of traditional concepts in coping with lateral relations can be told at the more specific level of line-staff relations. Robert T. Golembiewski provides the details in his "A New 'Staff' Model: A Synthesis From Behavioral Research." Golembiewski's critical argument has two foci, one on empirical regularities and another on values. Broadly, applications of the NII model of line-staff relations—the orthodox model—either create or aggravate difficulties in lateral relations between line and staff units. The selection stresses nine sources of tension between line and staff. In each case, the NII model comes off poorly in providing a structural framework within which these tensions can be reduced or eliminated.[16] Broadly also, Golembiewski illustrates the senses in which the NII model violates a set of values widely accepted in western societies. In short, the NII model is a loser on *the* two significant counts.

"A New 'Staff' Model" attempts to go beyond empirical and value criticism, moreover. That is, two sets of boundary conditions for a more empirically useful and more normatively acceptable model of line-staff relations are detailed. One set stresses empirical boundary-conditions for structural redesign; the second outlines values which any suitable structural arrangement should respect. In addition, the skeletal structure meeting these two sets of conditions is sketched and analyzed. The new concept—the Colleague model—implies substantial

---

[15] See Robert T. Golembiewski, *Men, Management, and Morality* (New York: McGraw-Hill, 1965), pp. 128–50.

[16] The model is elaborated in Robert T. Golembiewski, *Organizing Men and Power: Patterns of Behavior and Line-Staff Models* (Chicago: Rand McNally, 1967).

advantages in helping work through favorable lateral relations between line and staff. Indeed, the basic motivation of the Colleague model is to organize around flows of work. That is, the Colleague model's thrust is "horizontal." The NII model reflects a vertical bias, in contrast.

At this stage of the game, the Colleague model must be regarded only as a very promising structural alternative, contingent on extensive future research and experience. Relevant experience and research permits some confidence that the Colleague model is on the right track, however.[17]

---

[17] Robert T. Golembiewski, "Personality and Organization Structure: Staff Models and Behavioral Patterns," *Journal of the Academy of Management*, Vol. 9 (September, 1966), pp. 217–32.

What's Really Ahead for Middle Management*

Donald R. Shaul

During the past few years, thousands of hard-working middle managers have looked on with rising uneasiness while theoreticians of all hues have been cheerfully debating what effects the inexorable spread of electronic data processing will have on their future. Has the death knell sounded for middle management? A good many authorities have intimated as much, forecasting that, with the widespread reorganization necessitated by EDP, a vast number of middle-management jobs will either vanish altogether or become so structured that for all practical purposes their incumbents will become mere supervisors, denuded of their decision-making powers and stripped of their status.

Moreover, say these prophets of doom, much of the innovating and planning now being done by middle managers will be taken away from them by top management. The planning of work activities will become programed. The middle managers who remain will be highly specialized, adept at systems analysis, operations research, model building, and advanced EDP techniques. For the most part, their control function will be taken over by the computer itself.

The proponents of this school of thought have not had it all their own way, however. At the opposite extreme there are some authorities who maintain that, as a result of EDP, either more middle managers will be needed than ever or, at worst, that there will be a minimal change in the demand for them. These writers say that middle managers will have to be more able, that their decisions will become more important and far-reaching, and that their status will be enhanced. Between these two opposing viewpoints are the inevitable fence-straddlers, who have hypothesized that either side may be right in the long run.

There has been argument also over what effect the new technology will have on the locus of authority and decision making in the enterprise. One group believes that EDP must lead to the centralization of authority as well as of activities, and that the EDP elite will eventually make most of the decisions. Another holds that EDP should be used to assist individual managers at all levels to make better decisions and hence should remain decentralized.

Nearly all those who have written on the subject agree, though, on one thing: EDP will relieve middle managers of a vast amount of de-

* Reprinted with permission of author and publisher from *Personnel*, Vol. 41 (November-December, 1964), pp. 8–16.

tailed administrative work, since all decisions that do not require the exercise of individual judgment will be made by the system.

How do these varying speculations square with actual experience? With the aim of throwing some light on this question, I recently interviewed 53 middle managers and 14 top managers in eight companies, all of which had had at least two years' operating experience with an EDP system. The companies studied included representatives of both manufacturing and service industries—aircraft, petroleum, electronics (solely government work), radio and TV, banking, life insurance, finance, and telephone. All the managers interviewed had had several years' service with their companies.[2]

The interviews, which were conducted with the aid of a written questionnaire, focused on the effects of EDP on these aspects of the middle manager's job: (1) the nature and scope of his functions; (2) his decision-making authority; and (3) his status. Before I go on to discuss my findings in detail, I may perhaps summarize their general tenor by saying that the prophesied demise of the middle manager, like the reported death of Mark Twain, seems to have been greatly exaggerated.

Changes in Management Functions

To assess what effect EDP had had on the nature of the middle manager's job, I took as my yardstick the traditional executive functions—planning, organizing, staffing, directing, and controlling. Let's see now what changes, if any, my interviewees reported under each of these heads:

Planning. Sixty per cent of the managers interviewed said they work longer on planning activities now than they did before the EDP system was installed. This, they said, was due in the main to three reasons: (1) the increased volume and reliability of the data received; (2) the speed-up in the flow of information; and (3) the demands of their superiors for more detailed analyses, as well as for greater output from the system. All these pressures are compelling managers to plan more intensively and make more decisions than they used to before EDP came on the scene.

---

[2] For the purposes of this study, the term "middle manager" included any manager above the level of first-line supervisor and below the level of division manager or the equivalent. The term "EDP" was defined as a system that (1) makes an original entry or records data in an electronically or mechanically usable form, (2) communicates and processes these data automatically, and (3) integrates or coordinates all related data processing activities and procedures to provide swift and orderly information for managerial planning and control.

Some typical comments on this score:

> Things are moving much faster today. Our decisions must be made more quickly and yet our plans have to take into account the increased complexity of interrelationships involved in the information system.

> The computer is performing calculations that formerly were impossible, and I now use this information in formulating my plans.

> Just being an integral part of an information circuit forces us to plan more carefully as well as to make decisions more quickly.

Organizing. EDP seems to have had little effect on this function. Nearly all the managers reported that there had been practically no change in their organizing activities.

Staffing. Somewhat more change was noted here. EDP requires higher-caliber managers to fill the same positions now, my respondents said. Hence, additional time is needed to train people for them. Nearly everyone agreed that all managers should be familiar with the capabilities and limitations of their own company's EDP system.

Directing. A high percentage of the managers I talked with agreed that they now have to spend more time on directing the work of their departments. Several reasons were advanced for this change: (1) When a department is an integral part of an information circuit, the manager must have a thorough knowledge of its operations; (2) more complex relationships with interdependent departments have arisen because of the overriding influence of the EDP system; (3) there is more information to digest and use; (4) the addition of new activities has enlarged the manager's span of control; and (5) the increased reliance on EDP now makes it necessary for the manager to spend more time with his subordinates to insure that they are aware of the relationships involved in the new system, as well as what it can— and cannot—do.

As a result, the installation of an EDP system tends to expand the middle manager's personal contacts with his subordinate managers. As a rule, though, his contacts with his superiors at the top echelons are no more frequent than they used to be. Apparently, having discovered the wealth of information the computer can provide, top managers are now demanding more analytical studies, most of them in greater depth, than of old. They often ask, my respondents said, for information that has not hitherto been available, and demand to be supplied immediately with facts that actually take considerable time to extract from the tape files. Such requests usually entail more frequent consultations between the top-level middle manager and his subordinates, but do not require him to see his own boss more often than before.

Controlling. Approximately two-thirds of my interviewees agreed with the prediction that the computer will reduce the time managers need to spend on controlling. However, they rejected the notion that the middle-management ranks will be thinned as a result. In fact, they said, the computer has made it possible for managers to devote more time to their other (and previously neglected) functions. In general, the respondents felt that as more sophisticated techniques of computer usage were developed they would spend even less time controlling, because fewer exceptions requiring action would be brought to them for decisions. Thus, they would have more time for considering opportunities, because they would no longer be so preoccupied with solving problems. In any event, they said, human judgment would always have to make the final appraisal of the exceptions reported by computers. Moreover, they pointed out, the fact that computers were now helping in their control function did not relieve them of responsibility for the performance of their departments.

There was no evidence in these conversations substantiating the gloomy predictions that (1) the position of middle managers will become highly structured; (2) they will become mere specialists in computer techniques and operations; and (3) their job will take on the characteristics of straight leadership and supervision. It is true that the repetitive types of decisions, involving such matters as control of inventories, optimum shipping routes, product mix, credit checks, and maintaining quality-control standards, have been programed into the computer; but this accomplishment now permits managers to spend more time on important decisions—the decisions involving risk and uncertainty.

In fact, it appears that middle managers are being forced to go on making full use of their experience and judgment by the nature of the EDP system itself. In the first place, the increased volume of information forthcoming from the computer necessitates evaluation by experienced personnel if it is to be effectively used. Second, decisions are becoming increasingly complex because of the interdependency of relationships within the information system.

The effects of decisions on interdependent departments now have to be carefully weighed before action is taken. Managers are finding it increasingly necessary to confer with their peers on mutual problems—problems that involve the new information system as well as the departments themselves. As a result, *coordination*—the very essence of management—has become more vital than ever before to successful managerial performance.

In short, the experience of the managers I interviewed has not borne out the prediction that EDP would bring about basic changes in the nature of the middle-management job. No executive functions have been eliminated nor has the advent of the computer led to the creation of "functional" managers—one group for planning, another for organizing, and a third for control, for example. There has been a shift, though, in the amount of time middle managers spend on their individual functions. They now do less controlling and more planning, staffing, and directing. More time is available for motivating, leading, and training—functions the computer cannot handle—as well as for weighing new opportunities, and devising better work methods and better ways to provide service to customers or other departments.

Changes in Scope

Far from contracting the scope of the middle manager's job, EDP is expanding it, my respondents reported. A number of the managers I interviewed said that, on balance, more activities had been assigned to them since the system was installed. Many entirely new activities had been added, because the computer had made it possible to develop new services. Moreover, managers are now expected to make more thorough evaluations and to make more planning decisions because of the increased volume of information available to them.

Because middle managers are receiving more information—and more accurate information—faster than before, the expectation is that the quality of their decisions will improve. In some of the companies studied, an improvement in decision making has been noted, but this is not likely to become widespread for a long time to come. It will be many years before the EDP system will be available to middle managers seeking optimum solutions to simulation problems involving the use of different variables. The high investment in programed information, the heavy volume of work handled by the computers, and the higher priority of top management and staff work all preclude the use of the system at lower levels at the present time.

My respondents agreed with the prediction that EDP would increase the visibility and speed of business decisions and make it possible to "see" more in a shorter planning period. They also confirmed that a continuous and rapid feedback permits faster adjustment to new conditions. Plans can now be made for longer periods ahead; alternatively, more accurate forecasts are possible for the short run. Either way, the result is that middle managers are developing an increasing awareness of their responsibility to engage in planning decisions at their level, and they are making more planning decisions, not fewer, as some experts have prophesied.

Busy top managers, in fact, are finding the EDP system is an important aid in delegating decision making to their subordinates. From my interviewees' comments it seems evident that they will continue to do so.

Broader and Faster

Actually, then, EDP has made the middle manager's job more complex. Now, the manager must not only have some knowledge of the capabilities and limitations of the system itself; he must also be constantly coordinating his activities with those of other departments. Moreover, he is expected to react faster, make decisions more quickly (and take more facts into account in making them), and make more elaborate plans.

Almost half the middle managers I interviewed thought that EDP had definitely helped them to make better decisions. The rest said that they had not noticed any change. So far as planning was concerned, it was generally agreed that the system now enables detailed forecasts to be made for considerably longer periods ahead. On the other hand, because more accurate information is now available much faster than before, many operational activities do not have to be planned so far in advance.

Among the top managers interviewed, there was unanimous agreement that EDP itself does not create positions whose incumbents perform both line and staff functions; it has no effect on the number of middle managers rotated between line and staff positions; and it is not used to concentrate authority in top managers. However, this group was divided about the effect EDP had on rotating line and staff positions. Some felt that staff personnel would make the transition more easily because they had had the opportunity to familiarize themselves with all the ramifications of the information system, whereas line managers had a restricted viewpoint—the nature of their jobs and the vastly increased demands on their time did not permit them to become so familiar with the system's over-all operations. Other top managers took the view, however, that line managers are being kept sufficiently well informed of the operations and interrelations of the EDP system to make the transfer to a staff position without difficulty.

Changes in Authority

There has been a slight drift away from rigid enforcement of the rules governing middle managers' decision-making authority, my study shows. The computer has aided in this change by being instrumental in providing better controls. As superior managers gain confidence in their subordinates they sometimes grant approval, *ex post facto*, for actions taken during their absence. For example, one division manager now gives tacit consent to certain of his subordinates to exceed expenditure limits while he is away. On his return, he approves the transactions. But, in general, there has not been any change in the number of rules imposed upon middle managers.

Changes in the authority delegated to middle managers coincide with the increase or decrease in the number of activities assigned to departments, according to my respondents. The considerable reduction in the decision-making authority granted to middle managers predicted by some experts has not taken place. Apparently, the EDP system itself has had no significant influence upon the decision-making authority of middle managers.

In fact, half the managers studied are now using more of their experience and judgment in rendering decisions, while the rest are using at least as much as before. A number of reasons were offered in explanation of the greater demands on experience and judgment. There is more information now, and many new classifications to analyze; the manager must understand the EDP system and all interrelated activities to perform his job properly; new ways to use the information provided by the system are constantly being sought; decisions must be made faster and more often; and problems now have to be probed more deeply.

There was general agreement that middle managers are not sharing their decisions with top managers or staff specialists, nor are they being denied the opportunity to continue making decisions on subjects under their control. While corporate policies are being improved and better information is available to all levels of management much more quickly, the operating decisions continue to be made at the lowest level at which sound judgment, based on the available facts, can be brought to bear on the problem.

Changes in Status

My respondents were also unanimously of the opinion that, contrary to many predictions, the status of middle managers had not been lowered since EDP came on the scene. In fact, they pointed to a number of reasons substantiating the belief that, rather, the middle manager's status has been raised: (1) His job is more complex; (2) he has a greatly increased volume of information to analyze in greater depth; (3) he is using more experience and judgment; and (4) EDP has either added to his activities or replaced some with more responsible functions.

Several of the top managers interviewed made these points:

> The middle manager's job is more complex today because he has more controls to adhere to daily—quality, budget, cost. In effect, a manager today must have at least a working knowledge of the EDP system and is handling a job that a superintendent was handling before.

> Middle-manager jobs are more complex because there are more things going on in our department and they are more elaborate than they used to be. We do more of the total procedure now, instead of a simple part of it. Timing is much more important and reactions must be faster. What used to be one department is now three departments.

> The administration of the system will require managers to have a thorough knowledge of its operations, so that they can be placed in spots where they can coordinate activities that are not related to each other in their daily operations, yet, being an integral part of the information system, must be supervised so that no action is taken that would be detrimental to broad company goals. A production line can have only one person making decisions that affect the administrative processes.

From the above findings it should be evident that while EDP has undoubtedly eliminated a vast amount of monotonous, detailed administrative work, there has been no accompanying reduction in the need for middle managers. Indeed, some of the companies studied are now finding it necessary to establish new criteria for determining the salaries of middle managers instead of compensating them on the basis of the number of subordinates assigned to them. Where there have been reductions in the number of workers, these have usually been compensated for by new activities' being assigned to existing departments, or by the creation of new departments. Thus, the centralization of *activities* has not been accompanied by the elimination of managerial positions. On the contrary, the reorganization necessitated by the installation of EDP, and the new types of activities, coupled with the expansion of existing operations, all of which the system has made possible, have resulted in the addition of over 50 middle-management positions in the companies studied.

Moreover, in many of these companies the top managers are finding that they require more specialists. Several told me that the volume of data now being received may well require additional managerial personnel with the requisite experience to interpret it properly. One manager said he thought that in his company several supervisors and a few lower-echelon middle managers would eventually be eliminated; but he also visualized that the upper-echelon middle managers would require experienced staff personnel of their own.

All in all, then, instead of middle managers' facing a drastic reduction in their decision-making power and a lowering of their status, my survey indicates that this vital component of the management hierarchy is recognized as being more important than ever. Certainly, overall, no serious threat to middle managers seems to be posed by EDP. Their real menace is still the traditional causes of business failure, whether stemming from poor performance within the enterprise, from technological changes such as automation, or from external forces over which the company has little or no control.

Stretching the Span of Management[*]

Gerald G. Fisch

Some years ago, I attacked the line-staff concept for being obsolete.[1] An abstract term borrowed from the military and fitting business organizational realities only in part, it had, nevertheless, become somewhat of a sacred cow that no one dared to push out of the way.

Business is full of similarly dubious concepts. Not the least important of these is the *span of control* concept. Ever since Lyndall F. Urwick enunciated the principle that "no superior can supervise directly the work of more than five or, at the most, six subordinates whose work interlocks,"[2] the span of control concept has been debated throughout the literature and in the boardrooms of American industry. Arguments about it range from those who believe that a limited span produces excessive red tape[3] to those who fear it imposes prohibitions on democratic participation.[4]

I am more concerned, myself, with what Urwick's widely quoted statement really means, since it seems to assume that:

• All "supervisors," from the chairman of the board to the foreman, are alike in personal qualifications.

• Their jobs are so similar that they can be generalized about in the same breath.

• All types of subordinates require the same type of leadership.

Clear thinking about span of control decisions is important, since such decisions determine the number of people reporting to each manager. If this number is too large, the organization will be inefficient from lack of direction; and if it is too small, it will be top-heavy, expensive to operate, and stifling to initiative. Indeed, each added layer of supervision increases organization costs well beyond just salaries, introducing further fringe benefits, office costs, facilities costs, and communications costs, and proving, in the bargain, to be a barrier to communication throughout the organization.

---

[*] Reprinted with permission of author and publisher from *Harvard Business Review*, Vol. 41, No. 5 (September-October, 1963), pp. 74–85.

[1] "Line-Staff Is Obsolete," by Gerald G. Fisch, HBR September-October 1961, p. 67.

[2] *Scientific Principles and Organization* (New York, American Management Association, Institute of Management Series No. 19, 1938), p. 8; see also "The Manager's Span of Control," HBR May-June 1956, p. 39.

[3] Herbert A. Simon, *Administrative Behavior* (New York, The Macmillan Company, 1947), pp. 26–28.

[4] Harold Koontz and Cyril O'Donnell, *Principles of Management* (New York, McGraw-Hill Book Company, Inc., 1955), p. 98.

More Flexibility

In this article, I am urging a fresh, less rigid, not so oversimplified approach to span of control decisions. In fact, I would like to make the first step in this direction by coining the term *span of management* (which I shall refer to as SOM) to replace span of control, with its inflexible, militaristic connotations.

As a second step, I would like to isolate some of the pitfalls that most discussions of SOM fall into, in the hope that, by so identifying the hazards, I can keep what I say from being subject to the same objections. Specifically:

⁋ Many scholars of business organization tend to discuss span of management in the abstract, as if the people concerned were not part of a company, but part of a psychological experiment in small-group behavior conducted in the laboratory. Span of management decisions cannot be made in a vacuum, for they influence not only the structure of an organization as it is coldly reflected on the organizational chart, but its ability to centralize or decentralize, to control product diversification, to communicate, to develop leaders, to attract and retain independent managerial types, and, finally, even to operate efficiently.

⁋ Other people tend to think that the limits on SOM are set by purely psychological factors rather than by other factors as well, factors that have more to do with the nature of the work done, the type of business, the products handled, the capabilities of the subordinates supervised, and so on.

⁋ Still others debate generalized formulas . (like "not more than six subordinates") about *the* proper SOM, operating under the assumption that their preferred span can be applied equally effectively to *all* levels in the company hierarchy. This is so blatantly questionable that some writers restrict themselves exclusively to studying the number of subordinates who report to a top executive, and then assume that top executives in all kinds of businesses, with many differing types of personalities and styles of management, can also be subsumed under the "proper" formula.

⁋ Finally, many writers rule out large spans of management because of a fear that since communication between the superior and each of his subordinates would be diluted, the manager might lose control over his subordinates' work. Arguing just the reverse, other writers point out that a small SOM tends to result in a tall, narrow pyramid organizationally, so that communication from the bottom up is seriously impaired, if not actually precluded.

Faced with this welter of confusion, what should managers do who are genuinely concerned about the patterns of delegation to be followed by their companies? I suggest that it is about time for us to become less academic in our discussions of span of management, and to go to work to see just what generalizations can be advanced for the executives who must make organizational decisions.

Nature of Work

To date, our thinking in the area of SOM has been hindered by the assumption that all management levels are alike. Once we start categorizing management into different levels, however, I realize that we will be oversimplifying—but it will obviously be *far* less of an oversimplification than that which assumes all levels are alike in duties, relationships, and responsibilities. So, for convenience of discussion, let us now divide the management hierarchy into four basic groups:
Super managers.
General managers.
Middle managers.
Supervisors.
Then let us look closely at the unique characteristics of each group and see if we can formulate some general principles about SOM that are more realistic than those which have been formulated so far. But before we do, let me admit that this division of management into neat groups is only *generally* valid. Obviously, men move from one category to the next (both up and down). And in reality business life and the people in it are never so static as they seem to be when they are discussed in print.

Super Managers

We find super managers at the top or very near the top of super corporations—super organizations. Super organizations are companies with sales of a billion dollars or more, which have highly complex product lines, and whose operations are worldwide in scope. Typical might be the United States Steel Company, E. I. du Pont de Nemours & Company, Unilever N.V., Imperial Chemical Industries, Ltd., General Motors Corporation, General Electric Company, Westinghouse Electric Company, and Standard Oil Company of New Jersey, to mention only a few. Other typical examples of super organizations would be the governments of major nations.

What especially distinguishes the super manager? Not necessarily characteristics of the superman type, but particularly the nature of the job he does. Direct *personal* leadership is not the major job characteristic, though it might be in time of crisis, and certainly *is* during policy-making sessions with key high-level subordinates. But in neither of these instances is the leadership truly continuing. In the SOM sense, the only leadership that matters is the direct, day-to-day, personal contact between a boss and his subordinates. This type of leadership the super manager does not supply; he may symbolize the company, make its members proud to be working for him, but this is not leadership in the SOM sense at all.

Actually, the really important characteristic of the super manager's job is that he tends to manage through key subordinates on a *go, no go* basis. Take, for example, a Canadian super manager I know:

> Among this man's holdings is a complex of 20 manufacturing companies plus assorted retail outlets. Suppose he discovers that his profits are off in some of these enterprises. Does he call separate conferences with the entire management group of the errant companies? Nothing so complicated.
>
> He simply calls in the president of each company and decides whether to "go" or "not go" with him. If he decides to go along, he might give him a time limit in which to get the company moving. Next, he might call in a consultant, advise him of the situation, and instruct him to locate the problem areas in the company and assist the president with the solution. Following this, the super manager might appoint a monitoring board made up of managers from some of his other companies to review the work of both the president and the consultant. The monitoring board might be told that, since no major moves will be made without its approval, he is holding its members responsible also for getting results.
>
> At this point, the super manager will walk away and leave the detail work (and the human interrelationships) to others. Six months later, he might check on the president, the consultant, and the monitoring board to determine how much progress has been made. If their statements concur that the financial picture should look better in a short while, the super manager might give the president three months. At the end of this time, the situation will either have improved, or he will decide *no go* and bring in a new president, dismiss the consultant, or shake up the monitoring board. At this level, he is not concerned with executive development.

Such an entrepreneur makes essentially one decision regarding the management of any of the companies which he controls: Does he have confidence in the chief executive officer, or does he not? If *no*, he removes him; if *yes*, he supports him. The thought of personally leading each of his managers by the hand through the details of his duties is quite untenable, because it is utterly impossible in terms of the super manager's time or inclination.

This same method of operation is used by the head of the very large corporation. I include the chairman of the board, the president, and certain senior vice presidents (sometimes, as I will discuss later under group management, all these officers may be regarded in function as one super manager). These men do not have the time to begin to develop key subordinates. Each such subordinate is appointed because he has developed to the point where he is fully capable of operating at a high degree of effectiveness with a minimum of direction.

Instead of continued, direct, personal leadership uniting the top management of large super enterprises, the prime organizing force is supplied by policies, traditions, and administrative procedures (in the case of large corporations), and by laws and control practices (in the case of government). All the human interrelations problems spelled out by such writers as Urwick and A. V. Graicunas[5] just do not apply here. In the way the super manager operates, he is not concerned with the interlocking, human relations problems of his subordinates. His essentially *go, no go* methods enable him usually to hold just one person responsible for performance that is measured in generalized form (such as that afforded by the profit and loss statement), not in day-to-day details.

But, if we were to make a generalization about how many subordinates a super manager can control, what would we say? The answer is clearly a great many more than 6! In my experience I have known super managers who have controlled as many as 100 subordinates, although I would, quite subjectively, feel that 50 is about the uppermost limit that is workable.

General Managers

This group includes the top management level in medium- to small-size companies, as well as managers of subunits of very large corporations. Here is where Urwick's strictures on span of control most nearly apply. At this level, management is not generally conducted on a *go, no go* basis; there is teaching of subordinates going on. It is in this general management group that intimate contact with people

[5] "Relationship in Organization," *Bulletin of the International Management Institute,* 1933, reprinted in Luther Gulick and Lyndall F. Urwick, editors, *Papers on the Science of Administration* (New York, Institute of Public Administration, 1937), p. 183.

is a key factor—perhaps the determining factor—in SOM. Personal leadership does dominate the situation at the general management level.

Consequently, the factors that limit SOM at this level usually include the personality of the top man, the personalities and capabilities of his subordinates, and certain practical business realities like the complexity of the product line, the number of key locations, and the like.

Even so, a larger SOM than that advocated by Urwick is not only possible today, at this management level, but is increasingly common. EXHIBIT IA indicates, as proof of the pudding, that an SOM of over 10 is not unusual in corporations with sales of $100 million or more. EXHIBIT IB shows that this likewise is true when companies are measured by the number of their employees. These exhibits also confirm what was said before about the SOM in super corporations. Notice how the SOM increases as company size (measured both by sales and by number of employees) goes up. What this trend indicates actually is that the larger the company, the greater is the likelihood of diversification; and the greater the degree of diversification, the wider the SOM.

While much of the literature holding that the SOM is limited by "interlocking personal relationships" does apply to the general management level, we find in actual companies SOMs that are much larger than the "classical" 6. What accounts for this fact?

For one thing, speed (the extent to which people and goods can be moved) has been multiplied many times. Travel and communication are more efficient today than they were in the 1930's and before. Telephone networks are now more extensive, effective, and accurate, and the cost of cells has been substantially reduced. Our reporting capabilities, because of computers and EDP, have meant that increasingly complex operations which are widely separated geographically can be reported on in one central location with relative speed. Thus, technology has decreased the amount of "bother" and the amount of time wasted in supervising subordinates and has facilitated decentralization (and a widened SOM).

Middle Managers

The middle management group is even more complex in terms of SOM. By definition, this group is usually less autonomous than is the general management group. Its operations are involved, moreover, in coordination with a multiplicity of specialized services and staff

Exhibit I Trends in SOM by company size

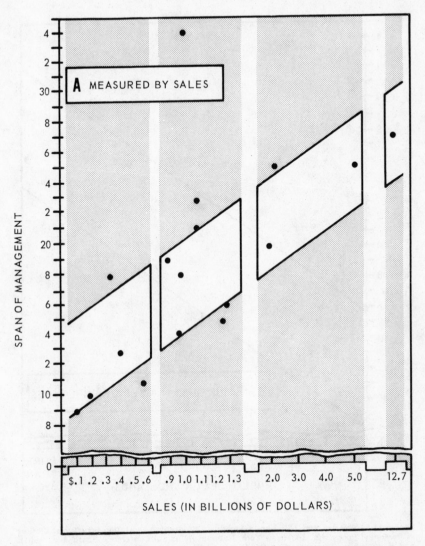

groups. Thus, the middle management group has the unique characteristic of being under extensive direction, while at the same time being
surrounded (in most instances) by a series of parallel (or support)
groups which can, depending on the circumstances, diffuse the direction of the basic line of authority, by doing some of the work
demanded.

In a large corporation, the marketing plans for a district might very
well be evolved and administered centrally, even though the district

Exhibit I Trends in SOM by company size

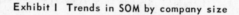

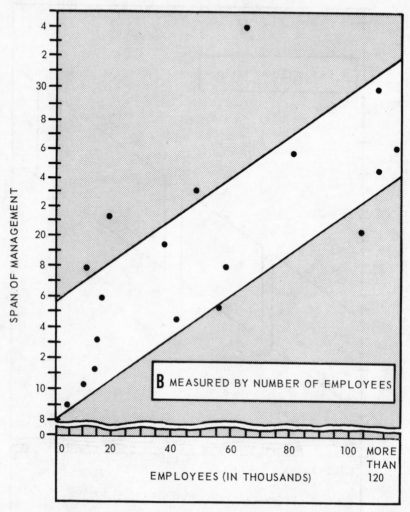

Source of Exhibit 1-A and 1-B: Harold Steiglitz, *Corporate Organization Structures, Studies in Personnel Policy*, No. 183 (New York, National Industrial Conference Board, Inc., 1961); and K. K. White, *Understanding the Company Organization Chart, AMA Research Study*, No. 56 (New York, American Management Association, 1963).

sales office was to be consulted. The work of the district sales office may be clearly circumscribed. For instance:

• The sales control system of the district sales office might be organized by a headquarters staff sales control group.

• Cars for the salesmen might be purchased under contract by the treasurer's department and might be turned in on a basis of regular company policy.

• Expense accounts and sales statistics might very well be processed by a corporate central information and data-processing center.

• Salesmen's compensation plans might be set by the central sales department.

• Even major accounts in the district might not be serviced directly from the district, but centrally, and classified as house accounts.

• The training of salesmen might be handled by a central training group.

• Finally, the warehouse which supplies the district might come under the general manager of distribution; while coordination might be required between this warehouse, the factory, and the district office.

The conditions under which we must determine the appropriate SOM in a situation such as this surely is in no sense parallel to those surrounding the super management or the general management groups and is indeed a distinct situation which calls for special treatment. For economy of presentation, let us defer our discussion of methods of determining the appropriate SOM for the middle management group until we look at the final management group.

Supervisors

The first line supervisors present a new situation. The people being supervised operate at the bottom of the organizational hierarchy, far below their superiors. Here we are dealing with unionized labor—with armies of clerical workers whose work is very carefully circumscribed, either by trade classifications or by job evaluation systems. So, too, the supervisor's work is less complex. Even the hiring of these workers may not be the prerogative of the supervisor, but that of the union hiring hall; or hiring may have to be done on the basis of a particular labor contract. The conditions of work are negotiated by the industrial relations department, not by the supervisor. Many of the problems of this class of workers may well be handled by the company's personnel department. Thus, the circumstances which determine the appropriate SOM for this group are again quite unique, as they are in the previous groups.

The "Proper" SOM?

In determining the SOM for the middle managers and supervisors, we can apply no hard and fast rules. Each company presents a unique situation in terms of the appropriate SOM. Each boss-subordinate group requires individual analysis to determine the optimum span.

But how does one go about determining, if not an optimum span, a reasonable one? Only by assessing three factors:

The business realities—How diverse functionally, operationally, and geographically are the company's operations?

The consistency and effectiveness of the management system—How effective is company planning and control? How free are managers and supervisors to delegate? How much information is at their disposal? How satisfactory is the remuneration structure?

The human realities—What are the capacities, the experience, and the personal characteristics of managers, supervisors, and each level of subordinates?

It should be obvious also that the maximum span of management under this formula can only be attained under conditions of almost ideal manning in a company which has a highly effective management system. The practical span can be determined in each situation after—

. . . a hard, accurate personnel assessment;

. . . a sincere attempt to make practical improvements in planning and control effectiveness;

. . . a long-range look at benefits that might arise from greater decentralization of functions or operations.

But while such a determination is the only way to achieve the best SOM answers for a particular company, are there no general observations about maximum SOMs for the middle management and supervisory levels? Once again the maximums that I give are based on my observations in the field and not on psychological or mathematical speculations. What I have seen in business leads me to state that the maximum SOM for middle management might well be 50, and for supervisory personnel as large as 100.

What about the limitation on SOM imposed by the interlocking of personal relationships? Perhaps these relationships are not so "interlocking" at the middle management and supervisory levels. At any rate, quite frequently, we see middle managers and supervisors in offices and plants who exercise effective control directly over many, many more subordinates than the classical 6.

As Exhibit II shows, the trick is to strike a balance between the economies afforded by the largest SOM possible and the cost of the necessary support activities as the SOM expands. In the case of the middle management and the supervisory levels, these economic factors can be significant. If a large corporation, because of some outmoded notions as to the benefits of a small SOM, is supporting an extra level of middle management or supervision, the cost is likely to be mea-

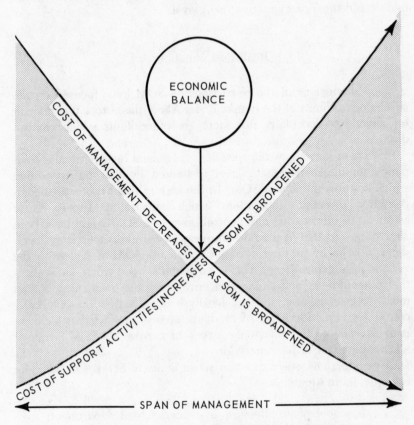

Exhibit II Striking an economic balance between SOM and cost of support activities

sured yearly in millions of dollars. And salaries, space costs, telephone charges, fringe benefits, and extra personnel to service this staff will not be the only elements involved. What is needed to keep the levels of management at a minimum? To do this means that the SOM for existing personnel must be as wide as possible. And the big dollar savings are actually attainable in the middle management and supervisory levels.

At the general management level (it is pointless, obviously, to discuss cutting down the super management level), great dollar savings will not be realized by eliminating one level—say, two vice presidents who earn $30,000 per year. This is not to deny, however, the possibility that better decisions resulting from this centralization of power might produce considerable savings. But these savings would not come as directly from enlarging the SOM as would enlargements made at the middle and supervisory management levels.

Realistic Limitations

Many discussions of the restrictions on SOM have focused on the psychological limits of the human brain. About this, I feel, it is difficult for anyone to speculate. But there are other limits which we can discuss.

EXHIBIT III shows how the span of management for a particular company's middle management level is limited by that one condition which requires the lowest SOM. In the case of this hypothetical company it is "diversity of operations" which limits the SOM to 10. As far as "effective information and control" goes, the SOM could have been 25. Notice also that at the middle management and supervisory levels diversification by product does not widen the SOM as it does at the general management level. This is easily understood when one realizes that the middle manager must concern himself more with details than must top management and can hardly be expected to be technically competent in a wide range of products. Hence, the fact that his company is widely diversified only serves to narrow his SOM, while it widens the SOM of his supervisors.

There are some other common sense limits to SOM. Consider, for example, these situations:

A school of architecture is divided into 2 departments (an architectural department and a planning department), each with a chairman. Therefore, the dean of the school has a predetermined SOM of 2. Another dean might have a similarly predetermined SOM of 10, if he had 10 chairmen reporting to him.

In other instances, the specialized nature of the work can reduce the SOM almost to zero. Imagine a famous physicist who is working in a highly advanced area of solid state research. It could be that, at some stage of his work, he would only be hampered by supervising the work of even one subordinate; yet the subordinate's work would be of great importance.

In other cases, the limiting factor might be something as mundane as the structure of a building. Take a situation where relatively small departments are mandatory merely because the rooms are small, rather than because of actual SOM considerations.

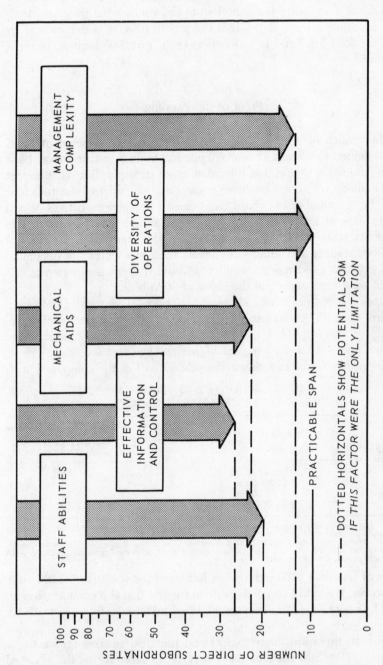

Exhibit III Determining greatest limiting factor on SOM

There are many possible types of limiting factors, but it is up to the individual managements themselves to determine what they are. Analysis by limits always shows that the practical SOM is determined by the "weakest link" and is widened as each "greatest" limiting factor is removed.

Proof of the Pudding

How much of a "straw man" has the "classical" concept of SOM (i.e., limited to 6) really been? All one has to do is to turn to any book on organization to find that it is taken quite seriously. But what impact has it made on actual business organizations? Perhaps one indicator may be the number of subordinates chosen by chief executives of real companies—at least this will give us some insight into the actual state of affairs at the super manager and general manager levels. But for the middle manager and supervisory levels, there is a scarcity of documentary evidence, and readers will have to use their own experience as a check on the pertinence of the classical SOM of 6.

Since many companies allow the National Industrial Conference Board, Inc., the American Management Association and similar research groups to publish their organization charts, there is no shortage of raw material for studying the higher management levels.

Exhibit IV seems to indicate that almost half of the companies with

EXHIBIT IV   ADHERENCE TO "CLASSICAL" SOM
AT TOP MANAGEMENT LEVELS

Group	Size of corporation (in millions of dollars of sales)	Percentage of companies in this size group with presidents whose SOM is within 1 to 6
I	Under $100	46%
II	$100–$499	4
III	$500–$999	25
IV	$1,000 and over	29

Note: The figures are derived from a random sample of 100 diverse U.S. and Canadian companies in terms of products, services, and size.
Source: Harold Steiglitz, *Corporate Organization Structures*, Studies in Personnel Policy, No. 183, op. cit.; and K. K. White, *Understanding the Company Organization Chart*, AMA Research Study, No. 56, op. cit.

sales of less than $100 million are following the less-than-7 SOM rule. However, it would be questionable to suggest that if a company has an SOM of 6 or less, it is because of blind adherence to some textbook rule.

In fact, there are many logical and practical reasons for having a narrow SOM, and none of them may be as arbitrary as the classical 6 rule. A few simple examples will suffice:

• One president likes to be free of all day-to-day management duties except public relations. Thus, he has reporting to him only an executive assistant, an executive vice president, and a director of public relations. Consequently, he has an SOM of 3. Yet there has been no arbitrary rule applied here.

• In another situation there are only 3 divisions at the general management level. The company, since it is small, groups all central staff functions, with the exception of finance, under a vice president of administration. Thus, there is an SOM of 5, and still no arbitrary rule has been applied.

EXHIBIT V expands the research shown in EXHIBIT IV to suggest a

EXHIBIT V   SOM RANGES IN COMPANIES OF VARIOUS SIZES

SOM	Percentage of companies in each size group (in millions of dollars of sales) with indicated SOM			
	Under $100	$100–$499	$500–$999	$1,000 and over
Over 16	0	13%	15%	41%
13–16	0	22	2	16
7–12	54%	61	58	14
1– 6	46	4	25	29

Note: The figures are derived from a random sample of 100 diverse U.S. and Canadian companies in terms of products, services, and size.
Source: Harold Steiglitz, *Corporate Organization Structures, Studies in Personnel Policy,* No. 183, op. cit.; and K. K. White, *Understanding the Company Organization Chart,* AMA *Research Study, No. 56,* op. cit.

specific trend in support of the conclusions made in this article. Note that 57% of super corporations (i.e., with sales over $1 billion) employ an SOM of more than 12, and that 41% use an SOM of 16 or more. One company in this sample employed an SOM of 26. Conversely, as the size of the company decreases, the incidence of the super span (that is, a span over 16) decreases also. In companies with sales under $100 million, 100% had an SOM of less than 13.

Perhaps the most interesting group of companies falls into the $100- to $499-million size range in sales. This group, large enough to be strong, yet small enough and young enough to be virile and aggressive, requires both flexibility and the rapid development of able executives. Consequently, these corporations seem to delegate authority freely to as wide a span as possible. Thus, we see a fascinating phenomenon in that 96% of these companies use a span of control from the chief executive to the next level in excess of the classical 6.

But this trend seems to focus on company size as the determinant of SOM breadth. It is important that this not be misunderstood. Companies organize in diverse ways, depending on their type of business, their history, their location, their facilities, and many other factors including the personalities of the top executives. But the positive relationship between company size and size of SOM is easily explained. *The larger the company, the greater is the likelihood of diversification; and the greater the degree of diversification, the larger the size of the SOM.*

To see this more clearly, consider the organization charts shown in EXHIBITS VI-A and VI-B. Take E. I. du Pont de Nemours & Company, for example. Here the president has 12 industrial departments and 11 auxiliary departments reporting directly to him—or an SOM of 23. When a company is as diversified in as many products as is Du Pont, it is, in effect, in a number of different businesses. In this case, the president must operate as a super manager on a *go, no go* basis. He could not possibly supervise the work of subordinates directly in so many different product areas.

The greatest advantage of a narrow, centralized SOM is *control*. In the case of Du Pont, the company achieves control by traditional, clearly established policies under which each general manager operates. Such policies, as EXHIBIT VI-A depicts, are established and enforced by four high-level committees. Scholars who worry about the loss of communication resulting from a wide SOM seem to fail to recognize that communication is not only *people talking to people;* it is every man knowing what is expected of him and knowing how the system operates. Because of vast product diversification, Du Pont has turned to wide SOMs. To ensure control and clear communication this company has established powerful policy committees which assist the president.

Now let us turn to General Motors Corporation for an example of a super corporation which, unlike Du Pont, is not extensively diversified in products. As you see in EXHIBIT VI-B the president has an SOM of 3 (not counting the administration committee). This suggests that the president's key function is over-all review of the activities of his key subordinates.

Then let us study the next lower level and see how wide an SOM is given to the executive vice presidents who report to the president. The SOM remains rather narrow. The executive vice president who is in charge of the automotive and parts division has an SOM of 9, and the executive vice president in charge of the operations staff has an SOM of 8; while the executive vice president in charge of other operating divisions has an SOM of 5. This narrow SOM results from the fact that General Motors is in one business—automobiles and their parts— a fact which lends itself to a consolidation of functions.

The Johns-Manville Corporation, on the other hand, is a highly diversified company with sales in the $100–$500 million range. And, as

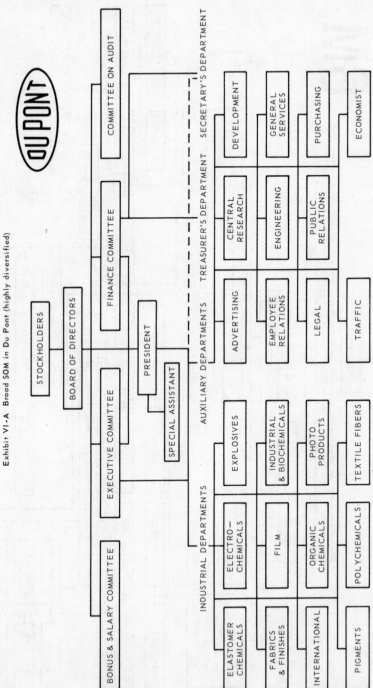

Exhibit VI-A Broad SOM in Du Pont (highly diversified)

Exhibit VI-B. Narrower SOM in General Motors (less diversified)

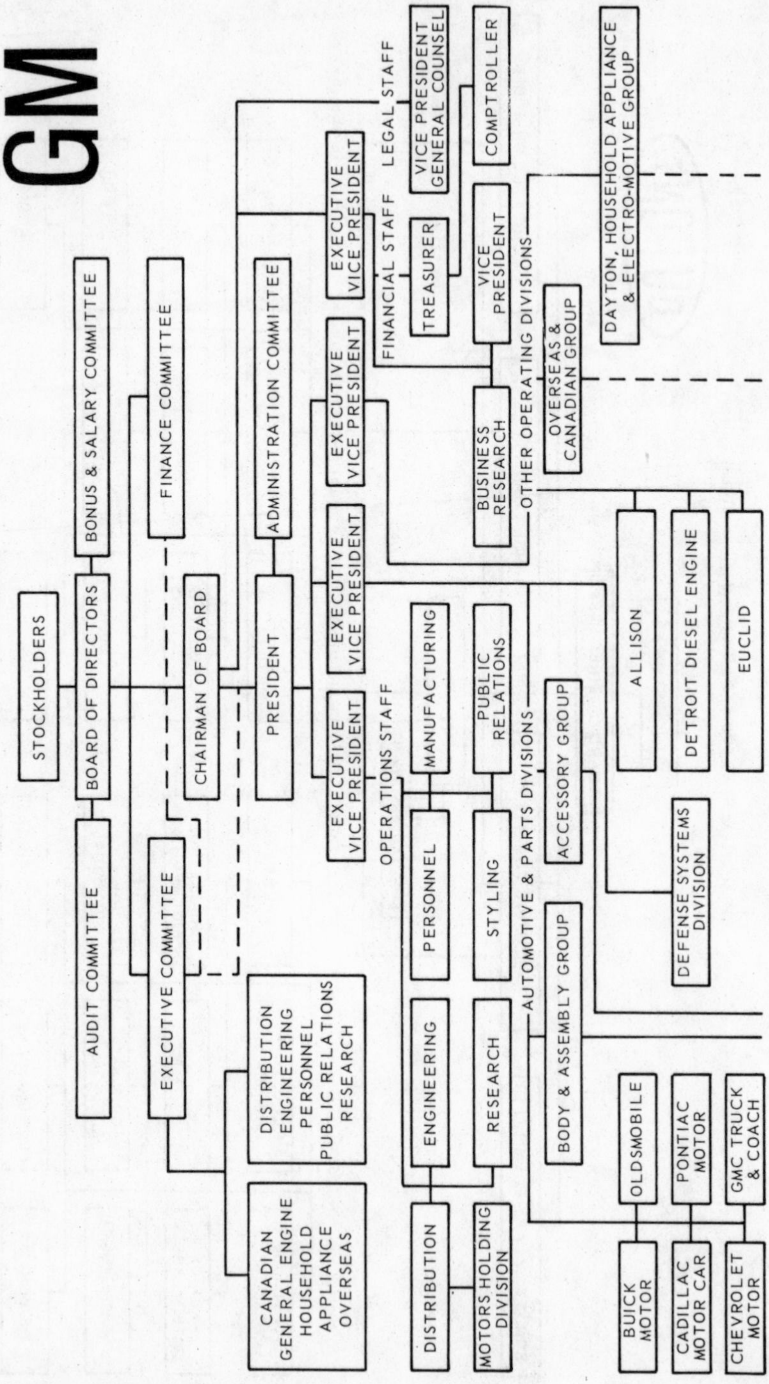

could have been predicted, EXHIBIT VI-C shows that the president's SOM is 17. The company is in a size range where, if it is going to grow in each of its diversified product areas, the general managers need a fair amount of autonomy. As was true of the much larger Du Pont Company, the president, because of diversification, operates as a super manager, relying on general managers to know the details of their businesses and their functions better than he does.

EXHIBIT VI-C also serves to introduce another aspect of SOM which we should not overlook. That is, how many of the subordinates have functions which actually support the president in the performance of his duties?

I realize that there is a danger that, by interpreting the SOM of the president of Johns-Manville as 17, I will fall into the same trap as have some other writers on SOM. One of the fallacies of the SOM rule of 6 is the implication that all executives shown reporting to the president on an organization chart can be classified as "subordinates" whom the executive must "supervise." A more meaningful breakdown of executives for SOM purposes is the following:

Top management—either individual or group management.

Support executives—including all personal assistants.

Action executives—usually with major profit or functional responsibilities.

In the Johns-Manville Corporation chart we see that the president has 9 *support* executives and 8 *action* executives reporting to him. Consequently, even though his SOM is 17, he is not performing his job without assistance.

EXHIBIT VI-D reveals another instance where the application of the classical rule of 6 gets confused. The Koppers Company, Inc., chart shows clearly that the "1" in the 1 to 6 rule can, when the company operates under the group management concept, be, as in this case, "4." This top management team, made up of the president and three executive vice presidents, shares an SOM of 16, a super span occasioned by the amount of product diversification.

Conclusion

In this article I have tried to put SOM discussions back into the context of practical business reality. Talk about limits imposed by the "human brain" and "interlocking direct personal relationships" seems to me to be based on drastic oversimplifications of the factors involved.

Much more pertinent, I feel, than such psychological limits are the following:

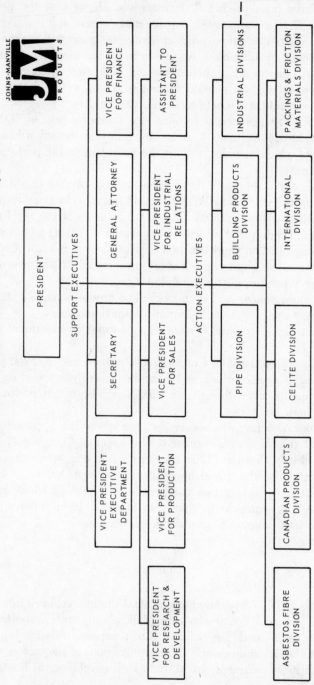

Exhibit VI-C Broad SOM in Johns-Manville (highly diversified, but not so large)

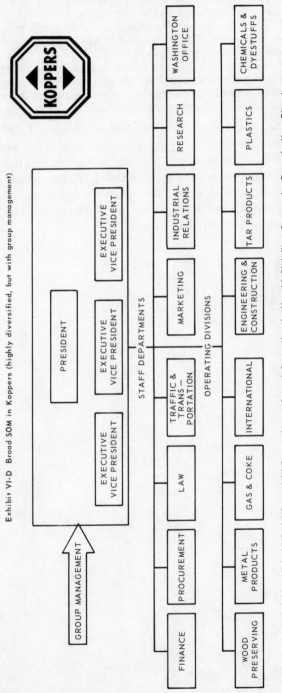

Exhibit VI-D Broad SOM in Koppers (highly diversified, but with group management)

Exhibits VI-A, VI-B, VI-C, and VI-D are drawn from information in Harold Steiglitz, *Corporate Organization Structures, Studies in Personnel Policy,* No. 183, *op. cit.,* pp. 68–69, 86–87, 90–91, 100–101.

(1) The type of managing to be done (by everyone from the super manager to the supervisor).

(2) The amount of diversification by products involved (as we have seen, larger companies are more likely to be diversified and hence have broader SOMs).

(3) All the other factors which influence the organizational structure of a company (its geographical dispersion, the complexity of its operations, the personality of its policy makers, and the effectiveness of its communication system).

Because of these complex and interrelated factors, I feel that it is impossible to make any sweeping generalizations about abstract and "proper" spans of management. (EXHIBIT VII summarizes the analytical approach to SOM advanced by this article). Today, when business is becoming ever more changing and more complicated, talking sense about delegation of authority, which the SOM reflects, has become a dollars-and-cents necessity to business.

GROUP	CLASSIFICATION	PERSONNEL INVOLVED	MAXIMUM RANGE OF SOM	ANALYTICAL METHOD RECOMMENDED
I	TOP MANAGEMENT (LARGE CORPORATIONS)	SUPER MANAGERS	50	OVER-ALL CONCEPTUAL ANALYSIS OF THE TOTAL ENTERPRISE AND ITS NEEDS NOW AND IN THE FUTURE
II	GENERAL MANAGEMENT (MEDIUM TO SMALL ORGANIZATIONAL UNITS)	GENERAL MANAGERS	12	SPECIFIC SITUATIONAL ANALYSIS OF THE OVER-ALL NEEDS OF THE UNIT AND PERSONAL LEADERSHIP REQUIREMENTS
III	MIDDLE MANAGEMENT (ALL SIZES OF ORGANIZATIONS)	MIDDLE MANAGERS	50	ECONOMIC ANALYSIS AND COST OPTIMIZATION OF THE TOTAL MIDDLE MANAGEMENT SYSTEM, BALANCING SAVINGS OF SOM INCREASES AGAINST RISING SUPPORT GROUP COSTS
IV	FIRST-LINE SUPERVISION (ALL SIZES OF ORGANIZATIONS)	SUPERVISORS	100	A. SPECIFIC FACTOR ANALYSIS OF EACH SITUATION OR GROUP OF SITUATIONS FOR SEPARATE ANALYSIS AND SIMPLIFICATION; THIS METHOD IS SIMILAR IN APPROACH TO THE COMMON INDUSTRIAL ENGINEERING SEQUENCE OF TIME STUDY, WORK SIMPLIFICATION, RESTUDY, AND STANDARD RATE SETTING B. SITUATIONAL EVALUATION USING ANALYTICAL TECHNIQUES SIMILAR IN KIND TO THOSE USED IN JOB EVALUATIONS

Exhibit VII The span of management and methods of determination

Generalist Versus Specialist:
Careers in a Municipal Bureaucracy[*]

William C. Thomas, Jr.

In the Autumn, 1958, issue of this *Review,* James W. Fesler noted that "a number of signs point to the revival of an old agenda item: 'the specialist and the generalist.' "[1] He went on to say that "the generalist 'school' won out over those arguing that a man must administer something and that a knowledge of that something is a necessary qualification for high administrative rank," but that now "new doubts are arising, or old doubts reviving." What follows here is an attempt to raise new and revive old doubts by reporting the findings of a study of the career paths of 90 bureau chiefs in New York City,[2] a jurisdiction in which the generalist school did not "win out."

Attempts to institutionalize the practical application of the generalist concept in the City have invariably been badly frustrated. The most recent effort was a proposal of the Department of Personnel to provide for lateral entry of college graduates as Municipal Internes. It was rejected, in 1955, largely because of the opposition of organizations of civil servants.

Official Career Philosophy

Meanwhile, the official philosophy of the City "career" system has strongly favored career paths which rise more or less vertically, with diagonal movement confined within departments. Appointments and promotions must be by competitive examination wherever "practicable."[3] Vacancies must be filled, wherever "practicable, by promotion

---

[*] Reprinted with permission of author and publisher from *Public Administration Review,* Vol. 21 (Winter, 1961), pp. 8–15.
[1] "Specialist and Generalist," p. 370.
[2] With three exceptions, all of the bureaus of fifteen City agencies were included. The agencies: The Departments of Air Pollution Control; Health; Marine and Aviation; Markets; Personnel; Public Works; Purchase; Sanitation; Tax; Water, Gas and Electricity; Welfare; the Comptroller's Office; the Housing Authority; and the Offices of the Borough Presidents of the Boroughs of Queens and Richmond. The word "department" is used generally in the text to refer to all of these agencies. Fifty-seven of the bureaus were line units and thirty-three were staff. The occupational specialities of the bureaus were as follows: Engineering, 22; Medicine, 11; Administration, 10; Accounting, 9; Real estate management, 6; Personnel administration, 5; Law, 4; Social work, 4; Skilled and semi-skilled labor (trades), 3; Unskilled labor, 3; Other, 14.
[3] Article V., sec. 6, *New York State Constitution.*

from among persons holding positions in a lower grade in the department in which the vacancy exists" and "due weight [must be given] to seniority."[4] There are also in-department experience requirements.[5] Among the exceptions allowed because of impracticability are the designations of some posts as belonging to the "exempt" and "noncompetitive" classes. Appointments to positions in the former category require no examination and those to the latter a "pass" examination—the candidate must be certified as qualified. But even in the cases of these categories—eleven of the ninety chiefs were in exempt posts and seven were in noncompetitive—the incumbents studied were found to have come up through the ranks more often than not, so strong was the philosophy of promotion from within. Although there is official provision for interdepartmental transfers, its degree of effectiveness may be indicated by quoting a now legendary comment of Mayor Fiorello LaGuardia: "It is more difficult to get an employee transferred from one department to another than it is to exchange prisoners of war." It is important to note that the main thrust of the official policy has erected and maintained barriers not to mobility from bureau to bureau, but only to that from department to department.[6]

Mobility in Practice

While the career paths of the ninety bureau chiefs were subjected to the influence of an official policy of such character, the men had, on their climb to chiefship, crossed departmental lines. Indeed, from a certain point of view, there had been a surprising amount of interdepartmental mobility. Eight had moved, by lateral entry, directly into bureau chiefships from employment outside the City service—the most obvious infraction of the principle of promotion from within. To further illustrate the point, twenty-nine bureau chiefs had served in only one department, twenty-seven had served in two, sixteen in three, and five, four, and one had served in four, five, and six departments, respectively.

---

[4] *McKinney's Consolidated Laws of New York, Annotated,* "Book 9, Civil Service Law" (Edward Thompson Co., 1958), sec. 52.

[5] *Rules of the New York City Civil Service Commission,* amended to Jan. 24, 1955, Rule V-X-4, 5.

[6] The *Rules of the City Civil Service Commission* specify that the Director of the Personnel Department "may limit eligibility in examination for promotion to persons employed in a certain bureau. ..." As amended to Jan. 24, 1955, Rule V-X-2. Examination of 60 per cent of the announcements of last promotion examinations taken by chiefs among the ninety disclosed no examination for which eligibility was restricted to any administrative unit smaller than a department.

However, this apparent mobility is seen only from a certain point of view, and that is a partial point of view. When timing is taken into account one finds that the movement tended strongly to take place at the earliest stages of the in-service careers—the lower administrative levels. Over two-thirds of all the City service experience accumulated by all of the subjects prior to their becoming bureau chiefs was acquired in the departments in which they became chiefs and as the last previous experience before becoming chiefs. In other words, over two-thirds of the City service experience was acquired under conditions of immobility so far as interdepartmental movement was concerned. For the fifty-three persons who had crossed departmental boundaries, the average length of assignments to departments other than the ones in which they became chiefs and prior to assignment to the department in which they ultimately became chiefs, was five years. For the same fifty-three the average length of the assignment prior to chiefship in the departments in which they became chiefs was fifteen years.

The pattern can be accounted for. The work done at the lower echelons required less independent judgment than that at higher levels and, therefore, less knowledge or experience. It was generally acknowledged that the lower skills used in one department were commonly used in others and were of approximately the same level of difficulty and interest in one department as in another. In the absence of machinery for the systematic rotation of personnel, movement was left largely to the initiative of the employees, but they found little to discourage them from seeking new departments to which they could shift. After a few years, however, they tended to find they had become habituated to the workways of the particular units in which they had been working, had an investment in their knowledge of them, and perhaps, had developed special interests in their work. It became more improbable that they would gain from a shift. This is the general contour, with the moves being concentrated in the early parts of the careers. There tends to have been a period of shuffling about, followed by a long period of horizontal immobility.

Mobility was also found between bureaus within the confines of departments. There are two striking differences, however, between the characteristics of these two kinds of horizontal mobility. First, it is not possible to identify any clear pattern of concentration of inter-bureau mobility in any particular time period of the careers. A shift from one bureau to another within a department appeared about as likely to occur at one stage of a career as at another. Second, instances of interdepartmental moves occurred twice as frequently as instances of the intradepartmental kind and were engaged in by almost twice as many persons.

Specialization Restricts Intradepartmental Mobility

The significance of these findings is that in a great number of instances the center of gravity of the law—the policy of promotion from within departments—was overcome by the informal dictates of diffusive, centrifugal specialization that characterized the requirements for bureau chiefships. With promotion examinations closed to those from outside a department, with the relative ease of formal interbureau transfers and of any requisite interbureau budgetary adjustments that might be necessary, and with the presumed greater familiarity of department heads with their own employees than with those of other departments, one would expect to find more flexibility in the making of assignments within departments than between departments. The reverse was actually the case because barriers of specialization were raised between bureaus and channels of specialization developed between departments.

Highly focused technical knowledge, intimate familiarity with some particular of the machinery of the City government, personal acquaintance with the special kinds of people who can help get the job done, relevant experience—these are the qualifications soberly considered necessary for the successful operation of a bureau. Because this specialization is within the bureau rather than the department, it tends to insulate the smaller organ from infiltration by other employees of the larger.

In some cases one of the desiderata is considered more important than the others, but whichever one, or combination, is regarded as the paramount qualification, the chief is expected to be more generously endowed with it than any other person in the bureau. As one becomes more qualified, one is likely to ascend the hierarchical ladder, so that those toward the top are most highly specialized. This condition is exemplified by the case of a chief who, in response to a query about what he regarded to be his most outstanding professional achievement, told of digesting the technical literature of his field and distributing it to his employees. He said that his staff not only did not have time to read the unabridged literature but would not read it even if they had time. He spoke with pride of a mailing list of people from all over the country who had requested his periodic releases of the digested material. Having the most of what is considered valuable for their par-

ticular bureau, those toward the top are less likely to be moved from
it and less easily replaced, than those at the bottom.

Greater Interdepartmental Mobility

Although within each department all of the same similar specialized
work processes are likely to be gathered into one bureau, departments
often employ many of the same kinds of work processes.

For example, a bureau of accounting will surely find a counterpart
in another department, as often will bureaus of personnel administration and maintenance. Many departments have engineering units
utilizing specialties which are found in other departments. There are,
therefore, channels for mobility which do lead to other departments
even though, like auto expressways, there may be no local stops. Concrete examples will illustrate the point. One chief, an auto transportation specialist, served successively in one bureau each in the Department of Parks, the Office of the President of the Borough of Queens,
and the Fire Department—and then went to a bureau in the Department of Plant and Structures which became part of the Department of
Public Works during a reorganization. Without a substantial down-
grading he could not conceivably have moved subsequently to another
bureau in Public Works because none utilized his skills. Similarly, an
engineer could work for the Board of Transportation reconstructing
sewers disturbed by subway construction, then move to the Parks
Department on drainage and irrigation, then go to design interception
sewers and treatment plants in a bureau of the Sanitation Department
which became, with the engineer along with it, part of the Public
Works Department in a reorganization. But after he arrived in Public
Works, had he moved again instead of becoming the bureau's chief, as
he did, it is almost certain he would have had to go out of the department, possibly to a Borough President's Office as one of his principal
subordinates did—since Borough Presidents' Offices also have some
responsibility for removal of sewage. For all of the work the Public
Works Department does that could utilize his special experience and
skills is in the bureau he heads.

This by no means exhausts the examples which might be given. Nor
does it note the exceptions—the few moves across departmental lines
which involved changing to a new kind of work. The moves within
departments were not usually gross departures from the work done
immediately before, but, interdepartmental moves were far more
likely to offer continuation of specialization. Such a conclusion is consonant with the finding that the instances of interdepartmental mobility decreased as the careers advanced but that intradepart-

mental mobility did not vary according to the stage of the career.

Although the specialty channels are narrow, they are long enough, on occasion, to reach past the boundaries of the City government itself and offer entrance opportunities to established outsiders. Most such entry was to a definite channel of specialization rather than to general operation within the City's hierarchy. For, by and large, those coming into the service who had spent a substantial proportion of their career outside had settled into a specialty there, had entered the appropriate channel within the service as a specialist and had not strayed from it. The kinds of chiefs who cleaved most strongly to specialties also tended to have spent larger proportions of their careers outside the service and, therefore, lesser proportions inside, than other kinds of chiefs.

Empirical Evidence

The validity of the foregoing conclusions can be supported. The ninety chiefs were divided into three groups, one consisting of the twenty-six who had engaged in the most professional activity,[7] one consisting of the twenty-six who had engaged in the most partisan political activity,[8] and a residual body of thirty-eight "less active" chiefs. Table 1 shows ninety chiefs classified according to group and to the proportion of their prechiefship career which was spent in the City service:

TABLE 1
BUREAU CHIEFS OF SELECTED NEW YORK CITY DEPARTMENTS
CLASSIFIED BY PROFESSIONAL AND POLITICAL ACTIVITY AND
PROPORTION OF THEIR CAREERS SPENT IN NEW YORK CITY
SERVICE PRIOR TO APPOINTMENT AS BUREAU CHIEFS

Proportion of Career in City Service	Profes- sionally Active	Politi- cally Active	Less Active	Total
All	—	4	5	9
Half but not all	15	16	28	59
Some but not half	6	4	4	14
None	5	2	1	8
	26	26	38	90

It is clear that the professionally active group was proportionately the object of the greatest amount of exception to the principle of pro-

---

[7] As indicated by the offices and committee posts they had held in professional societies and the professional writing they had done over and above that formally called for by their job.

[8] As indicated by posts held in political organizations and by campaign activity (only one chief qualified to be identified with both of these groups; the problem he presented was resolved by arbitrarily assigning him to the professionals).

motion from within, having engaged in more lateral entry than either of the other groups.[9]

Although they showed the greatest tendencies toward lateral mobility in their entry to the service, their conspicuousness in this regard declined markedly once they were in the service. The members of the politically active group were the most mobile there. Those of the less active group were next. The politically active made an interdepartmental move for each fourteen years of service they accumulated; the less actives made one such move for each twenty years and the professionals, also with a move for each twenty years, were as immobile. The fact that they moved at all, however, indicates the professionals as well as the others did have some facility for moving along specialty channels. And the figures on intradepartmental moves indicate the professionals had less total mobility and were more tightly bound to their specialties than the others. The politically active chiefs spent twenty-seven years in the service for each move within a department, about twice as many as for moves between departments; the less actives had thirty-four in-service years for each internal shift, approximately three-quarters again as many as spanned their interdepartmental moves; but the professionals accumulated fifty-nine years of in-service experience, virtually three times the twenty found between their interdepartmental moves, for each move made from bureau to bureau without leaving a department. That the professionals showed the least total horizontal mobility once in the service, and the greatest preponderance of interdepartmental over intradepartmental mobility, indicates by two measures that they, who tended to spend the greatest parts of their careers outside, were the group most likely to stay within specialty channels when in the service.

It is important to note that although the three groups varied as to the amount of horizontal mobility they engaged in, for each of the three groups there was less intradepartmental than interdepartmental mobility, indicating that members of all groups are more likely to slide along specialty channels, if they move at all, than to change to a different kind of work in the same department.

Channels Out of the Service

The specialty channels lead not only into but also out of the service. To illustrate, one chief rejected an opportunity to move up the

---

[9] This device for indicating lateral entry is used because the careers under observation had all reached chiefship before any standardized grade system was adopted in the City which would afford meaningful comparisons about entry levels.

ladder in another department because the proffered post would not allow him to make full use of his specialty. He expected to retire in four years, wanted to go into private practice as a consultant, and felt that the promotion offered could not compensate for the loss of reputation in his specialty he would suffer if he took it. "I know I have the number one job in my line in the country, so they say," he explained.

Many of the predecessors of the chiefs had earlier followed specialty channels to posts outside of the City service. Of the sixty-six persons who occupied chiefships immediately prior to the incumbents studied, nine resigned and twelve retired to continue working elsewhere. The City's retirement and pension policy makes it possible for many to retire at age fifty-five and by following this choice one may enjoy two incomes, one from a City pension and one from newly undertaken employment.

Rate of Upward Movement

The professionals were most favored by exception not only to the principle of promotion from within, as indicated by their amount of lateral entry, they were also the persons most likely to be excepted from the paced ascendancy up the hierarchical echelons of the service created by "due weight for seniority" and in-service experience requirements. This was due in part, of course, to the extent to which they effected lateral entry, conditions limiting the rate of climb being not so likely to prevail in employment outside the City service as in. However, it was also due to relatively quick promotions in the service. Table 2 supports this; it classifies the chiefs by professional and political activity and by time spent climbing to chiefship from the year of their self-supporting employment.

TABLE 2

BUREAU CHIEFS OF SELECTED NEW YORK CITY DEPARTMENTS
CLASSIFIED BY PROFESSIONAL AND POLITICAL ACTIVITY AND
TIME FROM FIRST SELF-SUPPORTING EMPLOYMENT TO
APPOINTMENT AS BUREAU CHIEF

	Up to 28 Years	28 Years or over	Total
Professionally Active	16	10	26
Politically Active	12	14	26
Less Active	16	22	38
	44	46	90

The existence of deviations from the career norm—promotion from within with due weight for seniority—was established by the tracing of the careers of the ninety chiefs. The professional group was identified as contributing the largest proportion of deviations. The professionals, however, had allies in their resistance to the established personnel policies; they could not have achieved the measure of deviation they did without substantial reinforcement from outside and from above.

Group Alignments

Wallace S. Sayre and Herbert Kaufman have described, in their recently published book, *Governing New York City*, how the leaders of the City's bureaucracies—particularly the leaders of employee organizations—have succeeded in their efforts to maximize and protect the career opportunities of their members. These leaders have extended, refined and guarded the rules growing out of the "primary doctrinal rationalization"—promotion from within—thereby increasingly confining the choices which department heads have in making appointments to those candidates who most closely fit their norms. In these efforts they have been protected by a mantle of neutrality and supported by the civil service reform tradition.[10]

The professional bureau chiefs, on the other hand, are backed by professional societies rooted outside the City service, that demand that professional qualifications be held by those who occupy positions which they, the societies, identify as within their special area of competence.[11] Allied with the professional societies are numerous civic bodies and other specialized interest groups who are dissatisfied with the level of expertise of the individuals who rise to the bureau chief echelon in the City hierarchy through the orthodox process.[12]

A consequence of an earlier victory by interest groups and professional societies is the professionalized department head. No less than seven of the fifteen department heads, in office at the time the bureau chiefs were studied, were people of high professional standing. As the official appointing officers their influence over the selection of bureau chiefs was, to say the least, significant.

The professional society, the private group closely interested in the

---

[10] (Russell Sage Foundation, 1960), see pp. 233–235, 405, 412–13.
[11] Sayre and Kaufman comment on these alliances and their standard-setting powers. *Ibid*. pp. 409, 410.
[12] Such organizations sometimes succeed in installing members of their own professional staffs in bureau chiefships. The groups and their tactics receive extensive treatment by Sayre and Kaufman. See particularly Chap. 13.

affairs of a bureau, and the professional department head—and more often than not the membership is overlapping—are frequently far more concerned with improving the quality (according to professional standards) of bureau chief competence and with increasing the amount of bureau chief energy than they are with matters of civil service morale, continuity in office, and preserving the sanctity of the vertical career system for whatever cause. To their ends they do battle with organized and unorganized career civil servants on such matters as allowing extra promotion credit for formal educational qualifications acquired in lieu of experience and the reclassification of a competitive position as non-competitive to accommodate a candidate with high professional qualifications.

There are, therefore, two camps in competition with each other to shape the career patterns of prospective bureau chiefs in New York City. The one, fostering a vertical pattern with a measured tread, is undoubtedly dominant. The other, promoting career paths which cut somewhat horizontally across the higher levels of the whole City bureaucracy, is nevertheless making its influence felt upon the career system. Both the paths, however, the vertical and the diagonal, are narrow and deep.

Desire for Achievement as a Factor

There is at least one further factor shaping career development that is important to this discussion—the relationship of the individual to his work under the public's expectation that its bureaucracy show some accomplishment. This may seem vague and amorphous, yet it is nonetheless real. It constitutes a pressure for men to do their best work. Even in instances where the influences of the opposing groups may be discounted, the men continue to behave as specialists, for the most part, under this pressure. Supporting evidence of this is shown by the fact that not only the professionally active group, but also the politically active and the less active groups, were far more likely to move from a specialized bureau in one department to a specialized bureau in another department than to a bureau with different specialization in the same department. Although the pro-professional groups undoubtedly foster such specialization, the career civil servant organizations undoubtedly have much more influence on the careers of the two groups of chiefs. On the other hand, the career civil servant organizations sponsored no wholesale interdepartment movement as against intradepartment mobility. Therefore, desire for achievement remains as an additional explanation.

If achievement-oriented specialization played a role in determining what kinds of moves were made, then it cannot logically be rejected as a factor *restricting* movement from bureaus. As a matter of fact, it would have been even more powerful in the latter role.

Conclusion

If it is true as a general proposition that administration grows more common with higher echelons and that one does not need to have knowledge of "something" to administer that something, it would be logical to expect to find some evidence of increasing leakage from the deep specialized career channels to outside positions as careers advanced to higher bureaucratic levels. None of any consequence whatsoever was found. Instead, a proliferation of pockets, or cones—bureaus—was found, within which the men selected at successively higher echelons tended to be the possessors of more and more particular kinds of experience and, presumably, particular knowledge and skill. What leakage there was tended to occur toward the bottom and flowed far more into what were specialized channels rather than general areas. These conditions obtained both within and without the spheres of influence of the groups identified as having impact upon career patterns.

This research, though narrow in base, strongly suggests a number of things. First, if pressures for specialization can do what the findings described above indicate they have done in New York City, where the policy barrier—"careers within departments"—has been raised across specialist channels, there is a probability they have been at least as strong in some other jurisdictions where no such barrier exists. Wherever massive complicated tasks are undertaken by large organizations no assumption that they are not as powerful as they are in New York is justified without some specific indication to the contrary. In other large cities, in states, and in the federal government are logical places to expect to find the same kind of development. Indeed, one collection of data pertaining to the federal level contains fragmentary evidence that the career paths of many federal bureau chiefs are grooves of specialization, deepening as they advance, as those of the 90 New York City Chiefs studied were found to be.[13]

Second, it suggests that the old question should be revived: What is it we want when we ask for a generalist? What qualities do we want our administrators to have and what values should they hold? Paul

---

[13] U.S. Commission on Organization of the Executive Branch of the Government, *Task Force Report on Personnel and Civil Service* (U.S. Government Printing Office, 1955), appendixes D, E.

Appleby has associated the root of "generalist," i.e., "general," with "political": As higher level administrators deal with broader areas of governmental structure and broader publics they deal with that which is more common, and therefore more general. And the more "generalist" administrators are, the ". . . more their functions have to do with weighing popular and organized opinion."[14] Implicit in the function of weighing opinion is a call for an acute awareness of the political nature of the many decisions which often masquerade as impartial or scientific matters. Also, there is implicit a promise of responsible behavior growing out of that awareness. But politics is not only the weighing of popular and organized forces, it also involves doing something about them once they have been weighed. It is ". . . the art of 'strategic obfuscation'" and requires ". . . creative powers to contrive a formula which, because it *does* mean different things to each side, may stop [a] quarrel, with the semblance of sameness, and may enable the factions to proceed peaceably."[15]

To raise, now, a newer question: Is the specialization of political awareness, skill and responsibility necessarily incompatible with specialization in "something" to be administered? Are we faced with a clear choice of either generalists or specialists at the bureau chief level? Probably, there is no full choice because the dominant forces in our complicated society are on the side of the specialists.

It never was contended that no specialist could be a good administrator. It stands to reason now that greater efforts to increase the numbers who are good administrators by imparting to them fuller appreciation of the political nature of the power they may wield as public servants, of the breadth and intensity of its impact and of their consequent responsibilities, would be a prudent course.

The increasing of specialists' sensitivity to considerations from outside their specialty channels can be encouraged in a number of ways. One, that bears closely upon the data reported in this piece, is the rotation of personnel from one administrative organ to another. There appears to be no reason to question its soundness as a tactic; if used judiciously, there would not necessarily be a waste of specialized qualifications employees might have and it would allow full advantage to be taken of all promotion possibilities for competent employees. Also, it could be expected to increase their appreciation of the variety and strengths of opinions and interests issuing from government and from the public. However, one cannot assume broad exposure from the sheer number of inter-agency jumps an employee has made. The

---

[14] *Policy and Administration* (University of Alabama Press, 1949), p. 50.
[15] T. V. Smith, *The Ethics of Compromise and the Art of Containment* (Starr King Press, 1956), pp. 41 and 43.

matter of when the moves were made is of importance. Ten years in one place may do much to limit and fix a man's attitudes and perceptiveness. And when most moves are made on the volition of the employees, as was the case with the New York chiefs—and is usually the case elsewhere—it seems unrealistic to expect them to gravitate to positions that will require serious adjustments in their habits of thought.

There are other approaches. Professional associations which have broadminded leadership can help. In-service training courses can, of course, be useful. A point of contact where more could be done is in the specialist schools and programs in our universities and colleges. Here future specialists could be influenced at a stage critical for the shaping of attitudes. Resistance to the subject matter may be severe, but if teachers can find ways to reach the students, the dividends could be rich.

However, all of these approaches taken together, though worthwhile, cannot insure the responsiveness and responsibility desired. It therefore seems advisable to strengthen the hands of chief executives, because they are generalists, responsible to the widest spectrums of considerations, in directing streams of policy. One way to approach this goal would be to work to broaden public recognition of the narrowness of the perspectives from which subordinate executives make their judgments.

Enter the Personnel Generalist*

Harry R. Knudson, Jr.

Traditionally, the hallmark of the personnel function has been specialization—a specialization which has its core in the highly trained,
experienced personnel man who is equipped to handle a specific type
of problem or assignment. A look at the personnel department's organization chart in almost any large company will reveal a veritable multitude of employment specialists, training specialists, wage and salary
specialists, employee relations specialists, pension and benefit specialists, and so on—their number and type depending, of course, on the
nature of the company's activities, its size, and the attitude of top
management toward the personnel function. In most cases, each of
these specialists reports to a functional manager (the employment
manager or the training director) and deals with all levels and types
of employees.

In many instances, this traditional arrangement has been unsuccessful, however, in accomplishing the stated objective of personnel administration: helping line management to maximize the profit potential by obtaining, maintaining, developing, and utilizing an effective
work force. In fact, while the traditional approach to personnel administration is meritorious in theory, it often prevents the personnel
organization from operating at its optimum effectiveness. Consider, for
example, the following disadvantages of specializing the personnel
function:

> In many instances, line management must deal with sev-
> eral representatives of the personnel department—a differ-
> ent person for each type of situation—thus preventing a
> high degree of rapport and empathy from developing be-
> tween personnel specialists and line management.
> The personnel specialist normally operates throughout
> the entire organization in his specialty. Thus, his contact
> with any particular line supervisor, or the line management
> of any given segment of the organization, is occasional and
> brief—again hindering the development of a close, continu-
> ing relationship between personnel specialists and line
> managers.
> The abilities and experience of personnel representatives
> at the "working level" are often too insufficient for them to
> obtain the confidence and respect of line management.
> Specialization limits even the best personnel representa-

* Reprinted with permission of author and publisher from *Personnel*, Vol. 37
(March-April, 1960), pp. 33–41.

tives to operating in a narrow, sometimes artificial, area of the employer-employee relationship.

Specialization increases the tendency for a personnel representative to perform his function from his own office, rather than in the work area, thus adding another block to effective communications and understanding.

Recognizing these and other limitations to the traditional organization of personnel activities, progressive managements have been experimenting recently with a new idea—the concept of the personnel generalist. While his appearance on the business scene has revealed him to be essentially similar to his predecessor, the traditional personnel man, some noteworthy differences in his activities and in the philosophy that underlies his existence mark his debut as a significant advancement in the theory and practice of personnel administration.

The concept of the personnel generalist is deceptively simple: A qualified personnel administrator is assigned to each significant segment or group of employees within the organization. Each of these personnel generalists is supported by a small, centralized personnel unit at the company level, each one reports to the manager of his group, and each is responsible for the major personnel functions of selection, orientation, employee appraisal and development, salary administration, employee relations, policy and procedure formulation, and so on, depending upon the nature of the unit to which he is assigned. Thus, the personnel generalist performs for his unit all but two of the usual personnel functions: (1) Supervision of clerical functions, such as record keeping, reports and announcements, and paperwork processing of new employees, which is the responsibility of the central personnel unit, and (2) recruiting, which is carried out on a companywide basis by a recruiting manager and his assistants.

In effect, then, the concept gives each personnel administrator or generalist a group of employees for whom he has primary personnel responsibility. He may, of course, ask for assistance from the central personnel department (which has already assisted him appreciably by undertaking the major clerical tasks) if unusually difficult situations arise requiring highly specialized treatment. Insofar as the employees of his group are concerned, however, he *is* the personnel department.

It is important to note that this new concept does not change the basic relationship between personnel and line management. The personnel administrator acts in a staff capacity to the line supervisor of his group—he does not usurp line management's authority; he does not make line decisions. His close relationship with the group enables him, however, to provide *continuing* service, thus making line management more effective. To emphasize the significance of this point, and to illustrate how the existence of the personnel generalist eliminates many of the disadvantages of the traditional personnel arrangement, let us examine some of the reasoning upon which the new concept is based.

First of all, let us consider the prime requirement of an effective personnel program: its acceptance by the employees. This acceptance depends mainly upon the extent to which the program satisfies the actual needs of the employees concerned, the extent to which key personnel have an opportunity to participate in the program, and the effectiveness of the personnel representative in advocating or implementing it.

Since the attitudes, abilities, work needs, values, and interests of employees differ from one group to another, it is imperative to give special attention to employee groups with similar characteristics and interests (for example, engineers and their supporting personnel) if the needs of the employees are to be satisfied. But the possibility of one personnel representative having the varieties of skills, insights, tools, techniques, and personal qualities to effectively deal with all these varying employee groups is somewhat remote. The concept of the personnel generalist is, therefore, a logical alternative.

The other two ingredients of an accepted and thus a successful personnel program—the participation of key personnel and the effectiveness of the personnel representative himself—are closely tied in with each other, since the effectiveness of the personnel representative is predicated upon his ability to win personal acceptance, which, in turn, rests upon his establishing and maintaining a close and continuing relationship with the employees. The personnel generalist is better able to fulfill these requirements than the traditional personnel man mainly because located as he is within the working area itself, he is in daily contact with the operating people. This gives him a first-hand opportunity to become acquainted with and share their problems and thus to provide continuing assistance in all areas of personnel administration. This principal feature of the concept of the personnel generalist—close physical proximity to the employees he is responsible for—cannot be overstressed. Its results touch upon many of the factors inherent in good personnel management.

Advantages of the Concept

For one thing, most personnel difficulties assume the proportions they do because of the traditional personnel man's failure to either anticipate their occurrence or to handle them properly in their early stages. The personnel generalist, however, because he works with operating personnel on a day-to-day basis, is in a good position to learn of potential problem areas and to suggest appropriate action before the problem reaches serious proportions.

Then, too, most successful management depends upon a supervisor's knowledge of the feelings, attitudes, and reactions of his subordinates. A personnel representative in daily contact with operating personnel and physically located within their domain is in a unique position to accurately interpret and advise management of the state of employee morale, and to suggest intelligent and practical approaches to keep it at a high level.

The personnel generalist also plays an important role in maintaining or increasing individual productivity. For example, effective work performance is often diminished because of problems inherent in the working environment or in the personal lives of the workers, such as friction between employees, between employees and supervisors, between one working group and another, or between a man and his wife. These problems can be minimized by understanding and intelligent counsel—but first, they must be brought out into the open. And the probability of an employee making his problem known is infinitely greater if the personnel representative is readily available, is personally known by the employee, and has the employee's respect, confidence, and acceptance.

Another main cause of employee dissatisfaction is misinformation or the lack of information. This may well result in low productivity, lack of teamwork, or excessive turnover and absenteeism. Again, a personnel representative who is in continuing contact with a particular segment of the work force is in an excellent position to advise management of the need for additional information within the segment, as well as to recommend methods by which the information could be more effectively disseminated. He is equally well placed to promote upward communications—an important aspect of employee relations that often gets little more than perfunctory attention at best.

Aiding Self-Development

Another key phase of personnel management upon which the concept of the personnel generalist leaves its mark is that of self-development. Many of the skills an executive must develop, if he does not already intuitively possess them, have to do with the management of people. Of fundamental importance here is an awareness and understanding of human behavior, to which there is probably no surer path than the endeavor to learn more about oneself. A personnel representative in daily contact with supervisory personnel is in a strong position to provide competent assistance and proper motivation and direction to line management in this crucial area of self-development.

Aside from placing the personnel administrator in the midst of the fray, so to speak, the concept of the personnel generalist has other features to recommend it. For one thing, a personnel representative, whose responsibilities encompass all the major personnel functions, is able to bring the experience and knowledge gained in one area into play in performing other duties. Thus, the concept of the personnel generalist provides an integrated personnel program in which all the important aspects in selecting, motivating, and developing employees become one continuing effort.

Also, under the generalist concept, since the personnel representatives do not purport to be specialists themselves, they are in a position to want, need, and make maximum use of the highly specialized and truly professional assistance available in the central personnel staff. This has the side effect of diminishing the friction that often occurs when one specialist attempts to assist another of lesser eminence.

Finally, under the new concept, a personnel representative is released in large measure from the overwhelming burden of paperwork that seems to characterize so many personnel operations. He is thus free to devote his time and energies to the more subtle problems involving the work force that often defy quantitative treatment, yet are the essential ingredients in a successful personnel program.

These, then, are the positive features of the concept of the personnel generalist. It will be admitted that they are impressive and reflect some serious thinking about the nature of personnel administration. But any new idea is bound to have some disadvantages and before going overboard with this one, it would be as well to see what the snags are, too.

Disadvantages of the Concept

The personnel generalist system has three principal drawbacks: (1) The difficulty of maintaining a uniform and consistent personnel program; (2) expense; and (3) the difficulty of finding capable personnel.

The first disadvantage has its root in the number of personnel administrators involved in the system. Because each one handles similar personnel functions and yet is relatively dissociated from the others, continuity and uniformity of action can be a problem. This dissociation, however, is inherent in the concept of the personnel generalist—

it is, in fact, the very heart of the concept. (The personnel administrator is not a member of the central personnel group—he reports only to the manager of the group he is serving.)

This disadvantage can be minimized, however, by a well-organized central personnel department with clear-cut policies and procedures and a capable personnel director who has an explicit understanding that one of his major responsibilities is to assure maximum communications between himself and each personnel administrator, as well as among the personnel administrators themselves. Without such direction, the generalist arrangement could lose much of its effectiveness, since each of its segments could conceivably be operating under significantly different policies and procedures.

The second disadvantage of the personnel generalist concept—its expense—follows from the type of person the program requires. While in actual numbers the new type of organization calls for about the same staff as is required in the traditional personnel department, the personnel generalist must be someone of considerably broader talents and experience than his traditional, specialist counterpart.

He must first be able to gain the acceptance of a whole group of employees, often of high caliber, on a continuing basis and then to take the appropriate actions to alleviate their personnel problems. In effect, therefore, the position of a personnel generalist requires someone capable of holding a position that would appear at a much higher level on a traditional personnel organization chart. This means higher salaries than would be paid to the general run of personnel specialists. But in relation to the significant investment in manpower that is becoming increasingly typical of most business concerns, the additional cost required to adequately staff a personnel organization that will yield a more effective personnel program is nominal indeed.

The third disadvantage—that of finding capable personnel to function as generalists—also arises from the high-caliber type of person required. This difficulty, while not insurmountable, should not be taken lightly, for it is crucial to the success of the program. The job of personnel generalist is not a training position for a junior personnel executive and must not be considered as such. If the system is to function effectively, it must be staffed by experienced, competent people fully capable of meeting the considerable demands of the job.

One Company's Experience

So far, we have discussed the concept of the personnel generalist in theory only. But what about its practicality—does it really work? To answer this question, suppose we take a look at the personnel program based on the concept of the personnel generalist that has been in operation at the Wayland Laboratory of the Raytheon Company since the summer of 1958.

Raytheon's Wayland Laboratory, with approximately 1,500 employees, is composed of several groups of highly trained electronic and technical specialists performing classified research on a contract basis for the government. The labor force consists primarily of graduate engineers and sub-professional technical employees, with the usual complement of support and clerical personnel. In dealing with Wayland's large number of highly educated professional workers—many working on the "team" basis typical of research activities and many having a common interest in and affiliation with professional societies outside the corporate structure—the shortcomings of the traditional specialist concept of personnel administration were very pronounced. It was in an attempt to find a better method of serving this unique, high-caliber group of employees that the personnel generalist system was initiated.

A personnel administrator was assigned to the manager of each of the Laboratory's larger departments. Each administrator was given the responsibility for all personnel functions for professional and sub-professional employees within his department, with the exception of recruiting and the following central office personnel functions: central processing activities, files, reports, employee benefit administration, coordination of employee services, and all personnel activities for clerical and support employees. Special technical assistance was made available from the corporate personnel staff as needed. The program has retained this organizational structure since its inception, although some personnel changes have taken place.

The personnel administrators were selected after extremely careful screening of prospects from the entire Raytheon organization. Each one had had several years' experience with the company in important positions, either in personnel or in general administration, or both. Some of the personnel generalists had basic technical backgrounds which, it was felt, would enhance their ability to deal effectively with technical people. All of them seemed to have an intuitive understanding of people—a quality that was specifically sought out in the screening process and one that has, undoubtedly, greatly attributed to the initial success of the program.

Results of the Program

In fact, the extensive screening process and the obvious capabilities of the personnel generalists probably accounted in large measure for their almost immediate acceptance by both the department managers and employees. The comments of the department managers, many of whom had extensive technical backgrounds, reflected an appreciation of the opportunity to have a qualified person working with them on a continuing basis to help them with problems that they themselves often felt less than expert in solving. The managers also expressed enthusiasm for having professional assistance in many areas which they felt were important, but to which they had not previously given adequate attention.

The employees, too, were uniformly enthusiastic about having someone to whom they could look for advice and assistance. Surprisingly, they showed no indications of dissatisfaction with the new arrangement. Thus, while unexpressed dissatisfaction may have existed, the employees apparently wholeheartedly welcomed the innovation. The addition to the department of a qualified person whose primary responsibility was their welfare seemed, in fact, to give them a feeling of prestige.

The high degree of enthusiasm on the part of the personnel administrators was also impressive. Although well aware that the results of the new system depended largely upon their own personal capabilities, they were, nevertheless, unanimously confident in its success. In other words, while they recognized the tremendous personal challenge in their new assignments, they also recognized the outstanding opportunity they were being afforded to contribute to the well-being of the organization.

The initial contacts of the administrators with their groups were characterized by seemingly endless demands for all kinds of specific information: "How often will my performance be evaluated?" "What effect will my extracurricular activities have on my progress with the company?" "How do I stand in the pension program?" "Will the company pay for graduate engineering courses?" These and similar questions were easily answered by the administrators. Incidentally, the extent of these questions, which was entirely unanticipated, indicated very clearly to management the shortcomings of their previous personnel operations—which, heretofore, were assumed to have been at least reasonably effective.

In addition to the demands for specific information, the administrators received a significant number of requests for general information about the company and its policies. It seemed that, in some instances, employees had received false impressions through misinterpretation of policy, rumor, or personal biases. Although this type of question was, of course, more difficult to deal with and often required more time and attention than a very specific question, the administrators were able, for the most part, to answer them satisfactorily. It was interesting to note that few employees attempted to use the new system to present obviously unfounded criticisms or unique considerations that would result only in their own personal gain. Evidently, the acceptance of the administrators was so complete that it almost precluded this type of action.

The personnel administrators did find, however, that many employees wished to discuss problems that were essentially personal in nature—problems ranging from their difficulties in finding housing to their children's poor school performance. Obviously, the administrators were not able to solve all these problems, but the employees now had a place to bring them for sympathetic understanding—and they seemed to be doing so.

Of particular significance was the tendency, on the part of many employees, to just "sorta talk things over" with the administrator, without discussing any particular problem. This was considered to be a positive indication that the administrator was becoming an integral part of his group. No only was he accepted passively, as a non-disrupting element, but he was actually considered a member of the group. While this may have been partly attributable to the physical availability of the administrators, it seems likely that their outstanding personal qualities mainly accounted for their complete acceptance.

Some Future Considerations

Though these initial successes were mostly confined to the area of improved communications with employees, some longer-range objectives of the program were also achieved to a rewarding degree. Each of the administrators spent considerable time with his department manager—giving advice on personnel problems, providing technical information, and generally being of assistance whenever possible. As a result of this close and continuing contact, many technically oriented managers have openly expressed a greater realization of the value of the human assets under their control. This may be only talk—but it is something of an achievement in so short a period of time, and certainly an encouraging harbinger of things to come.

It should be added that, as the program has progressed, the generalists themselves have revealed an increasing competence and confidence in handling all aspects of personnel administration rather than one specialized function. They have matured in their positions and feel that they have had a unique opportunity for their own development.

Of course, all has not been entirely smooth sailing, and there have been some problems mainly arising from situations in which there is a dual responsibility for personnel activities. For example, the individual administrators and the central personnel department share some responsibility in certain phases of employee processing, salary administration, employee counseling, and union activities. While some minor difficulties have been encountered here, viewed in the total achievements of the program to date, they are insignificant. Certainly, they can be eliminated as more experience with the generalist system is gained.

Although it is still too early to formally evaluate how far the Raytheon program is living up to expectations, all indications are that it will prove to be more effective than the traditional methods of personnel administration—at least in the Raytheon situation. Management has expressed a high degree of enthusiasm for it, and plans are currently being made to install similar programs in other Raytheon facilities.

To sum up, then, while the concept of the personnel generalist still has to meet the test of time, it is based on a well-thought-out philosophy of personnel administration and should, therefore, be of considerable interest to progressive managements dissatisfied with the traditional organization of the personnel function. Indeed, it may well turn out that the personnel generalist may prove to be *the* personnel man of the future.

Lateral Relations in Work[*]

Based on Leonard R. Sayles

The literature of organizational behavior places major emphasis on superior-subordinate relationships. This generalization applies not only to the classical school represented by Weberian scholars. It applies equally to the newer schools represented by such people as Simon, Presthus, Blau and Etzioni. Much of the research and writing on supervisory techniques, leadership styles, motivation and human relations also focuses narrowly on the authority-responsibility issues characteristic of vertical relations.

Emphasis or no, however, much of the interaction that takes place in an organization occurs "horizontally." These horizontal relations associate individuals who are not immediately tied together by the vertical chain of command. Rather these individuals are, in one way or another, dependent on each other in meeting suborganizational goals. Leonard Sayles has noted seven categories of such relationships. The seven categories that Sayles uses are:

1. trading relations
2. work-flow relations
3. service relations
4. advisory relations
5. auditing relations
6. stabilizing relations
7. innovating relations.

The inappropriateness of a fixation on vertical relations will be illustrated diversely. The demonstration may be previewed briefly. For example, the distinction between "line" and "staff" in organizations reflects a vertical emphasis. The "unity of command" is reserved theoretically to the "line" by making the "staff" advisory and service only. Practice is another matter, however. As will be shown, the lateral relations of line and staff are manifold, significant and in essential senses beyond the scope of vertical authoritative relations. Sayles's last five types of lateral relations reflect a particularly high potential for line-staff conflict, although that potential is high enough in the first two types.

We may briefly describe Sayles's seven categories of lateral relations, with particular emphasis on the inability of vertical relations to account for or to contain the required dynamic lateral interactions of

---

[*]Based on Leonard R. Sayles, *Managerial Behavior* (New York: McGraw-Hill, 1964), esp. pp. 58-82.

line and staff. According to Sayles, "trading" refers to the processes by which the terms of some future relationships are established. Trading relations have a high priority. Consider only a skeletal rationale based on the datum that many organizational units must meet specified goals in modern organizations, and usually under conditions of a high level of interdependence among units. Thus it becomes vital for each line manager to contact those in the organization who can "help" him in meeting the goals of his unit. Since help is seldom given without a concomitant responsibility or obligation—whether the help is provided by line or staff—it becomes necessary to work out formal or informal terms of a reciprocal relationship. As organizations become increasingly dependent on external groups in meeting goals, the trades that are crucial to successful management involve not only relations "internal" to the organization but also those with "external" suppliers or customers. This is particularly true, for example, when business firms work on a government defense contract.

The "flow of work" also requires ubiquitous lateral relations. Practically all work in a complex organization must be performed in an orderly sequence. That is, A must perform a function before B can perform his. B thus becomes dependent on A as, in turn, C is intimately dependent on B. Sayles calls such mutual dependencies among A, B, and C work-flow relations. Work-flow relations grow increasingly significant as an organization's skill-mix and product-mix become more complex, as when automation or computerization takes place.[1] Given that automation or computerization will become more and more intensive and extensive in tomorrow's organizations, work-flow relations will become increasingly critical.

"Service" relations are subtly distinguished from the lateral contacts required by the work flow. In the former, "multiple feeds" or inputs come to a service unit; outputs *in some order* go out to multiple customers. In either case, basically lateral relationships must exist among organizational peers. The strains and conflicts in these situations cannot be solved by the mere issuance of an order or by overhead impositions of priorities about who gets what and when.[2] Exceptions and flexibility often require less formal but workable relations. Thus conflicts often must be worked out by individuals of similar rank on a give-and-take basis. The successful manager in service relations is one who understands the "rules" that govern the game of compromise and who can negotiate successful trade of scarce resources. A preoccupa-

---

[1] See, particularly, George P. Shultz and Thomas L. Whisler, editors, *Management Organization and the Computer* (Glencoe, Ill.: Free Press, 1960).
[2] For a case study of some of the difficulties of overhead control, see Robert H. Guest, *Organizational Change* (Homewood, Ill.: Irwin-Dorsey, 1962).

tion with organizational dogma—e.g., that the "line" is formally superior to "staff"—is not particularly useful in such negotiations. Indeed, just such an insistence may be a major source of friction in lateral relations.[3]

The literature on "line-staff" is replete with examples of the delicateness of what Sayles terms "advisory relationships," although no more so than with service relations. The source of the difficulty is patent. In the traditional concept, staff personnel have no authority over line officials. Indeed, staff and line commonly report up separate hierarchies. Consequently, staff must depend on "selling" its ideas. This makes tense the process of developing advisory relations, for most students and managers recognize that only a fine line separates "advice" from "orders." Hence comes the usual counsel that staff personnel be circumspect in their dealings with line units lest staff violate their formal role. No one-way street exists, however, for line personnel can hardly neglect the often valuable aid that staff can provide, even if it has an "order" quality. Such resistance may only encourage staff to act as an informer to gain top management's support of staff programs. Hence the high potential for conflict in advisory relations develops.

Auditing, stabilizing and innovating relationships—like service and advisory relations—also involve delicate contacts between line and staff personnel. A quality-control unit which makes checks of output, or an accounting unit that performs a post-audit, exemplifies staff units involved in auditing relationships. Many line managers feel the relationship is one-sided, i.e., that power lies with the auditor. This makes the line manager's life difficult, for the successful "line" manager should use contacts with the auditor to improve the performance of his own unit and, perhaps, to dilute the severity of any criticism going "up the line." In the same breath, however, the line manager must recognize that his "helper" can be a "hurter" and an "orderer." Also, the line manager may have a limited ability to rectify the balance.[4] The conflict of reality with prescription can prove a great source of line-staff tension.

Stabilizing relations operate on a pre-audit or pre-clearance basis. This contrasts with the *post hoc* nature of the auditing relationship. Staff units created to examine and approve production plans, person-

[3] The point is illustrated neatly by George Strauss and Leonard R. Sayles, *Personnel: The Human Problems of Management* (Englewood Cliffs, N. J.: Prentice-Hall, 1960), p. 365.
[4] The "Corelli Case" presents a classic case of the lower-level line manager's disadvantage in a conflict with a staff unit. In John D. Glover and Ralph M. Hower, editors, *The Administrator* (Homewood, Ill.: Irwin, 1957), pp. 681–685.

nel changes or structural rearrangements are involved in stabilizing relations. Conflict in these relations results almost inevitably in delays in clearance, minute inspection of all submitted plans and a general hostile reaction to requests for timely decisions. Here staff service becomes control over the line. Favorable relations not only can speed requests for prior clearance but can result in advice and aid from the stabilization personnel.

Finally, staff units in modern organizations exist whose sole function is to innovate, to plan, to create, to research. Such groups usually try to stay aloof from other units in the organization in order to retain that independence and autonomy usually considered necessary for their work. Often, however, the research unit requires support in the form of data, personnel or other resources from other units. This dependence consequently also requires a reciprocal relationship in which staff and line must cooperate. That reciprocity is more intermittent than in service relations, for example, but it may be crucial.

The examples above establish the incidence and significance of reciprocal and lateral relations. Without denying the importance of vertical relationships, one can argue that the success or failure of a particular organizational unit depends as much on effective lateral relations with other line and staff units as it does on vertical command relations. At the very least, we know that lateral relations take up much of the time of managers at all levels.[5]

---

[5] Robert Dubin, "Business Behavior Behaviorally Viewed," esp. pp. 14–25, in George B. Strother, editor, *Social Science Approaches to Business Behavior* (Homewood, Ill.: Irwin-Dorsey, 1962).

Civil Service and Managing Work: Some Unintended Consequences*

Robert T. Golembiewski

Nature seldom allows us to get what we wish without paying her price. This truism is commonly illustrated by the delicate balance in animal life which often cannot be disturbed to satisfy man's wants (*e.g.*, for fox hunting) without demanding of man in return (*e.g.*, by increases in the rabbit population and in crop damage).

The several civil service systems in this country also illustrate this bittersweet combination of intended and unintended consequences. The argument here will not go to the extreme of one observer, in whose judgment the United States Civil Service Commission was the single greatest obstacle to the successful waging of World War II.[1] Rather, the focus here will be upon several characteristics of our civil service systems that have as presumably unintended consequences an increase in the burdens of managing work. For the most part, the analysis of management problems will derive from the research literature dealing with behavior in organizations, a field of study presently seething with activity.

I. The Goal-Matrix of our Civil Service Movement

The nature of these unintended consequences is suggested by the matrix of goals, or purposes, underlying our civil service movement. The primary goal, of course, was the separation of the management of public work from party patronage. Within this overriding goal, Sayre has noted three early subsidiary purposes of our public personnel systems:[2]

1. the guarantee of equal treatment of all employees and all applicants for employment;
2. the application of the logic (or theory) and methods of "scientific management"; and
3. the development of a public career service.

---

*Reprinted with permission of author and publisher from *American Political Science Review*, LVI (December 1962), pp. 961–973.
[1] John Fisher, "Let's Go Back to the Spoils System," reproduced in part in Dwight Waldo, ed., *Ideas and Issues in Public Administration* (New York, 1953), pp. 200–1.
[2] Wallace Sayre, "The Triumph of Technique Over Purpose," *Public Administration Review* Vol. 8 (Spring, 1948), pp. 134–35.

These goals define the field of my present effort. Detailed analysis later will demonstrate the significance for the management of work of the unintended consequences which derive from the ways adopted to achieve these purposes. I take this opportunity to suggest the general nature of these consequences.

Consider first the general tethers on the management of work implicit in the historical pursuit of the three purposes listed. The guarantee of equal treatment, to begin with, has never quite made peace with the managerially convenient notion that unequal contributions demand unequal reward. To take a recent and characteristic example, the teachers' union in Illinois has lately expressed violent opposition to a proposal for merit pay increases based upon performance. This opposition goes deeper than the convenience of seniority or of hours of graduate study as objective criteria for pay increases and far deeper than the blatant protectionism of hacks. However lofty the motives, their effect is clear. In practice, the struggle toward the "equal treatment" goal virtually forced public personnel systems into a monumental preoccupation with technique and mechanics. As Sayre concluded.[3]

> Its main effect has been to move personnel administration, in the words of Gordon Clapp, "into the cold objective atmosphere of tests, scores, weighted indices, and split-digit rankings" so completely that "these technical trappings have become symbols of the merit system."

The management of work pays a stiff price for such technical elegance. Work is notoriously insensitive to such easy capture, and the most subtly contrived managerial rewards and punishments might be frustrated by an awkward distribution of test scores. Moreover, these technical trappings put powerful weapons into the hands of "staff" people. That more than one "line" manager has been stymied by one of these "split-digit rankings" without accepting the results as divinely ordained, moreover, does nothing to lessen the often intense jurisdictional tugs-of-war encouraged by the traditional "line-staff" distinction. These tensions are apt to be increased by the time lag inherent in centralized administrative systems, and public personnel systems are usually operated centrally.

The logic and methods of "scientific management," second, tended to condemn managers to a treadmill even as it aided them. Scientific management was imported from the "practical" world of business where its impact was enormous.[4] But the impact was not one-way. Thus there is no denying the useful revolution in viewing work that

---

[3] *Ibid.*, p. 134.
[4] Dwight Waldo, *The Administrative State* (New York, 1948), pp. 47–64.

the methods of scientific management sparked. However, as recent research particularly demonstrates,[5] the assumptions in the logic (or theory) of scientific management concerning man and his work were mechanistic caricatures. Consequently, the manager tended to be less effective in direct relation to the degree that he patterned his behavior on the logic of the approach. That is, the reasonable methods of scientific management often were guided by an inadequate theory. Consequently, the usefulness of engineering a task with the methods of scientific management must be differentiated sharply from the usefulness of organizing a task's component sequential steps in terms of the theory of scientific management.[6]

The establishment of a public career service, third, also tended to have unintended and unfavorable consequences which counterbalanced the favorable and intended consequences. As Sayre put it,[7]

> Stated in its most positive terms, this objective represents an effort to provide the conditions of work which will attract and hold a public service of optimum talents. In its negative aspects, the goal has been translated into an elaborate system of protectionism. In the area of methodology the negative connotations have slowly but surely won the dominant position. . . .

Such protectionism, of course, often would bind the manager severely even as it safeguarded him (and his subordinates) from arbitrary removal.

In sum, then, striving toward the purposes of the civil service movement had its general costs. Three more specific sets of restrictions that burden the management of work in our civil service systems will concern us presently.

These costs of our civil service systems, however, must be kept in perspective. Today we can profit from hindsight and a sophisticated research literature. The efforts to achieve the separation of the civil service from patronage, in contrast, came before enough was known about the conceptual and operational problems of the description of organization, personality, or "position" to preclude an uncomplicated Tinker Toy approach to all three of these elements of personnel administration. That is, simple assumptions took the place of an understanding of empirical phenomena which were at least more complex and often essentially different from the assumptions.

Consequently, the early approach to public personnel administra-

---

[5] See my *Behavior and Organization* (Chicago: Rand McNally, 1962), esp. chs. 1–4.
[6] See my "Organizing Work: Techniques and Theories," *Advanced Management— Office Executive*, Vol. 1 (June, 1962), pp. 26–31.
[7] *Op. cit.*, pp. 134–35.

tion is understandable, if inadequate. The compulsions of life could not wait on the scientific explanation of the universe. However, necessity should not be suffered to be a virtue, lest the original simplistic assumptions become too deeply buried under a specialized literature. Students of public personnel administration, fortunately, have done considerable self-critical work of late. The determined, if preliminary, efforts since World War II to outgrow its early biases are a leading feature of the reorientation currently underway in public administration.[8]

II. Supervisory Power and Civil Service

Perhaps the most rewarding clue to supervisory effectiveness in recent research exploits the "power" concept. "Power" refers, in general, to the ability to control the job environment. Getting recommendations for promotion accepted, for example, indicates that a supervisor has relatively high power. "Power" thus conceptually complements "authority," which refers to the degree to which the formal organization legitimates a supervisor's control of the job environment. Typically, all supervisors at the same level monitoring similar operations have similar authority; and typically, these supervisors will differ in their power.

Power seems to be related to effective supervisory performance, whether it is exercised upwards, as influence with superiors, or downwards, as control of the specific job site. Pelz, for example, studied some fifty measures of supervisory practices and attitudes without finding any marked correlations with employee morale and attitudes. When the influence of a supervisor with his superior was specified, however, rather sharp differences were observed. High supervisory power was associated with effective performance.[9] Consequently, as Likert concluded, a supervisor must be an effective subordinate as well as an effective superior.[10] Otherwise, reasonably, a supervisor cannot be expected to influence his subordinates consistently.

Similarly, power expressed as control of the job site is associated with effective performance. Likert provides much supporting data. A comparison between the top third and the bottom third of departments

---

[8] The outlines of this reorientation are drawn sharply in O. Glenn Stahl, *Public Personnel Administration* (New York, 1956), pp. 577–82.

[9] Donald C. Pelz, "Interaction and Attitudes Between Scientists and Auxiliary Staff," *Administrative Science Quarterly*, Vol. 4 (December, 1959), pp. 321–36, and Vol. 4 (March, 1960), pp. 410–25.

[10] Rensis Likert, *New Patterns of Management* (New York, 1961), p. 114.

(ranked in terms of productivity) is particularly relevant here.. Personnel in the "top" departments, in contrast with the "bottom" departments, uniformly attributed greater influence over "what goes on in your department" to these four sources: higher management; plant management; department manager; and the workers themselves. Moreover, the "top" departments also desired that greater influence be exercised by all four sources than did the "bottom" departments. Significantly, the greatest differences between the "top" and "bottom" departments are in the power attributed to department managers (their primary supervisors) and in the power the men desired that department managers exercise.[11] These are reasonable results. A low-power supervisor has little leverage for motivating his men *via* his control over the job site. That is, the men have little reason to take him seriously.

If the reasons for the importance of supervisory power to effective performance seem clear enough, our civil service systems do little to ease the burdens of managing work *via* increases in supervisory power. This is particularly lamentable because much evidence suggests that the "power" variable may be influenced substantially by the design of the job, by the organization structure (of which more later), and by training. The supervisor's personality, in short, does not appear to be the crucial (or major) factor in determining power.

Although only empirical research can establish the point definitely, there seems ample evidence of this failure of civil service systems to respond to the need to facilitate the management of work by increasing supervisory power. On the broadest level, the first and third primary goals of the civil service movement certainly do not encourage supervisory power; and (as will be demonstrated) the application of the logic and methods of scientific management has the same effect.

To become more specific, these limitations on supervisory power have many practical impacts. For example, first-line supervisors seem to have less control over hiring and firing than their counterparts in business. The difficulty in business organizations of firing or reductions-in-force need not be underplayed, but the elaborate review procedures and the novel "bumping" arrangements[12] often found in our civil service systems probably admit of less flexibility in public agencies even on the part of officials at relatively high organizational levels. Raw turnover ratios seem to support this position.[13] Similarly, the emphasis upon seniority in promotions and pay increases in the

---

[11] *Ibid.*, pp. 56–57.

[12] James E. Drury, *The Displaced Career Executive Program* (Inter-University Case Program, University of Alabama Press, 1952).

[13] Stahl, *op. cit.*, p. 473.

public service plus the failures of supervisory rating of employee performance[14]—both common in our civil service systems—suggest that the environment in public agencies has not been conducive to the general heightening of supervisory power.

Some counterforces are at work, although they do not promise imminent change in the present condition of limited encouragement of supervisory power. Thus the federal program for rewarding superior performance permits a modest increase in supervisory power. Even in this case, however, apparently many agencies have preferred to ride very close herd over the recommendations of lower-level supervisors or (in at least one case of which I have personal knowledge) to neglect the immediate supervisor altogether. Thus this program not only died aborning as an opportunity to increase supervisory power, but its administration may even further reduce that power.

All this, be it noted, is not by way of an argument for arbitrary managerial or supervisory action. Just such abuses, of course, supplied motivation for the restraints emphasized above. The stress here, rather, is upon ways of reinforcing formal authority so as to permit greater effectiveness consistent with the policies of an agency. Just as in the case of any delegation, that is, attempts to increase supervisory power imply training and the development of suitable overhead controls. Moreover, "power" in the relevant research does not imply heavy-handed coercive techniques, which most subjects interpret as lack of control of the environment. Evidence such as that reviewed below in the context surrounding footnotes 48–51 supports this point.

The task of inducing high supervisory power, then, is more delicate than a mere reversal of gears toward the "spoils system" or advocacy of an administrative law of the jungle.

III. Job Design and Civil Service

Similarly, our civil service systems tend to limit the potential for increasing managerial effectiveness implicit in job design. The second primary goal noted above is the chief culprit, with strong support from the goal of "equal treatment." Their interaction in increasing managerial burdens can be illustrated in two ways, by considering specific job content, and by considering the place of the job in the broad organization structure.

In its doctrine about simplifying job content, particularly, the logic of scientific management makes difficulties for managing work effec-

---

[14] Felix Nigro, *Public Personnel Administration* (New York, 1959), p. 295.

tively. As in industry, at low organization levels, the process of routinization often has been carried too far in the public service. The effects of "job enlargement" on employee performance, at least in business concerns,[15] suggest the contribution to effective management that may be gained by adding content to a worker's responsibilities. This may be accomplished by increasing the scope of jobs or by rotating individuals through several jobs.[16] The crucial factor does not seem to be the number of task-elements given to an individual or the complexity of these elements. Patently, a job could become too complex. Rather, the significant point seems to be that various techniques of job enlargement, when they work, work because they increase the worker's control over his job environment.[17] Hence the success of plans for increasing the employee's control over factors which are not in his flow of work, such as that often called "bottom-up management."[18]

The effects of "job enlargement" may be explained in terms of the earlier analysis. In Likert's study, as already noted, employees in high-producing units felt that they themselves exercised and desired more power over their work than did individuals in low-producing units. This is consistent with the favorable effects on output commonly reported in the "job enlargement" literature, while it suggests an apparent paradox. Note that Hi-Pro units ranked themselves *and* three levels of supervisors as higher on "power" than did Lo-Pro units. This might seem curious, but only if one assumes that there is only so much "power" to be had, so that what superiors gain subordinates must lose. The fact seems to be, on the contrary, that a high-power supervisor can afford to (and usually does) allow his subordinates to exercise greater power also.[19] A low-power supervisor is in such an insecure position that he can seldom bring himself to be so generous. The real paradox, then, is that the apparently most straightforward way of adding to one's power is often the most direct way of reducing it. The common mechanical conceptions of organized activity implicit in scientific management discourage such thinking.

The often marked consequences of job enlargement may be illustrated briefly. Machine operations in an industrial concern, for example, had been plagued by an array of difficulties: productivity and quality were falling; and tension between operators and inspectors

---

[15] Chris Argyris, *Personality and Organization* (New York, 1957), pp. 177–87, summarizes many relevant studies.
[16] *Ibid.*, p. 177.
[17] *Ibid.*, p. 180.
[18] William Givin, *Bottom-Up Management* (New York, 1949).
[19] The point has been amply demonstrated in experimental situations. See James G. March, "Influence Measurement in Experimental and Semi-Experimental Groups," *Sociometry*, Vol. 19 (March, 1956), pp. 26–71.

was growing. The crucial factor was that the tool in this particular operation, when dulled to a certain point, would suddenly begin producing pieces which did not meet specifications. Inspectors were not always able to spot such sudden deteriorations in the product quickly, and operators (inspection not being *their* job) did not always cease work even when the quality was obviously unacceptable. Inspection reports helped little when they did come, the operators marking them down as "ancient history." The solution was easy. Simple gauges were given to operators to make periodic checks on their production, and the operators were allowed to decide when it was necessary to resharpen their cutting tools. The consequences: runs of defective products became shorter and less frequent; the nagging tension between inspectors and operators was reduced; and output zoomed.

Examples need not be confined to industrial operations. In a paperwork operation, similarly, a rather simple change increased output by 30 percent and reduced employee turnover by 70 percent.[20]

Although the design of the job could be an important means of reducing the problems of managing work, however, our civil service systems do not encourage the exploitation of such techniques as job enlargement. Consider only one feature which has an inhibiting effect, the very detailed job descriptions common in the public service. That these are an important part of the mechanisms for guaranteeing equal treatment of employees and for developing a career service does little to encourage flexibility in job design. Employee unions and the civil service commission staff can make much of these job descriptions, even in cases in which employees solidly favor changes of a job-enlargement sort. The difficulty is not necessarily avoided by job descriptions which conclude: "or other duties the supervisor may designate." Custom, employee unions, and an overprotective civil service commission can void such open-end descriptions.

Perhaps, however, this leans too heavily on personal (and limited) experience. Some administrators no doubt pay little attention to detailed job descriptions, except for such purposes as convincing the civil service commission that an individual deserves a multi-step promotion. And it may be argued that the significant point is not whether detailed job descriptions exist, but whether strong employee unions exist. Even in such cases, however, the detailed job description is part of the institutional framework within which management and union must function.

In determining the place of the job in the broad organizational pattern, our civil service systems also increase the problems of managing work. Consider two characteristics which tend to dominate pat-

---

[20] Peter F. Drucker, *The Practice of Management* (New York, 1954), pp. 291–92.

terns of organization in the public service, a limited span of control and organization by function or (at lower levels) by process. These characteristics largely derive from the impact of scientific management upon public personnel administration. Analysis of these two characteristics is particularly useful because it demonstrates, among other features, their tendency to reduce supervisory power.

The analysis of these two characteristics is facilitated by some simplified graphics.[21] Figure 1A presents the orthodox organization of

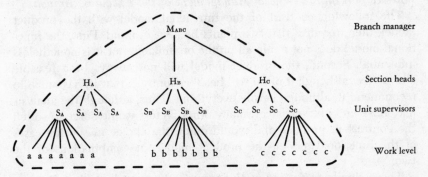

Figure 1A   Functional (Process) Organization with Narrow Span of Control.

functions (or processes) A, B, C—which may be taken to be any components whose integration is required to perform some administrative task—under the condition of a limited span of control. Figure 1B pre-

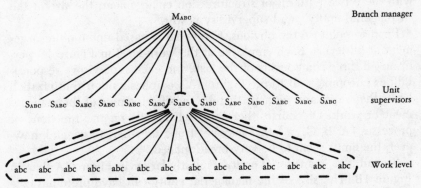

Figure 1B   Product (Discrete Sub-Assembly) Organization with Broad Span of Control.

sents the more unorthodox organization by product (or discrete subassembly), which permits a far broader span of control.

The functional model, with modest reservations, can be considered

---

[21] The parent of this analysis may be found in James C. Worthy, *Big Business and Free Men* (New York, 1959), pp. 90–99.

the pattern for government organizing. This does not do full justice to the diversity of actual organizational arrangements, admittedly. Various factors—size, pressure of work, geography, and the like—have encouraged significant deviations from the functional model. Thus the Justice Department long ago surrendered the fancy of having every government lawyer in the department. The functional model, however, is commonly encountered in practice and it is certainly the most commonly prescribed model in the literature, as in the Hoover Commission's *Report on the General Management of the Executive Branch*.

The following contrast of the functional model with the product model, then, requires that two points be kept in mind. First, the functional model does not guide all public organizing, but it is nonetheless influential. Second, the product model will not always be a feasible alternative, although it often will be. The contrast, that is, has much to recommend it, although hardly everything. Thus, although the analysis may have an either-or flavor, many other factors would serve to soften the contrast in practice and would guide the choice in specific cases of the functional model, the product model, or combinations of the two.

These simple variations in the organization of jobs in larger structures can have profound consequences for the management of work. In general, the type of structure common in most public agencies (see Figure 1A) incurs substantial costs avoided by the less familiar structure in Figure 1B. These costs derive from three features associated with these two patterns of structure: job enlargement; the size of the "managerial entity"; and supervisory power.

First, to point up the obvious, Figure 1B is based upon job enlargement at all levels. Each employee at the work-level in Figure 1B performs all three components of the task, and each supervisor's responsibilities encompass all three. Figure 1A's emphasis upon routinization limits the scope, and perhaps thereby the effectiveness of the management of work. Of course, there are some limits on the functions or processes (A, B, C, ...) that may be strung together. In general, however, the limits seem to be very broad indeed.[22]

Second, the "managerial entity" is vastly larger in Figure 1A than in Figure 1B. The size of the managerial entity can have profound consequences. It may appear, for instance, that the structure in Figure 1B puts too much strain on the capacities of management, because of the apparently greater demands it imposes upon the supervisors. In reality, however, structures such as that in Figure 1A often imply greater

---

[22] The point is supported by the example in Drucker, *op. cit.*, p. 291. See also Argyris, *op. cit.*, pp. 177–87.

(and different) demands upon management talent. Figure 1B structures reduce in significant ways the management burden carried by M_{ABC} and the supervisors as well. The difficulties faced by M_{ABC} in structures like that in Figure 1A cause considerable problems for supervisors, for example, by tending to reduce their supervisory power. Many of the problems associated with sizeable organizations, more generally, derive not from the aggregate size of the organization, but from the size of its component managerial entities. Thus the manager in our hypothetical organization in Figure 1A directs the work of 99 employees and encounters the difficulties to be enumerated below; the manager in Figure 1B oversees the work of 195 employees, yet significant problems facing the management of work are reduced.

The "managerial entity" concept warrants further analysis. Worthy defines it in these terms:[23]

> The administrative unit can be no smaller than that portion of the organization falling within the jurisdiction of an individual who controls enough elements of the total process to make effective decisions regarding the total process.

A high-level managerial entity might be organized around some total product, for example, water resource development in the Kings River Valley. The processing by each of several competing teams of all categories of mail received by the Government Printing Office, with each team handling all correspondence from writers whose names begin with designated letters of the alphabet, illustrates the kind of discrete sub-assembly around which a low-level managerial entity might be organized.

At whatever level of organization, then, a "managerial entity" contains that parcel of process-components necessary for the performance of some discrete task. The areas enclosed by the heavy dotted lines in the two figures above symbolize "managerial entities." Interpretively, any S_{ABC} in Figure 1B can "get all the way around" our hypothetical administrative task. In Figure 1A, in contrast, only M_{ABC} can do this job. M_{ABC} in Figure 1A has a managerial entity which contains 100 individuals; that of S_{ABC} contains only 15.

Many of the problems in sizeable organizations derive from the failure to restrict the size of the organization's managerial entities. Haire's analogy seems apt in this connection. He suggested the mushrooming problems caused by the growth in the size of organizations *via* the "square-cube law" applied to the story of Jack and the Beanstalk:[24]

---

[23] Worthy, *op. cit.*, pp. 92–93.
[24] Mason Haire, ed., *Modern Organization Theory* (New York: Wiley, 1959), pp. 273–74.

... Jack had nothing to fear from the Giant. If he were, as he is pictured, ten times as large as a man and proportioned like one, Jack was perfectly safe. The Giant's mass would be 10^3 or a thousand times a man's, because he was ten times as big in every dimension. However, the cross section of his leg bones would have increased in only two dimensions, and they would be 10^2 or a hundred times as big as a man's. A human bone simply will not support ten times its normal load, and the Giant, in walking, would break his legs and be helpless.

In a similar way, arithmetic increases in the size of the managerial entity seem to generate exponential increases in the problems of the management of work. Meeting these increases in size within the framework of the type of organization structure in Figure 1A does nothing to reduce these difficulties.

This general position can be elaborated. The size of the managerial entity, in sum, is likely to affect such significant features of administration as: the time lag between the perception of a problem and action on it, which influences supervisory power; the style of supervision; the measurement and the motivation of performance; and the training of subordinates.

Patently, first, decisions will tend to be pushed upward in an organization such as that in Figure 1A; for only M_{ABC} oversees all of the components which require integration. As a result, delegation to supervisors is all but restricted to routine matters, that is, those which involve the single component supervised by any supervisor and only that component.

The separation of decision-making from the action level often has significant costs. Overloading upper levels may make time-pressure a very serious factor, the more so if the stakes are high. A shutdown in any of the sections in Figure 1A might cause output to drop as low as zero. The manager, then, is under great pressure to assure that A, B, and C are integrated, and he is likely to exert that pressure downward. This does not encourage upward communication, in turn, which is difficult enough in the "tall" organization described in Figure 1A. (Notice that Figure 1B, with 69 per cent more people, has one less organization level than Figure 1A.) The efforts of the manager to fight the daily battle of integration of the components of his operation and to get the information required for his job, finally, will tend to undercut any efforts by the supervisors to gain high power. The common development of large "staff" units complements this tendency.

In contrast, decisions in Figure 1B organizations would strongly tend to be forced down to the action level, and certainly at least to the level of S_{ABC}. Indeed, M_{ABC} may have no other reasonable alternative, given his broad span of control. Upward communication and supervisory power often will be affected favorably. M_{ABC}, consequently, should be freed from the unremitting pressure of integration implicit in a Figure 1A structure. Downtime at any work station, for example, will not cause difficulty throughout the managerial entity. Output would fall at most by $1/N$. The manager therefore could devote himself to motivating superior performance, to training and counseling, and the like, rather than attempting to eliminate the possibility of error.

These comments on decision-making, second, suggest that the two types of structures encourage different styles of supervision. The structure in Figure 1A encourages "close supervision," *i.e.*, detailed instructions, persistent attempts to direct and observe performance, and the like. The limited span of control, of course, permits this, and the pressure for the integration of the task components may force it. The structure in Figure 1B encourages "general supervision," *i.e.*, monitoring performance in terms of results with considerable freedom for the employee so long as he is performing up to standard. Close supervision of janitors, for example, would require such directions as: "You will sweep from left to right, forty strokes per minute," and correspondingly close checks on performance. General supervision, in contrast, would assume competence and give such instructions as: "Sweep the floors in such time that you are able to get your other work done and so that the floor will reflect x units of light from a refractometer." The refractometer provides the check on performance. Acknowledgedly, this goes a little far. All of the components of general supervision are there, however, especially the measure of performance.

Structures of the type in Figure 1A pay a heavy cost to the degree that they in fact do encourage close supervision. In one study, for example, less than 30 percent of the work teams whose first- or second-level supervisors practiced close supervision had high output. Nearly 70 percent of the work units receiving only general supervision had high output.[25]

The reader may suppose, third, that the manager and supervisors in a Figure 1B organization would face an impossible task in motivating and measuring performance. For general supervision must be based upon performance standards, and what will keep standards high if the supervisor "gets off their backs?" But the several units headed by an S_{ABC}, each performing the same task, obviously set the stage for a relative measure of performance. They are in competition with each other,

[25] Dorwin Cartwright and Alvin Zander, eds., *Group Dynamics* (Evanston, 1953), esp. pp. 617–19.

which tends to keep performance high. This would complement the added contributions to be expected because of the job enlargement practiced in 1B-type structures. At the same time, reduced "line-staff" conflict seems implied by this potential for motivation and measurement, "staff" development being in large part due to top-level management's difficulties in motivating and, especially, measuring performance.

Figure 1A organizations do not offer the same possibilities. One might try to encourage competition within, for example, some S_A unit, or between the S_A units and the S_B units. But competition of that sort, as experimental studies suggest, is not likely to aid performance on most tasks,[26] since the tasks themselves are not comparable, and may indeed be incommensurable. The point may be driven home by considering this proposition: Assembling all As (or Bs or Cs) in organizationally separate units encourages the restriction of output and invites substantial jurisdictional conflict when the responsibility for an error must be assigned. Much evidence supports this proposition.[27] Responsibility is far more difficult to assign in a 1A-type structure, for at least three inspections would be required to permit accurate assignment of praise or blame, one after each of the component operations. Figure 1B organizations would require only one such inspection. Such considerations, and there are many others, attest to the difficulties of motivating and measuring performance in Figure 1A organizations.

These features of Figure 1B organizations suggest a way out of the objection that public agencies are not guided by "profit" and that therefore performance measurement is difficult. In Figure 1A organizations, in business, the measurement of macroscopic profit does little to determine the often crucial measurement of the effectiveness of constituent units. Hence many business enterprises have approached the type of organization sketched in Figure 1B by establishing "individual profit centers" within (for example) a plant. Their services are then "sold" internally, sometimes with the useful provision that outside purchase is possible if price or quality are not considered appropriate by the "buyer."[28] This encourages self-discipline of both "buyer" and "seller." Comptroller W. J. McNeil worked for years to install arrangements of this sort in the Department of Defense, for the provi-

[26] Robert T. Golembiewski, *The Small Group: An Analysis of Research Concepts and Operations* (University of Chicago Press, 1962), pp. 202–4.

[27] Eliot D. Chapple and Leonard R. Sayles, *The Measure of Management* (New York, 1961), pp. 18–45.

[28] W. H. Mylander, "Management by Executive Committee," *Harvard Business Review*, Vol. 33 (May, 1950), pp. 51–58.

sion of common procurement of goods and services, as a means of economy and of strengthening the Secretary's hand.

In any case, fourth, Figure 1B organization's seem to have a definite advantage in the training of subordinates. Patently, S_{ABC} faces training challenges not available to S_A (or S_B or S_C) in the normal course of events. Reasonably, then, organization structures such as that in Figure 1B should tend toward the early elimination of those without management ability, while it would attract the more able. Reasonably, also, high satisfaction and output should characterize Figure 1B organizations. These expectations, indeed, are supported by some research in the Sears, Roebuck chain[29] and elsewhere.[30]

Despite these (and other) advantages of 1B structures, our public personnel systems do not provide a congenial home for them. The dominant emphasis in these systems—and it is no doubt often a necessary emphasis—is negative rather than positive. As one observer with high-level experience in both government and industry noted.[31]

> ... no matter how well briefed on federal service peculiarities the private business executive may be, one of the first things he notices in public administration is this emphasis on procedure and routine. This emphasis is admittedly necessary and desirable provided it does not make method an end in itself. When it does, over-organized bewilderment results. The newcomer to top management positions in the federal service frequently feels that the organization and methods set up with the laudable idea of keeping him from doing wrong actually result in making it excessively difficult to do right.

This emphasis, despite its legitimacy, seems to have been overdone at all levels. Overdone or not, it is something to know what it costs to preserve the emphasis in Figure 1A structures.

Generations of organization theorists have labored hard to preserve the fiction of the unity of command in our public affairs, this being the very slender thread by which we demonstrate that the electorate really does control the administration through its election of the president. One may judge the impact of this theory upon supervisory practices from the longevity of the logically consistent but unrealistic notion that "politics" and "administration" are somehow separate. This no-

---

[29] See William F. Whyte, *Man and Organization* (Homewood, Ill.: Irwin, 1959), pp. 11–16.
[30] Ernest Dale, "Centralization versus Decentralization," *Advanced Management,* Vol. 21 (June, 1956), p. 15.
[31] Marver Bernstein, *The Job of the Federal Executive* (Washington, D.C.: Brookings Institution, 1958), pp. 34–35.

tion, of course, is the keystone of our civil service systems. Their failure to respect the realities of delegation hardly augurs for better treatment of this matter at lower organization levels. Comfortable as the fiction of unity of command may be to many, multi-line relations exist. We may choose to neglect this datum for various reasons, as the Hoover Commission did in arguing for a structure such as that in Figure 1A.[32] But this neglect may prove embarrassing,[33] and it is very likely that our theoretical simplicism has a high cost. Gaus long ago put the argument for a multi-line view in these convincing terms:[34]

> Such a theory . . . is the only one which fits the facts of contemporary delegation of wide discretionary power by electorates, constitutions, and legislatures to the administrators [who] must, of necessity, determine some part of the purpose and a large part of the means whereby it will be achieved in the modern state.

Finally, the accepted pattern of organization in public agencies (as well as in business concerns) is functional. This reflects the historic strength of the model sketched in Figure 1A and suggests the barriers which will restrain attempts to approach the Figure 1B model in organizing.

IV. Job Description and Civil Service

It says worlds, while it avoids an enormous complexity, to note that our civil service systems typically are based upon a duties classification, as opposed to a rank classification. Public personnel specialists have gone in for a duties classification with a sometimes uncritical zeal. As Nigro explains:[35]

> In a duties classification, the beginning point is a detailed analysis of the tasks required in the individual position. In fact, the tendency in the United States has been to make fairly minute investigations of job content.

The emphasis need not be exaggerated, for the specialists have providently refrained from stressing the content of all jobs. The handling of secretarial positions—whose importance is usually measured by secretaries and bosses in terms of what the boss does rather than what

---

[32] Hoover Commission, *Report on the General Management of the Executive Branch* (Washington, D.C., 1949), pp. 1, 3–4.

[33] As, *e.g.*, in *Morgan vs. United States*, 298 U.S. 468, where the Secretary of Agriculture was rebuked for deciding a case he had not heard in person.

[34] In Gaus, Leonard D. White, and Marshall E. Dimock, *The Frontiers of Public Administration* (University of Chicago Press, 1940), p. 91.

[35] Nigro, *op. cit.*, p. 85.

the secretary does—is perhaps the most striking illustration of what has been called the "realistic" approach to classification.[36] But the bias of job description in this country has not moved very far from the classic expression it was given, for example, in the 1932 classification plan for Philadelphia. Nigro called this "one of the best books of specifications on record." It listed twenty individual classes of clerks, for each of which specifications had been developed. Specifications also were stated for thirty additional classes of principal and chief clerks in the various city departments.[37]

The inspirations for this emphasis on job description in our public personnel systems seem clear enough. The logic and methods of scientific management—which encouraged the view of organization as a "delicate mechanism" of gear-like "positions" whose driveshaft was the line of command—clearly had their influence. Moreover, position classification provides the bases for equal treatment, general formal policies and procedures regarding recruitment, salary, promotions, and the like. Finally, position classification encourages the attempt to group similar jobs into a reasonable number of classes, sub-classes, and so on. This provided a ladder-like framework upon which a permanent career service could be built.

Despite its contribution to achieving the goals of our civil service movement, the American approach to job description has its unintended costs. Some obvious costs will be considered immediately; subsequent analysis will consider one less obvious set of costs in some detail.

Since one product of position classification was to be a manageable number of classes, first, this required a procrustean neglect of distinguishing job characteristics. The position approach, second, became the victim of its own imprecise terms. Consider the common observation that the "position" is the "universal building block of all organizations."[38] The observation has a certain validity, since all organizations contain positions. It tended to mislead the unwary, however, into supposing that "organization" is only a set of positions. The temptation to think of organization as some massive mechanical structure of positions linked by lines of authority was strong, since it apparently served to simplify the problems of personnel work.

The emphasis upon a duties classification, third, implies a substantial rigidity. Consider the difficulties of dealing with the many positions which have a kind of life cycle, with stages that impose varying

---

[36] Julius E. Eitington, "Injecting Realism into Classification," *Public Personnel Administration*, Vol. 15 (March, 1952), pp. 31–35.

[37] Nigro, *op. cit.*, pp. 98–99.

[38] Leonard D. White, *Introduction to the Study of Public Administration* (New York, 1948), p. 28.

demands on the incumbent. Developing an administrative role may be a very delicate task, while playing the role thereafter may be child's play. This phenomenon is difficult to accommodate within the framework of most of our public personnel systems. Some adaptations may be made quickly enough. But often it is necessary to waste a "big" man on a job too small for him or to give a "small" man a job too big for him. Similarly, the emphasis upon a duties classification makes it difficult to utilize positions for training purposes without the stretching of a point or two by the position analyst. The traditional question— What does the incumbent do?—is not appropriate for such positions, for he may, in fact, contribute little toward immediate task performance.

The abortive struggles toward a Senior Civil Service, and then a Career Executive Program, for the federal government, reflect the tenacity of the grip of these two types of inflexibilities.[39] For it was intended that the highly mobile and select corps of administrators in such programs would be used in both of the ways alluded to above, that is, as experienced "firefighters" and as trainees getting the "big picture." The rank-in-job bias in our civil service systems played not a little part in the lack of action.

Fourth and finally, the approach *via* a duties classification taken in this country is not the only available one. Indeed, in public administration, it appears that only Canada and Brazil follow our example closely. Many personnel systems—public and business—emphasize broad and general classes rather than narrow and detailed ones. Some of the spirit claimed for the British civil service, for example, is suggested by this open-end description of the few grades of "scientific officer" in Her Majesty's service:[40]

> It is not possible to define with precision the duties of the various grades but, broadly speaking, the duties of the grades above principal scientific officer include responsibility for the administration and direction of scientific work while the principal scientific officer and lower grades concentrate on the scientific work itself. . . .

> But the posts of senior principal scientific officer and above may, with Treasury authority, be created for outstanding individual research workers.

Not infrequently, on the business side, executives will take the more extreme ground that they will not tolerate even an organization chart

---

[39] Paul P. Van Riper, "The Senior Civil Service and the Career System," *Public Administration Review*, Vol. 18 (Summer, 1958), pp. 189–200.
[40] Royal Commission on the Civil Service, *Introductory Factual Memorandum on the Civil Service* (London: Her Majesty's Stationery Office, 1953), p. 54.

at their level, lest it force them into patterns of action which may become inappropriate, just as these patterns develop a vested interest in protecting personnel.

This general approach to job description has its virtues. For example, by all accounts, the British achieve great flexibility, avoid the sometimes gross artificialities of more "precise" efforts, and (one supposes) increase the power of the supervisors whose discretion is obviously emphasized. Their approach also seems to avoid that situation which haunts position analysts and outside observers alike: that an Einstein would have the same grade as any other physicist doing "similar work."

These problems of the American approach are known well enough, although they do not prove the inferiority of a detailed approach to job description in the lower classifications. These problems may have profound consequences for the management of work. At its worst, taking the mechanical aspects of job description too seriously can disrupt the flow of work. Moderation on the part of both "line" and "staff" seems indicated. The decentralization of much personnel work in the federal service suggests that just such a mature moderation has set in.

Others factors encourage a diluted devotion to the methods and theory implicit in the duties classification in this country. Here let us consider only this feature: it is not obvious that the common attempts at precision are precise about all (or most) of the elements of work which are important. This should encourage a healthy skepticism in developing and administering duties classifications. For, first, the technology of duties classification cannot support great precision now, nor is it likely to do so in the immediate future. Second, if a duties classification purports to describe the behaviors required for the effective performance of an organization's work, existing efforts commonly miss many significant possibilities. If it merely codifies existing practices it may not be worthy of vigorous support, for duties classifications are at least implicitly prescriptive.

The specific dimensions which characterize tasks are but imprecisely known. The usual guidelines for classification—level in the hierarchy, formal authority and responsibility, funds administered, and the like—are not sufficient for doing the job tidily. For example, they do not take into account whether Supervisor X is the informal as well as formal leader of his work unit. It is impractical and unjust to treat Supervisor X's job as the same whatever the answer to this question. Moreover, if a job description is prescriptive, a supervisor's socioemotional performance cannot be overlooked. We may fairly ask of an approach which preaches and seeks precision: Precision about what?

The question remains, what is significant in describing a task? It is a disarming question. Existing research does not suggest that it has an obvious or an uncomplicated answer. Factor analysis, a sophisticated mathematical technique, perhaps offers the most hope of developing a set of dimensions which will permit us to describe jobs precisely. A technical discussion of factor analysis hardly can be attempted here. In general, however, the technique permits an initial judgment as to the number of independent dimensions necessary to account for the variation in some batch of scores (*e.g.*, in rankings by several analysts of jobs in terms of the discretion they require incumbents to exercise). The technique has been utilized, for example, to isolate the various kinds of intellectual abilities measured by intelligence tests. There is no way to solve such problems *a priori*. Factor analysis, in sum, might well complement and direct the enormous amount of observation that normally goes into developing a duties classification and into keeping it current.

Applications of factor analysis to job description suggest the problems which must be met. The technique, for example, has been applied to the ratings of a very large number of characteristics of various jobs. Existing results do not suggest that a synthesis is imminent. A simple manual task, for example, required only a few factors to describe it in one study.[41] Another factor analysis of more complex tasks isolated twenty-three factors.[42] Yet only seven factors were considered necessary to describe the 4,000 jobs listed by the U.S. Employment Service.[43] Thus existing work does not suggest a clear pattern. To further complicate matters, there seem to be "families" of tasks for which individual sets of factor dimensions probably must be developed.[44]

Despite the inconclusiveness of such factor analytical work, two points seem clear. First, the dimensions isolated thus far do not closely resemble the guidelines implicit in much classification work. In fact, the factors need not have any obvious connection with "commonsense" notions.[45] Second, the isolation of such factors is only the initial step. Factor analysis provides a rough map of those things which are impor-

---

[41] A. W. Melton, *Apparatus Tests*, AAF Aviation Psychological Program, Research Report No. 4 (Washington, D.C.: Government Printing Office, 1947).

[42] L. L. McQuitty, C. Wrigley, and E. L. Gaier, "An Approach to Isolating Dimensions of Job Success," *Journal of Applied Psychology*, Vol. 38 (1954), pp. 227–32.

[43] E. J. McCormick, R. H. Finn, and C. D. Scherps, "Patterns of Job Requirements," *Journal of Applied Psychology*, Vol. 41 (1957), pp. 358–64.

[44] Launer F. Carter, William Haythorn, and Margaret Howell, "A Further Investigation of the Criteria of Leadership," *Journal of Abnormal and Social Psychology*, Vol. 45 (1950), pp. 350–58.

[45] The naming of factors is not always an easy task, for any factor normally has "loadings" of several variables. Hence the sometimes exotic designations of factorial structures.

tant descriptively. Successful prediction, however, is the crucial test. Such validatory work might take such a form: If the task has dimensions *a* and *d,* individuals which such-and-such training, proficiency, attitudes, and personality will prove to be high producers.

Even this preliminary factorial work has clear implications for our public personnel systems. Duties classification will have limited usefulness to the degree that task dimensions are not developed and the validatory work referred to above is not undertaken. The interim question of whether the pursuit of precision about characteristics—which may or may not be functionally important in describing the task—is worthwhile probably must remain open. The answer is not obviously in the affirmative. A fundamental reevaluation of the common approach to job description in this country seems required, while we await the scientific explanation which will permit great precision. It would seem useful to attempt to test whether general classification provides savings beyond the reach of the detailed classification.

If detail there must be in job description, many factors could fruitfully be included in the usual duties classification. One such is the style of supervision.

Different jobs seem compatible with different styles of supervision. On the available evidence, general statements under this head must be tentative, largely because we know so little about the dimensions along which tasks differ. An example, however, may be hazarded. Provisionally, jobs may be conceived as differing in the degrees to which their performance is programmed and to which their successful performance requires interpersonal cooperation. When a task is unprogrammed and requires high interpersonal cooperation, a permissive supervisory style has seemed most appropriate for those subjects tested. An authoritarian supervisory style will cause the least socioemotional dislocation on tasks which are highly programmed and require little interpersonal cooperation.[46] These are general relations, indeed, and require much specification of intervening conditions. Similarly, individuals with differing personality characteristics tend to perform most effectively under different supervisory styles.[47] Meeting the needs of employees *via* an appropriate supervisory style probably would serve to increase the power of supervisors, or at least to provide supervisors with a favorable environment in which to seek high power.[48]

---

[46] Robert T. Golembiewski, "Three Styles of Leadership and Their Uses," *Personnel,* Vol. 38 (July-August, 1961), pp. 38–39.
[47] Allen D. Calvin, Frederick K. Hoffman, and Edgar L. Harden, "The Effect of Intelligence and Social Atmosphere on Group Problem-Solving Behavior," *Journal of Social Psychology,* Vol. 45 (February, 1957), pp. 61–74.
[48] Likert, *op. cit.,* pp. 93–94.

The specification of such factors as the supervisory style congenial to a job is particularly important because the logic of scientific management encourages the choice of a generally inappropriate style. Thus close supervision—which is consistent with this theory—seems to be associated with high output in only a minority of cases, as already noted. If one had to make a choice between the two types of supervision, then, it is not crystal clear that one would be well advised to obey the logic of scientific management.

This analysis can be extended. Close supervision, patently, is encouraged by a structure such as that in Figure 1A. Supervisory pressure would seem to be most directly applicable in this model, which in turn might suggest high supervisory power. Things, however, do not seem to happen this way often. Likert reports that the more "unreasonable pressure" reportedly exerted by a supervisor, the less the power attributed to that supervisor.[49] Moreover, evidence suggests that greater supervisory pressure serves to isolate the supervisor from his men by increasing the danger of communication.[50] In addition, pressure seems inversely related to output. For example, ten of eleven departments in Likert's study which reported little outside pressure to control the pace of work were above-average producers. Nine of ten departments reporting great pressure were below-average producers.[51] Reasonably, then, job descriptions might well profit from the specification of such job-relevant factors as the style of supervision.

This discussion of two approaches to job description—through those factors normally included, and through those factors which are often neglected—permits of simple summary. There seem to be very substantial costs of commission and omission in the job descriptions common in our civil service systems. These costs complicate the management of work, however nicely the systems fit the three core goals underlying the American approach to public personnel administration.

V. Summary

Our federal Civil Service Commission has been accustomed to serve more than one master. As one commentator noted:[52]

"For whom does the Civil Service Commission work?" We used to reply, "Well, we think it works first for its congressional committees, second for the status employees, third

---

[49] Likert, *op cit.*, pp. 56–57.
[50] *Ibid.*, p. 45.
[51] *Ibid.*, p. 20.
[52] Bernstein, *op. cit.*, p. 76.

for the American Legion in support of veterans' preference laws, fourth for civil service employees' unions, and possibly fifth for the President." Since the end of World War II, the President has moved up in this list but it is difficult to tell just how far.

The analysis above, in essence, argues that yet another master requires service, the development of a work environment within which a professional manager can do his most effective job. Substantial revisions in traditional thinking and technique about our civil service systems will be required to that end.

A New "Staff" Model:
A Synthesis from Behavioral Research

Robert T. Golembiewski

To study nature rather than books, the existential rather than the speculative, often has proved good advice, but this advice, if necessary and convenient, is never sufficient. In the realm of human behavior, for example, consistent covariations of man's relations with men and with his environment are merely interesting *per se*. Whether consciously or unconsciously, values must and will guide the uses to which such empirical regularities are put.

This is common enough, but the dualism has caused uncommon mischief. For (to simplify only a little) those who emphasize the place of values commonly do not reflect deep awareness of the nature and findings of the "behavioralists,"[1] the validity of whose work cannot be judged in terms of *a priori* principles or textual criticism.[2] Those who have busied themselves with empirical research often have neglected values, whether for sufficient reasons,[3] naiveté,[4] or because of the blinding self-interest imputed to "servants of power." This basic bifurcation received strong reinforcement from a variety of sources.[5]

The general purpose here is to help scotch the mischief of compartmentalizing facts and values. Our specific approach is through the "staff" concept, an area of interest in organizational theory. By way of preview, five themes will be stressed. First, the traditional "staff" model will be sketched briefly, and a plausible ecology will be hazarded. Second, the spectrum of problems induced by the traditional concept, or compounded by it, will be outlined. Third, these problems will be analyzed to yield the empirical boundary conditions that must be respected by a more satisfactory "staff" model. Fourth, a set of

[1] For an exception, see Loren Baritz, *The Servants of Power: A History of the Use of Social Science in American Industry* (Middletown, Conn.: Wesleyan University Press, 1960).

[2] Herbert J. Storing, editor, *Essays on the Scientific Study of Politics* (New York: Holt, Rinehart and Winston, 1962), for example, generally neglects the point.

[3] As exemplified in what has been called "empirical work" elsewhere, as distinguished from "goal-based, empirical theory." See Robert T. Golembiewski, " 'The Group Basis of Politics': Notes on Analysis and Development," *American Political Science Review*, Vol. 54 (December, 1960), pp. 962–71.

[4] Leo Strauss aimed this scathing broadside at the "new political science": ". . . one may say of it that it fiddles while Rome burns. It is excused by two facts: it does not know that it fiddles, and it does not know that Rome burns." Storing, *op. cit.*, p. 327.

[5] Robert A. Dahl, "The Behavioral Approach," *American Political Science Review*, Vol. 55 (December, 1961), pp. 763–72.

values suitable for defining the ethical boundaries of such a more satisfactory "staff" concept will be suggested, and the common violation of these ethical boundaries by the traditional "staff" model will be demonstrated. Fifth, the design of an unorthodox model of "line-staff" relations will be attempted, relying on available behavioral research as a guide to the empirically attainable aspects that approach the normatively acceptable ones.

The five themes above constitute a considerable order, and this excuses three major conveniences adopted here. Thus this paper summarizes the results of a long monograph,[6] and documentation and illustration here will be sparse. Moreover, the model to be developed will apply most rigorously to "staff" units with a considerable involvement in "control activities," e.g., accounting, inspection and the like. Finally, the model developed will not be analyzed in detail to demonstrate that it does the required empirical and normative job, although illustrations of the full argument will be attempted.

The focus on "staff" is not trivial even if it is limited in scope and in execution here. This is the case in at least three major senses. Thus "staff" purposes are important indeed. One student outlined these purposes:[7] ". . . to increase the effectiveness of the chief executive through a larger and abler staff of assistants to reduce the load, making it possible for him to devote himself to broader issues and closer contact with his men and with others." Moreover, "line-staff" relations are perhaps the most unsatisfactory and vexing relations in contemporary organization.[8] Finally, scholars and practitioners have regarded the traditional "staff" model with the mixed feelings of the vice-president of personnel of a large pharmaceutical house who allowed, "I believe in the staff concept, up to a point." The precise locus of this point often lies somewhere beyond vigorous criticism of the concept but considerably short of structural innovation. There are few exceptions. Brech represents the common view. Thus he noted that "The more one endeavors to scrutinize the 'line and staff' concept analytically, the more one comes to the conclusion that—in the form in which it is advocated . . . in some quarters—it is an arbitrary and artificial notion whose implications have never been thought through." However he concluded that "The conclusion has, reluctantly, to be drawn that the

[6] Robert T. Golembiewski, *Organizing Men and Power: Patterns of Behavior and Line-Staff Models* (Chicago: Rand McNally, 1967).

[7] American Management Association, *Line-Staff Relationships in Production* (New York, 1957), pp. 7–8.

[8] Harold Koontz and Cyril O'Donnel, *Principles of Management* (New York: McGraw-Hill, 1959), p. 155, for example, put the matter strongly: "There is probably no other single area of management which in practice causes more difficulties, more friction, and more loss of time and effectiveness [than 'line-staff' relations]."

puzzle must remain unresolved, unless the view be accepted that the label serves no useful purpose and is therefore banished from the management vocabulary."[9]

The combination of significance of "line-staff" relations and incidence of unsatisfactory relations goads this analysis on to structural redesign.

The Traditional "Staff" Model:
Description and Ecology

The "arbitrary and artificial notion" that is the traditional "staff" model at least has the virtues of acceptance and simplicity. Despite many variations—both ingenious and ingenuous—a single "staff" model has captivated students of organization in both public and business adminstration. The model is simplicity itself, which may help account for its general acceptance. White described this model typically in these terms:[10] ". . . line authorities . . . are in the central elements of any administrative system; staff and auxiliary services are necessary in a large and complex organization, *but they are secondary*. They serve the line; the line serves the people." Consequently, I have elsewhere designated this model as the Neutral and Inferior Instrument (NII) concept.[11] The structural arrangements suitable for this model will be illustrated and discussed at several points below.

If the prevailing model of "staff" is straightforward, only a hypothetical (if plausible) approach suffices to suggest the forces that supported the development of the concept.

Six major factors in the model's ecological history may be hazarded with profit. *Logically*, the NII model may have been derived from—or at least fits exactly—such "principles" of classical organization theory as the unity of command and functional specialization. Indeed, this writer cannot conceive of any other "staff" model that could do the job.

Methodologically, the "principles" are internally contradictory, which does not clearly indicate a model derived from them or consistent with them. The ambiguity, uncommonly perceived, was therefore commonly tolerated.[12]

---

[9] E. F. L. Brech, *Organization: The Framework of Management* (London: Longmans, Green, 1957), p. 52.

[10] Leonard D. White, *An Introduction to the Study of Public Administration* (New York: Macmillan, 1955), p. 195. My emphases.

[11] Robert T. Golembiewski, "Toward the New Organization Theories: Some Notes on 'Staff'," *Midwest Journal of Political Science*, Vol. 5 (August, 1961), pp. 239–40.

[12] Herbert A. Simon, "The Proverbs of Administration," *Public Administration Review*, Vol. 6 (Winter, 1946), pp. 53–67, is the classic statement of these internal contradictions.

Historically, the period of the early acceptance of the NII model was characterized by a congenial and uncomplicated view of the role of the "specialist."[13]

Technologically, as compared to recent developments,[14] more simple and slower-paced "staff" specialities did not raise very pointed challenges to the neutral and inferior role prescribed by the traditional model. However, the NII model ill suits our new "information technology."[15]

Practically, the NII model avoided an open challenge to the supremacy of the old "line" supervisors and managers, who traditionally had very wide powers indeed and who would no doubt resist dilution of their authority by any "staff" model that did not plead neutrality and inferiority.[16]

Culturally, finally, the NII model well-suited the earlier massive acceptance of what has been called the ownership concept of authority.[17] Of late, compelling forces have increasingly shifted the locus of authority toward "the situation" or to the "expertise" and away from the person-owner. This shift patently provides more room for "staff" action and control.

The Traditional "Staff" Model:
Problems Induced by Structure

Given these inducing and supporting factors, rough sailing can be predicted for attempts to act upon the NII model, and rough sailing there has been. For example, a representative study concluded that only one of twelve companies *appeared* to have reasonably satisfactory "line-staff" relations.[18]

This spotty record may be explained. To this end, some nine common sources of "line-staff" friction underlying such findings will be considered here, and the ways in which the NII model creates or compounds difficulties will be outlined briefly.

1. Control is the correlate of service. This proposition has a cur-

[13] Dwight Waldo, *The Administrative State* (New York: Ronald, 1948), pp. 9–10.
[14] Walter Buckingham, *Automation,* (New York: Harper, 1961), pp. 19–46.
[15] Harold J. Leavitt and Thomas L. Whisler, "Management in the 1980's," *Harvard Business Review,* Vol. 36 (November-December, 1958), pp. 41–48.
[16] George Strauss and Leonard R. Sayles, *Personnel: The Human Problems of Management* (Englewood Cliffs, N.J.: Prentice-Hall, 1960), pp. 346–50.
[17] Mason Haire, "The Concept of Power and the Concept of Man," esp. pp. 171–73, in George B. Strother, editor, *Social Science Approaches to Business Behavior* (Homewood, Ill.: Irwin-Dorsey, 1962).
[18] Edmund P. Learned, David N. Ulrich, and Donald R. Booz, *Executive Action* (Boston: Divisions of Research Graduate School of Business Administration, Harvard University, 1951), p. 155.

rency of long standing,[19] and it refers to a phenomenon of high incidence and of considerable potential for mischief in organizations. Thus Hogan expressed a basic tension between the traditional model and practice in these terms:[20] "One of the principal tenets of the practitioners of modern management methods ... is the centralization of authority ... Yet the development of efficient management methods and their application ... are resulting in a new division of authority and responsibility with resultant cross purposes, and other evils which management methods are designed to eliminate." No doubt some degree of tension will inhere in the service/control dualism, no matter what the structural relations. However, patently, a "staff" model that denies the dualism is asking for trouble. The NII model does precisely this, and it pays the price in conflict.

2. "Staff" personnel and units handle and allocate scarce resources. The story should be a familiar one. Infinite are the ways in which control over scarce resources can become a source of influence for "staff," that is to say, a source of control over the "line's" program. Strauss and Sayles, for example, recount this delightful strategy of a Ship's Stores unit in handling those who made strong demands for a rapid service on complicated requisitions. The demanding units were forced to

> ... fill out in perfect detail the multi-copy, excessively complicated formal requisition sheets that were required by an official, but rarely observed, rule. These same pressuring groups also were denied their share of the special goods and goodies that were distributed, in part, at the discretion of the Stores Department: stationary, film, etc.[21]

Such adaptations by "staff" seem typical. The impact on "line-staff" relations is not eased by the NII model, which presumes "staff" is above such human use of resources possessed. "Line" use of similar resources, in contrast, is made legitimate by the NII model.

3. "Line" and "staff" activities tend toward differing time orientations. Orientations toward today and tomorrow, crudely put, tend to characterize "line" and "staff" units respectively. These differing orientations and their significant consequences are clear, for example, in Argyris' study of the budgeting process.[22] No doubt these differing orientations may be expected and are desirable under many circum-

---

[19] Frank M. Stewart, "Purchasing of Highway Equipment in Texas," *American Political Science Review*, Vol. 29 (May, 1930), pp. 409–15.

[20] Willard Hogan, "A Dangerous Tendency in Government," *Public Administration Review*, Vol. 6 (Summer, 1946), p. 235.

[21] Strauss and Sayles, *op. cit.*, p. 365.

[22] Chris Argyris, *The Impact of Budgets on People* (New York: Controllership Foundation, Inc., 1952).

stances, but the NII model does not facilitate the melding of the long run and the short run. Thus, under the generality of conditions, short-run considerations will tend to prevail. The NII model reinforces man's common temporal myopia by the inferior role it assigns to "staff." The likely consequences—as many studies show—are two: "staff" submissiveness and preoccupation with the trivial; or aggressive efforts by "staff" to gain informally what is denied formally, as by "getting the ear of the chief." Either adaptation is ill-suited, in many or most cases, to cooperative effort.

4. "Staff" personnel often are cast in the role of informants by specific design or they are tempted to play that role informally, and have the greater mobility that facilitates playing such a role. Consider only two commonly induced difficulties. First, the NII concept implies that "staff" is a glorified prosthetic device to enlarge the powers of the owner-manager. This places "staff" in an informant's role. Illustratively, "staff" reports "up, over and down" rather than "across." The consequences are many and significant. The lower-level "line," for example, understandably will be reticent to reveal information or aid "staff" investigators, given that the effect often will be punishment of the "line" and reward for the "staff."[23] The approach is psychologically and practically weak. Time may be sacrificed, for example, and indeed all opportunity for timely action may be lost.[24]

Second, playing the role of informant often is an effective way of gaining the support of the top "line," and particularly so because of the difficulties of the top "line" in measuring performance in an organization following the "principles" and the NII model.[25] The strategy, then, is a convenient way for the upwardly mobile "staff" man to compensate for his organizational inferiority. The unfortunate consequences of the NII model are also patent in this case. These consequences are not clearly overbalanced by the contributions to performance made in the process over the generality of cases.

5. The difficulty of measuring "staff" contributions, and the common rapid growth of "staff" personnel over considerable periods of an organization's growth, poses considerable and related problems for "line-staff" relations. A complex analysis would be required for the full development of the point. Crudely, however, the NII model and the "principle" of specialization by function and process combine to com-

---

[23] Harry D. Kolb, "Headquarters Staff Man as Consultant," pp. 144–45, in Mason Haire, editor, *Organization Theory in Industrial Practice* (New York: Wiley, 1962).
[24] The "line" supervisors in Argyris budgeting study, for example, echoed this refrain.
[25] Robert T. Golembiewski, "Organization Structure and the New Accountancy: One Avenue of Revolution," *Quarterly Review of Economics and Business*, Vol. 3 (Summer, 1963), pp. 29–40.

plicate the problems of the measurement of the performance of "staff" activities.[26] The growth pattern common to "staff" services ill suits these problems of measuring performance that are exaggerated by the NII model. As Haire roughly summarized the experience of a number of firms:[27] ". . . during the period when the line first doubled, the staff grew six times as large. When the line next doubled, the staff grew about five times; the next doubling of the line was accompanied by a tripling of the staff; and from then on they (approximately) each doubled."

The traditional model makes the worst of these two factors. Much of this growth pattern may be attributed to the "up, over and down" pattern of reporting implied by the NII model, which generates a need for paper-manipulating intermediary levels in "staff" hierarchies and in the "line" as well. In addition, the punitive environment encouraged by the NII model also commonly would generate a need for increasingly more "staff" aid to unearth increasingly lesser informational increments.

In sum, the NII concept does not ameliorate this fifth source of tension between "line" and "staff." In significant senses, indeed, the model heightens this tension.

6. "Staff" is oriented toward change, and the "line" toward stability. This source of tension seems pervasive and often is sharp. One budget official in Argyris' study, for example, put the matter in these terms: "We guard the fields. The budget department has to constantly strive to improve the goods and make the plant better. There is always room to make things better."[28] "Line" officials were less certain of his major thesis.

The NII model aggravates this source of tension. Note only that the NII model requires that changes often must be suggested to the "line" by "outsiders" from another organizational unit.[29] The implied dynamics are awkward, for they encourage resistance by the "line" who can at least note pointedly that the "staff's" suggestions for change can be made cheaply, for the "line" faces often painful problems of adaptation, and, if matters go awry, the "staff" always can plead lack of

---

[26] The difficulties and an example of possible measurement are provided by H. J. Helmer, "You Can Measure the Results of Production Training," *Factory Management and Maintenance*, Vol. 110 (March, 1952), pp. 128–30.

[27] Mason Haire, "Biological Models and Empirical Histories of the Growth of Organizations," p. 292, in Haire, editor, *Modern Organization Theory* (New York: Wiley, 1959).

[28] Argyris, *The Impact of Budgets on People*, p. 14.

[29] For an example of the difficulties associated with this role, see Alfred D. Chandler, Jr., *Strategy and Structure* (Cambridge: Massachusetts Institute of Technology, 1962), p. 154.

responsibility because it is "advisory only." Moreover, "staff" entreaties can be expected to grow all the more insistent, given reasonable "line" reticence and given "staff's" neutral and inferior role in the NII model. The point is not trifling, and some interesting recent work has demonstrated basic conflicting personality predispositions of "line" and "staff" in this particular,[30] perhaps a function of their roles under the NII model.

7. Significant cultural differences exist between "staff" and "line." These differences stem from a variety of sources: pressure of work, working conditions, education, identification with organization *versus* profession and the like.[31] In combination, these sources can serve to significantly fragment "line" from "staff." The NII model, of course, reinforces such difficulties by the common physical and organizational separation of "line" and "staff," as well as by the superior-inferior distinction upon which the model rests. In addition, cultural differences can feed on such consequences of the NII model as increased problems of communication.

8. "Staff" activities induce high levels of frustration that affect work adversely. Evidence is not conclusive on this point, but research and observation do permit some very strong suspicions.[32] Reasonably, for example, all of the preceding sources of tension could lead to high levels of frustration. The NII model, of course, is thus a probable villain. In addition, the NII model's implied separation of "thinking" from "doing" is psychologically awkward, for evidence suggests that "tension systems" will develop as the individual is prevented from completing some task.[33] In effect, of course, the NII model inhibits "staff" from extinguishing such tension systems by defining its role as advisory or service only. Further, evidence suggests that such extinguishing also can occur if a fellow group member completes the task.[34] The NII model, however, discourages "line" and "staff" from conceiving of themselves as members of a mutual group.

9. The integration of "staff" activities is a significant factor in increasing the delicacy of "line-staff" relations.[35] The causes are varied. No doubt the specialization by subfunction or process prescribed by

[30] Behavioral Research Service, Relations Services, General Electric Company, *Motive Patterns of Managers and Specialists* (February, 1960).

[31] Melville Dalton, *Men Who Manage* (New York: Wiley, 1959), pp. 87–99.

[32] *Ibid.*, pp. 95–99.

[33] Bluma Zeigarnik, "Uber das Behalten von Erledigten und Unerledigten Handlungen," *Psychologische Forschung*, Vol. 9 (1927), provides the classical experimental demonstration.

[34] David M. Shaw, "Size of Share in Task and Motivation in Work Groups," *Sociometry*, Vol. 13 (June, 1960), pp. 203–8, for example, permits this construction.

[35] O. Glenn Stahl, "The Network of Authority," *Public Administration Review*, Vol. 18 (Winter, 1958), pp. ii–iv.

the "principles" of organizational theory bears some major responsibility. Moreover, the several "staff" activities commonly are competing players in the organizational contest for power. The NII model does nothing to reduce the difficulties of integration. This model is derived from (or at least is consistent with) the "principles," and the NII model rises above recognizing the political demands of organized life. In addition, the NII model implies an "up, over and down" pattern of reporting. The problem then becomes the integration by the "line" of the efforts of several longish and separate "staff" hierarchies, the integration of which under the conventional theory must occur (if anywhere) at or near the top levels of organization although integration of "staff" services and "line" activities is most pressing toward the lower levels. The possibilities for integrative slippage are enoromus, consequently.

A New "Staff" Model:
Some Empirical Boundaries

This minianalysis of nine common sources of tension suggests a number of empirical conditions that must be improved upon, or induced, to facilitate "line-staff" relations. The task is of mixed difficulty. Thus much of the edge could be taken off the first two sources of tension by the simple expedient of rejecting the legitimacy of the NII model, as in Stahl's seminal contribution.[36] However, more satisfactory relations generally depend upon pervasive changes in traditional patterns of thought about organizing as well as upon changes in the "staff" concept. After all, the NII model is consistent with the "principles," and it seems reasonable that significant improvement in "line-staff" relations can come only as a consequence of fundamental changes in these underlying prescriptions that guide organizing.

Four gross empirical conditions to be approached outline the specific guides which the redesign of a "staff" model must respect. First, the new "staff" model must be grounded in a theory of organization that facilitates the measurement of performance. The "principles" of the traditional theory of organization do rather poorly on this score since they at once complicate the measurement of performance (by emphasis on functions and processes) while they attempt to compensate for the complication in ways that can be self-defeating (limited span of control, emphasis on authoritarian supervisory style, centralization and the massive reliance on "staff" to generate information and exercise oversight). Worthy summarily puts some of the mensural problems

---

[36] *Ibid.*

associated with the "principles," and their derivative interpersonal difficulties, in these terms:[37]

> ... where the internal structure of the organization is broken down into a series of functional [or processual] divisions, there are no "natural" standards of performance and management is forced to exercise considerable ingenuity in inventing controls which it can use for administrative purposes. Unfortunately, contrived controls such as these, so far from facilitating inter-divisional co-operation (which is one of their chief purposes) often become themselves a source of conflict. The individual supervisor or executive is under strong compulsion to operate in such a manner as to make a good showing in terms of the particular set of controls to which he is subject, and often he does so only at the expense of effective collaboration across divisional lines.

Relatedly, the redesign of a "staff" model should reflect a basic concern with the horizontal flow of work. In contrast, the "principles" are preoccupied with the vertical flow of authority. For example, the NII model seems to be a derivative of the desire to preserve the "unity" of the vertical flow of authority. Too, the "top–down" orientation of the "principles" is clear in prescribing departmentation by functions at the top level and processes at lowest levels and in the bias of the "principles" toward centralization. The awkward features of this "top–down" approach have been demonstrated elsewhere elegantly.[38] The redesign of a "staff" model might reasonably emphasize a "bottom–up" orientation and decentralization.

Additionally, structural redesign also must group all "line" and "staff" participants who contribute to a common flow of work. The "principles" and the NII model oppositely separate "line" and "staff" irrespective of the flow of work. The advantages of the former approach are numerous: it would facilitate the measurement of performance; it is a "bottom–up" approach; it can serve to reduce cultural differences and to avoid the "outsider" role with which "staff" often is saddled; and it can utilize the power implicit in group relations to increase output and satisfaction of members of an organizational unit that includes all of the necessary activities for some complete flow of work. The proposed emphasis, that is, may be conceived as the horizontal integration of all of the activities necessary for some industrial or administrative discrete subassembly.

---

[37] James Worthy, "Some Aspects of Organization Structure in Relation to Pressure on Company Decision-Making," p. 77, in L. Reed Tripp, editor, *Proceedings of the Fifth Annual Meeting of the Industrial Relations Research Association* (IRRA Publication No. 10, 1953).

[38] Eliot D. Chapple and Leonard R. Sayles, *The Measure of Management* (New York: Macmillan, 1961), pp. 18–45.

In contrast, the "principles" prescribe organizing around separate functional or processual contributions to undifferentiated flows of work. Social and psychological identifications, then, tend to be concentrated within monofunctional or monoprocessual units.[39] These identifications with separate units that contribute only partially to some discrete subassembly or product, as it were, vertically fragment the flows of work.

Finally, these first three conditions suggest much larger units of organization at the lowest levels than are implied by the limited span of control of the "principles." This, in turn, suggests a means of facilitating the integration of the several "staff" specialities and subspecialties. For example, one can conceive of the assignment of a "staff" official to a particular flow of work who would be responsible for integrating the full range of subspecialties of (for example) the personnel function. Considerable specialization, at the same time, could exist at high levels of organization of the personnel function. These lower-level "staff" officials would participate as coequal colleagues in significant decision making in teams built around the several flows of work at the lowest levels while they administer and integrate the full range (or many) of the subspecialties of the function they represent. These "staff" officials also would share responsibility for team performance.[40]

Our focus on the flow of work constitutes a grave violation of the "principles" and NII model in one sense and supports them in another. The working notion, crudely, is this. "Line" and "staff" colleagues would participate as coequals making decisions on matters of substantive concern to the entire team, and this violates the traditional theory. In addition, both "line" and "staff" officials would function more autonomously as the heads of their own subordinates in "technical" matters already a matter of consensus or of policies formulated at higher levels, thereby preserving the notion of unity of command.

Our approach to redesign of a "staff" model has a number of advantages. Thus the contributions to performance of "staff" activities by specific individuals on specific teams would be made directly and would stand out prominently with considerable discretion being given to the teams in the allocation of their budget among the several "staff" activities. This suggests some interesting possibilities of self-imposed control although it does not imply administrative chaos. The comparative performance of the several teams on similar flows of work assures that cases of inappropriate allocation will become evident soon enough.

---

[39] Dalton, *op. cit.*, pp. 58–64.

[40] This condition has been approached at some Raytheon sites. See Harry R. Knudson, Jr., "Enter the Personnel Generalist," *Personnel*, Vol. 37 (March–April, 1960), pp. 33–41.

In addition, some intriguing possibilities exist for developing "line-staff" bonus arrangements tied to the efficiency of the performance within their particular flow of work. Where attempted, the consequences (as in speedy provision of "staff" services) of such efforts have been salubrious indeed.[41]

The "principles" and the NII model discourage, if they do not preclude, such reasonable efforts, and generally the traditional theory provides much less leverage for motivating and rewarding behavior that contributes to the integration of the several "line" and "staff" activities in a flow of work. Rather, the bias of the "principles" and the NII model is toward the reward of individual efforts on some single and microscopic contribution.

A New "Staff" Model:
Some Normative Boundaries

The empirical boundary conditions above set a stern task for the redesign of a suitable "staff" structure, but they do not exhaust the limits that any redesign must respect. Table 1 conveniently provides

TABLE 1

BEHAVIORAL CONDITIONS ASSOCIATED WITH HIGH OUTPUT
AND HIGH SATISFACTION CONSISTENT WITH JUDAEO-CHRISTIAN VALUES
WHICH SHOULD GUIDE MAN-TO-MAN RELATIONS IN ORGANIZATIONS.

Values Guiding Man-to-Man Relations	Conditions Associated with High Output and with High Satisfaction
1. work must be psychologically acceptable, generally non-threatening	1. congruence of personality and job requirement 1a. compatibility of personalities of work-unit members
2. work must allow man to develop his faculties	2. job enlargement 2a. job rotation 2b. training, on and off the job 2c. decentralization
3. the task must allow the individual room for self-determination	3. job enlargement 3a. general supervision 3b. wide span of control
4. the worker must influence the environment within which he works	4. group decision-making 4a. peer representation in promotion 4b. self-choice of work-unit members 4c. decentralization
5. the formal organization must not be the sole and final arbiter of behavior	5. decentralization 5a. group decision-making

[41] Robert T. Golembiewski, "A Behavioral Approach to Wage Administration: Work Flow and Structural Design," *Journal of the Academy of Management*, Vol. 6 (December, 1963), pp. 267–77; and Seymour Melman, *Decision-Making and Productivity* (New York: Wiley, 1958), pp. 6–8.

the further specification necessary, it presents both a set of normative conditions that redesign should attempt to approach, and it lists some useful techniques that tend to be associated with high output and high employee satisfaction.[42] The proof of this happy congruence has been sketched elsewhere.[43]

The human tragedy, of course, may be written in significant measure in terms of the tension between the attainable and the desirable elements. Our present level of development, however, puts many desirable strategies within reach. This opportunity will not be neglected here. Thus the values to guide organizing (the left column in Table 1) are consistent with the empirical requirements suggested above for the new "staff" model. The persevering reader will find the strategies for organizing (the right column) reflected in, or consistent with, the design to be attempted below. Consider the former point. For example, job enlargement and job rotation are not encouraged by the "principles" or the NII model.[44] In contrast, the empirical boundaries for redesigning the "staff" concept would facilitate job rotation since a variety of jobs would be included on each team at the lowest level. Moreover, job enlargement is implied. Thus each "staff" representative on each team would have a job of increased content, as administrator and integrator of a wide range of subprograms (e.g.) in personnel. Moreover, because of the size of each team and the range of activities represented thereon, the job of the "line" supervisor also would be enlarged even though he would share in team making decisions as a colleague of "staff" officials.

A New "Staff" Model:
A Structure Illustrated

The preceding empirical and normative guidelines challenge the redesign of a more suitable structure for "line-staff" relations. The challenge is accepted here, albeit at the grave disadvantage of limited space. The analysis, therefore, will lean heavily on a single illustration encompassing the relative mischief of the traditional model as well as the relative advantages of an unorthodox model. This unorthodox

---

[42] Robert T. Golembiewski, "Organization as a Moral Problem," *Public Administration Review*, Vol. 22 (Summer, 1962), p. 54.

[43] Robert T. Golembiewski, *Men, Management, and Morality* (New York: McGraw-Hill, 1965).

[44] The often salubrious consequences of both techniques are, or should be, well-known. See Georges Friedmann, *The Anatomy of Work* (Glencoe, Ill.: Free Press, 1961), pp. 2–66.

model will be referred to as the "Colleague model," following the distinction introduced earlier.

The effort here is a modified "ideal type" analysis. That is, the Colleague model is not merely an exercise in logic limited by the empirical and normative boundaries sketched above, although this certainly is an important aspect of the present effort, for there are numerous cases of approaches in practice[45] to the Colleague model that have proved effective. This analysis builds upon these cases and extends them.

A typical assembly operation provides a convenient frame for the illustration here. Figure 1 depicts the conventional structuring of relations of such an operation.[46] The experiences with the formal structure in one case typify the problems to which it is heir, although determined efforts can avoid them.[47] In general, the integration of operations proved to be most delicate under the orthodox structural arrangements. Many controversies rattled their ways up and down the several and separate "line" and "staff" hierarchies, finally requiring the personal intervention of the vice-president of manufacturing. A bitter-end clash of personalities did not account for this significant and painful record. Rather, the orthodox structure made the vice-president the only officer who could make reasonable and nontrivial decisions relevant to the total flow of work. Further, the formal structure fragmented the flow of work, as in Figure 2.[48] The structure was built around separate functional and processual units that had their own interests and strategies. These units had to be integrated into a sequential flow of work, but there was no one short of the vice-president who had formal authority sufficient to attempt to force the integration.

The general picture may profit from specific illustration. For example, the 100% inspection clearly was in the flow of work, while the quality-control inspection need not disturb the sequence of operations. The pace of work at the 100% inspection—a quick, visual inspection— that is to say, had to be approximately the same as in the assembly sequences. Enormous reservoirs of good will could have surmounted the barriers to integration. However, the good will did not exist in such copious amounts. Such factors as different suborganizational interests often were barriers to integration, and particularly as they clashed over "objective dilemmas." "Objective dilemmas" include such pervasive

[45] Melman, *op. cit.*; and Adolph Vlcek, Jr., "Minimizing Line-Staff Friction at Martin-Baltimore: Functional-Operational Organization Structure," pp. 39–52, in American Management Association, *Line-Staff Relationships In Production.*

[46] See Chapple and Sayles, *op. cit.*, pp. 27–32.

[47] For an example, see Robert H. Guest, *Organizational Change* (Homewood, Ill., Irwin-Dorsey, 1962).

[48] Chapple and Sayles, *op. cit.*, p. 28.

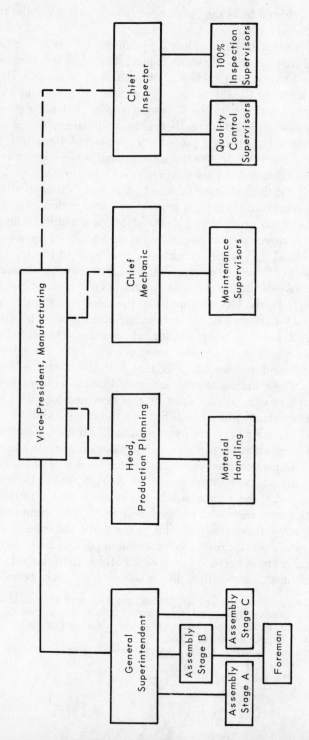

Figure 1 Organization of a typical assembly operation in terms of the "principles" and the NII model.

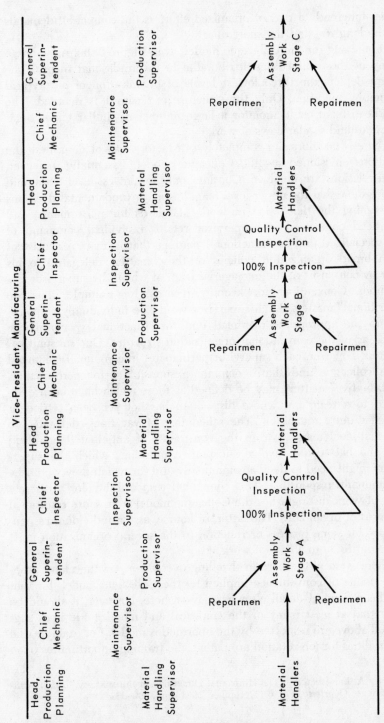

Figure 2 The fragmentation of the flow of work of a typical assembly operation by the "principles" and the NII model.

issues inherently a part of organized effort as the competing demands of the long run and the short run.[49]

Organizing for the Colleague model, as in Figure 3, helps moderate many of these difficulties attributable to the traditional theory. The figure depicts the three lowest levels of organization of our typical assembly operation. Only the structure of Team 1 is detailed. The overhead team could monitor a large number of similar teams organized around similar flows of work.

There is no short and completely satisfactory way of describing the relations envisioned for the Colleague model. Essentially, however, dual relations are involved. Consider only the lowest-level team, and also assume that the upper-level team has made fundamental decisions concerning the delegation of work, standards for performance and overhead controls. Each supervisor retains individual command of his specialized unit on "functional" matters, that is, matters consistent with broad organization policies or those matters delegated to his unit by consensus of the managerial team of which the supervisor is a member. Conventions for keeping records, for example, illustrate "functional" matters. Each supervisor would be individually responsible to the appropriate overhead unit for "functional" performance, much as in the conventional organization structure. On "substantive" matters, however, each supervisor participates in communal command as a colleague and shares common responsibility for performance. "Substantive" matters may be defined as those which have been delegated to a team but whose disposition has not yet been settled or which require redecision. The scheduling of vacations—delegated to the first-level teams, within the constraints of anticipated workload and the like—could involve substantive questions which the supervisors might need to decide communally and for which they would be communally responsible. This communal responsibility for a discrete flow of work distinguishes the Colleague model from more traditional patterns of organizing. The latter, of course, assign individual responsibility for some process or function to the several organization units that contribute to a flow of work.

There is no virtue here in dwelling overly long on the many probable points of convenience implied by the Colleague model, for that has been done in detail elsewhere. Even here, however, it should be clear that at least many of the empirical and moral guide lines suggested above are respected by the unorthodox model. For example, the possibilities for job rotation are patent, the training opportunities open

---

[49] Henry A. Landsberger, "The Horizontal Dimension in Bureaucracy," *Administrative Science Quarterly*, Vol. 6 (December, 1961), pp. 299–332.

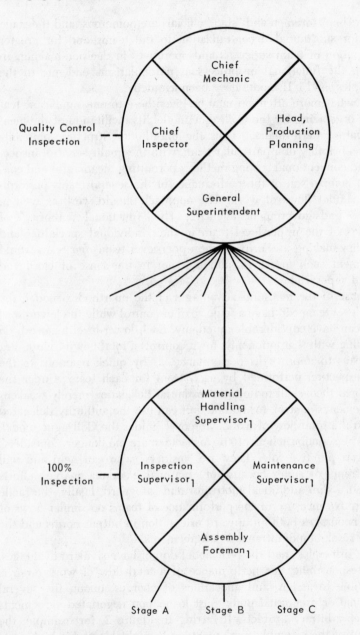

Figure 3 Organization of a typical assembly operation in terms of the
Colleague model.

to both "line" foremen and "staff" officials are numerous, and the stage is set for substantial decentralization to the teams and for greater participation of team superiors and operatives in decision-making. In general, the functional or processual particularisms endemic to the "principles" and NII model have been avoided.

Somewhat more attention may be given here to one significant feature of organizing for the Colleague model, its facilitation of the measurement of performance. Thus the unorthodox structure pinpoints the responsibility of a particular team, with the quality-control inspection and conventional costing methods permitting meaningful and convenient comparison of the performance of the several teams performing in similar flows of work. The approach should work as well in business and government agencies. The "functional authority" of members of the upper-level team in their individual specialties and the policy-making authority of the upper-level team *qua* team would supplement such measures, although not in the sense of close and detailed supervision.

Because of the mensural advantages of the unorthodox model, the upper-level team can have a wide span of control while the lower-level teams can have considerable autonomy. Each lower-level team can do something with that autonomy, for it controls a total flow of work, i.e., the means to improve its performance, as by quick reactions to the 100% inspection performed by each team for each team. Under the traditional theory, all too often substantial delegation merely weakens management's control, for no one unit can use the authority delegated to control a total flow of work. Moreover, under the Colleague model, "staff" personnel such as 100% inspectors are no longer "outsiders" playing a punitive role. They are "insiders" who can help and will profit from (or suffer because of) reasonable (unreasonable) efforts to do so. As an additional motivator and safeguard, finally, the facile comparative measure of the performance of teams on similar flows of work encourages both an upward orientation in output norms and the speedy resolution of intrateam disagreements.

The "principles" and the NII model do not have similar advantages. Thus responsibility for performance of a total flow of work often is impossible to assign, and allocations of charges among the several functional or processual units must lean upon negotiated agreements or other arbitrary artifacts. Referring to Figure 2, for example, the foreman of the assembly work at Stage B might blame his high costs on the awkward pace of work at A, or on the sloth of the inspectors and/or repairmen and/or material handlers. *Their* supervisors, however, often would take an unkindly view of such criticism of their own (and, of course, of themselves). Both charge and resistance often are safe in a sense, for such charges are notoriously difficult to establish. This datum encourages their use as defensive measures.

The traditional structure implies a high potential for conflict involving large units of organization, any one of whom could severely limit or completely stop production. Relatedly, the grouping of large numbers of personnel performing the same activity encourages the restriction of output. This follows the rule of thumb that the more possible is the more likely to occur. All units acting together can raise output in the traditional structure, but one willful unit in a strategic position can force it to lower levels.[50] The structure in Figure 3, in contrast, permits much less of this sort of thing.

An In-Process Summary

Such considerations suggest the usefulness of the Colleague model. However, considerable research will be necessary before one can be affirmative about many features of the model, such as the nature and incidence of the conditions under which it may be applied with reasonable expectations of success. Hence the title of this brief section is "An In-Process Summary." The purpose here was as much to provoke further investigation as it was to refine existing research and to approach certain normative goals.

---

[50] See the analysis of "strategic groups" in Leonard R. Sayles, *Behavior of Industrial Work Groups* (New York: Wiley, 1958).

Chapter 4

Managing by Thousands:
Developing and Maintaining an Institution

Many demands of organized life that can be sloughed off at lower levels, plus many demands far beyond the perspective or competence of lower levels, constitute the top-level executive workload. "Top-level" here refers to the chief executive officers of firms as well as of major departments of government, and includes officers of the larger subdivisions of both. At the lower boundary, for example, the plant manager of a multiunit decentralized firm is certainly in the business of managing thousands in the sense intended here, and some of his major department heads also might be carrying responsibilities greater than those of middle management.

Managing by thousands covers much organizational ground, then, and most of it is crucial ground indeed. Our approach to extensiveness and significance will be straightforward and undoubtedly too simple for the complexity of the relevant phenomena. However, we can hardly avoid some attempt to provide some structure that will aid in exploring the variegated executive realms. Our attempt will have three components. First, some of the characteristics of the work of top management will be outlined. Second, some major demands imposed on the individual operating at the executive level will be sketched. Third, some attention will be given to the peculiar executive problems that inhere in the characteristics of top management jobs and in the demands they make of incumbents. Characteristics and demands and problems, then, are seen as three aspects of that seamless cloth of reality we refer to as the management of thousands.

Caution is the order of the day when considering the characteristics of the job of the top-level manager. We shall be cautious while we attempt to say something relatively specific. Three characteristics of the executive job strike us as being particularly relevant. First, the activities of top-level managers influence thousands, although they may directly supervise small departments or even only a handful of individuals. Second, top-level management is preoccupied with developing and maintaining a social institution that gives organic meaning and continuity to technical procedures, formal policies, and paper procedures. Third, top management deals with matters of scope that often have broad and significant ethical implications. In this sense, the executive role sharply contrasts with the "organization engineering" orientation of middle management.

These three characteristics of the job of the top-level executive permit direct summary and imply the organizational demands experienced by incumbents. In sum, the management of thousands imposes such multifaceted and onerous demands on executives that their actions will have significant consequences on many people, whether for good or ill. The consequences are practical, social, and ethical; and they are uniformly profound. A summary consequence has a magisterial stature. Increasingly, man's freedom must be found in organizations if it is to be found anywhere. Top-level managers will help satisfy or will contribute to frustrating the quest for freedom of Organizational Everyman. Patently, there is no denying the crucial integrative role of the top-level executive.

Precise definitions of the derivative organizational demands on the top-level executive have no end, but two of these demands seem significant enough to set down. To an unusually high degree, to emphasize a first demand, the top-level executive has no place to hide from the problems that percolate up to his level. "The buck stops here," stated President Truman in expressing the major demand of his august office. To be sure, some executives follow Calvin Coolidge's opposed advice. When ten problems could be perceived as building up in intensity, Coolidge observed, the wise executive had only to wait and nine of them would somehow be resolved before they reached him. Nevertheless, that tenth problem can raise merry hell, and when it does the executive cannot escape its consequences.

Relatedly but independently the top-level executive must experience unique organizational demands because no one else sits exactly where he does.[1] It is he who can best attempt to balance the conflicting demands of the component activities of his organization simply because he is above direct identification with any one of those activities. This summarizes both opportunity and difficulty. In any case, and

---

[1] Richard E. Neustadt insightfully applies this notion to the office of the presidency. See his *Presidential Power* (New York: Wiley, 1960). Peter F. Drucker develops a similar analysis for the business executive in *The Effective Executive* (New York: Harper and Row, 1966).

make no mistake of it, the "view from the top" *is* different. The view from the top, because only the top man sits there, must be general and comprehensive. In contrast, even very high-level officials heading large functional units in centralized organizations may adopt—or may be forced by their subordinates to adopt—parochial and partial perspectives because of where *they* sit.

Sometimes, indeed, a single individual has the unusual opportunity to experience the varying demands made on "ultimate generalists" and "high-level specialists." Simon recounts the story of one Nelson Eckart of the San Francisco Utilities Department who wore three organizational hats: he was head of the Water Department; he served in the place of the recently deceased head of the Hetch Hetchy Power development; and he was acting Utilities Manager during the month-long absence of the department head Cahill who was in charge of a wide range of local utilities including water and power development. The experience was unnerving. On Cahill's return, Eckart quit. It was some time before the complex reasons for the move became clear to Cahill. As Simon summarized Cahill's search-and-discovery pattern:[2]

> He discovered, in fact, a letter Waterman Eckart had written asking for more water-works, another letter Hetch Hetchy Eckart had written asking for more HH dough, and a final letter Acting Utilities Manager Eckart had written denying both of his own requests. Naturally, Cahill asked what the devil. "From up here," Eckart explained, "things don't look the same as they do from down there."

The characteristics and demands of top-management jobs imply rather narrow boundaries within which the executive can operate effectively. Let us illustrate these boundaries in terms of two continua, the extremes of each of which the executive must labor to avoid. One of these continua may be labeled "stability/change." Patently, any organization has short-run objectives. These objectives cover a broad range: answering letters; building bridges; providing information. Thus the executive must create an organization that has some characteristics of the proverbial well-oiled machine. "Stability" thus becomes an executive guideline, but fixation on that objective must be avoided. Every organization also has longer-run goals such as adapting to a newer technology or to a developing organizational mission-and-role. Preparing the way for regular "change" then is an executive responsibility whose demands must be delicately traded-off against the demands of steady-state operations. Extremism on this continua definitely will get its come-uppance, in the short-run or the long.

---

[2] Herbert A. Simon, *Administrative Behavior* (New York: Macmillan, 1957), p. 214n.

The executive cannot console himself that he has but few such continua with which to contend. For example, a second continuum requiring executive tightrope walking may be called "chaos/conformism." That is, every functioning organization is infused with value. The same job may be done differently in two "similar" organizations, for example, and these differences reflect various sets of norms and values. These norms may have roots in the personalities of organizational members, in idiosyncratic common experiences, or perhaps even in minor variations in technology or architecture, but differences there will be.[3] Consequently, executive carelessness about the value aspects of an organization can be serious. At the very least, the executive will have missed the opportunity to consciously put his personal mark on his technical organization. At the worst, values may develop and persist which are in direct and major conflict with the organization's public objectives. Informally enforced restrictions on output, for example, typify the normative "chaos" that can result from an executive's shrinking from the task of infusing an organization with values he considers appropriate. On the other hand, rigid preoccupation with punctilious adherence to any organization's normative minutiae may result in an enervating "conformism" in which organizational members obligingly trudge into cooperative oblivion. Again, the executive must conceive *and* execute delicate trade-offs to avoid the costs of paying too much attention to one boundary condition or the other. The problem is not merely hypothetical, if we are to believe the many critical voices raised concerning our organizational revolution. Thus William H. Whyte's *The Organization Man* drew a very definite portrait of organizations tending toward one extreme of the chaos/conformism continuum, and he developed a convincing sketch of the attendant dangers both within the organization and outside.[4] Some have noted the lack of caution in Whyte's argument,[5] but he has his many followers. For example, Seidenberg not only argues that Whyte depicts what organizations are becoming; in addition, Seidenberg argues that matters cannot be otherwise.[6] Our organizational revolution is spiraling inward on itself, as it were, and this devolution into ever decreasing circles of flexibility will end only as organizations almost literally suffocate on their own immensity and rigidity.

[3] Many demonstrations of the point exist. Illustratively, see J. D. Thompson, "Authority and Power In 'Identical' Organizations," *American Journal of Sociology*, Vol. 62 (November, 1956), pp. 290–301.

[4] William H. Whyte, Jr., *The Organization Man* (Garden City, N.Y.: Doubleday Anchor Books, 1957).

[5] Robert T. Golembiewski, *Men, Management, and Morality* (New York: McGraw-Hill, 1965), esp. pp. 38–53.

[6] Roderick Seidenberg, *Post-historic Man* (Boston: Beacon Press, 1957).

The characteristics, demands, and problems of top-management jobs all point to their creative and crucial potential. This is the case whether we see the possibility of successfully coping with the contemporary organizational revolution, or whether at best we only hope that we can play for time within narrow limits. The exquisite dilemmas confronting chief executives can only be hinted at here, but that hint is suggestive. Consider the matter of emotional support. If a chief executive often must help create the conditions under which emotional support is provided members of the organization, his getting emotional support usually is problematic. One executive tersely put his view of the matter: "The top man in an organization has to have the capacity to love those he works with in an organization, and get his love elsewhere," he explained. There was no avoiding this central executive dilemma, as he saw it. He simply could not get that love from others in the organization. "There has got to be somebody to hate if things go wrong," he described his own major liability, "and he's it. So he has got to get his love from somewhere else."[7] Other chief executives may stress needs other than love, of course. But similarly—because of where the chief executive sits—satisfying those needs often will pose dilemmas for him. I have in mind a portly dean who cherishes his few moments of exercise on a bicycle. But because of his feelings about the dignity required by his office, the dean takes his precious exercise only late at night. Consequently, the little exercise he does get is gained only by sacrificing safety.

What the top-level executive must do, how he must do it, and who he is, consequently are issues of great moment, and we direct ourselves to these issues.

We approach these issues crabwise. We reject the traditional approach to executive selection and competence. This approach stresses the listing of traits that identify the successful executive or would-be executive. The interested reader can find these various listings in the literature. The number of necessary traits, for example, cover a substantial range. Stryher presents fourteen traits of successful executives;[8] Greenleaf and Mapel settle for only three.[9] The content of the traits also varies widely. Thus two students settled for these global traits: the courage to dream, the ability to organize and the strength to exe-

[7] Richard D. Hodgson, Daniel J. Levinson, and Abraham Zaleznik, *The Executive Role Constellation* (Boston: Division of Research, Harvard Graduate School of Business Administration, 1965), p. 376.

[8] Perrin Stryker, "On the Meaning of Executive Qualities," *Fortune,* Vol. 46 (June, 1958), pp. 116–19 and 136–39.

[9] R. T. Greenleaf and E. B. Mapel, "The Trained Executive: A Profile," in M. Joseph Dooher and Vivienne Marquis, editors, *The Development of Executive Talent* (New York: American Management Association, 1952), pp. 21–25.

cute.[10] Other observers are content only with categories complex enough to deter a Philadelphia lawyer, such as those categories deriving from the involved interpretation of depth-analytic techniques like the Rorschach.[11]

Despite their variety attempts to isolate traits for executive selection have common limiting biases. These attempts focus on the executive rather than on what he is executing. Moreover, the usual approach to traits admits only a few variables, and they narrowly focus on the executive. Finally, the trait notion is static. If an executive has the appropriate traits he will be successful, by implication, whatever the conditions.

We are more comfortable with an approach that is oriented around both the executive and his institution, that acknowledges multiple variables, and that is dynamic. David G. Moore's "What Makes A Top Executive" illustrates this second approach. For openers, Moore argues that typical lists of executive traits usually are "broad generalizations" about qualities of courage, morality, decisiveness, and the like. Since these qualities are characteristics of the emotionally mature individual, whether he is an executive or not, they are of limited value in isolating successful executives. Moreover, in any case, Moore is concerned with the interaction of organizational properties and executive characteristics, with a dynamic product rather than a static bundle of traits. The good sense of his approach can be established variously. The executive is a creature of his society; he operates in an organization that is part of that society; and he lives at a particular point in time.

These slim observations permit direct conclusions. The executive operates in a value-laden environment. Since he does, we can question whether a set of "executive traits" exists. Grossly, different organizations reflect different values at different points in time; and the same organization can change its operational values or they can be changed by external forces. Whether a set of traits would serve such various value-sets may be doubted.[12]

We can focus on the interaction of organizational properties and individual characteristics to develop one implication of Moore's argu-

---

[10] *Ibid.*

[11] Zygmunt A. Piotrowski and Milton R. Rokeach, *The Perceptanalytic Executive Scale* (New York: Grune and Stratton, 1963).

[12] This puts the position very mildly. Considerable evidence exists—supporting commonsense expectations—that different managerial attributes seem necessary and/or preferable in an "old" organization versus a "new" one, at various stages of the introduction of new technologies, and so on. See Floyd Mann, "Toward An Understanding of the Leadership Role in Formal Organization," pp. 68–103, in Robert Dubin, editor, *Leadership and Productivity* (San Francisco: Chandler, 1965).

ment. This does not presume that the former always determines the latter. Although the executive sometimes may range only on a short tether, he commonly can mold his value environment as well as maintain it. Charles H. Granger's "The Hierarchy of Objectives" develops one aspect of the point. He argues that one of the principal executive activities centers around establishing a rank-order of objectives for his organization. Without such a hierarchy, an organization wastes time on countless decisions which need not have been made, or which could have been made better if a hierarchy of objectives existed.

Philip Selznick's *Leadership In Administration* (parts of which are reprinted here) brings complementary attention to the full range of value-setting processes in organizations that define the executive's major focus for Selznick. His standards are high. Those in a position to articulate goals must do so, even if this means conflict within the organization and attack from outside. Nor can executives settle for superficial acceptance of the goals defining their institution. Although every executive must achieve minimum conditions for an organization's continued existence, Selznick argues, any executive fails if he does not recognize that he is primarily "an expert in the promotion and protection of values." The executive's primary value-oriented activities are:

1. defining the institutional mission and role;
2. developing an institutional embodiment of purpose;
3. defending the institutional purpose; and
4. managing internal conflict.

As the executive forfeits these tasks, he becomes an "organizational engineer." That is, by forfeiture, he acts like a middle manager rather than a top-level executive.

Let us sharpen one sense in which an executive's serving as "an expert in the promotion and protection of values" requires promoting and protecting new values. Here lies perhaps *the* distinctly executive task. Consider, by way of illustration, that organizations generally must grow in order to prosper. Alfred D. Chandler, Jr., in his *Strategy and Structure* develops the position that different *ways of growing* require different *ways of organizing*. Orderly growth, therefore, is a function of the appropriateness of an organization's structure for its growth "strategy," which Chandler defines as "the determination of the basic long-term goals and objectives of an enterprise and the adoption of courses of action and allocation of resources necessary for carrying out these goals." If growth strategies are consciously or unconsciously changed without appropriate changes in structure, organizational chaos is the major by-product.

The character and the significance of Chandler's strategies for growth may be detailed briefly. The strategies—roughly, in order of application and sophistication—include:

1. expanding production of a good or service at one site;
2. opening field units;
3. adding functions; and
4. diversifying into many product and service lines.

Strategy significantly influences the appropriateness of alternative structures. For example, the orthodox theory of organization is relatively appropriate where the basic strategy of growth is increased volume of a limited product line. Here, also, the narrow specialist has advantages that far outweigh his disadvantages. When the basic strategy of growth becomes the diversification of products or services, both the orthodox theory and its specialist-oriented human products have relatively greater costs than the unorthodox model and its generalist human products. Details supporting the summaries proposed by the preceding sentences may be found in Golembiewski, "Civil Service and Managing Work," reprinted in the previous chapter.

The executive managing thousands, that is to say, is enmeshed in the complex problems of developing appropriate strategic values to maintain his organization in the several tomorrows as well as in the compelling today. His failures are written in terms of a piling-up of outmoded organizations and obsolescent human skills and attitudes.

Chandler's approach does not want for cases in point. Frank J. McKenna's "Decentralization of Federal Disbursing Functions" provides a brief example of a structural change forced by an advanced strategy for growth. At one stage of the game, it was both possible and desirable to centralize the disbursing of federal monies. The advantages included economies of scale and closer surveillance of disbursing. As the service-mix was diversified and the workload grew, however, diminishing returns set in. The costs of these diminishing returns could be calculated in terms of delays and client complaints, for example. The rationale supporting the necessity of the centralized pattern, costs and all, was the orthodox model treated in Golembiewski's "Civil Service and Managing Work." A reorganization eventually was forced. It moved in the direction of the unorthodox model also touched on in that selection, but only grudgingly and incompletely. No doubt many organizational members still respect the traditional model, which helps explain the halting and hesitant nature of change.

McKenna provides detailed counterpoint to Chandler's generalized argument in two senses, one empirical and one normative, and both imply significant targets for executive action. Empirically, McKenna illustrates that managerial techniques and structural arrangements adequate at one stage of an organization's development become intolerable burdens at another. Empirically, also, most sizable organizations have passed the stage at which the orthodox model had its optimum usefulness. McKenna's article suggests the point which has been

massively supported in many other places.[13] These empirical considerations imply complex executive action. All too briefly, the derivative
demands on the executive in managing thousands are multiple in this
regard: to anticipate and to avoid the intolerable elements in the
future when managing today's work; to build toward suitable change
while steady-state operations continue; and to do so far enough in
advance to avoid organizational turmoil but not so far as to invite
rejection. Integrating diversity thus well characterizes the executive
job.

Normatively, McKenna's article also implies significant demands
for executive action. If decentralization is appropriate for advanced
strategies of organizational growth—and particularly for diversification
—decentralizing implies major changes in the values and attitudes of
many organizational members. Decentralization—like centralization—
must rest on a bedrock of appropriate attitudes and values. Decentralization—also like centralization—is not merely a technical matter.
Decentralization reflects a life-style; it is infused with value. The point
cannot be made fully. However, consider only this attempt to describe
decentralization. Two scholars observe that the social climate associated with decentralization defies easy cataloguing. "Such a social climate," they explain, "is full of contradictions and enigmas." Indeed, it
mixes apparently diverse values. "On the one hand it would seem to be
welfare-centered, with a certain flavor of devotion to human uplift,"
they explain. "On the other it retains the production drive and competitive atmosphere so characteristic of the industrial scene in the
past."[14] Therefore, the executive must face the task of combining the
diverse in infusing a decentralized organization with value.

Even the catalog above constitutes a substantial load of executive
"musts" in creating value-laden institutions appropriate to diverse conditions of organized existence, and real dilemmas challenge the executive at every turn. Consider, for example, that internal interest groups
or cliques in an organization "represent sources of energy ... [that
may] lend life and strength to an organization."[15] Such informal groups
—while they can facilitate the process of infusing with value a technical
structure—also can subvert the goals of an organization. The dilemma
is particularly real for the manager of thousands. Deprived of face-to-
face contact with and feedback from the organizational masses, that

---

[13] For example, in Alfred Chandler, Jr., *Strategy and Structure* (Cambridge, Mass.:
MIT Press, 1962).

[14] John M. Pfiffner and Frank P. Sherwood, *Administrative Organization* (Englewood Cliffs, N. J.: Prentice-Hall, 1960), p. 201.

[15] Philip Selznick, *Leadership In Administration* (New York: Harper & Row, 1957),
pp. 93–94.

is, the executive must take actions having profound consequences for informal groups of whose existence he may be unaware but which can influence performance in ways both subtle and significant.

The task of the executive managing thousands—stated in its most simple terms—is to recognize the existence of cliques, to use them when they contribute to the goals of the organization and to restrict them when they begin to subvert these goals. Melville Dalton helps in this complex task in his "Power Struggles In the Line." He identifies five different types of internal interest groups, or "cliques." They are: vertical symbiotic; vertical parasitic; horizontal defensive; horizontal aggressive; and random cliques. Of the five, the first two normally occur within a single department, but the remaining three cut across agency lines. Vertical cliques are the most troublesome in organizations and, unfortunately, they also are the most frequent.

Here, as at other points, the argument in this volume has doubled back on itself as it has built to the top executive level. The executive's dilemma in handling internal interest groups, for example, can rely on the preceding themes of this volume. That dilemma can be illumined by a knowledge of interpersonal and group dynamics, and structural innovations may "slip between the horns" of the dilemma. For example, the selection from McKenna and Golembiewski's "Civil Service and Managing Work" both imply ways of structuring work to take advantage of the social power of vertical cliques encompassing entire units of organization departmentalized in terms of product or in terms of total flow of work. Where function or process guides departmentation, vertical cliques can cause significant integrative problems to the degree that the functionally specialized formal units of organization also are effective social units. Therefore, the executive intent on limiting the arbitrary power of vertical cliques in a traditional structure often can do so only by attempting to destroy the internal interest groups that give "life and strength to an organization." Unorthodox structural arrangements help the executive avoid this cruel dilemma.

There is another way of noting the ways in which the argument has doubled back on itself. The whole of this volume argues for a "systems approach" to organizational phenomena. The piece by Edward S. Quade—"Progress and Problems In Systems Analysis"—reinforces this intention by reviewing the mechanics and some of the splendid gains made lately in "systems analysis." As Quade notes, much of the progress has been made via the use of mathematical tools. It is equally correct, as Quade also observes, that systems analysis admits of the full range of approaches to organizational phenomena. It is to this end that the selections of this volume contribute.

What Makes a Top Executive?*

David G. Moore

If you want to know what makes a top executive, don't ask the man who is one. He won't be able to tell you. Business executives are, after all, men of action; they are too deeply involved in their day-to-day affairs, the thrill of the chase, to introspect and dwell heavily on what makes them tick. To be sure, you do get some high-level generalities and abstractions. Once in a while, a business leader does get the time to write or propound his ideas at some conference or other. But in general, all that these utterances and pronouncements yield is a somewhat ponderous emphasis on such abstract qualities as courage, morality, broad-gauge thinking, decisiveness, and so on—the attributes, after all, of any emotionally mature individual and certainly not confined to businessmen alone. At the same time, it should be mentioned that the only really worthwhile theoretical statement on the subject was, in fact, written by a businessman, Chester Barnard, author of the classic *The Functions of the Executive*. More recently, there have been a number of other books by key executives that have considerable merit. But, even at his most articulate, the typical business executive has difficulty in describing what he does and how he acquired the necessary skills and abilities to perform his functions.

A variety of views about the functions of the executive has, however, emerged from other sources. Some say that the top executive is a generalist, whatever that means. This school of thought argues that he does not have to be a functional or technical expert—he can hire specialists to perform these functions. His job, therefore, is to preside over the organization, providing spiritual comfort perhaps to those who are getting their hands dirty. Others regard him as a coordinator, bringing divergent views together into one splendidly integrated set of goals. Again, it has been contended that he is a man who gets things done through people. All these definitions suggest somehow that the top executive doesn't really have to know anything—that his chief qualification is a somewhat vaguely defined leadership ability that binds together and coordinates the work and effort of the management team.

In contrast to these views, there are others that see the top executive as a "know-it-all," a man of vast knowledge, understanding, and ana-

---

* Reprinted with permission of author and publisher from *Personnel*, 37, No. 4 (July–August, 1960), pp. 8–19.

lytical ability who makes the final decisions. He sits at the center of an information and action network and like a great and exceedingly complex thermostat assesses conditions, both internal and external, and turns the heat on and off.

Barnard sees him as a man primarily concerned with maintaining the organization—both the work organization and the decision-making organization. Here the assumption is that, if the organization is functioning efficiently and effectively, all's right with the world and the top executive has done his job.

Finally, there are some who see the top executive simply as a figurehead, like the Queen of England, who operates in the public eye, a kind of ritualist who makes pronouncements, appears at public functions, and in general represents his organization in the important ceremonial activities of society. As a matter of fact, if you examine the way many top executives spend their time, there is some merit in this view. Indeed, there is some truth in all the above-mentioned notions about what an executive is. But we can approach the question more systematically, however, by examining the diverse environments in which the executive must operate. In this way we can perhaps penetrate more deeply than the stereotypes mentioned thus far.

The Executive's Value Environment

If the executive functioned like the TV detective, insisting only on "the facts, Ma'am," he'd be demoted to walking a beat. The most important environment in which the executive operates is what we might call the *value environment* of our particular society. An executive is a creature of our society; he operates in an institution that is a segment of our society; he is part of our ongoing history. Indeed, in some respects, he is a maker of history. He has risen to a key position in one of our most important social institutions. The decisions he makes will have important repercussions throughout society even though he may see them as affecting his own business alone.

Currently, there is great concern over the influence of business, particularly large-scale organization, on the emerging social character of American citizens, especially the American middle class. "Are we developing 'organization men'?" is a question that has been given great publicity in recent years. In its demand for loyalty, coordination, and unified action, is business developing a new kind of citizen—a citizen who owes his allegiance to particular companies, to special provinces, and to narrow interests that do not reflect the total values of our society? This is a very important value consideration because the ultimate test of the usefulness of any social institution lies in the kind of people it produces.

There is concern also about lower-level employees. Are we developing such a high degree of dependency at the lower levels of our business organizations that people are no longer able to function on their own, and would be incapable of surviving as individuals were they ever to be separated from their ant-hill society? Are we, with all our plenty, creating a nation of chronically frustrated, uncreative, dependent citizens who would fall apart under duress? Or do we still possess the power to build on our physical and economic prosperity and rise to new levels of spiritual, scientific, and creative achievement? On the surface, these would appear to be questions remote from the considerations of the business executive. Yet, it is not by chance that recent books written by top executives—Blough's *Free Man and the Corporation,* Worthy's *Big Business and Free Men,* Greenewalt's *The Uncommon Man,* Houser's *Big Business and Human Values*—deal precisely with such value considerations as these.

The world is confronted with two systems for solving the problems of famine, the material needs of people, and national strength. Both systems are obviously successful at the material level. You can take your choice on that score. Both systems have proved their capacity to produce. Differentiation from here on out must be made on achievements at a much higher level of human endeavor—that is, in the capacity of each system to produce men of character, intelligence, creativity, sanity, and love.

A Legacy of Values

Today's business executive operates not only within the evolving values of our own time, but also within an historical framework of past values that have become embodied in our institutions. His forebears were often deeply religious men who saw in work, in organization, and in the use of capital the revelation of God's will on earth. They could work a man from sunup to sundown and honestly believe that they were doing something for his moral character. Business in this country is in a very real sense the institutional embodiment of the Puritan mind. Even though they may not be consciously aware of the origins of their beliefs, many business executives are deeply convinced of the essential morality of discipline, service, efficient organization, and work. Articulate executives like James C. Worthy, of Sears, Roebuck, have turned directly to religion in their search for ideological justification for business and the free-enterprise system.

This recognition that many of the business executive's basic policy decisions have deep ethical and religious connotations having to do with the character of man and his relationship to his fellows can be observed in less articulate executives also. I remember participating on a panel once with a retired chairman of the board of one of our top companies. He was asked a question something like this: "Mr. Smith, how did you do it? To what do you owe your success and what can you pass on to us younger fellows who want to be successful, too?" The old fellow could do no more than dip into the Bible and come up with the Golden Rule—"Do unto others. . . ." He knew more than this, but this was his distillation of a lifetime of experience. Once he had sifted it all out, there remained only the deep ethical conviction that has guided him in those moments of tough decision: to cut, or not to cut, everybody's pay?

It is important to recognize that the business executive operates in this kind of value environment whether he is aware of it or not. The decisions he makes, whether they come out of his own thinking, *Fortune*, or the American Management Association, all have ethical implications. He may not know it, but as he guides his organization in its task of beating out tin cans, automobiles, or rockets, he is shaping the history of his country and the world.

The Institutional Environment

While the business executive is usually keenly aware that he acts in competition with other industries, he is less aware that he also competes with other institutions in our society—religious and educational institutions, unions, government, communities, and so on. He may see some of these other institutions as obstacles, but not strictly as competitors. Society is characterized, however, by a web of institutions that represents a network of competitive as well as cooperative relationships. Each institution is constantly striving to expand its own radius of operations. Each institution, in a sense, views society from its own vantage point and seeks to universalize its interests, ideologies, and functions. Thus, at one time, religious institutions dominated all the others. At the present time, in America, we have a kind of balance of power that in many ways was deliberately fostered by the Roosevelt administration over the dead bodies of many fallen business heroes. We have no doleful ballads commemorating these men; the struggle has shifted to more sophisticated levels, but the competition continues in the legislative foxholes, at the bargaining table, and so forth.

Businesses have taken on more functions than they ever dreamed of 25 years ago. In fact, some companies today perform the functions not only of business, but also of psychiatry, the funeral parlor, and the church. These days, a man can come into a company and not only be fed and clothed by it, but be buried by it and have official mourners to grieve at his passing. While I would not go so far as to say that business should not be involved in these essentially religious, ceremonial functions at all, they strike me nevertheless as more essentially the functions of other institutions in our society. The same observation might be made about the educational activities of a number of large corporations. Outstanding as some of these programs are, as a representative of the truly educational institutions of our society, I can't help wondering whether all the money being spent by companies in this manner might not better be used to bolster our existing educational structure. The same is true of certain aspects of research.

This is not the place, however, to enter into arguments about the functions of the various institutions of our society. It is enough to make the point that inter-institutional competition is an important environment in which the business executive operates and one with which he must come to grips. He must have a broad understanding of how a great society runs and the roles and functions of the various institutions that comprise it, and a statesmanlike grasp of the special interests and place of business in the larger whole.

The Company Environment

A third important environment in which the business executive operates is the culture of his own organization. Each company has a history, a way of doing things, a set of conventions, customs, and social habits that constitutes its character as a business. Executive development in many organizations represents a kind of acculturation process whereby the young executive is taught how this particular company operates—what its way is, what its character is, what kinds of things it will do, what kinds of things it positively will not do, what its policies, common symbols, ceremonials, and heroic figures are.

The difference between the young, immature executive, the fellow who doesn't know his way around, and the older one is often simply a difference in the degree of acculturation that has occurred. The latter knows the ins and outs of the organization, how to get things done, what symbols and conventions to invoke under varying circumstances;

he looks, speaks, and acts the part. The other man doesn't even know how to write a letter; he doesn't know business parlance, the lingo; he is unaware of all the sacred cows around the organization; he has no sense of the tempo of the place, how people dress, how they act, and how they get things done. There is an uneasiness about him because he has not yet learned the culture, symbols, and values of the organization.

The culture or character of a business and the understanding that executives and employees within the organization have of this culture are important controls. As a consequence, determining the character of an organization, which really means determining who you are, where you are going, and how you operate in this complex world, is likely to absorb a great deal of the attention of top management.

Environment of the Organizational Structure

A fourth environment that is extremely important to executive behavior is the organizational structure, particularly its hierarchical character. Every organization is a hierarchical system in which each individual, with the exception of the man at the top and the people at the very bottom, operates within an interacting triad of relationships in which some people are viewed as being in higher positions to him, some as being in lower, subordinate positions, and some as being at the same level. Dealing with these various levels and modifying behavior in appropriate ways in terms of the hierarchical system is one of the important skills of the executive. He has to learn how to get things done through the boss, how to approach him at the right time, how to avoid getting a definite *No,* how to sell ideas to him, how to motivate him, and so on. The executive who doesn't have these skills doesn't get much done. Every executive has to be a promoter of ideas; he has to be selling all the time.

By the same token, the executive has to learn how to deal with subordinates as well as with those at his own level With his subordinates, he has to learn how to sell the sometimes unpopular notion of work; he has to learn how to translate organizational ideas into goals that have meaning to those under him; he has to learn to balance the impersonal demands of the organization against the personal needs of his people. Above all, he has to learn how to deal with people in sympathetic but not emotionally involved ways. He has to avoid the sense of guilt that haunts many executives who cannot bring themselves to ask others to get the job done. He has to learn to exercise the power given him without projecting his own emotional needs into the situation. Any power position is potentially tyrannical, and the individual with power has to be either self-disciplined or, of necessity, outwardly controlled.

The business executive also operates within a system of mobility in which others are trying to get ahead. Even if they are really not trying to get ahead, they have to maintain the myth of getting ahead since this is an integral element of our kind of society. The colleagues of the business executive and his trusted subordinates are not only his friends, the people with whom he works and cooperates in getting the job done, but they are also his enemies. They are friendly enemies; everybody smiles and carries on as if nothing really were happening, but everybody is in competition.

In some companies, this competition is greater than in others. Some companies are made up of highly mobile, very aggressive fellows who push each other all over the place. If they're all bulls, they don't really mind this, but if there's a milquetoast among them, he is annihilated. But regardless of the degree of competition, executives in any company are in the strange situation of having to cooperate and compete at the same time.

This competition takes place not only at the personal level, but at the level of ideas as well. Pushing and trying to gain support for ideas are major activities of business executives since these represent socially acceptable ways of competing. This is why one of the most important skills of the business executive is being able to argue a point effectively. It also explains why the executive becomes preoccupied with the question of how radical he should be; either he can play it safe and stick to tried-and-true, conventional notions that no one can deny, or he can play for really big stakes and challenge the accepted ideas. If he loses, squoosh! If he wins, he's running the place.

One of the major problems of the top management of a company is achieving some kind of integration of the myriad of ideas that are being pushed by the various members of the management team. Nothing is more stultifying than that neat balance which some uninspired top executives achieve. This is the easy way out. Everybody is treated fairly, and everybody is frustrated. My own opinion is that dynamic imbalance is best. At least, there is movement; at least, some are hilariously happy and motivated, even if others may be deeply dissatisfied.

The Occupational Environment

The executive also operates within an occupational environment. Occupational influences are most obvious in the so-called professional groups in industry—the engineers, scientists, and other hired brains. These men owe allegiance not only to the company of which they are a part, but also to their profession. You find some highly dissatisfied, frustrated people in these professional fields in industry because they see themselves as being in direct competition with the administrators, the organization men. This situation is by no means confined to engineers and scientists, however. In the retailing field, for instance, there are display workers who regard themselves as artists, while advertising copywriters all seem to be frustrated Hemingways who might be writing best-selling novels if it weren't for the grinding necessity of drawing a regular pay check. You find it among other professional groups, too, wherever organizational demands come into conflict with professional, occupational ones. You certainly find it in universities.

Many occupational groups strive for professional status as a kind of way out—a means of achieving the security or recognition that would normally come from the companies of which they are a part. I suspect that some of these efforts toward professionalization are the result of the employee's not getting this kind of recognition from his company, or at all events, not getting the degree of recognition he expects. Under such circumstances, a man finds the recognition he needs, the sense of colleagueship and support, the feeling of understanding, of status, and of worth in his professional group.

Even those executives who do not see themselves as members of professional groups are influenced strongly by their occupational environment. An occupation is more than a function; it is frequently a way of life. It directs the interests of those engaged in it, shapes their values and attitudes, determines their relations with others, brings people of similar interests and often similar personalities together, and thus intensifies the interaction among them. The individual executive often personally identifies with his job. He is not just Joe Blow, business executive; he is a controller, a plant superintendent, a personnel man, a sales manager. An attack on his specialty is an attack on him. Moreover, he tends to universalize the special interests and values of his field and wonders why others are so stupid and so narrow, so impervious to his particular point of view.

The Decision Environment

Finally, the executive operates in a decision environment. There are several important aspects of this environment with which he must reckon. First and foremost, he is supposed to be rational.

Ideally, his decisions are expected to improve the company's competitive position—enhancing its growth, profits, stability, and all the other good things a well-run business should have. Furthermore, the choice of means to these various ends is presumed to be pinpointed, efficient, and precise. The executive is not supposed to be guessing and wandering around willy-nilly in a trial-and-error maze.

This intended rationality of executive decision and action, as Herbert Simon has put it, places a real burden on the business executive. It forces him to think and to rationalize and intellectualize what he is doing. A man can't do things simply because his gut-reaction tells him they are good; he can't make steel because he loves to make steel, or enjoys those belching, flaming chimneys, the stink, the sheer brute force of machines and power, the danger of bubbling metals, and the sense of satisfaction that comes from bringing Vulcan himself to his knees. Instead, he must wander about with papers in his hands, columns of figures, which he adds, subtracts, correlates, projects. He has to equate fun and emotions, and sadness and personal frustration, and love and hate with figures, particularly those with dollar signs in front of them, the ultimate denominator of business.

But with all the figures at his disposal, the business executive deals with fragments and pieces of information. He never has all the facts. He is part of unfolding history in which all the returns are not yet in and never will be. He is dealing with dynamic events—reactive phenomena that shift their courses as he shifts his.

Nonetheless, the executive must work with what he has, trying to build a picture from the fragments and pieces, trying to integrate them, and deciding courageously to move in one direction or another. The higher his position in the organization, the more fortunate he is, because the consequences of his decisions cannot be reckoned or assessed immediately. The ideal situation, of course, is the one where the decisions a man has made cannot be evaluated until after he has retired. But even here, there is always a gnawing anxiety.

I once had the opportunity to speak to former President Truman on this point. When I asked him how he rated his administration, he answered, "It's too soon to tell." He went on to say that a schoolboy's hindsight is better than a president's foresight. It is obvious that the actual consequences of the Truman administration or the Roosevelt administration or even the Hoover administration have not yet completely run their course. You cannot be sure just exactly what the Marshall Plan or the decision to drop the atomic bomb has done, or what the full consequences will be of any of these decisions made as far back as ten years ago.

The same is true of many business decisions. The really unfortunate fellow is the one whose decisions can be assessed five minutes from now—and that's the poor foreman, of course.

At any rate, the man who has heavy responsibilities—and this is true of most business executives—sometimes feels pretty lonely when he has to face this array of fragmentary information and finally say, "We're going to move this way." The tough part is when he has to make not the simple choice between right and wrong, but the choice between two rights or two wrongs. This is the ulcer-producing environment of our business society.

The Executive Personality

Though the environments discussed above are not the only ones in which the business executive operates, they are, I think, the most important. The questions now to be considered are: How does the executive adjust to these various environments? What are some of the successful ways of meeting these demands?

Some helpful clues are forthcoming here from what we already know about successful executive performance, that is, the kinds of personalities and skills that successful executives in established corporations appear to have. Professor William Henry, of the University of Chicago, who has made an extensive analysis of the executive's social personality, has provided us with some valuable insights into this question. His observations, modified in part by my own thinking, shape up something like this:

Ability to integrate. The executive has to have, first of all, the ability somehow to organize, or make sense of, the world that he perceives about him. This means that he has to be able to integrate what he perceives and to pull it together into some kind of picture. It doesn't make a lot of difference whether it is the right picture or the wrong picture. It is never completely right or completely wrong—only more or less plausible. (Nobody will ever know anyway, except through looking back at historical trends and past happenings.) But it does have to be a picture in which the argument is good and in which the details available for understanding the situation have somehow been effectively brought together.

We have all seen the difference between the man who can do this and the man who cannot. One man can move into a situation, get the details quickly, and put them together in some sensible way. Another, in a similar situation, starts turning over this, that, and the other thing, and never manages to tell you what it's all about. He may be able to tell you the 50 different things it might be about, but not what it is really all about. This means, then, that the successful executive has to be a well-integrated man—in Freudian terms, a man with a sufficiently strong ego to enable him to reach out, incorporate the world around him, say, "This is the way it appears to me," and stand by his convictions.

Obviously, he can do this at various levels. There are those business executives who can tell you all about a certain segment of the total problem. These are the men who can operate reasonably effectively, but who are going to miss all the finer points. They do not have the statesmanlike qualities, the ability to incorporate many different factors into the integrations they make. Often, they will skip over vital considerations. The fundamental requirement, however, is that the man be at least able to integrate something; the postgraduate requirement is that he be able to integrate on a broad scale.

Ability to decide. The second personality requirement that has emerged from Dr. Henry's analyses is that the man be able to reach a decision. There are many people who are afraid to decide. They have not been trained to reach decisions; they have been trained simply to analyze, which may be a valuable attribute in itself, but is not necessarily a virtue in a man who is required to reach a decision for his company. There are some very good staff men, incidentally, who can analyze what it's all about and say, "This is what I think should be done." But before they act they have to go to the boss and say, "Boss, what do you think?" If the boss says, "I think it's great," the man can move. Up to this point, he can't. The ability to decide seems to depend partly on ego, partly on conviction, and partly on a certain type of character.

Judgment. Still another factor that enters into the mental qualifications of the successful executive is judgment. Business is an ongoing activity, and there is a strong element of responsibility involved in it. A man may have some wild ideas, but he'd better not try them, not when the destiny of the company and all its employees is at stake. So judgment—practicality, the awareness of where we are now, where we're going, and what we might hopefully accomplish in a certain period of time—is essential. This includes awareness of the effects of decisions here on factors over there. Again, much of the difference between the mature and the immature executive lies in judgment.*

Ability to project. Another requirement is the ability to project or to forecast events. This is a very difficult psychological concept. I don't quite know how you spot it in a person, and yet there it is. There are

---

* For a more extended discussion of this point, see "The Older Manager: His Limitations and Assets," *Personnel*, 37, No. 4 (July–August, 1960), pp. 39–48.

some people who can perceive what is likely to occur if you do this, this, and this. They can put it together by a process that's not exactly logical, but that nevertheless still involves logic. They're certainly not clairvoyant, but they have a kind of insight into what is likely to happen.

Orientation toward work. As a rule, the successful executive is also work-oriented. He has a high degree of energy, which he can channel into his work. This distinguishes him from many people who can also think and make decisions, but who don't want to do it too often because it's too much of a strain. Take this example of a fellow who was sales manager for a company run by his family. He would come in to work once in a while, put his feet up on the window sill, and come up with an idea that, he said, paid his salary for that year and more. He used to say, "That was all I felt I should give to it." Then he would go back to pursuits that were more interesting to him. His 85-year-old father finally fired him.

There were other people in that organization who were charging about doing all kinds of things. The son used to say, "I think they have deep religious motivations of some kind. Certainly they are compulsive. I don't resent them; if they want to do that, God bless them—let them go ahead and do it. It just isn't for me." In short, he was lazy, with a capital "L," so far as business was concerned.

By work-orientation I don't mean that flurry of activity you sometimes find in many organizations. I mean the ability to channel the work. I've seen one top-notch executive sit down after a cocktail party and write three speeches for a convention the following day—one for the chairman of the board, one for the president, and one for himself. Obviously, all three had to be good. How he did it I'll never know, but he did it. Being able to produce at the crucial hour or moment demands the toughest kind of creative effort. Many top executives have this kind of drive, and many of them have tremendous physical stamina. They believe that work in itself is worth while; they value accomplishment for accomplishment's sake, not for the sake of the money that's in it, or the status, or the glory.

Maturity. Another factor in the executive's personality is his image of himself as a mature person. There are many men who envision themselves as young, frivolous clowns. They're wonderful people; it's fun to have them around an organization, but no one would ever think of putting them in charge of anything important. A successful executive has to see himself as mature and responsible. He's there to do the job.

Positiveness. Again, the executive's relationship with higher levels of authority, certainly in big companies, is positive. There is no deep, inner hostility toward papa. There is a definite feeling, "The guy up there is the old man; I've got a lot to learn from him. Some day I might be able to do better than he, but when all's said and done he's pretty able, and I want to be like him." That's the important point. Without this positive relationship, the executive runs the risk of ending up in the situation that confronted the hero of *The Man in the Gray Flannel Suit,* who, just at the point where he could have had the "old man's" job, said, "The hell with it; I couldn't take it. I think he's terrible, really."

Cooperativeness. Finally, cooperativeness in his relationships with his colleagues seems to be another important quality of the successful executive. Even though he may be a bull at heart, he's not going to fight every other bull in the place to get his own way. He's geared more to the cooperative level than to the highly individualistic level. Also, he can deal with his subordinates without having feelings of guilt. His attitude toward them is not so emotionally charged that he feels guilty assigning them jobs that he couldn't do himself. We've all seen men like this. They cannot run an organization because they will eventually usurp all the dirty jobs for themselves. In time, they'll wind up doing everything, and everyone else will be standing around watching them work.

While these observations are by no means conclusive or definitive, they do represent one kind of thinking that must be done if executive development programs are to be worth their salt. Just what training is required to equip men for positions of ever-broadening managerial responsibility is still a debatable question. Important new thrusts in business education may well be achieved through more intensive study of the elements outlined here.

The Hierarchy of Objectives*

Charles H. Granger

- Why is a conceptual framework of objectives important in decision making?
  - What are the most important characteristics of good objectives?
  - How should objectives be chosen and established?
  - How can objectives be used profitably by management?

We are all faintly amused by the aptness of the old quotation, "Having lost sight of our objective, we redoubled our efforts." Everyone admits to having been caught in this situation at one time or another. But is it possible that most large organizations are in this predicament a good part of the time?

Evidence indicates that this may indeed be true. The main trouble seems to be a lack of clear understanding of questions such as the above. In discussing these questions I shall use the term *objective* in the relatively broad, nonspecific sense which it commonly has in everyday business language. In this sense an objective is "an aim or end of action"; it is also used as an aim or guide to intermediate decisions and actions. For example, a sales manager might say, "Our objective is to have our salesmen make as many calls as possible"—but he might be very conscious of the fact that a more fundamental objective is to develop high sales volume.

Role & Importance

Everyone will admit that objectives are important. But is it really necessary to analyze them? Can they be taken for granted? On a larger scale we have evidence like this:

> In a $50-billion-a-year organization, Secretary Robert S. McNamara and professional military people are in serious dispute because of a new way of looking at objectives.
>
> The Roman Catholic Church has called some 2,500 of its highest officials from their pressing daily business to help rethink that organization's objectives.
>
> The American Telephone and Telegraph Company was perhaps saved from government ownership in the 1930's by having thought out its objectives.

* Reproduced with permission of author and publisher from *Harvard Business Review*, Vol. 42 (May–June, 1964), pp. 63–74.

Sears, Roebuck and Co. has expanded from being a catalog merchant into a fabulous range of services as a result of a continuing redefinition of its objectives.

Theodore Levitt proposes that some leading industries may be in danger of going the way of the railroads because of inappropriate objectives.[1]

Less dramatic examples, because they are so much more numerous, probably have even greater importance. Think of the waste from the countless decisions made every day which could have been made better if the desired objectives had been more apparent to the decision-maker. In many organizations, if you ask a number of managers to write down their principal objectives, you may get strongly conflicting answers. The results? Research and development money is sometimes spent on projects which are later abandoned because they are inconsistent with broader corporate objectives. Committees spend countless hours thrashing over problems unrelated to the over-all purposes of their organizations. Vacillation on acquisition policies is often attributable to inadequately defined objectives. And so on.

Organization planning, marketing planning, R & D planning, financial planning, to say nothing of total corporate planning, properly begin with the question, "What are our over-all objectives?" Moreover, proponents of Douglas McGregor's "Theory Y" stress the importance of integrating the objectives of the individual with the objectives of the organization. But how can this be done if the organization's objectives are not really known? It seems that there is a major opportunity for increased effectiveness if our objectives can be made clearer by even a small amount.

Subtle Conflicts

Clarity is not the only question. *Balance* is important, too. Thus:

Many a company is in trouble because customer-service objectives are not properly related to profit objectives.

One utility will tell you (privately) that it ran into a serious earnings problem because its managers overstressed customer-service objectives to the slighting of profit objectives, a condition that took some years to correct.

Some companies recruit too many top-rate college graduates to be consistent with the rather modest objectives of the over-all organization. When after a few years it becomes apparent to these high-potential individuals that the organization does not really intend to pursue very challenging objectives, the result is wasteful high turnover.

[1] "Marketing Myopia," HBR, July-August 1960, p. 45.

Lyndall F. Urwick sums up such problems in a refreshing and often-overlooked way:

> Unless we have a purpose there is no reason why individuals should try to cooperate together at all or why anyone should try to organize them. This, however, is very easily forgotten. Once an organization is set up, a human group is in being, all the individual and personal motives which have induced persons to join the group, which keep them in the game and playing the game, assume great importance in their minds. Most of us suspect that the main purpose of the undertaking which employs us is to provide us personally with a job.... People derive social satisfactions from working together. And they build up, often unconsciously, very elaborate codes of behavior, and loyalties, and affections and antipathies, which may have little or nothing to do with the formal organization of the undertaking, the official relationships which their superiors recognize.... Every organization and every part of every organization must be an expression of the purpose of the undertaking concerned or it is meaningless and therefore redundant.[2]

Is a Theory Necessary?

Management literature is teeming with titles such as "How to Set Objectives," "How We Set Our Objectives," and even with articles on the appropriateness of one objective as opposed to another—profits versus survival, volume versus customer-service, and the like. Less attention has been given to the structure of objectives, pseudo-objectives, and constraints. Some sort of conceptual framework embracing the whole range of objectives seems necessary if we are ultimately going to use objectives more effectively. In some orderly way we must relate the "grand design" type of objective with the much more limited objectives lower down in the organization. And we have to examine how one type of objective can be derived from another. Again quoting Urwick:

> We cannot do without theory. It will always defeat practice in the end for a quite simple reason. Practice is static. It does and does well what it knows. It has, however, no principle for dealing with what it doesn't know.... Practice is not well adapted for rapid adjustment to a changing environment. Theory is light-footed. It can adapt itself

---

[2] *Notes on the Theory of Organization* (New York, American Management Association, 1952), pp. 18–19.

to changed circumstances, think out fresh combinations and possibilities, peer into the future.[3]

Tests of Validity

How can the validity of an objective be tested? What should an objective accomplish? Here are some important criteria to be applied to an objective:

1. *Is it, generally speaking, a guide to action?* Does it facilitate decision making by helping management select the most desirable alternative courses of action?

2. *Is it explicit enough to suggest certain types of action?* In this sense, "to make profits" does not represent a particularly meaningful guide to action, but "to carry on a profitable business in electrical goods" does.

3. *Is it suggestive of tools to measure and control effectiveness?* "To be a leader in the insurance business" and "to be an innovator in child-care services" are suggestive of measuring tools in a helpful way; but statements of desires merely to participate in the insurance field or child-care field are not.

4. *Is it ambitious enough to be challenging?* The action called for should in most cases be something in addition to resting on one's oars. Unless the enterprise sets objectives which involve reaching, there is a hint that the end of the road may be at hand. It might be perfectly appropriate for some enterprises which have accomplished their objectives to quietly disband. However, for an undertaking to have continuity, it needs the vitality of challenging objectives.

5. *Does it suggest cognizance of external and internal constraints?* Most enterprises operate within a framework of external constraints (e.g., legal and competitive restrictions) and internal constraints (e.g., limitations in financial resources). For instance, if objectives are to be a guide to action, it appears that American Motors, because of its particular set of constraints, should have somewhat different objectives than General Motors.

6. *Can it be related to both the broader and the more specific objectives at higher and lower levels in the organization?* For example, are the division's objectives relatable to the corporate objectives, and in turn do they also relate to the objectives of the research department in that division?

If such tests as these are valid indications of the meaningfulness of objectives, then several further propositions become apparent. First,

---

[3] Ibid., p. 10.

objectives, as aims or ends of action, are intimately involved in a complex of other important considerations or guides to action, such as definitions of the business, internal and external constraints, measurements of success, budgets, and long-range plans. Secondly, there is a ranking or hierarchy of objectives, proceeding in concept from the very broad to the specific. Logically, the specific or more limited objectives should not be in conflict with the broad objectives. The second proposition in particular deserves further consideration.

Complete Framework

Much of the confusion which apparently exists about objectives can be alleviated by viewing objectives as a whole framework or complex of "aims or ends of action" and other guiding considerations. In this framework it is not helpful to think there is one overriding consideration, such as "profit," since we must also concede in the next breath that another objective is to "stay within the law." Profit may indeed be the factor to be maximized *in a particular case,* but it cannot be viewed as the sole objective. The concept of a hierarchy is illustrated in Exhibit i.

Leading Characteristics

Granted the existence of this hierarchy, what is significant about it? What are its important characteristics and implications?

1. *The full range of objectives and guiding considerations is distressingly broad.* No one individual in a large organization could consciously make each decision in light of the total framework of objectives and guiding considerations. Hence, in practice many managers are guided in their decision making by what they themselves view as their own key objectives. This creates quite a problem. Recognition that there is such a problem does not mean that we should shrug our shoulders and ignore the whole subject. It suggests the need for a greater effort to organize and compartmentalize objectives into classes that are useful for each decision-maker in the organization.

2. *The rate of change with time decreases as we go up the scale.* Short-term programs and budgetary objectives may change in less than a year. But long-range plans may exist for several years without major revision, and the "grand design" of an enterprise may last throughout the leadership tenure of its chief executive.

3. *For most enterprises even the broad objectives are subject to*

Exhibit I Hierarchy of objectives in terms of level of need or activity

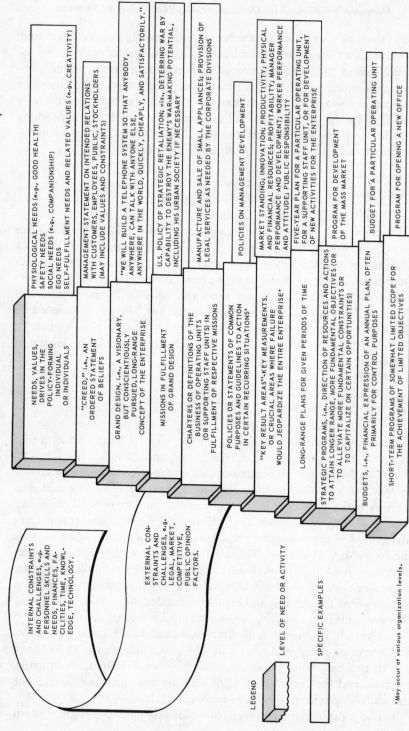

LEVEL OF NEED OR ACTIVITY

NEEDS, VALUES, DRIVES IN THE POLICY-FORMING INDIVIDUAL OR INDIVIDUALS
- PHYSIOLOGICAL NEEDS (e.g., GOOD HEALTH)
- SAFETY NEEDS
- SOCIAL NEEDS (e.g., COMPANIONSHIP)
- EGO NEEDS
- SELF-FULFILLMENT NEEDS AND RELATED VALUES (e.g., CREATIVITY)

"CREED," i.e., AN ORDERED STATEMENT OF BELIEFS
- MANAGEMENT STATEMENT ON INTENDED RELATIONS WITH CUSTOMERS, EMPLOYEES, PUBLIC, STOCKHOLDERS (MAY INCLUDE VALUES AND CONSTRAINTS)

GRAND DESIGN, i.e., A VISIONARY, BUT CONSCIENTIOUSLY PURSUED, LONG-RANGE CONCEPT OF THE ENTERPRISE
- "WE WILL BUILD A TELEPHONE SYSTEM SO THAT ANYBODY, ANYWHERE, CAN TALK WITH ANYONE ELSE, ANYWHERE IN THE WORLD, QUICKLY, CHEAPLY, AND SATISFACTORILY."

MISSIONS IN FULFILLMENT OF GRAND DESIGN
- U.S. POLICY OF STRATEGIC RETALIATION; viz., DETERRING WAR BY CAPABILITY TO DESTROY THE ENEMY'S WAR-MAKING POTENTIAL, INCLUDING HIS URBAN SOCIETY IF NECESSARY

CHARTERS OR DEFINITIONS OF THE BUSINESS OF OPERATING UNITS (OR SUPPORTING STAFF UNITS) IN FULFILLMENT OF RESPECTIVE MISSIONS
- MANUFACTURE AND SALE OF SMALL APPLIANCES; PROVISION OF LEGAL SERVICES AS NEEDED BY THE CORPORATE DIVISIONS

POLICIES OR STATEMENTS OF COMMON PURPOSES AND GUIDELINES TO ACTION IN CERTAIN RECURRING SITUATIONS*
- POLICIES ON MANAGEMENT DEVELOPMENT

"KEY RESULT AREAS"*KEY MEASUREMENTS OR CRUCIAL AREAS WHERE FAILURE WOULD JEOPARDIZE THE ENTIRE ENTERPRISE*
- MARKET STANDING; INNOVATION; PRODUCTIVITY; PHYSICAL AND FINANCIAL RESOURCES; PROFITABILITY; MANAGER PERFORMANCE AND DEVELOPMENT; WORKER PERFORMANCE AND ATTITUDE; PUBLIC RESPONSIBILITY

LONG-RANGE PLANS FOR GIVEN PERIODS OF TIME
- FIVE-YEAR PLAN FOR A PARTICULAR OPERATING UNIT, FOR A SUPPORTING STAFF UNIT, OR FOR DEVELOPMENT OF NEW ACTIVITIES FOR THE ENTERPRISE

STRATEGIC PROGRAMS, i.e., DIRECTION OF RESOURCES AND ACTIONS TO ATTAIN LONGER RANGE, MORE FUNDAMENTAL OBJECTIVES (OR TO ALLEVIATE MORE FUNDAMENTAL CONSTRAINTS OR TO CAPITALIZE ON CERTAIN OPPORTUNITIES)
- PROGRAM FOR DEVELOPMENT OF THE MASS MARKET

BUDGETS, i.e., FINANCIAL EXPRESSION OF AN ANNUAL PLAN, OFTEN PRIMARILY FOR CONTROL PURPOSES
- BUDGET FOR A PARTICULAR OPERATING UNIT

SHORT-TERM PROGRAMS OF SOMEWHAT LIMITED SCOPE FOR THE ACHIEVEMENT OF LIMITED OBJECTIVES
- PROGRAM FOR OPENING A NEW OFFICE

INTERNAL CONSTRAINTS AND CHALLENGES, e.g., PERSONNEL SKILLS AND NEEDS, FINANCES, FACILITIES, TIME, KNOWLEDGE, TECHNOLOGY.

EXTERNAL CONSTRAINTS AND CHALLENGES, e.g., LEGAL, MARKET, COMPETITIVE, PUBLIC OPINION FACTORS.

LEGEND

LEVEL OF NEED OR ACTIVITY

SPECIFIC EXAMPLES

*May occur at various organization levels.

change in 20 years. The argument is sometimes advanced that the very broad objectives of an enterprise are tied in with human values which are essentially immutable or subject to change only in terms of millennia. A good case could be made for this in terms of some organizations such as the Church. In other fields, however, the "grand design" even of many large organizations has changed within a leadership generation. The airframe industry, Sears, Roebuck and Co., the Tuberculosis Association, and the U.S. Air Force are examples. In smaller organizations it is not unusual to see the needs and values of the leader change —for instance, from financial security to esteem or creative contribution to society—with a discernible change in objectives of the organization. Management consulting firms are keenly aware of the fact that, when a new chief executive comes into power, there is considerable potential for consulting services in helping the organization to rethink and redetail its objectives in line with the new values, creeds, and grand design of the incoming chief executive.

4. *Debates on how specific an objective should be are not especially helpful.* One sometimes encounters the argument that an objective "to earn a fair return for the stockholder" is a pious but meaningless mouthing; 20% pretax return on invested capital (or some such specific target) is advanced as a more appropriate alternative. The scale of objectives in Exhibit i suggests that both of these are necessary (along with others). On the one hand, if we intend to use objectives as a tool for measuring progress, we are certainly much better able to do so if we have a certain percentage figure like 20% appropriate to the year. On the other hand, 20% (or any other fixed per cent) may be ridiculous for a recession year when nobody in the industry can even approach the figure; it then becomes meaningless. Thus, to derive a valid measurement we must fall back on our broader objective of fair return to the stockholders.

5. *Debates on the merit of one type of objective as opposed to another are only meaningful in light of the particular circumstances.* For example:

One frequently hears arguments as to whether profitability, public service, or perhaps customer-service or survival of the enterprise should be the ascendant objective. Arguments of this kind can quickly degenerate into a chicken-or-egg type of controversy.

Exhibit i suggests that the relative merit of a particular type of objective can only be evaluated in light of the particular circumstances being faced—the internal and external constraints, the values of the individuals who control the destiny of the enterprise, and so on. It might be entirely appropriate for a large undertaking, threatened with nationalization or government-directed splitting up which it deems against its best interests, to emphasize public service objectives more than profit objectives. H. Igor Ansoff points out that the near-term profits of many rather large firms are relatively secure anyway.[4]

6. *The obviousness of the need for stated objectives appears to decrease as we approach the upper end of the hierarchy.* Consider the experience of the Defense Department:

> Until the McNamara era, much Congressional debate centered around budgetary allocations in the traditional service categories (Army, Navy, Air Force, and so on), each broken down by personnel, operation and maintenance, procurement, R & D, and military construction. These traditional budget categories represent objectives of a sort and are still being used. But Secretary McNamara and his colleagues revolutionized the concept of objectives in government by taking this line of reasoning: It is not a fundamental objective simply to have so many men in the Marine Corps or to build such and such an Army base. The real objective is maximum national security. Within what might be called a grand design of national security, a number of "missions" were established, including strategic retaliation, continental air and missile defense, and general-purpose warfare capability. Now, for example, the Fleet Ballistic Missile System can be evaluated in terms of its contribution and cost/effectiveness relationships to the mission of the strategic retaliatory forces.

Although the advantages of evaluating the Defense Department program in light of its objectives seem obvious after the fact, and although such a system was long advocated by the Hoover Commission and other bodies, the Defense Department is the only major government department to have done this on a large scale.

This apparent casual approach to objectives is not a phenomenon of government organizations. How many talented leaders from business and other endeavors sit on boards of various churches, educational institutions, charities and the like, struggling with budgets in cases where the less obvious but more fundamental objectives have not been thought out? It is not an easy job. For example, one large church organization, after much preparatory staff work, required six early-morning-to-late-evening sessions of two days each (including the time of a large group of nationally prominent individuals) to redefine its objectives (the equivalent of grand design, missions, and charters in EXHIBIT I) and related matters.

While formalized statements of grand design and missions apparently exist only in a small percentage of business organizations,

---

[4] *Business Objectives* (Pittsburgh, Carnegie Institute of Technology, unpublished paper, 1962).

formalized charters and policy statements are relatively common; long-range plans are becoming much more so, and almost every business has a budget.

7. *The need for broad objectives of the grand design and mission type is not restricted to the very large company.* For example:

> One moderate-size New England company is founded on a variety of specialized technologies in mechanical sealing devices. The head of this company views its *grand design* as "stopping the leaks around the world." Bizarre as this first sounds, it is a perfectly workable concept for a grand design for a highly successful undertaking—which it already is on a moderate scale. From it are spawned *missions* relating to certain markets and applications. There is a network of *charters* relating to various operating divisions both in this country and abroad. This organization seems to have a unified sense of purpose and destiny which it would otherwise lack. The whole management team seems to know where it is going, and the individual managers are excited and enthusiastic about their common purpose.

The unfortunate cases are the organizations which lack such an over-all sense of purpose and are not doing anything to correct it; or perhaps their grand design is substantially accomplished or no longer appropriate to the current environment. These are the business enterprises in declining or static industries, the philanthropies for which the needs are now only marginal, and so on. The objectives of these organizations seem to be "to keep on doing what we have been doing," but the people in them are troubled and perplexed because they see that their results are not particularly satisfactory by a number of standards. A business enterprise in this situation may view its over-all objective as "10% net profit on stockholder investment"—but it does not have a ghost of a chance of achieving it on a consistent basis. People in the organization become engrossed in their personal objectives of holding onto their jobs. If only the board of directors in such cases would insist on having a written statement of the grand design!

8. *Objectives should not only guide action but also stimulate it.* Frederick R. Kappel, chairman of the board at AT&T, observes:

> Unless the business sets demanding and exciting goals, it runs a heavy risk of losing vitality. This is an area where people in top management positions have heavy responsibilities. . . . If these goals fail to stimulate, there is something missing at the top. . . . In the sense that I am using the word, a goal is something presently out of reach; it is something to strive for, to move toward, or to become. It is an aim or purpose so stated that it excites the imagination and gives people something they want to work for, some-

thing they don't yet know how to do, something they can
be proud of when they achieve it.[5]

Steps in Derivation

When we choose and establish directives, we cannot logically proceed in one step from a grand design to a budget, although companies
undoubtedly often attempt this. We are in effect confronted with a
situation of goals within goals within goals.

We must start with the given statement of the broader objective
(see EXHIBIT II). Next comes the process of setting up yardsticks, criteria, "key result areas," or some other form to measure the success of
the stated objective. Obviously the more tangible such yardsticks are,
the more usable they will be. But if they are going to be specific and
realistic (for example, so many dollars in world trade), then it is necessary to consider both the internal resources of the enterprise ("How
much physically can we export?") and the environmental conditions
("What share of which world markets can we obtain?"). Hence both
an analysis of internal resources and an environmental analysis are
called for in setting up realistic and adequately challenging criteria.

The next step requires that management define the range of possible
activities which it might use to accomplish the larger objective. For
example, the question for a furniture company might be: What balance of emphasis is best between office and home furnishings? The
alternatives must be weighed in terms of their effectiveness in accomplishing the objective, on the one hand, and of the consumption of
available resources, on the other hand.

As the preferred new subobjectives and subprograms begin to
emerge, one can expect numerous conflicts and inconsistencies. In the
case of the exporter, for example, protection of domestic sales may
not always be consistent with expansion of foreign trade. Hence some
sort of reiteration or recycling is called for to minimize the inconsistencies before the final subobjectives can be decided on.

So much for the general process. What are the problems of making
it work? What requirements must be observed?

Role of Creativity

Establishing even a subobjective within the framework of a broader
objective is a creative act. It involves the conceptual creation of a

---

[5] *Vitality in a Business Enterprise* (New York, McGraw-Hill Book Company, Inc.,
1960), pp. 37–38.

Exhibit II Process of deriving specific objectives from broader objectives

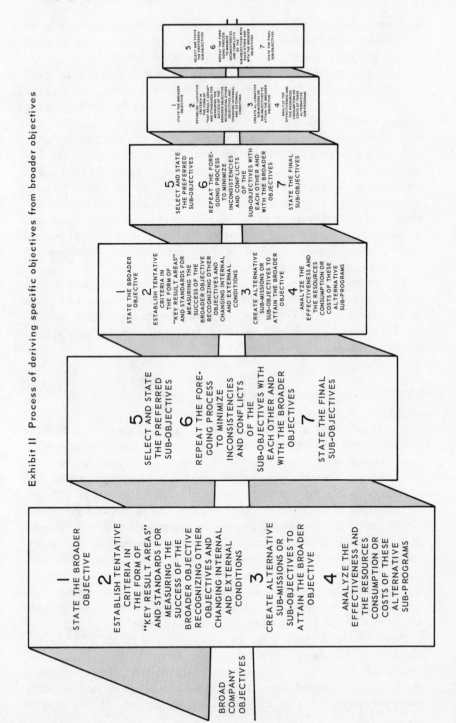

number of possible subobjectives, testing them against the realities of (1) consistency with internal resources, (2) consistency with environmental conditions, and (3) effectiveness/cost relationships in accomplishing the broader objective. Here we see the familiar concepts of creativity: exposure (to the broader objectives, internal and environmental constraints, and challenges), gestation, idea emergence, testing against reality, recycling.

Borrowing from the studies of creativity, we can see that the individual who is creative on the practical level, *provided he has had appropriate exposure to the company situation,* can be very helpful in establishing objectives. On the other hand, we have to beware of situations in which objectives are set without adequate *exposure* to environmental conditions (not all would-be staff planners are conscious of this); likewise we must beware of situations where objectives are set without adequate *analysis* of both internal and environmental conditions (not all line managers are conscious of this).

The creation of a workable grand-design type of objective thus emerges as an especially creative act. There are no broader objectives to be guided by. The creator of the grand design has as tools only his needs, values, and drives, and the company's environmental and internal constraints and challenges.

Motives & Appeals

In setting meaningful objectives, much help can come from creative people—those with high idea-emergence, good at censoring their own ideas against reality, persistent at recycling their ideas for improvement, having adequate exposure to internal and external factors, and possessing adequate drives. Moreover, Douglas McGregor's "Theory Y" approach to management suggests that the higher-order personal drives (such as those based on ego needs and self-fulfillment needs) of these people should be coupled with the objectives of the undertaking for the most effective accomplishment of the mission. This may be especially true in the higher echelons of a large organization. To oversimplify the thought, pay raises and threats of discharge may work with blue-collar workers, but the higher motives may be more effective with the financially more secure managers.

Frederick R. Kappel cites the visionary goal of AT&T—"the big dream stated without equivocation, the dream of good, cheap, fast, worldwide telephone service for everyone." He observes that such a goal is "not a wishful fancy. It is not a speculation. It is a perfectly clear statement that you are going to do something." He then points out three conditions which in his opinion favor setting the right goal at the right time:

1. An instinctive feeling for quality throughout the organization.
2. Freedom to make some mistakes.
3. A recognition of the pressure of external factors.

He further points out that "part of the talent or genius of the goal-setter is the ability to distinguish between the possible and the impossible—but to be willing to get very close to the latter."[6]

Eric Hoffer takes a stronger view, at least in regard to the goals of large undertakings or "mass movements." He suggests that the goals for a vital undertaking should be impossible of achievement (for example, achieving God's Kingdom on earth), and points out that the best climate for setting these visionary goals is among the groups who are down but not quite out.[7] For example, the Black Muslim movement apparently cannot reach the most abject Negroes, who seem to have little interest in anything beyond a day-to-day existence, nor does it apparently appeal much to Negroes who are currently "successful" in American society.

Does this apply to companies in the business world? Are there any indications that the downtrodden business organization, like pre-Hitler Germany, is most susceptible to a brilliant renaissance, and all that it lacks is a deliverer, a leader who electrifies its members with visionary goals? One could say that George Romney did something of this sort with American Motors. But such examples seem rare. Why aren't there more of them? There is certainly no lack of prospective candidates! Perhaps there is a lack of George Romneys, or perhaps they find themselves called into other fields. But any organization, in however severe straits, can probably boast a few young hotbloods who can establish visionary objectives, but who lack the other qualities of drive and leadership to carry them out.

Need for Renewal

There is probably merit in reestablishing objectives every so often just for the sake of reestablishing them. One might think that if objectives were once set, and if internal and external conditions did not change too much, the objectives would be valid for a good long time.

---

[6] *Vitality in a Business Enterprise* (New York, McGraw-Hill Book Company, Inc., 1960), pp. 40, 56–58.
[7] *The True Believer* (New York, Harper & Brothers, 1951).

But the same old objectives repeated over and over produce no impact, no challenge.

Perhaps this is a failing of many religious organizations. Canonical types of objectives, produced many years ago by undoubtedly brilliant churchmen, simply do not inspire the organization member of today unless he himself has gone through the process of thinking out the objectives and reached similar conclusions.

Some "Theory Y" practitioners have gone to an extreme; they favor changing the objectives at a given level and position every time a new individual comes into the job. In other words, the new appointee, along with his own superior and others with the need to know, sits down and writes a new job description including new objectives for the work. "Theory Y" practitioners claim to have encouraging results with this approach.

Locating Responsibility

Should the superior set the objectives for the individual groups that are subordinate to him? It is apparent that he must at least approve them if he is to discharge his own duties. Beyond this, he probably has broader exposure to internal and environmental conditions than his subordinates. But he may or may not be the creative type who can visualize a whole range of subobjectives, one for each of his various groups, the best of which are chosen after analyzing effectiveness and costs. Some of his subordinates may be better at this creation of alternatives than he is. Certainly they should have had greater exposure in depth (if not in breadth) to internal and environmental constraints, challenges, and opportunities. Accordingly, it would seem that to combine the best of these talents, the objectives for the subgroups should be worked out jointly by the leader of the subgroup and his superior.

How much help can staff give the line in this process? Certainly staff can conduct the internal analyses of resources and the environmental analyses of external conditions, always using the line for appropriate inputs in these analyses. Most line managers are accustomed to using their staffs in a similar capacity. Staff men can also propose and analyze a number of alternative subobjectives, and can sometimes make particularly brilliant contributions in proposing possible alternatives which might otherwise have been overlooked. This can be a major contribution of creative staff workers. Consultants, who are a form of temporary staff, do this frequently.

But the old principle holds true: the people with the ultimate responsibility have to make the ultimate decisions. Furthermore, they have to be brought into the decision-making process at sufficiently fundamental levels so they can have a full understanding of the context in which the final decision choices are being made. No responsible line man could be expected to accept ready-made objectives proposed by a staff person or researcher unless he, the line man, had personally weighed and debated the relation to internal and external conditions and the range of possible alternatives.

Working-Upwards Approach

Now suppose, as is often the case, that a company has not in recent years formally developed a written statement of objectives, and that (as should more often be the case) a member of the board of directors convinces his fellow members that they should have a written statement of objectives. *Where* should the job begin?

One might reason that logic calls for starting at the top of the hierarchy displayed in EXHIBIT I, starting with needs, values, and drives of the key individuals, and proceeding on down to creeds, grand designs, missions, and the like. For instance, Secretary McNamara and his associates, in the recent installation of program budgeting in the Defense Department, appear to have gone from a grand design to missions, to program elements (analogous to charters).

However, in our consulting practice with both business and non-business enterprises, my associates and I have found that as a practical measure the top of the scale is *not* the best place to start. We have found that profit objectives in terms of growth in earnings per common share are typically the most readily graspable starting point in business. They lead very understandably to environmental analysis (first in terms of profit results of comparable companies in industry, then to analysis of market requirements, technical trends, and competitive trends in the business environment) and analysis of internal resources.

People seem to have little difficulty in understanding the need and value of analyzing profit goals. Once this understanding has been obtained, it is not too painful to work up and down the hierarchy to fill it out; going *up* to other key result areas, charters, policies, missions, and even grand designs, and *down* to long-range plans, strategic programs, budgets, and short-term programs. Suddenly there is a new clarity to the growth directions for the enterprise, the type of management development needed, and the like.

As already indicated, there is a continual process of reiteration. In this reiteration one objective is adjusted in light of another, and in light of new developments in resources and in environmental conditions. Hence it does not really matter that some managers do not readily see the need for defining the higher-level objectives, and that attempts to attack the broader questions of creeds and grand designs make them squirm. When they start with some very tangible aspect such as profits, then work into the other types of objectives as the need to do so becomes demonstrated, they can achieve as good an understanding as anyone can.

Practical Uses

What are the practical uses of objectives? What tangible results come from giving thought and time to the clarification of objectives? An analysis was recently made by the American Management Association of companies that had developed formal company creeds.[8] In all too many cases this analysis indicated that the benefits were along the lines of "having opened up our thinking" or "a beneficial exercise for those who took part," but the practical results were rather hard to measure. This is unfortunate, for there are practical benefits indeed to be obtained.

Better Planning

Probably the most significant use of objectives is in planning. Not many organizations can conscientiously answer the question, "What should we be doing, and how much?" But carefully worked out objectives can narrow the target area, if not altogether pinpoint it. For example:

⁋ The new programing system in the Department of Defense is based on the nine types of missions or broad objectives of that organization (e.g., strategic retaliation). For the first time on an overall, formalized basis, the cost of each Defense Department activity has been related to its effectiveness in fulfilling these missions. Alternate systems are presented for top-level consideration in terms of cost and effectiveness analyses. The practical results include "thumbs down" for the RS-70, the Skybolt missile, and the Nike-Zeus antimissile system.

---

[8] Stewart Thompson, *Management Creeds and Philosophies*, Research Study No. 32 (New York, 1958).

❡ A major charity had been moving along on its natural momentum, doing an effective job in many ways, but not quite sure of just how large it should grow in the future, what new programs it should be undertaking, and what financial and other plans it should be making to ensure its future effectiveness. It has now developed a number of specific subobjectives in light of a definition of its broader objectives. Practical results are taking place in the way of organizational changes, staff recruitment and development, long-range financing plans, and development of new service programs—all based on a general agreement at the policy-making level of what the organization should look like in 1973.

❡ The management of Sears, Roebuck, in speaking of its objectives, says: "The Company sees itself not so much as a catalog merchant or retailer, but as an organized system for efficient and economical distribution, dedicated to serving the public with a broad range of *goods* and *services* [italics added], and to meeting any change in demand." Probably 90 out of 100 large organizations have some stated objectives of this general type. But the difference is that Sears not only states its objectives; it lives by them. In the last ten years the number of mail-order plants has remained steady at 11, and the number of retail stores has increased slightly from 694 to 748 (although many have been modernized and expanded). But the company is now upgrading itself into a style house, as its recent advertising demonstrates. Here are examples of the variety of Sears Roebuck activities—

It runs a fleet of 5,000 service and installation trucks.

Through Allstate it is the largest stock company insurer of automobiles in the country, and fourth largest in the fire and casualty field.

It is in the life insurance business.

The Allstate Motor Club and Allstate Tours operate in the travel field.

It has entered the savings and loan business.

Homart Development Company recently opened its first shopping center, with a half-dozen others in various stages of planning.

Sears, Roebuck Acceptance Corp. has about $500 million of installment contracts.

In short, Sears, Roebuck has not occupied itself with perpetuating its existing form. It has arrived at broad objectives and derived a wide and changing range of supporting missions, or subobjectives. All this has led to handsome results, with earnings per share increasing in eight out of the last ten years.

❡ A major drug company has staked out a grand design in the field of human health and well-being. In accordance with this broad objective, the research group has identified some 40 potential and actual program areas—e.g., cardiovascular ailments, fertility control, and cancer. In annual program planning reviews within the research group, scientists and managers go through a series of steps for deriving specific program objectives. They have environmental analysis material on hand—for instance, "If we develop a tranquilizer with such and such characteristics, it will capture X per cent of the market." They also have organized information inputs on the long-range needs in the health field (e.g., dermatology). At the same time they have conducted resources analyses so they know their abilities in certain specialized lines of research.

Choice of Alternatives

The hierarchy of objectives is also valuable in analyzing and choosing alternative courses of action. (This benefit is obviously related to the planning values just discussed, but it deserves separate emphasis.) To use the experience of the drug company again:

> To stimulate thinking about alternative courses of action, management encourages scientists to attend association meetings; invites a considerable number of outside technical consultants—usually university people—to meet with executives; and stresses the study of data from marketing research and the detail sales force.

> Three important questions stand out in the criteria for screening the wide range of alternate subprograms—

> 1. How important is the proposed program? Importance is usually measured in terms of profit potential.

> 2. Can we do it? This question is usually related to the availability of skills and knowledge to overcome the technical problems involved.

> 3. What will it cost? Here the company has what amounts to a cost/effectiveness analysis of alternative programs, much along the lines described earlier in the case of the Department of Defense.

> Of course, the process of exploring alternatives ends with a good deal of reiteration or recycling to cut out nonessentials here, fill out a program there, and to make the total research effort consistent with a practical budget. In practice, as might be expected, the general program areas do not change radically from year to year. Once a specialized staff and momentum are built up in a given area, a program may last for some time, uncovering new opportunities as time goes along. However, specific detailed

projects are changed, and the overall emphasis in the program also changes as a result of management's approach.

Management Development

One of the most interesting uses of a framework of objectives is in management development. Most executives are keenly aware that the difference between their organization and other organizations in its field is its personnel. They recognize that development of its own people is a key issue in the health and success of any enterprise.

Recent theory as well as actual practice in management development has stressed the concept of identifying the objectives of the individual with the objectives of the enterprise. It also stresses making these objectives as specific as possible, and measuring their exact success in meeting them. For example, contrast the effectiveness you might expect in an organization where a supervisor says, "I'm responsible for quality—whatever that means," with effectiveness in an organization where he says:

> I'm responsible for rejects which come off the rotary machines and I've agreed on the standard with the Chief Inspector. Each day I get an analysis of rejects so I can put things right. At present the General Manager and I agree on 2.7 per cent rejects as acceptable, but we have a plan to get this down to 2.2 per cent by next November.[9]

There is ample evidence that this concept of management by objectives and by specific results actually works, and works well. However, the question not always thoroughly explored is, "Are we doing the right thing to begin with?" Possibly the quality control supervisor in the foregoing example is inspecting beautiful products for which there is little demand, for a market where quality is not a key result area, in a situation where the products could better be purchased from the outside, or where the entire company would be better off merged into a larger organization.

If a framework of objectives has been worked out for the whole organization, there is not so much danger of misdirected effort. Top management can be assured that all employees are working toward common purposes which are mutually consistent, appropriately challenging, and realistic in light of both internal and external opportunities and threats. It can be assured that people's potentials are being developed along lines which will increase the effectiveness of the company.

[9] John W. Humble, "Programmitis and Crown Princes," *The Manager,* December 1963, p. 47.

Organizational Efficiency

It should not be inferred from the foregoing discussion that the formal organization structure should be rearranged to conform closely with objectives in various parts of the company. Rearrangement may or may not be appropriate, depending on the circumstances. For example:

> ❡ In the Department of Defense we find that both the B-52 and the Polaris submarines are program elements in the Strategic Retaliatory Forces. Nevertheless, organizationally they fit into conventional Air Force and Navy formats. Support elements of an organization (for instance, the payroll department) are frequently organized separately as one distinct entity supporting a number of departments or divisions which may have widely differing objectives. This is done for the sake of efficiency.
>
> ❡ Non-Linear Systems, Inc., a specialized California instruments manufacturer with 350 employees, has developed a curious form of organization which ties in closely with the theory of objectives.[10] The company has a president and seven vice presidents, each responsible for an area such as innovation, market standing, profitability, or productivity. It shows evidence of having excellent results with this system.

However, we must not forget that in business true efficiency—unlike the dictionary definition—is not merely producing a certain result at the lowest cost; worthwhile efficiency is producing a *desired* result at the lowest cost. It is a ratio in which cost is the denominator, and the degree of effectiveness in producing some desired result is the numerator. Thus we can hardly consider efficiency without considering a range of objectives. The cost/effectiveness studies in the Department of Defense and "value analysis" studies at General Electric[11] illustrate the application of such thinking to logical cost reduction and efficiency improvement.

Conclusion

It is curious that so many discussions of management begin with exhortations to clarify objectives, and then, as if the nature of objec-

---

[10] See, for example, Arthur H. Kuriloff, "An Experiment in Management, Putting Theory Y to the Test,"*Personnel*, November-December 1963, p. 12.

[11] See, for example, Hugh McCullough, "New Concepts in Defense Planning, Programming and Budgeting," *The Federal Accountant*, September 1962, p. 70; also, L. D. Miles, "Purchasing Must Analyze Values," *Purchasing*, January 4, 1960, p. 65.

tives were well known, proceed to explore some other aspect of the matter at hand. In reality we know very little about the nature of objectives. And it is abundantly clear that we cannot quickly set up some objectives for an enterprise and then proceed on the assumption that they will be meaningful guides to action.

Taking stock of the little knowledge we do possess, we find that we know a few bare essentials. For instance, there are certain minimum tests which an objective, or a set of objectives, should pass. Thus, objectives—

> ... need not begin with the broad grand design of the enterprise, but all objectives in the hierarchy should be consistent with it;
> ... should make the people in the enterprise reach a bit;
> ... should be realistic in terms of (a) the internal resources of the enterprise, and (b) the external opportunities, threats, and constraints;
> ... should take into account the creative conception of a range of alternatives and the relative effectiveness and cost of each;
> ... should be known to each person so that he understands the goals of his own work and how they relate to the broader objectives of the total enterprise;
> ... should be periodically reconsidered and redefined, not only to take account of changing conditions, but for the salutary effect of rethinking the aims of organizational activities.

Objectives, properly developed and applied, can tell us in what paths, new and old, our total undertakings should be moving. They can guide both the day-to-day activities and the personal development of individuals in an organization. If we in management can clarify the objectives of our undertakings by even a small amount, we can greatly increase the effectiveness and efficiency of our businesses.

Leadership in Administration[*]

Philip Selznick

Leadership is not a familiar, everyday idea, as readily available to
common sense as to social science. It is a slippery phenomenon that
eludes them both. What leaders do is hardly self-evident. And it is
likely that much failure of leadership results from an inadequate
understanding of its true nature and tasks. Most of this essay will be
devoted to identifying and analyzing the chief functions of institutional leadership. By way of introduction, however, it may be helpful
to state a few simple guiding ideas here.

1. *Leadership is a kind of work done to meet the needs of a social
situation.* Possibly there are some individuals more likely to be leaders
than others, possessed of distinguishing personal traits or capacities.[1]
Whether or not this is so, we shall here be concerned with leadership
as a specialized form of activity, a kind of work or function. Identifying what leaders do certainly bears on (and is perhaps indispensable
to) the discovery of requisite personal attributes; but the questions
are of a different kind and may be treated separately.

To know the nature of the work done by leaders, we must know
something about the social situations they are called upon to handle.
This immediately suggests that there must be a very wide variety of
activities associated with leadership.[2] However, it does not follow that

---

[*] Reprinted with permission of author and publisher from *Leadership in Administration* (New York: Harper & Row, 1957), pp. 22–28, 33–43, 62–64, 149–154.
Copyright © 1957 by Harper & Row, Publishers, Incorporated. (Footnotes have
been renumbered.)

[1] This problem has received considerable attention, with largely negative but still
inconclusive results. See Ralph M. Stogdill, "Personal Factors Associated with
Leadership: A Survey of the Literature," *J. Psychology*, 1948, 25: 35–71; also
William O. Jenkins, "A Review of Leadership Studies with Particular Reference
to Military Problems," *Psychological Bulletin*, 1947, 44:54–77.

[2] Indeed, the current literature on this subject, in part as a reaction against the
"trait" approach, in part due to the influence of "situational" or "field" theory in
social psychology, has made this a central conclusion. Thus Jenkins, *op. cit.*, p. 75,
finds: "Leadership is specific to the particular situation under investigation. Who
becomes the leader of a given group engaging in a particular activity and what
the leadership characteristics are in the given case are a function of the specific
situation, including the measuring instruments employed. There is a wide variation in the characteristics of individuals who became leaders in similar situations,
and even greater divergence in leadership in different situations." But note the
following by Stogdill, *op. cit.*, p. 65: "The evidence suggests that leadership is a
relation that exists between persons in a social situation, and that persons who
are leaders in one situation may not necessarily be leaders in other situations.
Must it then be assumed that leadership is entirely incidental, haphazard, and
unpredictable? Not at all. The very studies which provide the strongest arguments

the *nature* of leadership varies with each social situation. If that were so, there would be nothing determinate about it; its study would be a scientific blind alley. In fact, of course, we must assume that significant leadership patterns are relatively few; and that these patterns are related to *types* of social situations. This means that certain very general activities of leaders—e.g., facilitating communication within the group—reflect equally general characteristics of all human groups; and that the functions of leadership will be understood only as we develop a better understanding of the main types of groups and the recurrent problems they face. In other words, a theory of leadership is dependent on a theory of social organization.

We shall not be concerned here with all leadership, but with leadership in large-scale organizations. This will require some consideration of the nature of such enterprises, including the characteristic problems that arise within them. It will be necessary to understand the institutional aspects of large-scale organizations, for the central argument will stress the close connection between these aspects and the key functions of leadership. Although institutional leadership must share the general characteristics of all leadership, we shall not deal with the latter problem directly.

2. *Leadership is not equivalent to office-holding or high prestige or authority or decision-making.* It is not helpful to identify leadership with whatever is done by people in high places. The activity we have in mind may or may not be engaged in by those who are formally in positions of authority. This is inescapable if we are to develop a theory that will be useful in diagnosing cases of inadequate leadership on the part of persons in authority. If this view is correct, it means that only some (and sometimes none) of the activities of decision-makers are leadership activities. Here again, understanding leadership requires understanding of a broader social process. If some types of decisions are more closely related to leadership activities than others, we should learn what they are. To this end in this analysis let us make a distinction between "routine" and "critical" decision-making.

3. *Leadership is dispensable.* The word "leadership" has its own halo, easily inviting the tacit assumption that, being a good thing, it is always in order. It may indeed be that all human groups require at all times *some* leadership activities. But if leadership is anything determinate, we should know how to distinguish its presence from its absence; similarly, if there are some social situations that especially require leadership, we should know how to tell them apart from other

---

for the situational nature of leadership also supply the strongest evidence indicating that leadership patterns as well as non-leadership patterns of behavior are persistent and relatively stable."

social situations. The idea is developed in this essay that leadership is not equally necessary in all large-scale organizations, or in any one at all times, and that it becomes dispensable as the natural processes of institutionalization become eliminated or controlled. This will provide some clues to the general conditions that call for leadership decisions.

These premises emphasize the futility of attempting to understand leadership apart from the broader organizational experience of which it is a phase. A theory of leadership will necessarily reflect the level of sophistication we have reached in the study of organization. We are dealing with an activity, with a function, with work done; we can make no more sense of it than is allowed by our understanding of the field within which that activity takes place.

The Default of Leadership

When institutional leadership fails, it is perhaps more often by default than by positive error or sin. Leadership is lacking when it is needed; and the institution drifts, exposed to vagrant pressures, readily influenced by short-run opportunistic trends. This default is partly a failure of nerve, partly a failure of understanding. It takes nerve to hold a course; it takes understanding to recognize and deal with the basic sources of institutional vulnerability.

One type of default is the failure to set goals. Once an organization becomes a "going concern," with many forces working to keep it alive, the people who run it can readily escape the task of defining its purposes. This evasion stems partly from the hard intellectual labor involved, a labor that often seems but to increase the burden of already onerous daily operations. In part, also, there is the wish to avoid conflicts with those in and out of the organization who would be threatened by a sharp definition of purpose, with its attendant claims and responsibilities. Even business firms find it easy to fall back on conventional phrases, such as that "our goal is to make profit," phrases which offer little guidance in the formulation of policy.

A critique of leadership, we shall argue, must include this emphasis on the leader's responsibility to define the mission of the enterprise. This view is not new. It is important because so much of administrative analysis takes the goal of the organization as given, whereas in many crucial instances this is precisely what is problematic. We shall also suggest that the analysis of goals is itself dependent on an understanding of the organization's social structure. In other words, the purposes we have or can have depend on what we are or what we can be.

In statesmanship no less than in the search for personal wisdom, the Socratic dictum—know thyself—provides the ultimate guide.

Another type of default occurs when goals, however neatly formulated, enjoy only a superficial acceptance and do not genuinely influence the total structure of the enterprise. Truly accepted values must infuse the organization at many levels, affecting the perspectives and attitudes of personnel, the relative importance of staff activities, the distribution of authority, relations with outside groups, and many other matters. Thus if a large corporation asserts a wish to change its role in the community from a narrow emphasis on profit-making to a larger social responsibility (even though the ultimate goal remains some combination of survival and profit-making ability), it must explore the implications of such a change for decision-making in a wide variety of organizational activities. We shall stress that the task of building special values and a distinctive competence into the organization is a prime function of leadership.

In this sense, the leader is an agent of institutionalization, offering a guiding hand to a process that would otherwise occur more haphazardly, more readily subject to the accidents of circumstance and history. This is not to say that the leader is free to do as he wishes, to mold the organization according to his heart's desire, restrained only by the quality of his imagination and the strength of his will. Self-knowledge means knowledge of limits as well as of potentialities.

The default of leadership shows itself in an acute form when *organizational* achievement or survival is confounded with *institutional* success. To be sure, no institutional leader can avoid concern for the minimum conditions of continued organizational existence. But he fails if he permits sheer organizational achievement, in resources, stability, or reputation, to become the criterion of his success. A university led by administrators without a clear sense of values to be achieved may fail dismally while steadily growing larger and more secure.

Finally, the role of the institutional leader should be clearly distinguished from that of the "interpersonal" leader. The latter's task is to smooth the path of human interaction, ease communication, evoke personal devotion, and allay anxiety. His expertness has relatively little to do with content; he is more concerned with persons than with policies. His main contribution is to the efficiency of the enterprise. The institutional leader, on the other hand, *is primarily an expert in the promotion and protection of values.* The interpretation that follows takes this idea as a starting point, exploring its meaning and implications. . . .

Drawing on general psychoanalytic theory, Erich Fromm distinguishes "static" and "dynamic" adaptation:

> By static adaptation we mean such an adaptation to patterns as leaves the whole character structure unchanged and implies only the adoption of a new habit. An example of this kind of adaptation is the change from the Chinese habit of eating to the Western habit of using fork and knife. A Chinese coming to America will adapt himself to this new pattern, but this adaptation in itself will have little effect on his personality; it does not arouse new drives or character traits.[3]

This may be compared with the idea of routine psychological processes suggested above. Static adaptation is not static, strictly speaking: it is, one might say, "everyday" dynamics. It is routine learning, and the study of it centers on such factors as motivation, practice, etc. It is ordinary, responsive behavior, subject to such normal tendencies as stimulus generalization. Most human responses are of this routine sort. It is natural that, wherever the training and control of large numbers is involved, as in industrial or military life, the students of these processes will have the major role.

Yet certain critical areas of experience belong to a different realm:

> By dynamic adaptation we refer to the kind of adaptation that occurs, for example, when a boy submits to the commands of his strict and threatening father—being too much afraid of him to do otherwise—and becomes a "good" boy. While he adapts himself to the necessities of the situation, something happens in him. He may develop an intense hostility against his father, which he represses, since it would be too dangerous to express it or even to be aware of it. This repressed hostility, however, though not manifest, is a dynamic factor in his character structure. It may create new anxiety and thus lead to still deeper submission; it may set up a vague defiance, directed against no one in particular but rather toward life in general. While here, too, as in the first case, an individual adapts himself to certain external circumstances, this kind of adaptation creates something new in him, arouses new drives and new anxieties. Every neurosis is an example of this dynamic adaptation.[4]

"Dynamic" here connotes more than simple activity, change, or growth. It suggests certain impelling forces that have a quite different origin and role from the routine tissue tensions of hunger, toothache, and sex. In dynamic adaptation, there is no simple one-to-one relation between an isolated stimulus and its response, a particular drive and

---

[3] Erich Fromm, *Escape from Freedom* (New York: Rinehart, 1941), p. 15.
[4] *Ibid.*, pp. 15–16.

its satisfaction, even if one accepts the idea that to some degree the total organism is implicated in all responsive behavior. The point is not the degree of involvement, but the reconstruction of need, the change in posture and strategy, the commitment to new types of satisfaction.

The relevance of these remarks for organizational theory is not far to seek. "Static adaptation" occurs in organizations as well as in personalities. The day-to-day functioning of the organization requires the continuous solution of problems. For the most part, the existing structure—both the informal human relations and the more formal patterns of communication and control—is competent to meet issues as they arise *without internal crisis*. As the daily work proceeds, changes occur, but normally these do not significantly affect the nature of the enterprise or its leadership. Even changes to top personnel may not be significant, if succession is orderly and fundamental policy is firmly established. The corporation grinds out sales and products; the union continues its ceaseless round of negotiations; the government agency extends approved services to assigned publics. Within broad limits, we sometimes say, these large organizations "run themselves"; yet we understand that this holds only for routine activity. In organizational life, just as in individual behavior, this routine functioning and adaptation is quantitatively preponderant. And the proper tooling of everyday activity is a legitimate and necessary preoccupation of management.

Yet in organizations, too, it is plainly necessary to focus attention on dynamics, to study less routine kinds of adaptation. There is a vital sector of organizational experience that cannot be understood as simple problem-solving in which the organization remains essentially intact. Rather, in this sector we find such adaptations of leadership to the interplay of internal and external forces as result in basic institutional changes. This is the area of "character-defining" commitments, which affect the organization's capacity to control its own future behavior. The range of discretion becomes limited, often in unanticipated ways; or it may be significantly broadened. For example, a government agency may adapt itself to a potentially hostile clientele by appointing representatives of the clientele to the agency staff. This has far-reaching consequences for policy, and is not understandable as simple "economic" personnel procurement.

In organizations, "dynamic adaptation" takes place in the shadowy area where administration and policy meet. We must take this, not in the obvious sense that administrative devices execute and form policy, but rather in the sense that organizational processes profoundly influence the kinds of policy that can be made, and policy in turn shapes the machinery of organization in ways that cannot be accounted for on the premises of efficient functioning. At the same time, this is precisely the area of "critical experience" upon which we wish to ·focus.

When we discuss the bearing of military unification on strategy, the social composition of administrative staffs, the restrictive consequences of administrative alliances, the abandonment of old agencies for new ones, the relation of autonomy to the defense of a program, the unorthodox administrative practices of Franklin Roosevelt, and similar matters, we find ourselves outside the area where administration can be made routine. We are squarely in the field where leadership counts and where managerial *expertise* is of secondary importance.

The term "leadership" connotes critical experience rather than routine practice. This is suggested in the following comment by Barnard:

> The overvaluation of the apparatus of communication and administration is opposed to leadership and the development of leaders. It opposes leadership whose function is to promote appropriate adjustment of ends and means to new environmental conditions, because it opposes change either of status in general or of established procedures and habitual routine. This overvaluation also discourages the development of leaders by retarding the progress of the abler men and by putting an excessive premium on routine qualities.[5]

However, it is easy to overemphasize the *personal* element. While personal qualities are important, and reflect differences in self-conception, too much attention to them may obscure the essential distinction. Even the person free of "routine qualities" may in fact be performing a routine function if he devotes his main energy to greasing the wheels of organization, albeit in human terms. In thinking of leadership, we too often have in mind the personal relation of leader and follower, especially as it involves such psychological mechanisms as identification. This emphasis leads us away from the role of leadership in the making of critical decisions.

It is in the realm of policy—including the areas where policy-formation and organization-building meet—that the distinctive quality of institutional leadership is found. Ultimately, this is the quality of statesmanship which deals with current issues, not for themselves alone but according to their long-run implications for the role and meaning of the group. Group leadership is far more than the capacity to mobilize personal support; it is more than the maintenance of equilibrium through the routine solution of everyday problems; it is the

---

[5] C. I. Barnard, *Organization and Management* (Cambridge: Harvard University Press, 1948), pp. 204 f.

function of the leader-statesman—whether of a nation or a private association—to define the ends of group existence, to design an enterprise distinctively adapted to these ends, and to see that that design becomes a living reality. These tasks are not routine; they call for continuous self-appraisal on the part of the leaders; and they may require only a few critical decisions over a long period of time. "Mere speed, frequency, and vigor in coming to decisions may have little relevance at the top executive level, where a man's basic contribution to the enterprise may turn on his making two or three significant decisions a year."[6] This basic contribution is not always aided by the traits often associated with psychological leadership, such as aggressive self-confidence, intuitive sureness, ability to inspire.

The Concept of Organization Character

Our general perspective may be clarified further if we continue the psychological analogy. In particular, the process of "character-formation" seems worth exploring for the insights it may yield to students of institutionalization and critical decision-making. When we have seen the connection between these two phenomena we shall be in a better position to analyze the nature and tasks of institutional leadership.

The idea of "character" as used by personality analysts is not altogether clear, but its usefulness is scarcely in doubt. There seems to be general agreement on four attributes.

First, character is a *historical* product. "The character as a whole," writes Fenichel, "reflects the individual's historical development."[7] Character is the "ego's habitual ways of reacting." In this sense every individual has a unique character.

Second, character is in some sense an *integrated* product, as is suggested by the term "character-structure." There is a discoverable pattern in the way the ego is organized; and the existence of such a pattern is the basis of character analysis.

Third, character is *functional*, in the sense that it is no mere accidental accretion of responsive patterns. Character development fulfills a task set by the requirements of personality organization: the defense of the individual against inner and outer demands which threaten him. "Biologically speaking, character formation is an autoplastic function.

---

[6] E. P. Learned, D. N. Ulrich, and D. R. Booz, *Executive Action*, Harvard University Graduate School of Business Administration, Boston, 1951, p. 57.

[7] Otto Fenichel, *The Psychoanalytic Theory of Neurosis* (New York: Norton, 1945), p. 470.

In the conflict between instinct and frustrating outer world, and motivated by the anxiety arising from this conflict, the organism erects a protection mechanism between itself and the outer world."[8] Whatever the special content of varying theories of character-formation, they share an emphasis on the *reconstruction of the self* as a way of solving anxiety-laden problems.

Fourth, character is *dynamic* in that it generates new strivings, new needs and problems. It is largely through the identification of these needs that diagnosis proceeds, as when the discovery of excessive dependency or aggressiveness suggests that the patient has a particular type of character-structure.

Now let us compare these attributes of character with the discussion above of how organizations become institutions. The following points were emphasized there:

1. The technical, rational, impersonal, task-oriented formal system (the "organization") is conditioned by the responsive interaction of persons and groups.

2. In the course of time, this responsive interaction is patterned. A social structure is created. This patterning is *historical*, in that it reflects the specific experiences of the particular organization; it is *functional* in that it aids the organization to adapt itself to its internal and external social environment; and it is *dynamic*, in that it generates new and active forces, especially internal interest-groups made up of men committed to particular jobs or policies.

3. Organizations become institutions as they are *infused with value*, that is, prized not as tools alone but as sources of direct personal gratification and vehicles of group integrity. This infusion produces a distinct identity for the organization. Where institutionalization is well advanced, distinctive outlooks, habits, and other commitments are unified, coloring all aspects of organizational life and lending it a *social integration* that goes well beyond formal co-ordination and command.

The study of organizational character-formation is, then, a phase of institutional analysis. Here the emphasis is on the embodiment of values in an organizational structure through the elaboration of commitments—ways of acting and responding that can be changed, if at all, only at the risk of severe internal crisis. As in the case of individuals, the emergence of organizational character reflects the irreversible element in experience and choice. A great deal of management practice, as in the hiring of personnel, may be viewed as an effort to hold down the number of irreversible decisions that must be made. On

---

[8] Wilhelm Reich, *Character-Analysis*, New York, 1949, p. 159.

the other hand, a wise management will readily limit its own freedom, accepting irreversible commitments, when the basic values of the organization and its direction are at stake. The acceptance of irreversible commitments is the process by which the character of an organization is set.

We have suggested that "critical" experience is closely related to organizational self-definition and self-reconstruction. This experience reflects the "open-endedness" of organizational life—the existence of alternative ways of responding and changing. Critical experience calls for leadership. Experience is less critical, and leadership is more dispensable, when the range of alternatives is limited by rigid technical criteria. The more limited and defined the task, the more readily can technical criteria prevail in decision-making. That is one reason why critical experience increases as we ascend the echelons of administration, where decisions based on broader interests must be made. But when the organization is not so limited, when it has the leeway to respond in alternative ways, there is room for character-formation, which enters to give structure to precisely this area of freedom.[9] Hence leadership, character, and critical decision-making are linked as aspects of the same basic phenomenon: the institutionalization of organizational life.

Perhaps the most obvious indicator of organizational character as a palpable reality is the abandonment of old organizations and the creation of new ones when changes in general orientation seem required. A new program does not always call for a new organization, but where a new point of view is to be embodied, there is often recourse to a fresh start. The fear is that the character of the old organization will create resistances to the full development of the new program. In practical terms, this usually means that the new program, even if accepted in good faith, may be threatened by personnel or budgetary procedures, and by many other operating routines that are uncongenial to it. An organization requiring considerable flexibility in personnel practice may find itself seriously hampered as part of a larger enterprise that must, considering the interests of the whole, enforce

---

[9] Cf. Karl W. Deutsch, "Communication in Self-Governing Organizations," in *Freedom and Authority in Our Time* (New York: Harper, 1953): "The importance of memory is the greater, and the effects of its loss the more severe, because a functioning memory implies the probability of eventual *individuation*. Two organizations might set out with exactly the same structure, and yet the different experiences from the outside world would eventually produce different stocks of memories in each, and eventually different kinds of behavior even in the presence of identical stimuli. Then such organizations might function in some respects similarly to individuals with peculiarities of personality; and as their memory-guided behavior might influence their intake of subsequent memories, such organizations might be capable of considerable internal evolution" (p. 275).

more rigid standards. Or, where long-established habits of work prevail, a new program may find itself quickly redefined into terms that sustain the received patterns. Issues of this sort were involved when the Roosevelt administration set up many new agencies, as in agriculture, instead of channeling new programs through existing organizations.

Character as Distinctive Competence

In studying character we are interested in the *distinctive competence or inadequacy* that an organization has acquired. In doing so, we look beyond the formal aspects to examine the commitments that have been accepted in the course of adaptation to internal and external pressures.

For purposes of illustration, let us examine briefly two rather different organizational experiences which have been previously investigated and reported, and in which the phenomenon considered here was studied. We may then consider some further applications and theoretical implications.

1. *Policy and character in the TVA experience.* In a study of the Tennessee Valley Authority,[10] the policy of channeling a federal program through local agencies was examined. In particular, the agricultural activities of the Authority were carried out in co-operation with the Extension Services of the land-grant colleges in the seven Valley states. This co-operation was extensive; in effect, the Extension Service organizations became the operating arm of the TVA in the agricultural field. In assessing the consequences of this arrangement, it was necessary to inquire into such commitments of the Extension Services as (1) might affect the way in which the TVA agricultural program was administered, and (2) might have a broader influence on policy-making in the TVA as a whole.

The "character" of the Extension Service was reflected in the following set of related commitments: (1) The involvement of the county agricultural agent in "courthouse" politics; (2) the intimate relation between the Extension Service and the American Farm Bureau Federation; (3) a tendency of the extension agents to deal with the relatively more prosperous elements of the local farm population and to reflect certain dominant attitudes, such as those toward farm tenancy; (4) a shift in the role of the Extension Service from a primarily edu-

---

[10] Philip Selznick, *TVA and the Grass Roots* (Berkeley and Los Angeles: University of California Press, 1949).

cational emphasis to the acceptance of responsibility for "action" programs. These and related commitments, it was found, significantly
affected the ability of the TVA to achieve an agricultural program that
would be free of restrictive pressures. In addition, the TVA's commitment to the Extension Service involved it in the national struggle for
control of the U.S. agricultural programs, drawing it into the Farm
Bureau camp. Further, the commitment created a group *inside* TVA
that defended general Extension Service attitudes and objectives and
successfully exerted pressure on other TVA programs....

[TVA gained considerable advantages from such concessions as re-
serving a strip of land around reservoirs for public access, recreation,
and conservation. These advantages included the support of important
local interests and of a powerful national lobby. Such are the fruits of
developing a distinctive organizational competence that make it a key
responsibility of executive leadership.]

The relation of leadership to organizational character may be more
closely explored if we examine some of the key tasks leaders are called
on to perform:

1. *The definition of institutional mission and role.* The setting of
goals is a creative task. It entails a self-assessment to discover the true
commitments of the organization, as set by effective internal and external demands. The failure to set aims in the light of these commitments is a major source of irresponsibility in leadership.

2. *The institutional embodiment of purpose.* The task of leadership
is not only to make policy but to build it into the organization's social
structure. This, too, is a creative task. It means shaping the "character"
of the organization, sensitizing it to ways of thinking and responding,
so that increased reliability in the execution and elaboration of policy
will be achieved according to its spirit as well as its letter.

3. *The defense of institutional integrity.* The leadership of any
polity fails when it concentrates on sheer survival: institutional survival, properly understood, is a matter of maintaining values and distinctive identity. This is at once one of the most important and least
understood functions of leadership. This area (like that of defining
institutional mission) is a place where the intuitively knowledgeable
leader and the administrative analyst often part company, because
the latter has no tools to deal with it. The fallacy of combining agencies on the basis of "logical" association of functions is a characteristic
result of the failure to take account of institutional integrity.

4. *The ordering of internal conflict.* Internal interest-groups form
naturally in large-scale organizations, since the total enterprise is in
one sense a polity composed if a number of sub-organizations. The
struggle among competing interests always has a high claim on the

attention of leadership. This is so because the direction of the enterprise as a whole may be seriously influenced by changes in the internal balance of power. In exercising control, leadership has a dual task. It must win the consent of constituent units, in order to maximize voluntary co-operation, and therefore must permit emergent interest blocs a wide degree of representation. At the same time, in order to hold the helm, it must see that a balance of power appropriate to the fulfillment of key commitments will be maintained. . . .

Creative Leadership

To the essentially conservative posture of the responsible leader we must add a concern for change and reconstruction. This creative role has two aspects. First, there is what we have called the "institutional embodiment of purpose." Second, creativity is exercised by strategic and tactical planning, that is, analyzing the environment to determine how best to use the existing resources and capabilities of the organization. This essay has not treated the problem of externally oriented strategies. On the other hand, what can be done to establish policy internally depends upon the changing relation between the organization and its environment.

The inbuilding of purpose is a challenge to creativity because it involves transforming men and groups from neutral, technical units into participants who have a peculiar stamp, sensitivity, and commitment. This is ultimately an educational process. It has been well said that the effective leader must know the meaning and master the techniques of the educator. As in the larger community, education is more than narrow technical training; though it does not shrink from indoctrination, it also teaches men to think for themselves. The leader as educator requires an ability to interpret the role and character of the enterprise, to perceive and develop models for thought and behavior, and to find modes of communication that will inculcate general rather than merely partial perspectives.

The main practical import of this effort is that *policy will gain spontaneous and reasoned support*. Desired ends and means are sustained and furthered, not through continuous command, but as a free expression of truly accepted principles. This presumes that at least the core participants combine loyalty to the enterprise with a sensitive awareness of the principles by which it is guided. Loyalty by itself is not enough, just as blind patriotism is insufficient. There must also be an ability to sense when a course of action threatens institutional integrity.

To be sure, this ideal of rational, free-willed consent is virtually impossible to achieve in organizations that have narrow, practical aims and whose main problem is the disciplined harnessing of human energy to achieve those aims. But such organizations, just because of this narrowness, are but meagerly institutionalized and have correspondingly little need for executive statesmanship. The creativity we speak of here is particularly necessary—and peculiarly possible—where, as discussed earlier, the transition from organization to institution is in process or has occurred.

To create an institution we rely on many techniques for infusing day-to-day behavior with long-run meaning and purpose. One of the most important of these techniques is the elaboration of socially integrating myths. These are efforts to state, in the language of uplift and idealism, what is distinctive about the aims and methods of the enterprise. Successful institutions are usually able to fill in the formula, "What we are proud of around here is...." Sometimes, a fairly explicit institutional philosophy is worked out; more often, a sense of mission is communicated in more indirect but no less significant ways. The assignment of high prestige to certain activities will itself help to create a myth, especially if buttressed by occasional explicit statements. The specific ways of projecting a myth are as various as communication itself. For creative leadership, it is not the communication of a myth that counts; rather, creativity depends on having the will and the insight to see the necessity of the myth, to discover a successful formulation, and above all to create the organizational conditions that will sustain the ideals expressed.

Successful myths are never merely cynical or manipulative, even though they may be put forward self-consciously to further the chances of stability or survival. If a state university develops a concept of "service to the community" as its central ideal, as against more remote academic aspirations, this may have its origins in a sense of insecurity, but it will not be innocent in application. To be effective, the projected myth cannot be restricted to holiday speeches or to testimony before legislative committees. It will inevitably color many aspects of university policy, affecting standards of admission, orientations of research, and the scope of the curriculum. The compulsion to embody the myth in practice has a dual source, reflecting inner needs and outer demands. Externally, those who can enforce demands upon the institution will not be content with empty verbal statements. They will expect conformity and the myth itself will provide a powerful lever to that end.

The executive acts out the myth for reasons of self-expression, but also for quite practical administrative reasons. He requires *some* integrating aid to the making of many diverse day-to-day decisions, and the myth helps to fulfill that need. Sharp discrepancies between theory and practice threaten his own authority in the eyes of subordinates; conformity to the myth will lessen "trouble" with outside groups. Not least important, he can hope that the myth will contribute to a unified sense of mission and thereby to the harmony of the whole. If the administrator is primarily dedicated to maintaining a smooth-running machine, and only weakly committed to substantive aims, these advantages will seem particularly appealing.

In the end, however, whatever their source, myths are institution builders. Making the myth effective willy-nilly entrenches particular objectives and capabilities, although these may not be the ones that initially inspired the sponsors of the enterprise. Myth-making may have roots in a sensed need to improve efficiency and morale; but its main office is to help create an integrated social organism.

The art of the creative leader is the art of institution-building, the reworking of human and technological materials to fashion an organism that embodies new and enduring values. The opportunity to do this depends on a considerable sensitivity to the politics of internal change. This is more than a struggle for power among contending groups and leaders. It is equally a matter of avoiding recalcitrance and releasing energies. Thus winning consent to new directions depends on how secure the participants feel. When many routine problems of technical and human organization remain to be solved, when the minimum conditions for holding the organization together are only precariously met, it is difficult to expend energy on long-range planning and even harder to risk experimental programs. When the organization is in good shape from an engineering standpoint it is easier to put ideals into practice. Old activities can be abandoned without excessive strain if, for example, the costs of relatively inefficient but morale-saving transfer and termination can be absorbed. Security is bartered for consent. Since this bargain is seldom sensed as truly urgent, a default of leadership is the more common experience.

On the same theme, security can be granted, thereby releasing energies for creative change, by examining established procedures to distinguish those important to a sense of security from those essential to the aims of the enterprise. Change should focus on the latter; stability can be assured to practices that do not really matter so far as objectives are concerned but which do satisfy the need to be free from threatening change. Many useless industrial conflicts have been fought to protect prerogative and deny security, with but little effect on the ultimate competence of the firm.

If one of the great functions of administration is the exertion of cohesive force in the direction of institutional security, another great function is the creation of conditions that will make possible in the future what is excluded in the present. This requires a strategy of change that looks to the attainment of new capabilities more nearly fulfilling the truly felt needs and aspirations of the institution. The executive becomes a statesman as he makes the transition from administrative management to institutional leadership.

Strategy and Structure*

Alfred D. Chandler, Jr.

[The ways organizations grow affect their structures.] Until the volume or technological complexity of an enterprise's economic activities had so grown as to demand an increasing division of labor within the firm, little time needed to be spent on administrative work. Then the resulting specialization required one or more of the firm's executives to concentrate on coordinating, appraising, and planning these specialized activities. When the enterprise expanded geographically by setting up or acquiring facilities and personnel distant from its original location, it had to create an organization at a central headquarters to administer the units in the field. When it grew by moving into new functions, a central office came to administer the departments carrying on the different functions. Such a central administrative unit proved necessary, for example, when in following the policy of vertical integration a manufacturing firm began to do its own wholesaling, procuring of supplies, and even producing raw materials. Finally, when an integrated enterprise became diversified through purchasing or creating new facilities and entered new lines of business, or when it expanded its several functional departments over a still larger geographical area, it fashioned a number of integrated divisional units administered by a general office.

The thesis that different organizational forms result from different types of growth can be stated more precisely if the planning and carrying out of such growth is considered a *strategy,* and the organization devised to administer these enlarged activities and resources, a *structure. Strategy* can be defined as the determination of the basic long-term goals and objectives of an enterprise, and the adoption of courses of action and the allocation of resources necessary for carrying out these goals. Decisions to expand the volume of activities, to set up distant plants and offices, to move into new economic functions, or become diversified along many lines of business involve the defining of new basic goals. New courses of action must be devised and resources allocated and reallocated in order to achieve these goals and to maintain and expand the firm's activities in the new areas in response to shifting demands, changing sources of supply, fluctuating economic conditions, new technological developments, and the actions of competitors. As the adoption of a new strategy may add new types

* Reprinted with permission of author and publisher from *Strategy and Structure* (Cambridge, Massachusetts: The M.I.T. Press, 1962), pp. 13–16.

of personnel and facilities, and alter the business horizons of the men responsible for the enterprise, it can have a profound effect on the form of its organization.

Structure can be defined as the design of organization through which the enterprise is administered. This design, whether formally or informally defined, has two aspects. It includes, first, the lines of authority and communication between the different administrative offices and officers and, second, the information and data that flow through these lines of communication and authority. Such lines and such data are essential to assure the effective coordination, appraisal, and planning so necessary in carrying out the basic goals and policies and in knitting together the total resources of the enterprise. These resources include financial capital; physical equipment such as plants, machinery, offices, warehouses, and other marketing and purchasing facilities, sources of raw materials, research and engineering laboratories; and, most important of all, the technical, marketing, and administrative skills of its personnel.

The thesis deduced from these several propositions is then that structure follows strategy and that the most complex type of structure is the result of the concatenation of several basic strategies. *Expansion of volume* led to the creation of an administrative office to handle one function in one local area. Growth through *geographical dispersion* brought the need for a departmental structure and headquarters to administer several local field units. The decision to expand into new types of functions called for the building of a central office and a multidepartmental structure, while the developing of new lines of products or continued growth on a national or international scale brought the formation of the multidivisional structure with a general office to administer the different divisions. For the purposes of this study, the move into new functions will be referred to as a strategy of *vertical integration* and that of the development of new products as a strategy of *diversification*.

This theoretical discussion can be carried a step further by asking two questions: (1) If structure does follow strategy, why should there be delay in developing the new organization needed to meet the administrative demands of the new strategy? (2) Why did the new strategy, which called for a change in structure, come in the first place?

There are at least two plausible answers to the first query. Either the administrative needs created by the new strategy were not positive or strong enough to require structural change, or the executives involved were unaware of the new needs. There seems to be no question that a new strategy created new administrative needs, for expansion through geographical dispersion, vertical integration, and product diversification added new resources, new activities, and an increasing number of entrepreneurial and operational actions and decisions. Nevertheless, executives could still continue to administer both the old and new activities with the same personnel, using the same channels of communication and authority and the same types of information. Such administration, however, must become increasingly inefficient. This proposition should be true for a relatively small firm whose structure consists of informal arrangements between a few executives as well as for a large one whose size and numerous administrative personnel require a more formal definition of relations between offices and officers. Since expansion created the need for new administrative offices and structures, the reasons for delays in developing the new organization rested with the executives responsible for the enterprise's long-range growth and health. Either these administrators were too involved in day-to-day tactical activities to appreciate or understand the longer-range organizational needs of their enterprises, or else their training and education failed to sharpen their perception of organizational problems or failed to develop their ability to handle them. They may also have resisted administratively desirable changes because they felt structural reorganization threatened their own personal position, their power, or most important of all, their psychological security.

In answer to the second question, changes in strategy which called for changes in structure appear to have been in response to the opportunities and needs created by changing population and changing national income and by technological innovation. Population growth, the shift from the country to the city and then to the suburb, depressions and prosperity, and the increasing pace of technological change, all created new demands or curtailed existing ones for a firm's goods or services. The prospect of a new market or the threatened loss of a current one stimulated geographical expansion, vertical integration, and product diversification. Moreover, once a firm had accumulated large resources, the need to keep its men, money, and materials steadily employed provided a constant stimulus to look for new markets by moving into new areas, by taking on new functions, or by developing new product lines. Again the awareness of the needs and opportunities created by the changing environment seems to have depended on the training and personality of individual executives and on their ability to keep their eyes on the more important entrepreneurial problems even in the midst of pressing operational needs.

The answers to the two questions can be briefly summarized by restating the general thesis. Strategic growth resulted from an awareness of the opportunities and needs—created by changing population, income, and technology—to employ existing or expanding resources more profitably. A new strategy required a new or at least refashioned structure if the enlarged enterprise was to be operated efficiently. The failure to develop a new internal structure, like the failure to respond to new external opportunities and needs, was a consequence of over-concentration on operational activities by the executives responsible for the destiny of their enterprises, or from their inability, because of past training and education and present position, to develop an entre-preneurial outlook.

One important corollary to this proposition is that growth without structural adjustment can lead only to economic inefficiency. Unless new structures are developed to meet new administrative needs which result from an expansion of a firm's activities into new areas, functions, or product lines, the technological, financial, and personnel economies of growth and size cannot be realized. Nor can the enlarged resources be employed as profitably as they otherwise might be. Without admin-istrative offices and structure, the individual units within the enter-prise (the field units, the departments, and the divisions) could un-doubtedly operate as efficiently or even more so (in terms of cost per unit and volume of output per worker) as independent units than if they were part of a larger enterprise. Whenever the executives respon-sible for the firm fail to create the offices and structure necessary to bring together effectively the several administrative offices into a uni-fied whole, they fail to carry out one of their basic economic roles.

The actual historical patterns of growth and organization building in the large industrial enterprise were not, of course, as clear-cut as they have been theoretically defined here. One strategy of expansion could be carried out in many ways, and often, two or three basic ways of expansion were undertaken at one and the same time. Growth might come through simultaneous building or buying of new facilities, and through purchasing or merging with other enterprises. Occasionally a firm simultaneously expanded its volume, built new facilities in geo-graphically distant areas, moved into new functions, and developed a different type of product line. Structure, as the case studies indicate, was often slow to follow strategy, particularly in periods of rapid expansion. As a result, the distinctions between the duties of the dif-ferent offices long remained confused and only vaguely defined. One executive or a small group of executives might carry out at one and the same time the functions of a general office, a central office, and a de-partmental headquarters. Eventually, however, most large corpora-tions came to devise the specific units to handle a field unit, a func-tional department, an integrated division, or a diversified industrial empire. For this very reason, a clear-cut definition of structure and strategy and a simplified explanation or theory of the relation of one to the other should make it easier to comprehend the complex realities involved in the expansion and management of the great industrial enterprises studied here, and easier to evaluate the achievement of the organization builders.

Decentralization of Federal Disbursing Functions[*]

Frank J. McKenna

A new approach to handling check-disbursing functions in the federal government is currently being put to test, with the Railroad Retirement Board serving as the "proving ground." The basis for the idea was the belief that substantial savings in both time and money would be achieved if the check-disbursing operations performed by the Treasury Department for those agencies which issue repetitive benefit payments or a large volume of single payments could be decentralized.

The idea started in September, 1952, when a survey group was set up at the request of the Appropriations Committee of the House of Representatives to study the check-disbursing operations performed by the Treasury Department for the Railroad Retirement Board in the payment of retirement benefits. The survey group consisted of representatives of the staff of the House Appropriations Committee, the General Accounting Office, and the Treasury Department. However, studies indicating the potential savings of such a program had been made by the board itself as far back as 1947.

The Railroad Retirement Board, an independent agency of the federal government, located in Chicago, Illinois, is charged with the administration of a system of social insurance for the nation's railroad workers. The board derives its authority from two laws—the Railroad Retirement Act and the Railroad Unemployment Insurance Act. Under the Railroad Retirement Act, benefits are paid to aged and permanently disabled employees and their wives, and to the widows, widowers, children, and parents of deceased employees. This benefit program is to all intents and purposes self-supporting, being maintained by taxes collected in equal shares from the railroads and their employees. The taxes for the retirement system are collected by the Internal Revenue Service under a third law—the Railroad Retirement Tax Act—and are credited to a special Treasury account designated as the railroad retirement account.

Under the Railroad Unemployment Insurance Act, benefits are paid to railroad employees who are unemployed or temporarily disabled. The costs of these programs are paid entirely from contributions collected by the board from the railroads.

In terms of the number of people served and the amount of money involved, the board's programs are not nearly so large as the general

* Reprinted with permission of author and publisher from *Public Administration Review*, Vol. 16, No. 1 (Winter, 1956), pp. 37–39.

social security system; but the types of protection are much more comprehensive. The board pays benefits to about 1,000,000 persons a year. In the fiscal year which ended June 30, 1955, well over 1,000,000 people drew benefits totaling $750,000,000. A majority of these beneficiaries received repetitive monthly payments.

The mission assigned to the survey group was restricted to the development of necessary cost and procedural data in both the administrative agency and the Treasury. It had no decision-making authority. Specifically, the phases which the group was directed to study fell into three important categories, as follows:

1. Any reductions in costs which could be achieved under the existing system, in which the disbursing operations were centered in the Treasury. This phase was necessary from the point of view of establishing an adequate basis against which to compare further possibilities for saving through physical consolidation of operations.

2. Savings, added costs, and other advantages or disadvantages which would be realized if the total operation was physically moved into the Railroad Retirement Board building under Treasury management.

3. Savings, added costs, and other advantages or disadvantages which would result from the integration of the disbursing function with the accounting function under the management of the Railroad Retirement Board.

The group examined all post-adjudication operations related either directly or indirectly to the disbursement of retirement payments which were performed by the board and the Chicago disbursing office of the Treasury. The activities involved in these operations were quite varied. Among the specific operations studied were the certification and processing of awards; the issuance of single, accrual, and recurring payment checks; the processing of change-of-name-and-address requests, termination and suspension notices, and returned checks; the remailing and cancellation of checks; and the control, verification, and reconciliation of these payments. The functions relating to the disbursement of payments under the Railroad Unemployment Insurance Act were excluded from this study.

The results of the study satisfied the survey group that the proposal for integration contained sufficient potentialities for economy to warrant a "test run." Based on the conclusions of the survey group, the Treasury Department approved the transfer of the checkwriting and related operations to the board on a test basis. Operations were to be evaluated after a transitional period of ninety days. Under these arrangements, the board began writing checks on a limited scale in December, 1953; and when all necessary records were transferred from the Treasury Department to the board, the program was expanded to include all benefit payments under the Railroad Retirement Act.

After the transitional period, detailed time-and-cost records were maintained for a three-month test period beginning in April, 1954. The cost records for this three-month test period were carefully evaluated by a cost committee consisting of representatives of the Railroad Retirement Board, the Treasury Department, and the General Accounting Office. The findings of the committee showed that substantial savings were being achieved.

In arriving at its evaluation, the committee analyzed detailed operations for the purpose of arriving at actual costs, both direct and indirect; the basis used in allocating overhead charges and segregating costs between the disbursing and accounting functions; and the methods employed in projecting costs to annual amounts for fiscal years 1953 and 1954. Direct costs in the Railroad Retirement Board were the product of two ninety-day time studies—one of the old system and the second of the new system. Every effort was made to conform to the cost system existing in the disbursing office of the Treasury Department and to include all elements of cost, both actual and theoretical, except such items as postage which would have been identical under any system. On the basis of the committee's findings, the Secretary of the Treasury formally delegated to the board the authority to continue checkwriting under the Railroad Retirement Act.

In the short operating history of the integrated system, substantial economies have emerged. Specific examples of changes which have contributed to the major savings as well as numerous short cuts are the following:

1. The elimination of duplicate recordkeeping through the consolidation of several different types of records made possible, for example, the elimination of some 500,000 individual payee punch cards which were maintained by the board for the purpose of reconciling the recurring monthly payments processed by the division of disbursements.

2. The addition of only seven people to the regular staff of forty, who, before the integrated operations, maintained records and payment lists and performed other work preliminary to the disbursing operation, enabled the board to perform the entire operation itself and to save a substantial part of the money which would have been paid to the Treasury Department for the checkwriting service.

3. The establishment of a later cut-off-date in each month for the preparation of checks allowed more time to process such actions as changes of name and address, in order to reduce the number of corrections required after the checks were printed.

4. The reduction in number of forms, or copies of forms, resulted in savings from the elimination of their handling and filing.

These are only a few of the more significant economies of operation that resulted from the integrated system. There have been others which, while not extensive in themselves, have brought about many economical and lasting changes.

By December of 1955, over 14,200,000 checks covering a wide range of payments had been issued by the board. These included not only all of the system's retirement and survivor benefit checks, but also its own "housekeeping" checks (salaries for board personnel, maintenance of equipment payments, rent, etc.). In addition, the board has taken over the payroll savings bond program for its own employees from the Treasury Department.

The Treasury Department disbursing offices in the various cities in which the board has regional offices continue to write the checks for unemployment and sickness benefits which are certified under the Railroad Unemployment Insurance Act. The feasibility of having the regional offices of the board assume the responsibility for checkwriting under these programs is currently being tested in the board's Chicago regional office.

Although further improvements are still to be explored, those which have been effected thus far have demonstrated the soundness of the idea of transferring railroad retirement disbursement operations to the Railroad Retirement Board.

Power Struggles in the Line[*]

Melville Dalton

Although the term "clique" *denotes* a small exclusive group of persons
with a common interest, it too often *connotes* a group concerned with
questionable activity. Without these moral overtones, the term can
aptly apply to the initiating nucleus of many group activities in and
out of industry. Certainly the negative feeling associated with the term
is carried too far, for cliques and secrets are inseparable and essential
for group life. We would question, for example, whether parents
covertly checking on their children's activities in school and community are "conspirators"; whether the indirect attempts all of us make to
learn more of our acquaintances than they voluntarily tell us is "immoral"; and whether the widespread "manipulations" by both leaders
and followers in all areas of life in competitive societies to win ends
is "villainy." Villainy may develop in all these cases, but not necessarily. Cliques may work for moral as well as immoral ends. Whether
or not we are able to preach what we practice, the organization will
fall apart without sustaining action by some clique. All organizations
must have "privy councils" similar in some sense to the meaning of that
phrase in feudal times. One may well ask, what organization is without secrets held by some members, usually the more responsible, from
other members with the intent and eventual result of helping all *loyal*
members? Too often uncertainty hallows and hides the developing
defects of official doctrine for changing situations. Responsible members must nevertheless try to fit the department, or firm, to inescapable
conditions. And in doing this they necessarily "socialize" and "discuss
problems," which is easily seen by opponents as "clique" activity "un-
dermining" the organization.

More of this later, but for now let us think of a clique as the informal association of two or more persons to realize some end. The end
is usually a calculated one, but it may be multiple and differ for some
members. Typical ends in an industrial plant are: to increase the status
and reward of one or all members; to get more support in job activities; to find social satisfactions; to hide facts or conditions that would
be frowned on by superiors; to escape unpleasant situations or annoy-
ances; to get more privileges, especially those peculiar to higherups;
and to share the limelight with superiors.

Many factors contribute to the rise of cliques. A few that are intrinsic

[*] Reprinted with permission of author and publisher from *Men Who Manage*
(New York: John Wiley & Sons, Inc., 1959), pp. 52–67. (Footnotes have been
renumbered.)

or recur and that can be summarized quickly include: (1) division of labor, (2) variations in identification with the firm, (3) changes in the industrial community, and (4) compulsions of growth.

Division of Labor

Formal division of labor and assignment of responsibility encourages cliques, especially in a society stressing equal opportunity. Isolation of personnel in this way provokes a given group to magnify the importance of its function in the system and to ignore and minimize that of others. This leads to challenges and defenses. Work groups and their supervisors compare and rank contributions to the organization. This is particularly true of newer departments, and is of course not confined to industry. In the FWD, for example, there were numerous tiffs among material men, expediters, estimators, and job analysts, with each very status-conscious, defending his contribution as *the vital one.* The condition is probably commoner where education is higher and contribution is less tangible, for the repetition and intensity of defenses seem greater in staff than line. In both, however, departmental boasting extends to accomplishments and competence of the department head.[1] In Milo's chemical department—and in at least two of the chemical firms in Mobile Acres—there were disputes between chemists on the one hand, and samplers and vat operators on the other, about whose function "is most important" and who "actually produces." This job identity forces personnel into defensive action to get their share of credit and honors. Leaders call on subordinates for help to protect departmental interests and to expose the errors of others. Though seen as a distinct unit, the department is compared with others in performance of assignments, original contributions, etc., all of which encourages clique effort to conceal shortcomings and preserve appearances.

Clique action usually accompanies reorganization and the new divisions of labor that come with expansion. Departmental resistance to the new system is often apprehension that new procedures will limit old personal arrangements and "rights." Some supervisors are thrown into panicky opposition by talk of formalizing loose practices. They mouth platitudes about the threat to "democratic" relations, when they really fear the change and the unpleasant lag before they can build a new reservoir of unofficial advantages and in some measure again control the deference of subordinates. They argue that "for-

---

[1] There is of course nothing "unnatural" about such behavior, but it is contrary to expectations. On the other hand, loyalty to the system rather than to the unifying leader, or department head, may handicap him severely. See M. E. Dimock, *The Executive in Action,* Harper and Brothers, New York, 1945, p. 249.

malizing things" will force them to "work for" instead of "working with" the company.

Differences in Feeling for the Firm[2]

Variations in the emotional ties of personnel with their firm are unavoidable. Differences in age, ability, expectations, and personal and community responsibilities lead to a *differential identification*. Given human agents in close association, with similar standards of what is desirable, and obviously they will clash over available rewards. Whatever the goals of the organization, there will be rivalry for higher posts, a voice in policy, and recognition from leaders. Without benefit of formal rules, and even forbidden, rivalries find expression in cliques.[3] Moreover, the individual's identification with the firm will vary with success or failure. The gap between his expectations and reality can never close, because our society almost demands that he never be satisfied. With this fluctuating identification a given employee is willing to engage in action at one time that he would not at another. We may say, overneatly, that his view of the firm changes with his success in advancing and protecting himself through participation in the inescapable aggressive and defensive cliques.

Other factors influence the degree of organizational attachment. Some members are in a department by chance and are looking elsewhere. Some entered by choice but are disillusioned and remain to please their families, or because they feel "too old to make a change," or "could not get the same money" elsewhere, or "have too much seniority." Some are indifferent or resigned and say, "All jobs are alike when you have to work for somebody else." Others are embittered and glad to see superiors embarrassed with problems. In other words, some officers are devoted career members, some are lukewarm toward the firm, while some hardly identify at all.

Changes in the Industrial Community

A changing market and technology, with plant expansion and turnover of personnel, promotes and requires cliques. New personnel and

---

[2] For general remarks on "identification," see [C. I.] Barnard, [*Functions of the Executive*, Harvard University Press, Cambridge, 1938] pp. 83–86; H. A. Simon, [*Administrative Behavior*, The Macmillan Company, New York, 1948,] pp. 110–112, 204–214; C. L. Shartle, *Executive Performance and Leadership*, Prentice-Hall, Englewood Cliffs, N.J., 1956, pp. 156–161. And though expressed in different terms, see L. Reissman, "A Study of Role Conceptions in Bureaucracy," *Social Forces*, 27:305–310, March, 1949.

[3] C. I. Barnard notes the potential for covert action in democratic organizations. See his *Organization and Management*, Harvard University Press, Cambridge, 1948, pp. 39–47.

methods may make the organization more desirable for some but less so for others, so that one finds a range of commitments to the organization, as well as the department. This of course means that responsible officers cannot count equally on all members. Having to depend on some more than others their "interaction rate" is consequently much greater with some than with others. Hence despite formal equality, prescribed relations, and assumed objectivity, they draw closer emotionally to some and share community as well as job experiences with them. During work crises these persons turn to each other spontaneously. They share knowledge of developing events and judiciously withhold information from the untried, and especially from those who have "talked out of turn" or are likely to. Their ties are, of course, seen and variously interpreted. Some of the other members may be alienated and, intentionally or not, aggravate differences in the department. But in any case departmental affairs will be dominated by the necessarily small closed corps of officers who become the center of influence and attention, or a clique in our sense of the word.

Rapid turnover of personnel even in an otherwise relatively stable firm naturally weakens group unity. One finds "old-timers" drawing together into cliques because they "have been through things together" and "can count on each other." Irregular transfers of individuals in and out of departments, or the sometimes required systematic shifting of personnel around a circuit in the firm, gives a certain vagrant character to the movers and creates social instability and demand by some for closer relations. As a threat to existing informal arrangements these "floaters" are seen as strangers of a kind.

Under these several conditions demands for "loyalty" force departmental and subgroup identifications. But for some, or even many, this allows only tenuous concern with the organization as a whole, and limited or distorted awareness of departmental affairs. Alert and driving cliques then become the generators of action.

Compulsions of Growth

Organizations have an expansive force and they act to preserve themselves.[4] Milo's action toward its Office was a case in point, and we shall see in the next chapter that this also holds for departments. Often disparagingly termed "empire building," these strains of growth are typical and may be quite lawful, but they jar the organization and induce various clique actions. Two practices always present in organi-

[4] [M. E.] Dimock, [*The Executive in Action,* Harper and Brothers, New York, 1945,] pp. 53–68; Herbert Blumer, "Group Tensions and Interest Organizations" in Milton Derber, ed., *Proceedings of the Second Annual Meeting, Industrial Relations Research Association,* 1949, pp. 150–159.

zations, decision making based on limited information and avoidance of decision when possible, increase with the firm's rate of expansion.

Repeatedly middle level executives must act on limited knowledge. Some pressures forbid delay: the placating of powerful associates or influential union officers; the creation of a suitable post for an able but impatient subordinate; the handling of covert internal practices long ignored but now suddenly big with threat to the firm. Here any action may seem like a gamble. These problems become more acute when carried to a superior who refuses to act, but directly or indirectly penalizes the subordinate officer for failure to act successfully on his own. As head of the department the latter turns to his subordinates for loyal support. At each level this is really a request (*a*) for closer ties to conceal current departmental actions and alternatives from outsiders; (*b*) for the keeping of secrets from emotionally marginal members who may be both ambitious and incompetent enough to exploit debatable points of policy; and (*c*) for obedience to understood orders. In effect it calls forth an action clique from the mixture of fit, half-fit and unfit subordinates.

Avoidance of decision may fall into several types, but two are noteworthy and stimulate clique action. In one of these, *sympathetic avoidance,* supervisory subordinates know that their chief is upset by decisions calling for ingenuity or marked departure from formal routine. Yet they see that official procedures are inadequate for meeting his demands. So to prevent the complications that might follow from forcing a decision on him, they develop clique action to protect him as well as to evade him. Their practices require that they keep key persons among interlocking departments informed of changes in unofficial methods, and that, at the proper time, they teach new members the distinctions between their practices and *official misleading instructions.*[5]

---

[5] Quite apart from decision making, this coaching in the finesse of workable illegalities may be given in any organization. For example, embarrassing disturbances often result when new conductors come on the job and disrupt established practices between older conductors and daily commuting passengers on the interurban railway systems in metropolitan areas. Usually the commuter from the suburb to downtown on such trains carries a fifty- or sixty-ride monthly commutation book of tickets. Because the tickets are sold at reduced rates, the company declares tickets void that are presented separately from the book. That is, officially the conductor is to take the book from the passenger, tear out the ticket, and return the book. However, because trains at rush hours are usually full to standing room only, passengers, with the blessing of the conductor, speed up collection by tearing out the ticket and having it ready for him. Ignorant of this arrangement, the new conductor follows official precept and rejects tickets removed from the book. Passengers and conductor are of course outraged with each other. Fellow conductors in adjacent cars allow this to continue for some time, apparently as part of a hazing ordeal required of the newcomer, and to insure that he is sound before they acquaint him with their "illegal" but effective technique.

In the other escape from decision, *avoidance by misdirection,* the department chief or similar high officer wishes to elude a subordinate, or colleague in another department, who seeks to force a decision on him. To escape, the chief calls his closest associates to aid him by telling pursuers and telephone callers that he is where he is not—in some part of the plant or in the community "looking after company business." The chief's motivation frequently is fear of making changes in response to pressures from one quarter that will only bring pressures from another. Hence he engages in clique action to avoid action. Sometimes, too, he works on the theory that his pursuers will "cool off" and find a solution "if they are given a little time and *have* to." . . .

P. F. Drucker[6] praises skill in avoiding action and holds that in some cases any action would be equivalent to a "surgical operation." Also instructive are the comments from a roundtable of executives.[7] One executive says:

> Life in a large corporation is pretty much like politics. A fellow gets along pretty much on what kind of an organization he has been able to gather around him. . . . As far as I am concerned the lone wolf with no friends will get nowhere, either in business or politics.

Types of Cliques

Though cliques arise from dynamic situations and engage in many actions, they can be classified roughly. Typing may be in terms of their recurrence, what they do, the situations they spring from, or their effects. Probably the simplest relevant scheme, however, is to label cliques chiefly on the basis of their relation to the formal chart and the services they give to members. Such a scheme is, of course, not exhaustive or exclusive.

Approached in this way, cliques fall into three general groups: *vertical, horizontal,* and *random.* Vertical cliques can be broken down to vertical *symbiotic*[8] and vertical *parasitic;* and horizontal to horizontal *aggressive* and horizontal *defensive* cliques. Vertical cliques

---

[6] Peter F. Drucker, *The Practice of Management,* Harper and Brothers, New York, 1954, p. 361.
[7] Eli Ginzberg, ed., *What Makes an Executive?* Columbia University Press, New York, 1955, p. 148.
[8] The term *symbiotic* is adapted from the biological term *symbiosis* (*syn,* together, and *bios,* life) which refers to a mutually beneficial *internal* partnership between two different kinds of organisms. This is related to the term *commensalism* (*con,* together, and *mensa,* table) which is reserved by some students for *external* associations between two quite different kinds of animals, who live together in effect as messmates or fellow boarders. Examples of commensalism are the tie between the Dor beetle and its blind mite partner, the hermit crab (some) and sea-

usually occur in a single department. The tie is between the top officer and some of his subordinates. It is vertical in the sense that it is an up-and-down alliance between formal unequals. It could be represented as a rectangle with the altitude greater than the base, e.g., □. Horizontal cliques, on the other hand, cut across more than one department and embrace formal equals for the most part. The horizontal clique can be symbolized as a rectangle with a base greater than its altitude, e.g., ▭.

Vertical Symbiotic Clique

In this relation, the top officer is concerned to aid and protect his subordinates. He does this by concealing or minimizing their errors, occasional lapses, etc. He does what favors he can to meet their immediate needs and to solidify their future in the firm. He interprets their behavior favorably to critical members of the department and to his own superiors. He humanizes the painful impersonal situations and the demands he must make.

The subordinates fully advise him of real or rumored threats to his position. They tell him of current work situations, confer on ways of dealing with "troublemakers" outside the clique, and discuss interdepartmental maneuvers. When urgency demands action and the chief is unavailable or there is no time for consultation, lower members confer and make moves with the chief's welfare in mind, and in terms of his known attitudes. Thus for all levels involved, there is a satisfying exchange of services. This is the most common and enduring clique in large structures. It is more than "team work" because only a nucleus of departmental personnel is involved. As it sweeps other members along they may follow gratefully, indifferently, or with some hostility. It is most effective when lower members are relatively indifferent about promotion or reasonably patient in waiting.

Vertical symbiotic cliques formed the real power centers in Milo, and they occurred at the divisional as well as the departmental level. Though not quite ideal because of Taylor's resentment, the Blanke-Dicke-Peters clique was an example extending into the divisional level,

---

anemones, the Nile crocodile and one of the plovers, and the "tuatara" lizard and the petrel. Symbiotic relations include those between heather and its fungus partner, and termites and their flagellates. Our aim is not to force rigid parallels or to precisely follow biological usage. See R. W. Hegner, *College Zoology*, The Macmillan Company, New York, 1942, 5th edition, pp. 155, 702–703, and use of the term by sociologists: R. E. Park, "Symbiosis and Socialization: A Frame of Reference for the Study of Society," *American Journal of Sociology*, 45: 1–25, July, 1939; E. Gross, "Symbiosis and Consensus as Integrative Factors in Small Groups," *American Sociological Review*, 21: 174–179, April, 1956.

and the Hardy-Springer-Ames clique was another. However, several things make the clique less important at divisional levels. Personal ambitions and opportunities to move to other plants, for example, make the clique less stable there than at departmental levels. More subject to direct claims from the top, too, division heads usually want no official knowledge or part in taboo activities below them that they are sure department heads can contain. The latter understand that they are to serve as screening stations for conversion of unavoidable irregularities into reports befitting divisional dignity. Despite the weakness of a symbiotic vertical tie extending into the divisional level, these heads are caught in unofficial actions. . . .

Vertical Parasitic Clique

This is *the clique* of popular thought, the one that writers of supervisory manuals have in mind when they make such statements as, "No person may work under the direct or indirect supervision of an officer to whom he is related by blood or marriage."

This is a negative approach which assumes that collusive behavior is inevitable among persons with kinship ties who are in certain job relations. Apparently the implied dangers are thought to be confined to such persons and situations. This is not the case, and the approach explains nothing about how the clique works, or of its relation to other unmentioned cliques that may preserve it in some form. If this kind of clique is regarded as organizationally harmful, it deserves more study.

The term "parasitic" is used because the exchange of services between lower and higher clique members is unequal. The lower ranked person or persons receive more than they give and may greatly damage the higher officer. This clique need not be a family affair. It may be based on a friendship developed earlier in the plant or elsewhere, when the current higher and lower ranking officers were on the same job level. The subordinate person owes his position to one of his superiors. He reports to this person what he regards as pertinent facts in his work area. His information may be of use to the superior, but often its importance is exaggerated. It is useful where it is accurate and the higher officer has real need of it—but in such cases the clique relation moves toward the symbiotic type. The problem arises when the lower member is thought to "carry tales" to the higher, whether he does or not. In this event his rejection by the group leads him to resentful distortion and overstatement.

Since management theoretically places members on merit only, the belief that special aid is given the lower member of the clique obviously inspires fear in associates that he has advantages they lack and will win still more by informing on them Where this feeling is widespread, the group resists the chief and misinterprets his best efforts. He may exchange aid with the lower member, but group alertness to hide things from the lower member cuts the volume of favors he can send up as compared with that coming down to him. Much of the harm of this clique to the firm stems from its interference with operation of the symbiotic type. Given the values of personnel, the fringe identification of some members, and the incentives applied by higher management, *a symbiotic clique is essential for a given department to compete on a par with other departments* for favors from higherups and to set up workable arrangements with other departments.

The uneven exchange holds when the clique includes members of the work groups. In at least two cases in Milo, workmen informed to general foremen with whom they had been intimate before the foremen entered management. The foremen granted favors that eluded vigilance of the union and were repaid with information and cooperation on rush jobs. But the exchange showed a more tangible balance in favor of the workmen.

Formal regulations against the action we ascribe to this clique are evaded in various ways to allow the solicting member to receive special aid and favors. An arrangement used at Milo, similar to what is described below as an aggressive horizontal clique, worked in effect to establish the parasitic clique in at least six situations. That is, two or more higher officers on comparable levels agreed to aid each other's relatives or friends on an exchange basis. One officer made a place in his department for the solicitee of the other, or promoted the person ahead of others, or gave him more desirable work or more freedom from regulations in exchange for like aid for *his* protégé from a colleague. This cooperation, of course, promotes other understandings and joint action across departments.

Horizontal Cliques

Horizontal Defensive Clique

Cutting across departments and including officers, as we noted, of nearly the same rank, this clique is usually brought on by what its members regard as crises. Threatened reorganization, introduction of disliked methods or a control such as that of the FWD or the Office, efforts by lower and middle management to shift responsibility to each other for problems that have developed, or opposition among the same groups as reassignment of duties is made after a reorganization, are all conditions that bring on crises. This clique may also arise across departments when day and night supervision hold each other responsible as the source of illegal strikes, serious accidents, rejection of the product by a customer, etc.

Usually this clique is strong for only the limited time necessary to defeat or adjust to a threat. Since nothing is served by its persisting longer, it lapses to dormancy until another crisis, but when active it forces the symbiotic cliques into quiescence. However, it is inherently weak because of the vertical breaks likely to occur from action by resurgent symbiotic cliques. That is, as a horizontal structure the clique is made up of departmental segments, each restrained temporarily by the chief's preoccupation with interdepartmental action.

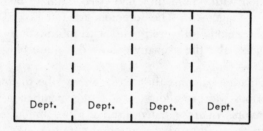

Figure 7 Horizontal clique.

Horizontal Aggressive Clique

This type is distinguished from the defensive clique chiefly by its goals and the direction of its action. Its members are the same, and they are likely to have some ties based on past cooperative victories in getting favors and outwitting others. Their action is a cross-departmental drive to effect changes rather than resist them, to redefine responsibility, or even directly shift it. As with defensive action, interdepartmental friction subsides as the clique becomes a mutual aid bloc. Its goals may be to get increased operating allowances; to bring on advantageous reorganization or to win favored consideration over other units of the corporation; to obtain an advantage in forthcoming union-management negotiations; to check the expansion of some staff group; or to advance some member to a higher post so he can help the clique. And of course any executive level, top management, division chiefs, department heads, spontaneously forms this clique when it sets out to correct extreme action by other cliques at lower levels.

When advancement of some member is successful his placement graphically distorts the clique toward the vertical form, but this does not of course necessarily destroy old horizontal ties. For in his new post, the promoted officer frequently finds that his present assistants do not measure up to his earlier ones.[9] He may then contrive to bring one of his former associates closer to him formally. Obviously the continuation of old ties and understandings hinders adjustment to a new circle. Where the promoted officer does work to draw advantages from earlier associations, he and its members behave remarkably like campaigning politicians. They introduce praise and blame into the stream of plant gossip where it will bring highest returns. If conditions allow, the upgraded officer criticizes the state of the product as it enters his department. He attributes defects to laxity under the responsibility of the person to be discredited. He cooperates with his favorite chiefs to decrease their costs at the expense of others. He talks and exchanges favors with intimates among the superiors of those he wishes to aid, as in the cases above where rules against nepotism were reinterpreted. To aid his own candidates he may omit the subtleties of faint praise and positively damn the chances of others by attacks on their personal untidiness, excessive drinking, extramarital activities; or their disgraceful family squabbles, unmanageable children, impossible personality, and the like. Or, if the condition is known to exist, he may stress the person's stomach ulcers as proof of his shortcomings.

Blanke, Geiger, Meier, and Boesel were an aggressive horizontal clique. At one time they were all in the same division. As we noted, Blanke was then departmental chief with Geiger as his assistant. Meier and Boesel were assistant heads in other departments. When Blanke moved to head another division, Geiger succeeded him. Then with two other officers eligible in service and experience, Boesel became the next department head. Conversations with Geiger and others indicated that Blanke and Geiger greatly aided Boesel and that the three of them

---

[9] Frequently there is reluctance to break old emotional ties and to face the problems of developing new ones. His feeling is understandable if there are strong differences in attitude between his earlier and present associates on the issue of literal or loose interepretation of official doctrine. He may also be committed to aid one or more of his earlier associates. This last is related to a kind of spoils system and has been observed by numerous executives. See H. Frederick Willkie, *A Rebel Yells*, D. Van Nostrand Company, New York, 1946, pp. 186–88, and Eli Ginzberg, ed., *What Makes an Executive?* Columbia University Press, New York, 1955, p. 156, where it is noted that changes in top leadership often mean that the "new man promoted his own associates" to the detriment of other well-qualified individuals. Sometimes correction of this evil creates others.

worked for Meier who came last to full superintendency. As superintendents, Meier, Boesel, and Geiger then cooperated closely to win favors from Revere. Through strong support from Boesel and Meier, Geiger had as much influence in the division as Revere. Although Blanke was in a different division and all faced new distractions, the old ties were revived on occasion to surmount official barriers.

The Random Clique

This clique is called *random* because its members usually cannot be classified in terms of formal rank, duties, or departmental origin, though they associate intimately enough to exchange confidences. Typically they have no consciously shared formal goal in the plant or point of company policy they are working to change, but the attraction is clearly friendship and social satisfaction. This can of course also exist in the other cliques, but friendship is not their end and may be hardly present. As compared with the more functional cliques this one is random in the sense that its members may come from any part of the personnel, managers and managed, and that they do not anticipate important consequences of their association.

As a rule, members of the random clique are not solidly in any of the more functional cliques. And usually they have never been in them, or if so, they are rejectees for indiscreet talk and failure in action. They are most often apathetic persons who are not sure why they are in the department. But being there they are given things to do, including the less desirable tasks, and they mechanically follow the routines. Consequently they resent, and do not fit into, the changing informal arrangements around them. They would like to escape the confusion to find simpler and more permanent recreational relations. As a result they get away from their jobs when possible to indulge in unguarded talk about people and events.

Their friends are like themselves. From the cafeteria to the showers they meet and gossip about their home departments and their dissatisfactions. Though only on the rim of events they do interact superficially with members of the other cliques. As would be expected, they learn few if any important secrets because of the barriers between themselves and these pivotal groups. And they may miss the meaning for larger issues of what they do learn. Nevertheless this relatively aimless association is important in plant affairs. As small unattached gossip groups moving freely around the firm, these cliques are both a point of leaks from the functional groups as well as a source of information for them. As such, the random clique intensifies informal activities in the plant.[10] The incomplete bits of information members exchange may mean little out of their larger context to an apathetic person, but much to an alert member of some functional clique. Discrete items supplied by a random clique on, for example, cost manipulation, or "gentlemen's agreements" at some level of union-management trading, may fit so well into the puzzle of an interested action clique that its members will clinch or change their pending action.

Instances from Milo show the circuitous routes of information leaks and the effects on others. The assistant chief chemist, Miller, received a confidential monthly salary "adjustment" of a hundred and twenty-five dollars. He wished to hide this from his subordinates, who were also pressing for salary increases to maintain the gap between themselves and the surging unionized stillmen and samplers. However, Miller did tell his wife, who belonged to a woman's club in the community. She told members of the club, one of whom was the wife of Sand, a line foreman from a third department. Sand was intimate in the plant with Wheeler, one of the samplers. Wheeler played golf with Sand and spent considerable time in Sand's office. Sand eventually passed the secret from his wife to Wheeler. Apparently seeing it as a joke on the chemists, Wheeler told them. Angered at Miller's "unfairness," some of the chemists wanted to face him with their knowledge and use it as a lever. Others overruled this, but "to get even" all cooperated with the samplers to conceal line errors and deviations from Miller, and to reduce the number of their own analyses.

In another case, superintendent Smith learned from his neighbor, Haller, a Milo employee whose loquacity was guarded against in his own department and encouraged elsewhere, that Boesel had arranged with his grievance committeeman to promote a workman contrary to the seniority record. Smith sought a similar deal with his own grievance man but was refused.[11] Smith's anger struck fear in Boesel and his union ally that Hardy and the president of the union local might be called in. They returned the promoted workman to his old position temporarily, though later both Boesel and Revere made deals with the union adverse to seniority principle. This incident made enemies of Smith and Boesel, and Boesel never learned the source of the leak.

---

[10] The random clique is not, of course, the only source of leaks. Under stress, members of the functional cliques may tell things they would not normally, and for calculated purposes they may deliberately pass a secret to a known "two-way funnel." . . .

[11] It is common (. . .) for grievance officers and managers to pair off in cliques and to oppose like cliques as all pursue peaceful informal adjustments with small concern for their official roles under the contract.

Control of Cliques

Given the nature of personnel, and the official frameworks they create, even the cliques essential for intertwining official and informal actions occasionally get out of hand and must be curbed. These are the vertical symbiotic and the two horizontal forms. They normally function (*a*) to build working harmony from the differing skills and abilities, private feuds, and shifting identifications of employees in endless turnover; and (*b*) to adapt the personnel and changing technology to each other. But when this function fails, or other factors give one department a force in events unwarranted by its contributions, eventual action by a high level horizontal aggressive clique corrects the distortion.

Clique correctives are perforce applied expediently. Conflicting reports on the clique, questions of who the members are and their degree of involvement, and the indispensability of constructive clique skills, work to order the steps taken and to grade the rigor of correctives.

Restrictive action is typically initiated by (1) guarded attacks on the effects of the clique's expanding influence, and followed by a hint, from the presiding officer at a formal meeting, that not all sins are pardonable. If this is ineffective, and conditions permit it, (2) efforts are made to hold the structure as it is and to contain the clique. Greatly influenced by impersonal factors as well as the rank, quality, and extra-clique ties of members, this is a first step in some firms, a last resort in others. Failure to contain the clique may lead to (3) transfer or promotion of the clique leader, and, as in the case of Nevers in Chapter 7, he may receive surprising aid from the firm when he moves to another unit or another company. (4) If pretext and expediency interlock well, clique members may be dispersed about the firm. (5) Sometimes an offensive clique is nullified by neatly justified withdrawal and rotation of members about the firm. In other cases, (6) conditions and matching ingenuities may dictate direct or indirect change of structure or method in adjacent work areas to disrupt clique routines and thus weaken it. Instead of changes, circumstances may call for (7) informal punishments adapted to known sensibilities of key members. (8) Where the corrective clique agrees that certain members of the disruptive clique are expendable, demotions are made, with and without pretext, and members may abide by the change or quit the firm.

Since human ingenuity seems inexhaustible, and managerial structures and industrial technologies are so varied, these corrective steps obviously represent only some of the actions that are taken. Some of these points require further comment.

For example take the first point—complaints against an injurious clique in the hierarchy. Direct communication to top officers is taboo, as everybody knows, because intermediate levels may be involved. Formal "open door" policy may welcome detoured grievances, but subordinates fear leaks of their message and hidden reprisal from those they by-pass. The theory that each supervisor must know all that goes up through his level is sound but incomplete: it has not been news for at least two thousand years that the intermediate levels of various hierarchies wish to interpret and color reports on the way up to protect themselves and to please higherups.[12] Hence initial opposition to a hurtful clique usually resorts to anonymous communication by a letter typed on an outside machine and handled entirely by a non-employee. If the letter shows enough knowledge of irregular behavior, action of some kind is sure to be taken. Even though the behavior reported has been ordered or tacitly acquiesced to by the addressee, some changes must be made to preserve organizational decorum.

Containment is sometimes accomplished by setting up problem committees that include one or more clique members,[13] who share assignments, meet deadlines, prepare progress reports, and otherwise work with the group, which weakens the clique and promotes organizational consciousness.

Transfer or promotion of the clique's key member is sometimes possible and effective. New abilities are suddenly discovered in him that fit him for another post, usually staff, where it is hoped that neither the function nor new associates will channel his genuine abilities into aberrant action. The post may entail standard duties or be only a sinecure. As we saw with Blanke, who was not promoted to break up a clique, this may not entirely check old horizontal aggressive clique actions, but the new preoccupations are a powerful restraint. Sometimes intercompany relations allow cooperative transfers of gifted incorrigibles, as was done between Milo and Fruhling.

Where all members of a deviant clique are considered indispensable and above the humiliation of what cannot be concealed as obvious disciplinary action, all may be dispersed to different parts of the firm, or incorporated into some kind of rotating system to limit expression of

---

[12] See the actions of Sejanus in Tácitus, *Historical Works*, E. P. Dutton & Co. (Everyman's Library), New York, no date, especially Vol. 1, book iv, sections 1, 2, 3, 8, 39–59, book v, sections 6–9; and Frederick the Great's countermeasures in W. S. Dorn, "Prussian Bureaucracy in the 18th Century," *Political Science Quarterly*, 46: 403–423 (1931), 47: 75–94, 259–273 (1932); B. B. Gardner and D. G. Moore, *Human Relations in Industry*, R. D. Irwin, Homewood, Ill., 1955, 3rd edition, pp. 95–101.
[13] C. L. Shartle, *Executive Performance and Leadership*, Prentice-Hall, Englewood Cliffs, N. J., 1956, p. 60.

excessive clique skills or to use them where they are needed. The potential tumult of dispersal may be more disruptive than the clique. But decisions usually favor the risk, for one finds the expanding firm expediently creating new posts for this purpose, and the more static company maintaining a reserve of active and dormant sinecures as a safety valve for this and other pressures.

Rotation as a remedy also has its pros and cons. It does hasten the breakup of undesirable cliques, hinders the formation of others and offers new promise to frustrated officers. But used injudiciously, it disturbs essential personal ties. The common pretext for its employment, "Everybody is more valuable to the organization because they know more about plant operations," is often suspected as a "trick" or resisted as "pushing people around," as any change is likely to be seen. In theory the rotated persons "get a fresh outlook." By the time they return, if they do, both they and the earlier situations have changed. Rotation is of course not always a mask, but is also used for broadening individual perspectives.

When personnel shuffles are inadequate or impossible, changes are made in methods and duties to balance pressures, reduce inequities, or to bring less troublesome realignments. Sometimes the problem area is seemingly ignored while the personnel and methods in an interlocking department are reorganized as needed to break routines of the troublesome clique and refocus its interests.

Where clique members are not regarded as indispensable, but their rank is such that a blunt release would raise questions about the original appointing officer's judgment, some one of the group may be singled out as a link to be broken, and as an example. Such a person habitually will not receive the information or aid he requires to function, or new "temporary" and logically sound but impossible assignments will be given to him. With calculated aid from others he will involve himself in trouble, grow weary of the job, become suspicious of clique members, and ask for a transfer or quit.

As implied earlier, almost never would an able executive be discharged for clique activity. Higher managers value these skills as necessary for cutting a way through or around chaotic situations. Public relations and the equalitarian ideology may require denial, but top managers are more disposed to pardon than punish occasional excesses of the social skill required for organizational coherence and action.

Progress and Problems in Systems Analysis*

Edward S. Quade

It is not easy to tell someone how to carry out a systems analysis. We lack an adequate theory to guide us. This must be expected, for systems analysis, even more than operations research, is a new discipline. History teaches us that good theory usually comes late in the development of any field and after many false starts.

The attention of the practitioners, when it has turned to methods, has been focused mainly on the development of mathematical techniques for handling certain specialized problems, common in operations research, rather than on an attempt to build a basic theory for the treatment of broad context questions such as occur in defense planning. This attention to technique has met with great success. Models have become easier to manipulate, even with many more variables represented, and the computational obstacles in operations research now cause comparatively little difficulty. The more philosophical problems, however, such as occur in providing assurance that the model is meaningful, in devising schemes to compensate for uncertainty, or in choosing appropriate criteria, are most troublesome. Therefore, the many important and useful mathematical techniques of operations research are treated very cursorily in this book, although Chapter 13 tries to give some indication of their nature and limitations. Concepts and understanding—areas where the analyst as well as the user is more likely to err—are emphasized instead.

When the possibility of preparing a lecture on the procedures of analysis was first considered, the proper approach seemed obvious: Examine all available studies carried out to help military decision-making and extract the principles and methods common to the successful studies. In other words, isolate the ideas that make an analysis a good one. This effort did not turn out to be very productive. Either the sample was too small or we were not sufficiently perceptive, or (what now seems more likely) no universally accepted set of ideas existed. It was even difficult to decide which studies should be called good or successful.

One hope for guidance is to turn to science. In fact, it is frequently argued that operations research should be considered a science. But the goals are different. Science is concerned primarily with the pursuit of truth and a better understanding of the world we live in. Operations

* Reprinted with permission of author and publisher from *Analysis for Military Decisions* (Chicago: Rand McNally & Co., 1964), pp. 149–176.

research, almost without exception, is concerned with policy, that is, with more effective manipulation of the real world—even if this may have to be accomplished without full understanding of the underlying phenomena. Its purpose is seldom merely to understand or to predict.

There is little difference in method:

> ... Both the exact scientist and the operations analyst tend to make use of what is sometimes called a mathematical model of the subject matter; in the case of the scientist such a model is apt to be part of the well-confirmed body of our scientific knowledge, whereas an operations research model is of a more tentative, *ad hoc*, character. In other words, even if the current status of science provides no well-established theory for the phenomena to be dealt with by the operations analyst, the latter must nevertheless construct a model as best he can, where both the structure of the model and its numerical inputs may be based merely on intuitive insight and limited practical experience by the analyst himself or by whatever expert advisers on the subject matter may be available to him. As further insights accrue and more experimental data become available, the operations analyst has to be ready to discard his first model and replace it with an improved one. This tentative procedure, dictated by pragmatic considerations, is thus essentially one of successive approximation. In this regard, operations research has a status similar to that of the so-called inexact sciences, of which medicine, engineering, and most of the social sciences are examples.
>
> Therefore, in comparing operations research with an exact science, it is with regard to exactness that operations research falls short, but not necessarily with regard to the scientific character of its methods. ... [1]

Operations research attempts to use the methods of science. This means in essence that it strives for the same traditions. Scientific tradition holds that (1) results are obtained by processes that another scientist can duplicate to attain the same results; (2) all calculations, assumptions, data, and judgments are made explicit and thus subject to checking, criticism, and disagreement; (3) the scientific method is objective; its propositions do not depend on personalities, reputations, or vested interests; where possible it is quantitative and experimental. For operations research and systems analysis, however, these are still unachieved goals.

---

[1] Olaf Helmer, *The Systematic Use of Expert Judgment in Operations Research,* The RAND Corporation, P-2795, September 1963.

Engineering and Systems Analysis

Operations research and, to an even greater degree, systems analysis seem to be more nearly engineering than science. For the purpose of making a distinction here, one might say that science finds things out, while engineering uses the results of science to do things cheaply and well.

While there are similarities between the typical engineering problem and the typical military systems analysis or operations research problem, there are important distinctions. Most of these are of a quantitative rather than of a qualitative nature. In military systems analyses

1. There are relatively many more factors that can only be estimated rather than measured or experimented with. Consider as an example the design of a "flyaway" kit, that is, a package of spare parts, tools, and equipment to be airlifted into the field to support a tactical bomber. Among a host of factors, the design depends upon the character of the war in which the bomber is to be used. But the pattern of future wars in which a tactical bomber might be used is a real uncertainty—not something that can be experimented with.

2. Even when measurements can be made, the results of field tests or of experiments made on the proving ground are likely to differ radically from results obtained under combat conditions.

Again refer to the flyaway kit problem; the peacetime demand for spare parts does not necessarily reflect the wartime demand the kit should be designed to meet.

3. The time period after which the answers become worthless is almost always extremely brief.

In these days weapons become obsolete rapidly. If we spend enough time in testing even to establish the peacetime demand for spares for our flyaway kit, we may have our answer too late to be of any help.

The time limit is important to the engineer also, but ordinarily not to the same extent. To the academic scientist, time may not be of particular consequence. He is after a high degree of confidence in his results, and whatever time it takes to get the degree of confidence he is after, he can usually take. The military analyst, on the other hand, must frequently reach his best possible conclusion in a limited time.

4. There is frequently no way to verify the conclusions of the study.

If we are lucky, before there is a war our flyaway kit will be replaced by another to complement a more modern aircraft, and we will never find out whether the original kit would have been satisfactory.

5. The value concepts are much more troublesome. Like engineering, the military analyses seek to help someone take action; unlike

most engineering, however, the determination of objectives, costs, and criteria represents a difficult problem.

6. In military analysis, as opposed to its civilian counterparts, the interaction of the enemy's alternatives, objectives, and costs with our own is usually the major problem, and the interaction between our own alternatives, objectives, and costs is relatively minor. While the need to treat *conflict* aspects of the problem does not necessarily make the analysis more difficult, it does introduce an additional set of uncertainties and complexities.

There are also some more subtle differences.

> For one thing, systems analysis is engineering at a high level in the sense suggested by the following example. A glass engineer successfully plans the production of certain kinds of optical glass on the basis of chemical knowledge; a lens-designing engineer designs camera lenses on the basis of a knowledge of optics, the techniques of lens manufacture, and the general capabilities of the glass engineer; a camera engineer designs a camera on the basis of his knowledge of many things, including what the lens designer can do; the aeronautical engineer designs a reconnaissance plane, using, among other things, his knowledge of what he can expect from the camera designer; the systems analyst designs a reconnaissance system knowing what he can expect from the plane designer. Of course, there is communication up and down the list.

> Military systems analysis may differ from ordinary engineering in its enormous responsibility, in its relatively poor data, and in the unusual difficulty of appraising the value system applicable to its problems, but these differences are not violent; they are quantitative, not qualitative. All the difficulties referred to occur in some measure in the humblest engineering problem such as designing a simple dog kennel.[2]

Perhaps no set of lectures has ever been directed toward those who employ civil, mechanical, or chemical engineers, and while it would not be impossible to imagine such a course being useful, it is significant that it is nonexistent or rare.

> If a city hires an engineer to design a bridge, it may perhaps have his work checked by another engineer, but the city fathers will not presume to study his report with a view to seeing for themselves whether the proposed bridge is likely to collapse. They believe, with more or less reason, that the field of civil engineering is sufficiently well devel-

---

[2] Unpublished communication from L. J. Savage commenting on an earlier version of this chapter.

oped and a licensed engineer so likely to be firm in his science that his judgment in this matter is overwhelmingly better than their own. Similarly, they will trust the authority of their engineer that the clearance, carrying capacity, safety, and durability of the proposed bridge cannot all be increased without an increase in cost. The trade-offs among these values might in principle concern the city fathers, and in special cases they will. But, by and large, there will be none among them capable of or feeling the responsibility for going deeply into these matters. Where, however, a defense system for the nation is concerned, tradition cannot be relied upon; for there is too little of it. The trade-offs between the various values involved are properly felt to be high concerns of the nation and the immediate responsibility of high government officers. Of course, even in the case of the bridge, there are some trade-off considerations that the city fathers cannot dodge. They must make some decisions that depend on their estimates of the political temper of the city and of its probable future growth—decisions for which the civil engineer has no particular competence.[3]

The Philosophical Aspects of Analysis

Systems analysis, particularly of the type required for military decisions, is still largely a form of art. An art can be taught in part, but not by means of fixed rules which need only be followed with exactness. Thus, in these analyses, we have to do some things that we think are right but that are not verifiable, that we cannot really justify, and that are never checked in the output of the work. Also we must accept as inputs many relatively intangible factors derived from human judgment, and we must present answers to be used as a basis for other judgments. Whenever possible, this judgment is supplemented by inductive and numerical reasoning, but it is only judgment nonetheless.

In fact, to a large extent, systems analysis and operations research are successful aids to policy determination in areas such as national security, where there is no accepted theoretical foundation, precisely because they are designed to make systematic and efficient rather than haphazard and unguided use of judgment by specialists or experts in the fields of interest. The essence of their method is to construct a "model" appropriate to the problem; such a model—which may be a game, a computer program, or a politico-military scenario—introduces a precise structure and terminology that serves primarily as an effective means of communication, and, through feedback—the counter-

---

[3] *Ibid.*

moves in a war game, for instance—helps the experts to arrive at a clearer understanding of the subject matter and the problem.

There is a distinction here between operations research and what we term systems analysis. To be more explicit, consider what might be called a "typical" operations research problem by many of its practitioners. Although there may be several resource variables which are subject to choice, the problem usually can (by making enough assumptions) be put in a form where there is only one dependent variable—termed the criterion or measure of merit (frequently cost); this is to be optimized subject to some set of constraints. The relationship between this dependent variable and the resource variables is formulated mathematically. This allows trade-offs between resources to be investigated. On the other hand, the "typical" systems analysis problem is often first: What is the problem? It is frequently difficult to formulate a criterion because the objectives may be multiple and conflicting. Trade-off may have to be investigated between objectives as well as between resources. Moreover, it may be impossible to describe the relationship between objectives and resources in terms of known mathematical functions or even to describe it numerically or graphically. Without a means for expressing the relationships between these classes of variables, the only recourse for investigation of trade-offs lies in the judgments and intuitions of experts. Such judgments in systems analysis are, of course, in addition to those which are inherent in even the simplest operations research problem—for example, judgments about the scope of the problem.

To emphasize further this distinction between operations research and systems analysis, we quote (in essence) from one military report.

> The participants were asked to project their experience and thinking into an uncharted future where formal doctrine offered little or no guidance and where concepts of future war would not necessarily be limited by practical considerations of current organization, weapons, and budgets. *The work of the group, therefore, was not operations research.* Concepts and hypotheses were presented and discussed that could not be supported immediately by facts and figures or be analyzed in terms of experience or experimental data, simply because the necessary data did not exist.[4]

Again, from another source.

> The formulation of objectives and the action on the recommendations are not properly included in the activity of the operations analyst, being literally boundary conditions imposed on the freedom of his operation.[5]

---

[4] Italics supplied.
[5] Thomas L. Saaty, *Mathematical Methods of Operations Research*, McGraw-Hill Book Company, Inc., New York, 1959, p. 4.

While such activities may not be operations research, they are part and parcel of the activities which go on under the name of systems analysis.

This suggests that analysis in support of defense decisionmakers at the national policy level is different from operations research as traditionally viewed. As one participant puts it:

> ... The traditional formulation of operations research problems in terms of ends and means—how can I maximize the' achievement of an objective or a set of objectives for a given cost, or alternatively, how can I minimize the cost of achieving a certain set of objectives?—is proper, but limited. At the national policy level, the major part of systems analysis is the exploration of the interaction of ends and means. By that interaction is meant that what are objectives from one point of view are means from another; that what is worth trying to do depends on what is possible to do, or on how effective the means for doing it are; and that any given objective is likely to be one of a number of alternative ways of achieving a still broader objective.[6]

Decisions pertaining to choices of alternative weapon systems or force structures and the strategies for their employment, made five to ten years in advance, are essentially matters of economic choice. Certain elements are common to such problems, although these elements may not always be explicitly identified by the analyst. . . .

1. *The objective* (or objectives). Systems analysis is undertaken primarily to suggest or, at the very least, to help choose a course of action. This action must have an aim or objective. Policies or strategies, forces or equipment are examined, compared, and preferred on the basis of how well and how cheaply they can accomplish the aim or objective.

2. *The alternatives.* The alternatives are the means by which it is hoped the objectives can be attained. They need not be obvious substitutes or perform the same specific function.

3. *The costs.* Each alternative means of accomplishing the objectives implies the use of specific resources which cannot then be used for other purposes.

4. *A model* (or models). The model is a representation of the situation under study designed to predict the cost and performance of each alternative. It abstracts the relevant features of the situation by means which may vary from a set of mathematical equations or a computer program to an idealized description of the situation in

---

[6] Alain C. Enthoven, "Operations Research and the Design of the Defense Program," *Proceedings of the Third International Conference on Operational Research,* Dunod, Paris, 1964, pp. 531–538.

which judgment alone is used to assess the consequences of various choices.

5. *A criterion.* A criterion is a rule or test by which one alternative can be chosen in preference to another. It provides a means for using cost and effectiveness to order the alternatives.

It is easy to find statements in the literature of operations research which imply that analysis to aid any decisionmaker is really nothing more than the "scientific method" extended to problems outside the realm of pure science. Even though it is by no means clear that there is any unique method which might be termed the "scientific method," what is usually meant is that the analysis advances through something like the following stages:

Formulation — Defining the issues of concern, clarifying the objectives, and limiting the problem.

Search — Determining the relevant data, looking for alternative programs of action to resolve the issues.

Explanation — Building a model and using it to explore the consequences of the alternative programs, ordinarily by obtaining estimates of their cost and performance.

Interpretation — Deriving the conclusions and indicating a preferred alternative or course of action. This may be a combination of features from previously considered alternatives or their modification to reflect factors not taken into account earlier.

Verification — Testing the conclusion by experiment.

A systems analysis always involves the first four of these stages but frequently must omit the last. For military problems, experiment, other than a pseudo experiment by simulation, may simply not be available. . . .

Formulation

Formulation implies an attempt to isolate the questions or issues involved, to fix the context within which these issues are to be resolved, to define the meaning of the variables or factors that are operative, and to state relationships among these factors. The relationships may be extremely hypothetical because empirical knowledge may be in short supply, but they will help make the logical structure of the analysis clear. In a sense, this is the most important stage, for the time spent restating the problem in different ways, redefining it, or expressing its limits brings to light whether it is spurious or trivial and points the way to its solution. The tendency all too frequently is to accept the original statement of what is wanted exactly as proposed, and then to set about building a model and gathering information, scarcely giving a thought to how the answer will contribute to the decisions which it is trying to assist. In fact, because the concern is with the future, the major job may be to decide what the policymaker should want to do. Since systems studies have resulted in some rather important changes, not only in how the policymaker carries out his activity but in the objectives themselves, it would be self-defeating to accept without inquiry the customers' or sponsors' view of what the problem is.

An analogy with medical practice may be drawn. No doctor ignores a patient's description of his symptoms, but he cannot allow the patient's self-diagnosis to override his own professional judgment. The medical analogy is not entirely applicable, however; the businessman or military commander ordinarily knows more than anyone else about his actual operations and what, if anything, might be wrong with them.

How then is the analyst to know his formulation of the problem is superior? *His only possible advantage lies in analysis.* That is, the process of problem formulation itself has to be the subject of analysis. The system analyst always has some idea as to the possible solutions of the problem; otherwise, he probably should not be working on it, for his analysis will prove to be too formal and abstract. At this early stage the analyst essentially makes an attempt to solve the problem before the facts are known. It is this attempt which gives him a basis for better formulation.

Let us take an example of how an analyst might go about problem formulation. Take the choice of a criterion. It may be hopelessly impossible to think out a good one in advance. The practical way may be to take a rather crude value scale, see what solution its use leads to, and then, if the solution is not in accordance with common sense, revise it. For instance, consider the analyst who needed to lose weight and set out to use a linear programming model to evolve an optimal reducing diet. He decided that an ideal criterion would be to get the most volume within the constraints of the necessary nutrients and calories. Well, he put his model on the machine, ground away, and came up with watermelon. That showed him he had better consider dried weight to exclude water. When this was done he came up with bouillon cubes, which consist largely of salt. Since this would not be very palatable and might be injurious to health, he made still another choice, and continuing in this way, he finally evolved a satisfactory rule of choice.

The problem itself does not remain static. Interplay between a growing understanding of the problem and of possible developments will redefine the problem itself. Primarily, as the result of discussion, the original effort to state the problem should suggest one or more possible solutions or hypotheses. As the study progresses, these original ideas are enriched and elaborated upon. Each hypothesis serves as a guide to later results—it tells us what we are looking for while we are looking. The final statement of the conclusions and recommendations usually rests on a knowledge of facts about the problem which are not known to the analyst at the start. Frequently, a hypothesis must be discarded and an entirely new one considered. In the early stages it is not a mistake to hold an idea as to the solution; the pitfall is to refuse to abandon such an idea in the face of mounting evidence.

The process of analysis is thus an *iterative* one—a cycle of problem formulation, selection of objectives, design of alternative systems, data collection, model building, a weighing of costs against effectiveness, the questioning of assumptions and objectives, the opening of new alternatives, reformulation, etc. Figure 8.1 attempts to indicate the iterative character of systems analysis. The various stages are ordered only with respect to a single cycle; the approximate solution we obtain at the end of the first cycle helps us to better prepare a second formulation. Thus, in a sense, it is impossible to formulate a problem completely before it is solved, or, in other words, the final problem statement may have to be written simultaneously with the final answer.

In the problem of choosing objectives, the iterative character of systems analysis stands out. It is impossible to select satisfactory objectives without some idea of the cost and difficulty of attaining them. Such information can only come as part of the analysis itself.

It is a common error to believe that goals should, and can, be set independently of the plans to attain them. Yet there is overwhelming evidence that ultimate objectives are, more often than not, the result of opportunities that possible alternatives offer rather than a source of such alternatives. The point is that only part of the consequences of different goals can be anticipated without analysis.

Military analysis must frequently be undertaken with only partial information about the objectives, criteria, and preferences at higher levels. At the highest level, official statements of national objectives are likely to be either nonexistent or so vague that they are not very helpful. This is a situation that gives rise to "suboptimization"—that is, the selection of intermediate objectives and criteria for the problem that are consistent with and that approximate in some sense or other those at the higher level. Given limitations on time and manpower, a suboptimization may be the only feasible approach. For example, a

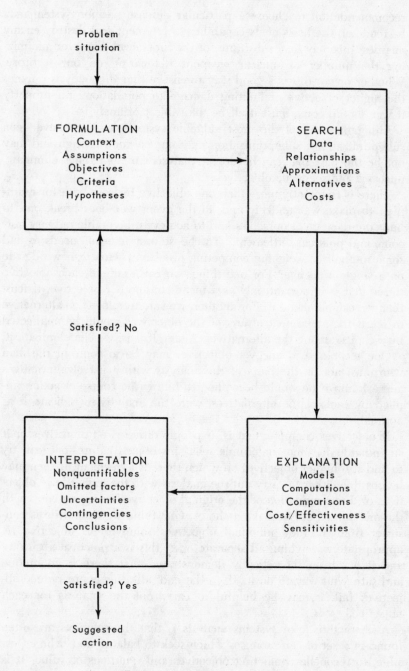

Fig. 8.1 Activities in analysis

recommendation to choose a particular defense weapon system may be made on the basis of its capability to intercept and destroy enemy missiles; this may be a substitute for the broader objective of minimizing the number of nuclear weapons detonating on our territory. Whether or not this is a good way to ensure that the analysis pursues the higher objective of limiting damage to population and property if war should come must itself be the subject of analysis.

Although many of the most valuable systems analyses have been suboptimizations, suboptimization may not be good enough and may not be the best that can be done. Analysis can sometimes eliminate, uncover, and reconcile objectives.

There is frequently more than one objective for a system; for example, "to make war unlikely and, in the event war does break out, to limit the damage to ourselves and to achieve a favorable military outcome and political settlement." To choose a system one needs to find some method of weighing competing objectives. How can we decide on a single objective? For one thing, we can examine each objective to see if it is important only as a means to another objective; if it is, then we can eliminate it. For another, we can examine each alternative to see if the attainment of any of the objectives would be unaffected by a choice among the alternatives. Again, if it is, we can eliminate it.

One technique to uncover objectives may be to confront the man who must act on the basis of the analysis with a list of alternatives and ask him if he would be willing to follow the course of action implied by each of the alternatives, were the analysis to indicate it as optimal.

If objectives compete, that is, if people disagree on objectives or if an individual cannot determine what his objectives are—one can try to find still higher objectives on which there is agreement. It then may be possible either to carry out the analysis with the higher level objectives or, by examination of the original objectives for consistency with the one agreed on, to make a choice. One thing we cannot do is construct from all the individual objectives some group objective by appropriately weighing all separate ones; this is a practical absurdity and it has been theoretically demonstrated that there is no unique and satisfying way to do it. If, in the end, all attempts to reduce objectives fail, it may be helpful to carry out the analysis for each objective.

A characteristic of systems analysis is that the solutions are often found in a set of compromises which seek to balance and, where possible, to reconcile conflicting objectives and questions of value. It is more important to choose the "right" objective than it is to make the "right" choice between alternatives. The wrong objective means that the wrong problem is being solved. The choice of the wrong alternative may merely mean that something less than the "best" system is being chosen. Frequently we must be satisfied with merely a demonstration that a suggested action is "in the right direction," anyway. This may be all that is possible.

To choose among alternatives, we must do more than determine which alternatives can attain a desired objective. Some criterion or test of preferredness must be employed; say, a rule to select for us the alternative (or alternatives) that yields the objectives for the least expenditure of costs or resources.[7]

Two rules for guidance in choosing a criterion, originally stated by C. J. Hitch,[8] are

1. A criterion used in a lower level problem should be consistent with that appropriate to the next higher level.
2. A criterion should not have to be repeatedly hedged by constraints to prevent it from giving absurd results.

As an example to illustrate the first rule, in determining a parking lot policy for an amusement park, the policy at the level of the people running the lot might be that of maximizing net revenues from parking. But this may well be different from the policy of the people running the park whose criterion might be to maximize the net revenues from the amusement park as a whole. In considering parking lot revenues, lack of parking for a few people, who then go elsewhere, might lead to considerable savings in land costs for parking and in salary for attendants, and thus in greater revenue for the lot, but the loss of good will might result in considerable loss of revenue for the park as a whole. A policy more consistent with the higher level, and thus a better policy for the lot, might simply be to provide parking for all who come—or even to provide this parking free of charge.

We cannot know a priori, however, that income from a parking lot should be small relative to income from the facility it serves. Whenever there is little opportunity of visiting the facility except by private car, the possibility of disguising a significant general admission charge as a parking charge may merit serious consideration.

As an example to illustrate the second rule, we can take any "ratio"

---

[7] See, in addition to Chapter 5, C. J. Hitch and R. N. McKean, *The Economics of Defense in the Nuclear Age,* Harvard University Press, Cambridge, Mass., 1960; and Hitch, "Economics and Military Operations Research," *Review of Economics and Statistics,* vol. XL, no. 3, August 1958, pp. 199–209.

[8] "Comments by C. J. Hitch," *Operations Research,* vol. 4, no. 4, August 1956, p. 427. His statement is paraphrased here.

criterion where a constraint must be imposed to keep the denominator away from zero.

Cost must be treated as a major element:

> Furthermore, there has long been a tendency in the Defense Department to state military requirements in absolute terms without reference to their costs. But the military effectiveness or military worth of any given weapon system cannot logically be considered in isolation. It must be considered in relation to its cost—and in a world in which resources are limited, to the alternative uses to which resources can be put. Military requirements are meaningful only in terms of benefits to be gained in relation to their cost. Thus, resource costs and military worth have to be scrutinized together.[9]

The costs to be considered in choosing among alternatives, moreover, should be the "new" costs, that is, the net additional resource drain or "incremental cost" that would be incurred because of the choice of a particular alternative. Because a certain system may inherit facilities, personnel, or equipment from previous systems, its incremental costs may be much lower than what it would cost if it were to exist "in isolation." Also, in a comparison of military capabilities, costs have sometimes been computed on the basis of what the various systems would cost independent of the existence of other systems or other capabilities. In this light consider, for example, a Navy supercarrier. In a paper comparison to estimate its value in a limited-war role, if no credit were assigned to its central war capabilities, then on a cost-effectiveness basis it would be handicapped unfairly in comparison with a weapon system that had only a single role.

Great attention must be paid to initial conditions; that is, to the assumptions that limit the problem and set the background against which the initial attempt at a solution is to be made. The situation is not like that of an empirical science, which starts with observed facts, but more like that of mathematics, where the results take any "validity" they might have in the real world from the initial assumptions. The difference is that for the systems analysis to give correct guidance, it is important that the assumptions be the "right" assumptions.

Even for small-scale problems, the number of factors under consideration at any one time must be reduced until what is left is manageable. In systems analysis, the complexity of the "full" problem fre-

---

[9] Charles J. Hitch, Assistant Secretary of Defense (Comptroller). Testimony in *Systems Development and Management (Part 2)*, Hearings before a Subcommittee of the Committee on Government Operations, House of Representatives, 87th Congress, 2nd Session, U.S. Government Printing Office, Washington, D.C., 1962, p. 515.

quently far outruns analytic competence. To consider in detail anything like the complete range of possible alternative solutions may be impossible. The vast majority will obviously be inferior, hence there is no harm in leaving them out. The danger is that some alternative better than that uncovered by the analysis will also have been left out. Constraints must be imposed on the number of alternatives to be examined, but by preliminary analysis, not by arbitrary decree. Such constraints must be regarded as flexible so that they may be weakened or removed if it appears in later cycles that their presence is a controlling factor.

Sometimes problems can be reduced by factoring out subproblems. This can be done when a group of variables having relatively little interdependence with the other variables can be treated separately.

Once the problem has been broken down into its components—which is what analyzing the problem means—some of the components can be further analyzed, using various techniques; but others may defy analytic techniques. In that case, because the problem has been broken into smaller pieces, the systems analyst may be able to find individuals who have direct, sound experience and on whose "considered" judgment he can rely.

Considered judgment differs from ordinary or intuitive judgment in that the logic behind the opinion is made explicit. Both are based on an individual's experience and background, but when the reasoning is explicit, an observer can form his own opinion from the information presented. Judgment permeates systems analysis—judgments as to which hypothesis is better than another, or which approach is more fruitful, or what facts are relevant. The ideal is to keep all judgments in plain view.

One methodological aspect of operations research, the reliance on expert judgment, has received little attention.[10] Only by replacing the surreptitious use of expertise by explicit and systematic application of it can objectivity be safeguarded.

Usually two or more experts are available. When they differ, there are several ways to try to bring them together. Using the consensus approach they can work individually and then seek methods for the best combined use of their findings; or they can work jointly in a

---

[10] Except by Olaf Helmer. For additional information, see Helmer, *The Systematic Use of Expert Judgment in Operations Research*, The RAND Corporation, P-2795, September 1963; Helmer and Nicholas Rescher, "On the Epistemology of the Inexact Sciences," *Management Science*, vol. 6 no. 1, October 1959, pp. 25–52; N. Dalkey and Helmer, "An Experimental Application of the Delphi Method to the Use of Experts," *Management Science*, vol. 9, no. 3, April 1963, pp. 458–467. (The discussion on the use of experts presented in this chapter is based on Helmer's paper.)

group exercise—ranging from simple round-table discussions to reacting through a sophisticated simulation model—to obtain expert judgments from the group as a whole. Operational gaming, or simulation involving role-playing by the participating experts, is particularly promising when it is desirable to employ several experts with varying specialties in a context in which their forecasts cannot be independent but are likely to interact. Here the game structure or model furnishes the experts with an artificial, simulated environment within which they can jointly and simultaneously experiment, acquiring through feedback the insights necessary to make successful predictions within the model environment and thus indirectly about the real world.

Another method, falling somewhere between individual and group action, is the so-called Delphi technique. It needs further development and testing but is regarded by this author as very promising. It tries to improve the basis consensus method by subjecting the experts' views to each other's criticism without actual confrontation and all its psychological shortcomings (such as specious persuasion, an unwillingness to abandon publicly expressed opinions, and the bandwagon effect of the majority). The Delphi technique replaces direct debate by a carefully designed program of sequential individual interrogations (best conducted by questionnaires) interspersed with information and opinion feedback derived by computed consensus from the earlier parts of the program. Some of the questions directed to the respondents may, for instance, inquire into the "reasons" for previously expressed opinions, and a collection of such reasons may then be presented to each respondent, together with an invitation to reconsider and possibly revise his earlier estimates.

Systems analysis, as the name suggests, must be systems oriented. It is important to recognize that anything going on in one part of an activity, organization, or weapon system will likely affect what goes on in every other part. The natural inclination might be to factor out parts of the problem and analyze each separately, neglecting their interactions. However, the aim of analysis is to extend the boundaries of the system as far as required, determine which interdependences are significant, and then evaluate their combined impact.

For this reason, and because the context is naturally broad anyway, systems analysis usually calls for an interdisciplinary team consisting of persons with a variety of skills. This is not required merely because many factors and aspects are involved. Even more important is that a problem looks different to an economist, to a mathematician, and to an engineer, and different ways of looking at a problem are important in finding a solution.

Uncertainty in long-range military planning problems being as great as it is, it is well—particularly early in the study—not to attach much significance to small differences in cost and effectiveness of alternative systems. Specifically, it is important to look for differences that have a chance of surviving *any* likely resolution of the uncertainties. Rather than ask precisely how much better one alternative is than the others, the question to address is which alternatives have a clear advantage or even, initially, which will move us forward.

Search

This phase is concerned with finding the facts, or evidence, on which the analysis is based. It is necessary to look for ideas (and evidence to support them), including the invention of new alternatives, as well as to look for facts. Unless we have alternatives and ideas about them, there is nothing to analyze or to choose between. If in the end we are to designate a preferred course of action, we must have discovered earlier that such a course exists. In long-range problems, the total number of alternatives may be endless, and we must use judgment to eliminate those that are unreasonable.

Many facts are hard to come by. The actual operational performance of future weapons in combat cannot be predicted with any degree of certainty. Purely theoretical studies or operations research of weapon characteristics must be depended upon. In systems analysis, as contrasted with most other forms of engineering, a great many more inputs depend on judgment than on measurement or engineering analysis.

For many problems it is the availability of the facts which makes a solution possible. Consider, for example, the flyaway kit problem we mentioned earlier. The computation per se of the optimum kit according to some standard of performance, measured in terms of the expected loss in combat effectiveness attributable to kit shortages during the support period, is a relatively trivial problem. Surprisingly enough, the difficulty comes in getting the input data. This may involve such a seemingly easy item as getting a complete list of spare parts, as well as such an acknowledgedly difficult one as getting the data that tell how frequently particular spares are needed.

Indeed, even if the analysis is never completed, the collection of facts and their orderly presentation in tables and graphs can sometimes make the solution obvious.

It is sometimes said that when all the facts are known, the problem is solved. This may be true in a philosophical sense, but in a practical sense the real work may have only begun.

In practical problems for systems analysis, however, all the facts are never known. For example, to recommend a preferred interceptor combat radius, it is necessary to study interceptor and performance characteristics, radar coverage requirements, effectiveness, and cost as functions of combat radius. This involves a study of the possible target systems the enemy might select and the pattern of enemy attacks. Such things as radar, costs, proper deployment, interceptor armament, attrition, and the effect of other weapons must then be considered.

When should an inquiry stop? It is important to remember that in this sort of a problem, inquiry is rarely exhaustive. Inquiries are partial, and the decisionmaker must get along without the full advantage of all the potentiality of operations research and the scientific approach. Inquiries cost money and time; they cost in whatever values are concerned. They can cost lives; they can cost national security. It might be interesting to know what the Russians could do if we dropped an armed Atlas on Moscow. It might be an easy observation to make, but some of the costs seem to prohibit this type of investigation. One should never fall into the error of feeling that inquiry is free of cost. There are many contexts in which we can ignore the cost of inquiry; but paradoxes arise if we allow ourselves to forget that almost all inquiries must stop far, far short of completion either for lack of funds, of time, or of justification for spending further funds or time on them. It is out of the question to collect all the information that is required for exhaustive analysis, and it is out of the question to process it.

As an analogy, consider the example of a physician who uses a clinical laboratory to help him decide whether or not his patient has one of several ailments that have many similiar symptoms. Even when all the reports are in, the doctor's inquiry may not be complete. He could probably do a lot more laboratory analysis or call in a specialist for consultation. If the problem is simply one of diagnosis, one of the best procedures might be to slaughter the patient and perform a thorough autopsy. The cost here is prohibitive, not only by the standards of modern society but simply by the fact that the physician's goal is to help the patient live a longer and fuller life. He would only frustrate himself if he bought knowledge at the price of the life he was trying to guard.[11]

---

[11] This is not to say he might not risk life in trying to guard it; he might order such tests as a spinal puncture or a liver puncture, or other inherently dangerous procedures. Many diagnostic procedures are dangerous and are used when the danger is justified, but a doctor will not make a complete sacrifice of what he is trying to protect.

Explanation

After obtaining some idea of what the facts and alternatives are, it is necessary to build up some way to explain them and to determine their implications.

In order to make much progress with real-world problems, we must ignore a great many of the actual features of a question under study and abstract from the real situation certain aspects—hopefully, the relevant ones—and their interaction, which together make up an idealized version of the real situation. This idealization we call a "model."

In the general process of formulating a problem and gathering data about it, the analyst will have developed some ideas of what the major influencing factors are, that is, the factors which provide discrimination with respect to the possible courses of action. To produce quantitative results, it is necessary to assign a scale of measurement to each factor and to show its dependence on certain parameters. Next, the interaction of the factors must be described. Then we have a model. In other words, isolating those factors pertinent to the problem or the decision at hand, abstracting them, assigning a scale of measurement, and then describing their interactions build the model.

The difficulty in model building is that we do not know at the start what is superfluous and what is relevant. We must proceed on the basis of experience and trial with preliminary models, conducting pencil and paper experiments to illuminate our preliminary judgments. Analysis, being iterative, is self-correcting; as the study goes on, the original model is refined and replaced so that behavior of the relationships being investigated is represented with greater accuracy.

For most phenomena, there are many possible representations; the appropriate model depends as much *on the question being asked* as on the phenomena about which it is asked. . . . A town can be modeled by a map if the question being asked is how to walk from A to B; but if the question is how to speed up the flow of traffic between the same two points, a much more elaborate model may be needed. There are thus no "universal" models—that is, say, no one model that can handle all questions about a given activity.

Sometimes representation by the model is mathematical, by means of a series of equations. At other times, particularly where detailed specification of the relationships between factors is extremely difficult —for example, in studying the behavior of human organizations—the representation may be by simulation or by a war game.

In operations research parlance, the term simulation is applied to the process of representing, without using formal analytic techniques, the essential features of a system or organization and analyzing its behavior by operating with the representation. Simulation is a broadly inclusive word used to describe various physical or analogue devices, such as a Link trainer, or a computer program which traces a strategic campaign through Monte Carlo operations, or a group of people or machines acting as if they were an air defense control center.

If working with the representation or model has some of the aspects of playing a game, particularly if human players are involved, the simulation is called a game. A gaming model cannot be expected to tell us what an optimal response to an uncertain state of affairs might be, but it can do much to make the players aware of such uncertainties and of the necessity of formulating their plans in such a way as to cope with all foreseeable contingencies. Indeed, an important asset to all systems analysis is the spirit of gaming. This consists in explicitly looking at possible moves and countermoves, in examining and designing a wide range of alternatives, and in looking for substitution possibilities—all against a hostile opponent.

Simulation, although relatively new in wide-scale applications, is an established operations research technique, which uses quasi-experimentation in an artificial environment for actual experiment in the real world. Its outstanding virtue is that it can be used to tackle seemingly unmanageable or previously untouched problems where a traditional analytic formulation appears infeasible. It is ordinarily an inefficient technique, however, to use in determining a sharp result, and it yields only a quasi-empirical form of knowledge, inferior to the functional relationships built up through the more traditional approach of using an analytic model. Simulation is a device appropriate to use before one has an adequate theory, for it provides a means to use the intuition and advice of experts in a systematic fashion and a way to go about building an analytic model by approximating the behavior of the random numbers, or physical counters, or human players with mathematical expressions.

The primary function of a model is "explanatory" rather than descriptive. Frequently it is not used to guide computation but solely to organize our thinking.

It should be emphasized that, in many important systems analyses, no need arises to build formal models, explicitly. When such cases occur, the analysis may be extraordinarily effective since it can be completely understood by the policymaker. The essence of systems analysis is not mathematical techniques or procedures. A computing machine or a technique such as linear programming may or may not be useful, depending on the problem and the extent of our information. The essential thing is a listing of the alternatives and an examination of their implications and costs so that they can be compared. What we say about models thus does not have much significance for analyses that require no more than a listing of alternatives and their implications, but is included because many difficult problems do require the use of well-defined models to guide computation.

The widely useful operations research techniques for optimization, when they are used at all in systems analysis, are used much more extensively in component studies than they are at the heart of the overall problem. Before any mathematical technique can be applied to a real-world problem, we must construct a quantitative model of the processes involved. This model expresses the effectiveness of the alternatives under examination as a function of a set of variables, some of which are under control. Once this is done, a solution can be determined mathematically, since formal statements of relationships between the variables exist. The solution obtained from such a model will be a usable solution to the real-world problem if and only if the model is a reasonably accurate representation of the real-world situation with respect to the question at issue. In situations of great complexity, such as those associated with major military decisions, only pieces of the problem can be represented with confidence. The submodels for these pieces or components can frequently be put into a form in which they can be handled by such techniques as dynamic programming or queuing theory. But even here, the new and more advanced techniques, while they are useful and promise to become more so, are seldom necessary since—except in relatively few instances —more elementary tools are usually adequate.

The design of models to assist in the decision process is in large measure an art. Wide experiences and the collaboration of many people are helpful, but it requires selection or composition, plus instinct and a sense of form, to achieve a desired effect.

Rules for model building are few in number and not very helpful. For example, it is sometimes suggested that the analyst should try to find models which explain more and more things within the same context. In operations research this leads to the construction of overly big models and attention to the model and not to the problem.

In building a model, assumptions are frequently made in order to handle something that is too difficult to investigate. For example, in the missile comparison of Appendix B, the model was built up step-by-step by a process of "simplification by assumption." Each target, for instance, was taken to be like every other target. This meant that in the model the targets (1) were of equal value to the offense, (2) required the same bomb yield to destroy, (3) were at the same range, (4) were protected by the same defense, and (5) were isolated so that destruction of one did not imply destruction of another. In essence, we made use of the assumption, fundamental to working with models but seldom stated, that by studying a simplified hypothetical situation we will get approximately the same answer we would get by studying the most realistic situation imaginable.

All of the assumptions of a model must be made explicit. If they are not, this is a defect. A mark of a good systems analyst (or any wise person communicating with others) is that he state the basis on which he operates. This does not imply necessarily that he makes better assumptions, but only that his errors will be more evident.

The contrast between the relative amount of time usually spent on designing a model and that spent in computing its consequences can give bias in judging what is important. The design of the model and the faithfulness with which it represents those aspects of the phenomena being modeled are significant for the question under consideration, not how far we push the computation.

The military analyst does not have, and cannot be expected to have, the precise and flexible means available to the physical scientist for testing his models experimentally. He cannot, for example, experiment with an actual war. The best he can do is to test his models by their workability. For example, he can try to determine answers to the following questions.

1. Can the model describe correctly and clearly the known facts and situations?
2. When the principal parameters involved are varied, do the results remain consistent and plausible?
3. Can it handle special cases in which there is some indication as to what the outcome should be?
4. Can it assign causes to known effects?

Whether or not one model is better than another does not depend on its complexity, realism, or computability but solely on whether it gives better predictions.

"Working" the model, trying out various strategies and concepts of operation, is the closest systems analysis comes to scientific experimentation. Deductions based on operating with the model frequently suggest new directions of effort. That is to say, starting with the relatively few parameters that characterize a system in terms of the model, it is sometimes possible to show that changes in these would improve the performance of the system as measured by the model, and then to suggest corresponding changes that could be made in the real system which would lead to improved performance in the real world. In this way, working the model contributes to system design.

It is also important to go outside the model: to contemplate changes that violate its assumptions and, in so doing, achieve a better model.

Two aspects of model building are particularly troublesome: quantification and the treatment of uncertainty.

Some variables are difficult to quantify, either because they are not calculable, like the probability of war, or because no scale of measurement has been set up like the effect on NATO solidarity of some unilateral U.S. action. This leads either to their neglect, for they tend to be ignored, or to their recognition only through a qualitative modification of a solution reached by manipulation of quantified variables. Thus, when the problem of what action to recommend on the basis of the solution from the model arises, effect of the quantitative variables is built in, while the nonquantitative ones may be easily lost in the welter of qualitative considerations that must be weighed.

One argument for the omission of a particular variable is that the solution of the problem is virtually insensitive to it. The fact that many variables fall into this category makes analysis possible. If the results were *not* insensitive to all but a relatively small number of variables, analysis would have to yield completely to guesses and intuition. Insensitivity can occur either because a factor is irrelevant or trivial in its quantitative effects or because it has roughly the same effect on all the alternatives under consideration. *The point is that this insensitivity must be discovered.* Sometimes logical reconnoitering is sufficient, but usually analysis is required, possibly with arbitrary values assigned to factors we are unable to calculate.

If nonquantitative variables are not to be neglected without mention or dismissed with some spurious argument, such as the one that they act in opposite direction and hence cancel out,[12] then how are they to be treated? The usual method is to attempt to take them into account through modification of the solution rather than to incorporate them into the model. But this in itself represents a particular method of quantification, for, by altering the solution to take account of the previously omitted variables, the analyst is implicitly valuing them. Since we always have some insight into the range of values that a factor might take, we can, even in the worst cases, assign the factors an arbitrary value and observe the effect on the solution. It seems to be an empirical fact that actions taken on policy questions are based on the available numbers, no matter how relevant or sound they may be; consequently, every effort should be made to quantify.

Most aspects of problems of choice in national security require numbers; others do not. But the real issue is one of clarity of understand-

---

[12] It is not enough to know that two variables act in opposite directions; their quantitative impact must also be estimated.

ing and expression. Numbers are part of our language. When a quantitative matter is being discussed, the greatest clarity of thought is achieved by using numbers instead of by avoiding them, even when uncertainties are present. Only in rare cases is it possible to make a convincing comparison of alternatives without a quantitative analysis of the relevant numbers.

Systems analysis is concerned with problems in which the essence is uncertainty about the future; not only uncertainties about technical and operational parameters and the actions of the enemy, but also conceptual uncertainties. Such analysis, as well as any other attempt to answer the same questions, must necessarily face this uncertainty squarely, treat it as an important element in the problem, and take it into account in formulating recommendations. The treatment of uncertainty is not merely a difficulty in principle, but is a considerable practical problem. Somehow the number of cases made necessary by the presence of uncertainty must be limited and the total effort kept within reasonable bounds.

There are different degrees of uncertainty but for discussion here we will recognize two categories: We will call them, for want of better terms, statistical uncertainties and "real" uncertainties.

Statistical uncertainties—those having a more or less objective or calculable probability of occurrence—can be handled in the model by Monte Carlo or other methods. For instance, our knowledge of the situation may be complete and accurate, but a quantity may be stochastic or "noisy." An example might be the accuracy of a missile system. Alternatively, the quantity involved may have a unique value, but the determinate factors may not be measurable. Then again the quantity involved may be related to measurable factors in such a complex way that it is beyond our mathematical or engineering power to describe, and we must approximate the real situation by a simple description. For example, take the "lethal radius" concept of a nuclear bomb. Such uncertainties, like those in cost or missile accuracy, lead to risks that can be estimated and accepted. They can be annoying but not devastating, like, say, the uncertainties due to ignorance or to competition associated with the prediction of what the environment may turn out to be or the enemy may do during the lifetime of the systems under consideration.

Uncertainties about human factors, which have no necessarily logical construction, or about the future behavior of things, which is beyond the practical ability of analysts to predict, belong to the class of real uncertainties. Under real uncertainty, we consider events—like the probability of war—to which individuals may attach subjective probabilities, but which we cannot calculate. With regard to air defense, for example, real uncertainty involves such questions as "Will we have warning? If we get it, will we believe it? What surprises does the enemy have?" For such uncertainties, there is frequently widespread disagreement about the pertinent probabilities, and even confusion and vagueness within any one individual.

As a simple example, my son when he had just turned sixteen wanted to drive the car. Since he could not walk through a room without bumping into the furniture, the problem I faced was whether to let him drive or not. Here I had uncertainties as to how not driving would affect his personality and character during the next year or so, as well as those about his capability to survive in freeway traffic. This was uncertainty about empirical facts that were not and would not be available and that could not be made available to me by a realistic or thinkable course of inquiry. Therefore, my solution to this problem had to involve guesses and judgments which would never be confirmed, and even now I do not know whether I chose a good solution or not.

There is no foolproof recipe for handling uncertainty, but there are almost always measures that can be taken to make the consequences of possible mistaken prediction less devastating.

With regard to my son's driving, for instance, there were various ways in which I might have sought a good solution. For example, I might have (1) deferred granting the driving privilege for a while to see his reaction, or (2) set up a policy in which a near accident as well as an accident would result in revocation of his privileges, or (3) required him for a period to drive only in specified areas or at specified times. The last, incidentally, would have been not so much a way of getting data as a way of keeping him out of dangerous traffic while he acquired proficiency. I chose still a fourth way, requiring him to pass a course in a driving school reputed to have high standards (rather than teaching him myself and passing my own possibly bad driving practices on to him), and then taking the recommendation of the instructor that if he passed the test for a license, he be permitted to drive without restrictions.

In the analysis, as a prelude to finding ways to compensate for uncertainty, an effort can be made to *forecast* or map the many possible futures, rather than to *predict* a future environment in the sense of specifying a *single* sequence of events. Since the future is inherently unpredictable, it is too hazardous to proceed solely on the basis of a "best estimate" about the future military-technological-political environment. Instead, the analysis must reckon with the wide scope of possible developments and serious uncertainties that the future holds.

To do this, as far as the technical and operational parameters are concerned, one way is first to explore their limits and then make the calculations in terms of the range of uncertainty, using an upper and lower estimate in addition to a best guess. Although initially it is usually necessary to design the system or strategy primarily on the basis of best estimates, this type of investigation, through feedback, helps to modify them so that their performance will not be sensitive functions of parameters whose values are essentially unknown. And it must be kept in mind that alternatives are to be evaluated also by their flexibility to meet the unforseen, rather than solely by their optimality in meeting expectations. In cases of doubt, to overestimate one's opponent and to underestimate our own capabilities is not necessarily the safe thing to do. Overestimates do not necessarily lead to safety and insurance. They are just as likely to lead to despair and loss of morale, to the feeling that the attainment of certain policy objectives is hopeless, and thus to "strategies of desperation."

Of course, the best way to compensate for uncertainty would be to "invent" a better system or policy which would provide insurance against the whole range of possible catastrophes; the difficulty is to discover how to do this.

In view of the uncertainties present in any operations research model, how can one obtain useful information? This fundamental question confronts every scientist and requires *sensitivity* and *contingency* analysis. In addition to calculating initially with a range of values, it is necessary to find out how changes in the information put into the problem and the assumptions made affect the results.

In "sensitivity analysis" an attempt is made to determine how sensitive the results are to variations in key parameters and assumptions. The hope is to obtain a dominant solution in which the ranking of the preferred alternative is essentially insensitive to reasonable variations in values of the parameters or assumptions in question. "Contingency analysis" investigates how a system chosen with one assumption about the environment measures up to the performance of its alternatives when radical changes in the environment occur. Thus, sensitivity analysis might test the alternatives for a wide range of enemy capabilities or for the consequences of having planned for one level of capability when another is experienced. Contingency analysis might test the alternatives under a change in criteria or compare them in an environment in which France, say, had become part of the Communist Bloc.

Since a systems analysis is a study which attempts to influence policy, it must in the end present a convincing comparison of the relevant alternatives. Although it may be clear to the analyst that a certain course of action A is better than alternative possible courses of action B, C, D . . ., it may not be clear to someone who has not "lived" with the problem. One way to show that under any reasonable assumption the system or policy designed or selected by the analyst is indeed to be preferred is to use either an a fortiori or a "break-even" analysis.

To make an analysis a fortiori, we bend over backward in making the comparisons to "hurt" the system we think is best and to "help" the alternative systems. If it then turns out that after we have done this we can still say we prefer the handicapped system, we are in a strengthened position to make recommendations. Sometimes we cannot do this—say, if we concede the exaggerated performance claims for rival systems and the pessimistic estimates about the systems we like. In this case, we might try a *break-even* analysis: We decide what assumptions must be made about important values in order to make the performance of the two systems essentially the same. Then we can simply ask people to judge whether these assumptions are optimistic or pessimistic. As Kahn and Mann put it:

> *More than any other single thing, the skilled use of a fortiori and break-even analyses separate the professionals* from the *amateurs.* Most analyses should (conceptually) be done in two stages: a first stage to find out what one wants to recommend, and a second stage that generates the kind of information that makes the recommendations convincing even to a hostile and disbelieving, but intelligent audience.[13]

Interpretation

After a solution has been obtained from a model, this solution must be interpreted in the light of considerations which may not have been adequately treated by the model, since the model was but a single representation of the real world chosen by the analyst. For example, the systems analyst (or for that matter the designers of the strategic offensive force) may have established the requirement that a force assure the destruction of, say, 95 per cent of the targets at a minimum cost under a certain range of contingencies. But many questions occur. Perhaps the minimum cost is too high; maybe the tasks of deterrence and limiting damage could be better done by spending less on strategic forces and more on air defense. The 95 per cent may be too high, or too low. Someone must translate the percentage of target destruction into its implications in terms of more meaningful criteria, such as the balance of military forces, the will to continue fighting, and the effect

---

[13] H. Kahn and I. Mann, *Techniques of Systems Analysis,* The RAND Corporation, RM-1829 (DDC No. AD 123512), December 3, 1956.

on our diplomacy. The analyst may be able to help here, but the responsibility is someone else's.

The solution that has been simplified and possibly reduced to mathematical form by drastic idealization and aggregation is not necessarily a good solution of the original problem. A different model might be called for. At this stage, not only does the analyst attempt to interpret his work, but the sponsor or the real world gets into the iterative cycle again, to counteract the analyst's ignorance and thus produce better answers.

To form a basis for recommendations, any military systems analysis must at the very least give adequate consideration to

1. The objectives both of the nation as a whole and of the forces that are to implement these national objectives.
2. The military capabilities required to attain these objectives.
3. The enemy capabilities and objectives.
4. The technological possibilities.
5. The effectiveness of each posture, system, or plan considered.
6. The costs or resource implications of the choices.
7. The uncertainties in the above.

These things, of course, cannot be specified absolutely. They depend on each other, on the degree of security deemed adequate, and on the enemy's interpretation of our objectives and the actions we take to implement them; and they vary over time. Moreover, the entire structure is based on a set of assumptions, hopefully not arbitrary but objective. If action is to be taken on the basis of the analysis, it is important that the assumptions, as well as the goals, be the right ones.

There are special problems associated with military questions. Many factors used in the computations are not and cannot be measured. Sometimes this is because of time limitations; other times it is because factors such as the enemy defense strength, or degradation in combat of complicated man-machine combinations, are not accessible to measurement but have to be assessed on the basis of experience or pooled judgment. The results of computations must be examined to see if they depend critically upon estimations such as these.

In military problems, there are always considerations not subject to any sort of quantitative analysis. To achieve efficiency in a military context, factors other than cost-effectiveness are important—discipline, morale, esprit de corps, tradition, and organizational behavior. Such problems involve more than purely military questions. The size, composition, location, and state of readiness of forces influence our foreign policy and the freedom of action we have there. They also have a major impact on our domestic economy and public morale. The men who must somehow integrate these factors with the study are really doing systems analysis, but at a level so high it is hard to consider it as such.

It is important for the user of analysis to distinguish between what the study shows and the recommendations for action the analyst makes on the basis of what he thinks the study implies. Frequently, when new minds—management, for example—review the problem, they bring new information. Even though the solution obtained from the model is not changed, recommendations for action based on it may be. A model is only an indicator, not a final judge. . . .

There are numerous reasons why an interpretation is necessary. Mainly it is because major decisions, in the field of economic or military policy, are part of a political as well as part of an intellectual process. Consider, for instance, the following.

The relationship between "cost" and "effectiveness" of a weapon system for some given objective typically plots as in Fig. 8.2.

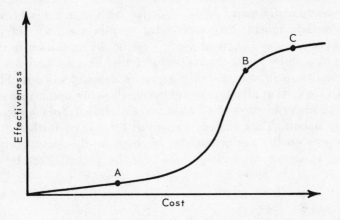

Figure 8.2 A typical cost-effectiveness curve

If a weapon system plots at A, then clearly the objective is too ambitious for the budget and someone must decide to look for a less ambitious objective or to abandon the system, or, as another possibility, to decide to spend a lot more money to get it to B. If at C and we still have money to spend, clearly we've put more money into the system than was economic and should look for another system and more ambitious objectives.

If, in the judgment of the analyst and those who use his analysis, the alternative ranked highest by the model is good enough, the process is over; if not, more and better alternatives must be designed or the objectives must be lowered. Analysis is sufficient to reach a policy conclusion only when the objectives are agreed upon by the policymakers.

In defense policy in particular, and in many other cases as well, objectives are not, in fact, agreed upon. The choice, while ostensibly between alternatives, is really between objectives or ends, and nonanalytical methods must be used for a final reconciliation of views. Although the consequences computed from the model may provide guidance in deciding which objectives to compromise, such decisions are not easily made, and judgment must again be applied.

In the end, military decisionmaking, like systems analysis itself, is an art. After a certain stage, calculation may no longer be helpful. There are always considerations that cannot be measured—say, the importance of military gains against political losses, or public reaction to a temporary setback against the enhanced chances of a long term gain. Moreover, there are always considerations that have been measured or determined by judgment but not to the decisionmaker's satisfaction.

By definition, no judgment is known to be correct. Because systems analysis ordinarily goes beyond objective analysis, it relies heavily on considered judgment. No matter what may be the hopes of professional analysts, the judgment applied by the decisionmaker in the last phase of a study limits the influence of the previous analyses. At its best, analysis can only embrace a part of a broad-scope problem; it gets no foothold at all on many subjective elements, and before it organizes an understanding of all objective elements it becomes too complex to handle. Thus analysis can go so far and no further. But the restrictions on the use of analyses imposed by the refusal of policymakers to use it when they should can be pushed back by better analysis.

Author Index

Adams, S., 178, 197
Allen, L. A., 14
Ansoff, H. I., 346
Arensberg, C., 163
Argyris, C., 23, 41, 43, 54–56, 58, 59,
  60, 63, 64–90, 77, 83, 91–94,
  104, 125, 157–160, 164, 210,
  211, 279, 282, 300, 301, 302
Atkinson, J. W., 99

Babchuck, N., 165
Bakke, E. W., 24, 33, 92, 93
Bales, R. F., 172
Bamforth, K., 166
Baritz, L., 296
Barker, R., 73, 92
Barnard, C. I., 43, 44, 47, 48, 134,
  326, 327, 366, 387
Baumgartel, H., 181
Beer, S., 27
Bentley, A. F., 43
Berkowitz, L., 99, 184, 189
Bernstein, M., 287, 294
Bertalanffy, L. von, 30
Bibby, D., 211
Black, K., 19
Black, R., Preface
Blake, R., 69, 83
Blau, P. M., 39, 43, 49, 125, 153–
  156, 176, 179, 269
Bloom, A., 38
Blough, R. M., 328
Bond, N., 107, 113
Booz, D. R., 299, 367
Boulding, K. E., 28
Bradford, L. P., 68
Brech, E. F. L., 14, 15, 19, 297, 298
Bronfenbrenner, W., 91, 92
Brown, R., 10
Buckingham, W., 299
Bunker, D. R., 83
Burlingame, J. F., 207

Cadwallader, M. L., 26
Calvin, A. D., 182, 192, 293
Campbell, D. T., 48
Canavan, F., 38
Carter, L. F., 183, 292
Cartwright, D., 285
Chandler, A. D., 302, 322, 323, 324,
  376–380
Chapple, E., 11, 164, 286, 305, 309
Christensen, P. R., 107, 113
Christie, R., 183
Coch, L., 20
Coker, F. W., 40

Collins, O., 163
Cottrell, L., 10, 19
Couch, A., 9, 183
Crockett, W. H., 177
Cropsey, J., 47

Dahl, R. A., 296
Dale, E., 287
Dalkey, N., 415
Dalton, M., 18, 166, 303, 306, 325,
  385–400
Davis, K., 16, 17, 20, 204
Davis, L. E., 63
Davis, R. C., 15
de Baca, P., 117, 121
Demerath, N. J., 186
Deutsch, K. W., 25, 27, 369
Deutsch, M., 99, 191, 192
Devine, J. V., 117, 121
Dickson, W. J., 16, 21, 154, 179
Dimock, M. E., 288, 386, 388
Dorn, W. S., 399
Doult, J. T., 20
Drucker, P. F., 280, 282, 317, 390
Drury, J. E., 277
Dubin, R., 96, 272

Easton, D., 30
Eddington, Sir A., 31, 33
Eitington, J. E., 289
Elliott, J. D., 211
Ellis, H. C., 116
Enthoyen, A. C., 407
Erikson, E. H., 91, 92
Etzioni, A., 269
Evan, W. M., 41

Fantz, R., 110, 113
Fenichel, O., 367
Fesler, J. W., 246
Festinger, L., 19
Finn, R. H., 292
Fisch, G. G., 205, 206, 223–245
Fisher, J., 273
Follett, M. P., 41
Form, W. H., 16
Fowler, I., 168
Frederiksen, N., 11
French, J. R. P., Jr., 20
Friedmann, G., 308
Fromm, E., 364
Fryer, D. H., 176

Gaier, E. L., 292
Gardner, B. B., 16, 18, 134, 138, 399
Gibb, C. A., 185

Subject Index

Allstate Motor Club, 355
American Legion, 295
American Management Association, 214, 259, 326, 329
American Telephone and Telegraph, 350–351
Appropriations Committee, House of Representatives, 381
Atmosphere, 181–183, 162–172
 (*See also* Groups)
Authoritarianism, 182–190
 analytical problems with, 183
 and leadership, 189–190
Authority, 154–155, 162–163, 180–182, 279–282, 298–304
 and dependence, 162–163
 and leadership styles, 180–182
 concept of, 154–155, 279–282, 298–304
 (*See also* Orthodox organization theory.)
Autokinesis, 179n

Balance, 25–27
 as a construct in organization theory, 25–26
Break-even analysis, 427

Canadian Civil Service Commission, 206n
Centralization, 206–212, 259–268, 276–288, 323–324, 381–384
 and electronic data-processing, 206–207
 and federal disbursing, 323–324, 381–384
 properties of, 261–262, 279–284
 some consequences of, 210–212, 262–264, 276–281, 284–288
 structure suitable for, 259–268, 279–284, 304–315
 (*See also* Growth, strategies for; and Orthodox organization theory.)
Change, guidelines for, 105
Civil Service Commission, U.S., 273, 294–295
Civil service movement, 276–294
 effects on job description, 288–294
 effects on job design, 279–288
 effects on supervisory power, 276–279
Cliques, 324–325, 385–400
 control of, 398–400
 description of, 324, 385
 relation to division of work, 386–387

types of, 325, 391–397
 horizontal, 393–396
 random, 396–397
 vertical, 391–393
 (*See also* Lateral relations.)
Cohesiveness, 177–178
 as a group property, 177–178
 relation to productivity, 177–178
Colleague model of line-staff relations, 104–108, 212–213, 304–315
 described, 104–108, 212–213
 some advantages of, 308–315
 (*See also* Orthodox organization theory.)
Command group, 162
Communication, 55–59, 64–94
 and "pyramidal values," 58–59, 65–67
 feedback as crucial in, 65–66, 73–74
 "unfreezing" via lab training, 67–69
 (*See also* T-groups.)
Compatibility, 128–129, 184–185
 and "self-choice," 129
 as criterion for work assignments, 128–129, 184–185
Computers, 204–207, 214–222
 (*See also* Electronic data processing.)
Conditioning learning, 62–63, 115–121
Controllership Foundation, 157
Coordination, 39–42
 theoretical bases of, 39–42
 as central direction, 40–41
 as reciprocal relation, 41–42
Creative interdependence, 92
Creativity, 9–11, 372–375
 impact of organization on, 9–11
 in infusing organization with value, 372–375
Cybernetics, 27–28, 33–34

Decentralization, 206–207, 213–222, 258–268, 279–284, 304–315, 323–324, 381–384
 and electronic data-processing, 206–207, 213–222
 and federal disbursing, 323–324, 381–384
 some consequences of, 265–268, 279–284
 structure suitable for, 259–268, 279–284, 304–315
 (*See also* Growth, strategies for; and Orthodox organization theory.)

PRINTED IN U.S.A.